BÉLA BARTÓK

The Ernest Bloch Professorship
of Music and the Ernest Bloch Lectures
were established at the University of California
in 1962 in order to bring distinguished figures
in music to the Berkeley campus from time to time.
Made possible by the Jacob and Rosa Stern
Musical Fund, the professorship was founded
in memory of Ernest Bloch (1880–1959),
Professor of Music at Berkeley
from 1940 to 1959.

THE ERNEST BLOCH PROFESSORS

1964 Ralph Kirkpatrick
1965 Winton Dean
1966 Roger Sessions
1968 Gerald Abraham
1971 Leonard B. Meyer
1972 Edward T. Cone
1975 Donald Jay Grout
1976 Charles Rosen
1977 Alan Tyson
1980 William P. Malm
1981 Andrew Porter
1982 Ton de Leeuw
1983 James Haar
1985 Richard Crawford
1986 John Blacking
1987 Gunther Schuller
1988 George Perle
1989 László Somfai
1993 Susan McClary
1994 Wye J. Allanbrook
1995 Jonathan Harvey

LÁSZLÓ SOMFAI

BÉLA BARTÓK

Composition, Concepts, and Autograph Sources

UNIVERSITY OF CALIFORNIA PRESS

Berkeley   Los Angeles   London

The publisher gratefully acknowledges the contribution provided by the General Endowment Fund of the Associates of the University of California Press. Publication of this book was also made possible in part by a generous grant from the American Musicological Society.

University of California Press
Berkeley and Los Angeles, California

University of California Press, Ltd.
London, England

© 1996 by
The Regents of the University of California

Library of Congress Cataloging-in-Publication Data

Somfai, László.
    Béla Bartók : composition, concepts, and autograph sources /
László Somfai.
      p.   cm. — (Ernest Bloch lectures ; 9)
      Includes bibliographical references and indexes.
      ISBN 0-520-08485-3 (alk. paper)
      1. Bartók, Béla, 1881–1945 — Criticism and interpretation.
    2. Bartók, Béla, 1881–1945 — Manuscripts. I. Title. II. Series.
    ML410.B26S59 1996
    780'.92 — dc20   95-6043

Printed in the United States of America

08   07   06   05   04   03   02   01
9   8   7   6   5   4   3   2

The paper used in this publication meets the minimum requirements of ANSI/NISO Z39.48-1992 (R 1997) (*Permanence of Paper*). ∞

To Dorka, my wife

CONTENTS

List of Facsimile Plates   ix

Preface and Acknowledgments   xiii

Abbreviations   xix

1.   Introduction   1

2.   Bartók on Composition, His Concepts, and Works   9

3.   A Survey of the Sources   25

    The existing sources · The function of different types
    of manuscripts · Reconstructing the chain of sources

4.   Sketches and the Plan of a Work   33

    Terminology · Destroyed and lost sketches or no sketches? ·
    Separate preliminary memos · Preliminary memos in context ·
    Side sketches in drafts · Memos extended into continuity
    sketches · Working with a sketch-book · Partial sketches for the
    final texture or the instrumentation · "Plans" and "calculations"?

5.   Fragments, Unrealized Plans   83

6.   Paper Studies and the Micro-Chronology of the Composition   96

7. The Key Manuscript: The Draft   113

General characteristics • Formation of a work: *String Quartet no. 3, Ricapitulazione della prima parte / Piano Sonata, the beginning of Movement I / String Quartet no. 4, the beginning of Movement I / Violin Concerto, the 12-tone melody / Recapitulation strategies in Piano Concerto no. 2, Movement I / Development section strategies / Formation of the coda in Piano Sonata, Movement I / Draft complex of piano pieces from 1926 / Corrections in the draft of String Quartet no. 6, Movements III & I, and String Quartet no. 5, Movements III & II* • Reorganization of the form: *String Quartet no. 5, Scherzo / Deleted movements and episodes / Endings for the Violin Rhapsody no. 1 and the Violin Concerto / New retransition in the 2-piano Sonata / Endings for the Concerto for Orchestra and for the Violin Rhapsody no. 2*

8. Final Copy, Orchestration, Reduction, Arrangement   204

Autograph fair copy and copyist's copy • The Bartók copyists • Working with *Lichtpausen* • Orchestration • Piano reduction • Arrangements, authorization of arrangements made by others

9. Editing and Correcting Process   229

Introduction • Maturing the final version • Editing and proofreading • Corrected and revised editions

10. On Bartók's Notation and Performing Style   252

Tempo, metronome, duration • Selected problems of Bartók's notation • The significance of Bartók's own recordings

Appendix: List of Works and Primary Sources   297

Index of Basic Terms   321

Index of Bartók's Compositions   323

General Index   329

FACSIMILE PLATES

FACSIMILE 1. Folio 8ᵛ of the *Black Pocket-book*, sketches from 1908   42

FACSIMILE 2. Folio 9ʳ of the *Black Pocket-book*, sketches from 1908   43

FACSIMILE 3. Folio 11ʳ of the *Black Pocket-book*, sketches from 1908   45

FACSIMILE 4. Sketches for *The Wooden Prince*   46

FACSIMILE 5. Sketch page from 1926 with unused thematic ideas probably for Piano Concerto no. 1 and the themes of the finale of the Piano Sonata   49

FACSIMILE 6. Sketch from 1926, the first notation of the "Ostinato" (*Mikrokosmos* no. 146)   51

FACSIMILE 7. Sketches from 1926, unused ideas for Piano Concerto no. 1 and the beginning of Movement III   52

FACSIMILE 8. Bartók's handwriting with six birdsongs; no. 6 used in Movement II of Piano Concerto no. 3   55

FACSIMILE 9. Sketches from 1939 for Movements III, I, and II of the Divertimento   59

FACSIMILE 10. First page of the draft of the Violin Concerto (no. 2), 1937   62

FACSIMILE 11. First page of Movement I of the draft of Piano Concerto no. 3, 1945   65

FACSIMILE 12. Sketches for Movement II in the draft score of Piano Concerto no. 2, on the page with the end of Movement I, 1930 or 1931   67

FACSIMILE 13. Folio 27ᵛ of the *Black Pocket-book* with sketches for the Sonata for Violin and Piano no. 2, 1922   72

FACSIMILE 14. Folio 28ʳ of the *Black Pocket-book* with the continuation of the sketches for the Violin Sonata no. 2   73

FACSIMILE 15. Draft with sketches of Movement II of the Sonata for Solo Violin in the Arab field-book, 1944   78

FACSIMILE 16. Partial sketches to the score of the *Dance Suite*, 1923   79

FACSIMILE 17. One-page fragment of a piano piece, ca. 1918   88

FACSIMILE 18. Fragment of a piano piece, among the sketches for the Piano Concerto no. 1   90

FACSIMILE 19. Fragment in the Turkish field-book, 1943, among the sketches and the draft of the Concerto for Orchestra   92

FACSIMILE 20. Orchestral fragment ca. 1943 (?), planned as an episode for the orchestrated version of the chorus "Hussar"   93

FACSIMILE 21. Fragment perhaps for String Quartet no. 7 (?) in the Arab field-book, 1944 or 1945   94

FACSIMILE 22. Corrections and sketches for the beginning of Movement I in the draft of String Quartet no. 6, 1939   108

FACSIMILE 23. *The Wooden Prince*, p. 31 of the draft, ca. 1916   123

FACSIMILE 24. *Four Orchestral Pieces*, the last page of Movement IV in the draft, ca. 1912   124

FACSIMILE 25. Violin Concerto (no. 2), p. 4 of the draft, 1937   125

FACSIMILE 26. Viola Concerto, p. 1 of the draft, 1945   126

FACSIMILE 27. Piano Concerto no. 3, p. 7 of the draft   127

FACSIMILE 28. Piano Concerto no. 2, p. 11 of the draft score   128

FACSIMILE 29. *Music for Strings, Percussion, and Celesta*, p. 40 of the draft score, 1936   129

FACSIMILE 30. Piano Sonata 1926, the beginning of Movement I in the draft   130

FACSIMILE 31. Piano Sonata 1926, the beginning of Movement I in the first autograph copy   131

FACSIMILE 32. The draft of "Bagpipe" (*Mikrokosmos* no. 138), ca. 1937   132

FACSIMILE 33. String Quartet no. 6, the first page of the draft   133

FACSIMILE 34. Draft of "Wandering," from Twenty-Seven Choruses, 1935 or 1936 and a sketch for *Mikrokosmos* no. 98   134

FACSIMILE 35. String Quartet no. 5, the beginning of Movement II in the draft   135

FACSIMILE 36. String Quartet no. 1, p. 3 (Movement I) of the draft, 1908–1909   136

FACSIMILE 37. Sonata for two Pianos and Percussion, sketchy page of the draft, 1937   137

FACSIMILE 38. Sonata for two Pianos and Percussion, p. 35 of the draft   138

FACSIMILE 39. *Contrasts*, for violin, clarinet, and piano, the end of Movement III in the draft, with a side sketch for Movement II, 1938   139

FACSIMILE 40. Suite op. 14, for piano, the discarded original Movement II in the draft, 1916   140

FACSIMILE 41. String Quartet no. 5, the beginning of the first version of Movement III in the draft, 1934   141

FACSIMILE 42. Piano Concerto no. 1, p. 1 of the original full score   208

FACSIMILE 43. Piano Concerto no. 1, p. 1 of the autograph copy of the full score   209

FACSIMILE 44. Bartók's copyists. Samples of handwriting by family members   210

FACSIMILE 45. Bartók's copyists. Samples of handwriting by copyists Anon. Y and Anon. X, Jenő Deutsch, Erwin Stein, and Tibor Serly   211

FACSIMILE 46. Violin Concerto op. posth., the solo violin part written by Anon. Y   212

FACSIMILE 47. Sonata for Violin and Piano no. 1, Márta's copy of the violin part, 1921, with Bartók's additions and corrections   212

FACSIMILE 48. Piano Concerto no. 2, handmade 2-piano reduction based on the *Lichtpausen*, ca. 1932   217

FACSIMILE 49. *The Miraculous Mandarin*, p. 9 of the draft   222

FACSIMILE 50. *The Miraculous Mandarin*, p. 22 of the autograph copy of the piano 4-hand reduction   223

FACSIMILE 51. Violin Concerto (no. 2), Movement I, p. 11 of Bartók's violin-and-piano-form working copy   224

FACSIMILE 52. Violin Concerto (no. 2), Movement III, p. 31 of the draft   225

FACSIMILE 53. J. S. Bach's Sonata VI (BWV 530), autograph of Bartók's transcription   234

FACSIMILE 54. *Seven Sketches*, first page of the corrected proof sheets of the Rozsnyai edition   241

FACSIMILE 55. String Quartet no. 1, excerpt from Movement I in the Rózsavölgyi pocket score edition and in the draft   242

FACSIMILE 56. Violin Concerto (no. 2), p. 51 of the corrected proof sheets of the Boosey & Hawkes full score   244

FACSIMILE 57. String Quartet no. 4, the beginning of Movement III in the sketchy draft, full draft, and autograph copy   271

PREFACE AND ACKNOWLEDGMENTS

This book is the extended form of six public lectures delivered in the Ernest Bloch Lecture Series from September 18 to October 23, 1989, in the Department of Music at the University of California at Berkeley. To my regret, the presentation of this expanded version, which for the most part I had finished by the end of 1992, is somewhat overdue, but not without good reason. For an American publication I found that I could not help but produce, if I may say so, a magnum opus, a summary of three decades of Bartók studies, thereby offering grateful, if belated, thanks to the University of California and to my colleagues and students at Berkeley. It was probably the happiest time of my life: I had the honor not only of presenting the music of Béla Bartók but also, at a turning point in Bartók studies, of outlining the tasks awaiting future research on his oeuvre before the most resonant, expert audience I have ever met outside of my country, Hungary — the homeland of Bartók.

Coming half a century after the death of the composer, this is the first book dedicated to the study of Bartók's compositional process to be based on the complete existing primary source material. Therefore, a great many things need to be accomplished simultaneously: a description of the sources (chapter 3) as well as the first reliable list of manuscripts (in the appendix); an extensive discussion of Bartók's sketches and drafts (chapters 4 and 7); an introduction to auxiliary research fields as for instance in paper studies (chapter 6). And although this book is primarily aimed at musicologists, I could not disregard the possible questions of a performer about the problems posed by Bartók's metronome markings and other such issues (chapter 10).

There is, however, no extensive bibliography in the present book, which is perhaps unorthodox in a study of this size. The list of abbreviations includes the literature to which I repeatedly refer, and in the notes to chapter 1 there is a survey of the basic Bartókiana that has directly or indirectly influenced my studies. Nonetheless, we are going to work largely on the basis of original sources, notably an immense amount of unpublished material to which I have been fortunate to have access. Quotations from Bartók's correspondence with his publishers, if no printed edition has been given, are based on the originals or photocopies contained in the American and the Budapest Bartók Archives. Translations of already printed versions of Bartók's letters and essays have been tacitly revised, if the original meaning had been distorted considerably. Titles of Bartók's compositions will occasionally be shortened (thus "2-piano Sonata," instead of "Sonata for two Pianos and Percussion"). Titles may also appear in an English version different from, but more authentic than, that generally used in sheet music editions (such as "Evening in Transylvania") or in a hitherto unpublished, corrected form taken from the original sources (thus BB 106 *Székely Folksongs,* instead of "Székely Songs"). The appendix, a list of works and primary sources, is organized according to my new numbering of the Bartók compositions, namely, the BB numbers of the planned thematic catalogue, and contains a great amount of unpublished data relating to chronology and other matters.

One cannot compile a work of this complexity without assistance from many quarters: institutes, libraries, owners of the manuscripts, workshops of Bartók research and performance, musician and musicologist friends. To begin with the occasion that ignited my work on this book, I should like first to acknowledge my friends at Berkeley for inviting me to be the eighteenth visiting Ernest Bloch Professor: Daniel Heartz, who put forward the proposal; Bonnie C. Wade, chair of the Department of Music at the time of the invitation; Philip Brett, the chair in the fall of 1989; Richard F. Taruskin, the host at the lectures and, together with Joseph W. Kerman and Anthony Newcomb, a keen critic during the discussions; and Madeline Duckles, whose house was our home and whose friendship assured me that I could get over my inhibitions and work together with an elite group of musicologists.

To my own institute, the Bartók Archives (which I head) at the Institute for Musicology of the Hungarian Academy of Sciences in Budapest, I am also grateful. Past and present directors of the home institution, Bence Szabolcsi, József Ujfalussy, and Zoltán Falvy, established the conditions conducive to creative work, including freedom in planning and chances to lecture on Bartók abroad. I can still rely on the advice of my predecessor, Denijs Dille, on two former assistants, Vera Lampert (Lampert-Deák) and Tibor Tallián, on our trusted colleague Adrienne Gombocz (Gombocz-Konkoly), on the stimulation of András Wilheim, and on the help of young members of my present staff. The Budapest Bartók Archives gave me the opportunity to meet scholars from abroad and exchange views. Two further centers of my activity should be mentioned here: the Department of Musicology at the Liszt Academy of Music in Budapest, with its broad-minded chairman, György Kroó, where as a professor I have an opportunity to test new ideas and to train young people in Bartók research; and the yearly International Bartók Seminar in Szombathely, Hungary, directed by Tamás Klenjánszky, where the ideas of Bartók scholars are discussed and tested by a special group of Bartók interpreters and teachers, including György Kurtág, Péter Eötvös, and Zoltán Kocsis. This contact with performance practice, which started with interviews of Bartók's intimate partners in music, above all Zoltán Székely, has a sobering and at the same time stimulating effect on my efforts to determine the proper role and goals of musicology.

Without access to the sources this book could not have been written. I am deeply indebted to the sons of Béla Bartók, who own the overwhelming majority of the primary sources, for their interest in my work and for their permission to reproduce many facsimiles of Bartók's manuscripts from their collections. Béla Bartók Jr. (d. 1994) supported this work for many years; he even allowed me to examine sources in the collection at his home. I am also very grateful to Peter Bartók for giving me access to copies of manuscripts in his collection as well as assisting my examination of the originals in Florida. The Siemens Foundation, Munich, provided financial aid for a research trip to the United States and for travel in Europe. Many libraries and collections kindly gave me permission to survey original manuscripts or sent me copies, but I would like to express my special appreciation to Paul Sacher, founder of the Paul Sacher Foundation, Basel. For their expert help, I would also like to thank James W. Pruett at the Library of Congress, Washington, D.C.; J. Rigbie Turner at the Pierpont Morgan Library, New York; Arthur Searle at the British Library, London; and Ernst Hilmar at the Stadt- und Landesbibliothek, Vienna.

Since English is not my mother tongue and the production of a major musicological study on Bartók involves special difficulties, the preparation of this book has entailed extraordinary work on the part of its publisher. I must therefore thank the Editorial Committee of the University of California Press for accepting the book for publication. I also extend my gratitude to the readers of the rough version, Ingrid Arauco and Reinhold Brinkmann, for their advice. I am grateful as well to my editors at the University of California Press: Doris Kretschmer, for her encouragement of this project; Rose Vekony, for her guidance through editing and production; and Edith Gladstone, for her considerable improvements to the English of my text. Special thanks are due to Richard F. Taruskin, who read and corrected the final copy with an expert eye and great empathy.

Last, but by no means least of all, I wish to express my deepest thanks to my wife, Dorka, who has always fostered a way of life for me in which, independent of the outside world, I could pursue dedicated work. She has urged me to undertake great challenges and remain faithful to my labor-of-love topics, even in my years of frustration with the Bartók situation; she has always been my first reader and, being herself a colleague and an expert musicology editor, the first critic of my writings.

All music examples and the drawings in figures, if not facsimiles of Béla Bartók's autograph works, are reproduced in my handwriting. Facsimile reproductions of sketches and drafts of Bartók's compositions from the collections of Béla Bartók Jr. (Budapest) and Peter Bartók (Homosassa, Fla.) are used by permission. For permission to reprint copyrighted material or publish pages from the original sources of copyrighted compositions in facsimile, acknowledgment is due to the publishers of Bartók's compositions:

Allegro barbaro (for piano). Copyright 1918 by Universal Edition; renewed 1945. All rights in the U.S.A. owned by Boosey & Hawkes, Inc. Used by permission.

Bach–Bartók, Sonata VI, transcribed for piano (1929). Copyright 1930 by Rózsavölgyi és Tsa, Budapest; copyright assigned 1950 to Editio Musica Budapest. Used by permission.

Cantata Profana. Copyright 1934 by Universal Edition; renewed 1961. All rights in the U.S.A. owned by Boosey & Hawkes, Inc. Used by permission.

Concerto for Orchestra. Copyright 1942 by Hawkes & Son, Ltd.; renewed 1973. Used by permission.

Contrasts for Violin, Clarinet, and Piano. Copyright 1942 by Hawkes & Son, Ltd.; renewed 1969. Used by permission.

Dance Suite. Copyright 1924 by Universal Edition; renewed 1951. All rights in the U.S.A. owned by Boosey & Hawkes, Inc. Used by permission.

Divertimento for String Orchestra. Copyright 1940 by Hawkes & Son, Ltd.; renewed 1967. Used by permission.

Four Dirges (for piano). Copyright 1923 by Rózsavölgyi és Tsa, Budapest; copyright assigned 1950 to Editio Musica Budapest. Revised edition: copyright 1945 by Delkas Music Publishing Co.; copyright 1950 in the U.S.A. by Boosey & Hawkes, Inc. Used by permission.

Fourteen Bagatelles (for piano). Copyright 1908 by Rozsnyai Károly, Budapest; copyright assigned 1953 to Editio Musica Budapest; copyright 1950 by Boosey & Hawkes, Inc. Used by permission.

"Hussar," for choir and orchestra. Copyright 1942 by Hawkes & Son, Ltd.; renewed 1969. Used by permission.

Improvisations, op. 20 (for piano). Copyright 1922 by Universal Edition; renewed 1949. All rights assigned to Boosey & Hawkes Music Publishers Ltd. Used by permission.

Mikrokosmos (for piano). Copyright 1940 by Hawkes & Son, Ltd.; renewed 1967. Used by permission.

The Miraculous Mandarin. Copyright 1925, 1927, 1955 by Universal Edition; renewed 1952, 1955, 1983. All rights in the U.S.A. owned by Boosey & Hawkes, Inc. Used by permission.

Music for Strings, Percussion, and Celesta. Copyright 1937 by Universal Edition; renewed 1964. All rights in the U.S.A. owned by Boosey & Hawkes, Inc. Used by permission.

Nine Little Piano Pieces. Copyright 1927 by Universal Edition; renewed 1954. All rights in the U.S.A. owned by Boosey & Hawkes, Inc. Used by permission.

Out Doors (for piano). Copyright 1927 by Universal Edition; renewed 1954. All rights in the U.S.A. owned by Boosey & Hawkes, Inc. Used by permission.

Petite Suite (for piano). Copyright 1938 by Universal Edition; renewed 1965. All rights in the U.S.A. owned by Boosey & Hawkes, Inc. Used by permission.

Piano Concerto no. 1. Copyright 1927 by Universal Edition; renewed 1954. All rights in the U.S.A. owned by Boosey & Hawkes, Inc. Used by permission.

Piano Concerto no. 2. Copyright 1933, 1941 by Universal Edition; renewed 1960, 1968. All rights in the U.S.A. owned by Boosey & Hawkes, Inc. Used by permission.

Piano Concerto no. 3. Copyright 1946 by Boosey & Hawkes, Inc.; renewed 1974. Used by permission.

Rhapsody no. 1 for Violin and Piano. Copyright 1930 by Universal Edition; renewed 1957. All rights in the U.S.A. owned by Boosey & Hawkes, Inc. Used by permission.

Rhapsody no. 2 for Violin and Piano. Copyright 1929 by Universal Edition; renewed 1956. Revised version: copyright 1947 by Hawkes & Son, Ltd.; renewed 1975. All rights in the U.S.A. owned by Boosey & Hawkes, Inc. Used by permission.

Rumanian Folk Dances (for piano). Copyright 1918 by Universal Edition; renewed 1945. All rights in the U.S.A. owned by Boosey & Hawkes, Inc. Used by permission.

Seven Sketches (for piano). Copyright 1912 by Rozsnyai Károly, Budapest; copyright assigned 1954 to Editio Musica Budapest. Used by permission.

Sonata for Piano (1926). Copyright 1927 by Universal Edition; renewed 1954. All rights in the U.S.A. owned by Boosey & Hawkes, Inc. Used by permission.

Sonata for Two Pianos and Percussion. Copyright 1942 by Hawkes & Son, Ltd.; renewed 1969. Used by permission.

Sonata for Violin and Piano (1903). Copyright 1968 by Editio Musica Budapest. Used by permission.

Sonata for Violin and Piano no. 1. Copyright 1923 by Universal Edition; renewed 1950. All rights in the U.S.A. owned by Boosey & Hawkes, Inc. Used by permission.

Sonata for Violin and Piano no. 2. Copyright 1923 by Universal Edition; renewed 1950. All rights in the U.S.A. owned by Boosey & Hawkes, Inc. Used by permission.

String Quartet no. 1. Copyright by Rózsavölgyi és Tsa, Budapest. Copyright 1956 by Editio Musica Budapest. Used by permission.

String Quartet no. 2. Copyright 1920 by Universal Edition; renewed 1948. All rights in the U.S.A. owned by Boosey & Hawkes, Inc. Used by permission.

String Quartet no. 3. Copyright 1929 by Universal Edition; renewed 1956. All rights in the U.S.A. owned by Boosey & Hawkes, Inc. Used by permission.

String Quartet no. 4. Copyright 1929 by Universal Edition; renewed 1956. All rights in the U.S.A. owned by Boosey & Hawkes, Inc. Used by permission.

String Quartet no. 5. Copyright 1936 by Universal Edition; renewed 1963. All rights in the U.S.A. owned by Boosey & Hawkes, Inc. Used by permission.

String Quartet no. 6. Copyright 1941 by Hawkes & Son, Ltd.; renewed 1956. Used by permission.

Suite op. 14 (for piano). Copyright 1918 by Universal Edition; renewed 1945. All rights in the U.S.A. owned by Boosey & Hawkes, Inc. Used by permission.

Three Burlesques, op. 8c (for piano). Copyright 1912 by Rozsavölgyi és Tsa, Budapest. Copyright 1954 by Editio Musica Budapest. Copyright 1950 by Boosey & Hawkes, Inc. Used by permission.

Three Studies for Piano, op. 18. Copyright 1920 by Universal Edition; renewed 1945. All rights in the U.S.A. owned by Boosey & Hawkes, Inc. Used by permission.

Viola Concerto (viola and piano). Copyright 1949, 1950 by Boosey & Hawkes, Inc.; renewed 1976, 1977. Used by permission.

Violin Concerto no. 1, op. posth. Copyright 1958 by Boosey & Hawkes, Inc.; renewed 1986. Used by permission.

Violin Concerto no. 2. Copyright 1941, 1946 by Hawkes & Son, Ltd.; renewed 1968, 1973. Used by permission.

Wandering & Hussar, from Twenty-Seven Choruses a cappella. Copyright 1935 by Magyar Kórus; renewed 1960 by Editio Musica Budapest. Used by permission.

For permission for use of further copyrighted material, grateful acknowledgement is also made to the following:

Corvina Press, Budapest, for material from *Béla Bartók Letters* (copyright 1971), and Tibor Tallián, *Béla Bartók* (copyright 1988). Used by permission.

Editio Musica Budapest, for excerpts from *The Black Pocket-book* (copyright 1987), and for material from Tibor Tallián, ed., *Bartók Béla Írásai I* (copyright 1989). Used by permission.

St. Martin's Press, New York, for material from Benjamin Suchoff, ed., *Béla Bartók Essays* (copyright 1976). Used by permission.

ABBREVIATIONS

Antokoletz/1984
Elliott Antokoletz, *The Music of Béla Bartók: A Study of Tonality and Progression in Twentieth-Century Music* (Berkeley: University of California Press, 1984)

Archive Edition
Piano Music of Béla Bartók. The Archive Edition. Series 1–2, ed. Benjamin Suchoff (New York: Dover, 1981)

B & H
Boosey & Hawkes

Bartók/*Családi levelek*
Bartók Béla családi levelei [BB's family letters], ed. Béla Bartók Jr. and Adrienne Gombocz-Konkoly (Budapest: Zeneműkiadó, 1981)

Bartók/*SP*
Béla Bartók, *Slovenské l'udové piesne / Slowakische Volkslieder*, vols. 1–2 (Bratislava: Academia Scientiarum Slovaca, 1959, 1970)

BB
Béla Bartók Thematic Catalogue number

BBA
Budapest Bartók Archives (Bartók Archívum, Budapest)

B. Bartók Jr./*Apám*
Béla Bartók Jr., *Apám életének krónikája* [The chronicle of my father's life] (Budapest: Zeneműkiadó, 1981)

BBI/1
Bartók Béla Írásai [BB's writings]. Vol. 1: *Bartók Béla önmagáról, műveiről, az új magyar zenéről, műzene és népzene viszonyáról* [BB on his life, work, the new Hungarian music, the relation between art music and folk music], ed. Tibor Tallián (Budapest: Zeneműkiadó, 1989)

BBLevelei

Bartók Béla levelei [BB's letters], ed. János Demény (Budapest: Zeneműkiadó, 1976)

Black Pocket-book

Black Pocket-book. Sketches 1907–1922, by Béla Bartók, ed. László Somfai (Budapest: Editio Musica, 1987)

BÖI

Bartók Béla Összegyűjtött Írásai [BB's collected writings], ed. András Szőllősy (Budapest: Zeneműkiadó, 1967)

Bónis/*Így láttuk*

Így láttuk Bartókot: Harminchat emlékezés [Bartók remembered: 36 recollections], ed. Ferenc Bónis (Budapest: Zeneműkiadó, 1981)

Centenary Edition

Centenary Edition of Bartók's Records (Complete), ed. László Somfai, Zoltán Kocsis, and János Sebestyén, vols. 1–2 (Budapest: Hungaroton, 1981), LPX 12326–33, 12334–38

DD

Dille number in Dille/*Verzeichnis*

Dille/1939

Denijs Dille, *Béla Bartók* ([Antwerp]: Standaard-Boekhandel, 1939)

Dille/1990

Denijs Dille, *Béla Bartók. Regard sur le passé*, ed. Yves Lenoir (Louvain-la-Neuve: Institut Supérieur d'Archéologie et d'Histoire de l'Art, Collège Érasme, 1990)

Dille/*Verzeichnis*

Denijs Dille, *Thematisches Verzeichnis der Jugendwerke Béla Bartóks 1890–1904* (Budapest: Akadémiai Kiadó, 1974)

DocB/1–4

Documenta Bartókiana, ed. Denijs Dille, vols. 1–4 (Budapest: Academy Press; Mainz: Schott's Söhne, 1964–1970)

DocB/5–6

Documenta Bartókiana, ed. László Somfai, vols. 5–6 (Budapest: Academy Press; Mainz: Schott's Söhne, 1977–1981)

EMB

Editio Musica Budapest (=Zeneműkiadó)

Essays

Béla Bartók Essays, ed. Benjamin Suchoff (London: Faber and Faber, 1976)

Gillies/*Remembered*

Malcolm Gillies, *Bartók Remembered* (London and Boston: Faber and Faber, 1990)

Lampert/*Quellenkatalog*

Vera Lampert, "Quellenkatalog der Volksliedbearbeitungen von Bartók." In *DocB/6*, 15–149

Letters
Béla Bartók Letters, ed. János Demény (Budapest: Corvina Press, 1971)

Maramureş/1975
Béla Bartók, *Rumanian Folk Music*, ed. Benjamin Suchoff. Vol. V: *Maramureş County* (The Hague: Nijhoff, 1975)

M K
Magyar Kórus

ML
Music and Letters

MQ
The Musical Quarterly

OSZK
Országos Széchényi Könyvtár (Széchényi National Library), Budapest

PB
Peter Bartók's archive (Homosassa, Florida)

R
Rozsnyai

RFM
Béla Bartók, *Rumanian Folk Music*, ed. Benjamin Suchoff. Vol. I: *Instrumental Melodies;* vol. II: *Vocal Melodies* (The Hague: Nijhoff, 1967)

Rv
Rózsavölgyi

SM
Studia Musicologica Academiae Scientiarum Hungaricae

Somfai/*19th-Century Ideas*
László Somfai, "Nineteenth-Century Ideas Developed in Bartók's Piano Notation in the Years 1907–14." *19th-Century Music* 11, no. 1 (Summer 1987): 73–91

Somfai/*Allegro barbaro*
———, "Die 'Allegro barbaro'-Aufnahme von Bartók textkritisch bewertet." In *DocB/6*, 259–275

Somfai/*Exhibition*
———, *Bartók's Workshop. Sketches, Manuscripts, Versions: The Compositional Process.* Exhibition of the Budapest Bartók Archives (Budapest: Bartók Archives, 1987)

Somfai/*Influence*
———, "The Influence of Peasant Music on the Finale of Bartók's Piano Sonata: An Assignment for Musicological Analysis." In *Studies in Musical Sources and Style. Essays in Honor of Jan LaRue*, ed. Eugene K. Wolf and Edward H. Roesner (Madison, Wis.: A-A Editions, 1990)

Somfai/*Liszt's Influence*
———, "Liszt's Influence on Bartók Reconsidered." *The New Hungarian Quarterly* 17, no. 102 (Autumn 1986): 210–219

Somfai/*MS vs. Urtext*

—, "Manuscript versus Urtext: The Primary Sources of Bartók's Works." *SM* 1981: 17–66

Somfai/*Piano Year*

—, "Analytical Notes on Bartók's Piano Year of 1926." *SM* 1984: 5–58

Somfai/*Rubato-Stil*

—, "Über Bartóks Rubato-Stil: Vergleichende Studie der zwei Aufnahmen 'Abend am Lande' des Komponisten." In *DocB/5*, 193–201

Somfai/*Strategics*

—, "Strategics of Variation in the Second Movement of Bartók's Violin Concerto 1937–1938." *SM* 1977: 161–202

Somfai/*Tizennyolc*

—, *Tizennyolc Bartók-tanulmány* [18 Bartók studies] (Budapest: Zeneműkiadó, 1981)

Somfai/*Vázlatok I, II, III*

—, "Bartók vázlatok" I–III [Bartók sketches, I–III (Piano Sonata Mov. I; Sonata for Violin and Piano no. 1; fragments in the *Black Pocket-book*)]. In *Zenetudományi Dolgozatok* (Budapest: MTA Zenetudományi Intézet) 1984, 71–81; 1985, 21–36; 1986, 7–18

Somfai/*Viola Concerto*

—, *Viola Concerto*, by Béla Bartók. Facsimile Edition of the Autograph Draft with a Commentary by László Somfai and Fair Copy of the Draft with Notes Prepared by Nelson Dellamaggiore (Homosassa, Fla.: Bartók Records, 1995)

Sz

Szőllősy number of the works

Tallián/1988

Tibor Tallián, *Béla Bartók, the Man and His Work*. Translated by Gyula Gulyás; translation revised by Paul Merrick (Budapest: Corvina, 1988)

UE

Universal Edition

W

Waldbauer number of the works

W.Ph., W.Ph.V.

Wien: Philharmonia Partituren

1 · INTRODUCTION

The sheer volume of writing on Bartók is staggering. The complete bibliography of books, studies, and doctoral dissertations written since his death, not to speak of publications of his letters, along with the mass of documentary essays and articles, often written by nonmusicians, on biographical connections, on the ethnomusicological angle, and on the composer's aesthetics, has grown to truly overwhelming proportions.

This immense Bartók literature is, however, disturbingly uncoordinated and controversial. First of all there are serious language barriers: the larger part of the extant Bartókiana has been written not in major world languages but in Hungarian. Owing primarily to the restricted access to sources and partly to the narrow horizons of interest of several dedicated specialists, from the beginning until recently a gap has existed in Bartók research between the study of the biography and the work, between source studies and style analysis. Very few of the acknowledged Bartók scholars have made use of studies by other authors. Thus, instead of evolving as an organic whole, Bartók studies have branched into rather isolated individual approaches, necessarily on extremely different professional levels.

The postwar political circumstances in Hungary have also been responsible for the unhealthy growth of Hungarian Bartókiana, and for unnecessary discourses even in serious analytical studies. Bartók's personality, music, and aesthetics have been used or rather abused as a symbol of matters he would hardly approve. His endeavor to create world music on a national basis became the ideal of the next generations. Yet Bartók's enthusiasm for peasant music has also been used as justification for an oversimplified concept of the folk-music movement. Even his own oeuvre has been victimized by extremist aesthetes of the period who divided it in two parts, praising the works based on folk music or "of a folk-music simplicity" and condemning the modern, "formalist" works. All this in turn provoked as an opposition a great amount of shadowboxing even in the best Bartók literature of the period. Thus in his own small country the Bartók phenomenon, the weighty legacy of a famous son, far exceeded the interest in Bartók's music.

In spite of these peripheral issues, considering the relevant Bartók studies alone, the main stumbling block has been the lack of access to the sources at the time Bartók research began, right after the composer's death in New York City on September 26, 1945. The bulk of his manuscripts has been shared between Budapest and New York: they were either in the possession of his elder son, Béla, and his widow, Ditta, in Budapest, and later on as their deposit in the Budapest Bartók Archives (Bartók Archívum), or in the American Béla Bartók Estate, housed in the Béla Bartók Archives in New York, under the directorship of the trustee, Victor Bator, and after his death, Benjamin Suchoff. As a result of the policy of the management of the two collections, aggravated by cold-war politics, the endless litigations in the 1960s and 1970s, family and legal matters, mixed-up roles of trusteeship, directorship, and scholarship, coupled with personal rivalry, the autograph sources (even their photocopies) were available for public research only to a very limited extent.

These circumstances led in turn to an unwanted specialization on fields that could be exploited without the primary sources or that have been based on a limited number or circle of available sources. For decades there was a proliferation of two kinds of so-called Bartók specialists. The one, generally working in a single isolated field based on accessible documents, collected local biographical data or speculated on extramusical aspects of Bartók's life and work; this approach was more common in Hungary. The other, most often encountered in Germany or in the United States, was the curious musician, looking for a dissertation topic or a less competitive field in which to present his analytical methods. These would-be scholars often became interested in Bartók's music only because it seemed in so many respects to be refreshingly different from the mainstream of Western music.

Moreover, the hard core of the Bartók studies had not been flawless either. The majority of the authors of the best books, analyses, and essays to emerge in the first generation of postwar Bartók studies had not been professional musicologists. They did not belong to the trained musicologists who would have cared about the interconnection of their work with the main trends in historical musicology; who would have been concerned with the compatibility of Bartók style analysis with the standard approaches, and terminology; who would not have been satisfied with commercial editions of the score but would at least have insisted on the scholar's right to see the autograph sources of Bartók's compositions.[1]

A survey of the approaches characteristic of the still often-quoted pioneering

1. It is a great pity that Otto Gombosi could not complete his Bartók book, on which he worked intensively until his death in 1955; see László Somfai, "A Major Unfinished Work on Bartók," *New Hungarian Quarterly* 1981: 91ff.

essays reveals the truth of this progress report.[2] One thinks of the first monographs by Serge Moreux (1949) and Halsey Stevens (1953);[3] analyses written by composers, notably Mátyás Seiber (1945), György Ligeti (1948), Milton Babbitt (1949), George Perle (1955), Allen Forte (1960), András Mihály (1967), and Lajos Bárdos (1969);[4] documentary studies without any institutional backing by a self-made music scholar, János Demény (1948), and a composer-philologist, András Szőllősy (1948);[5] the approaches of the first generation of dedicated young musician-scholars who gathered around the musicologist Bence Szabolcsi but were without regular musicological training, such as Ernő Lendvai (1947), a pioneer in style analysis, and József Ujfalussy (1962);[6] the first wave of German dissertations and books on Bartók by Hans Ulrich Engelmann (1953), Jürgen Uhde (1954), Roswitha Traimer (1956),[7] and others. The very promising studies of Colin Mason (1950) came to a sudden end;[8] analytical approaches similar to Leo Treitler's (1959) were rare;[9] and a study dedicated to the genesis of a work based on an autograph manuscript, like the one by István Szelényi (1954), was an exception.[10]

2. The references that follow are not intended as a survey or evaluation of the complete Bartók literature. For an extensive survey, with annotations, see Elliott Antokoletz, *Béla Bartók: A Guide to Research* (New York: Garland, 1988).

3. Serge Moreux, *Béla Bartók: sa vie, ses oeuvres, son langage* (Paris: Richard-Massé, 1949); Halsey Stevens, *The Life and Music of Béla Bartók* (New York: Oxford University Press, 1953).

4. Mátyás Seiber, *The String Quartets of Béla Bartók* (London: B&H, 1945); György Ligeti, "Bartók: Medvetánc" [Bear dance], *Zenei Szemle* (Budapest) 1947: 216ff.; Milton Babbitt, "The String Quartets of Bartók," *MQ* 1949: 377ff.; George Perle, "Symmetrical Formations in the String Quartets of Béla Bartók," *Music Review* 1955: 300ff.; Allen Forte, "Bartók's Serial Composition," *MQ* 1960: 233ff.; András Mihály, "Metrika Bartók IV. vonósnégyesének II. tételében" [Metrics in Mov. II of B's String Quartet no. 4], *Muzsika* (Budapest) 1967, nos. 10–12: 18ff., 34ff., 35ff.; and Lajos Bárdos, *Harminc Írás* [Thirty essays] (Budapest: EMB, 1969), 9ff.

5. János Demény, ed., *Bartók Béla levelek, fényképek, kéziratok, kották* [BB's letters, photos, manuscripts, scores] (Budapest: Magyar Művészeti Tanács, 1948), and his subsequent editions of Bartók's letters (1951–1976), including *BBLevelei* and *Letters*, as well as the documentary studies in *Zenetudományi Tanulmányok II, VII, X,* ed. Bence Szabolcsi and Dénes Bartha (Budapest: Akadémiai Kiadó, 1954–1962), etc.; András Szőllősy, ed., *Bartók Béla válogatott zenei írásai* [BB's selected writings on music], (Budapest: Magyar Kórus, 1948), and enlarged editions, including *BÖI* (1967). Szőllősy is also the author of the list of the Sz numbers of the Bartók works in Bence Szabolcsi, ed., *Bartók, sa vie et son oeuvre* (Budapest: Corvina, 1968), 299ff., and in subsequent revised editions.

6. Ernő Lendvai, "Bartók: Az éjszaka zenéje" [Night's music], *Zenei Szemle* (Budapest) 1947: 216ff., and subsequent analytical studies, including his first book, *Bartók stílusa* [B's style] (Budapest: Zeneműkiadó, 1955); József Ujfalussy, "A híd-szerkezet néhány tartalmi kérdése Bartók művészetében" [Semantics of the bridge-form in B's music], in *Zenetudományi Tanulmányok X* (Budapest: Akadémiai Kiadó, 1962), 541ff., as well as his later essays, books, and documentary volumes.

7. Hans Ulrich Engelmann, *Béla Bartóks Mikrokosmos: Versuch einer Typologie "Neuer Musik"* (Würzburg: Triltsch Verlag, 1953); Jürgen Uhde, *Bartóks Mikrokosmos: Spielanweisungen und Erläuterungen* (Regensburg: Bosse Verlag, 1954); and Roswitha Traimer, *Béla Bartóks Kompositionstechnik dargestellt an seinen sechs Streichquartetten* (Regensburg: Bosse Verlag, 1956).

8. Colin Mason, "Béla Bartók and the Folksong," *The Music Review* 1950: 292ff.; and idem, "An Essay in Analysis: Tonality, Symmetry, and Latent Serialism in Bartók's Fourth Quartet," *The Music Review* 1957: 189ff.

9. Leo Treitler, "Harmonic Procedure in the Fourth Quartet of Béla Bartók," *Journal of Music Theory* 1959: 292ff.

10. István Szelényi, "Bartók Zongoraszonátájának kialakulása" [The genesis of B's Piano Sonata], *Új Zenei Szemle* 1954: 20ff.

If scholarly work on Bartók was thus long impeded by the difficulty of access to original sources, misconceptions in policy and practice also beset the research carried out internally in the two archives, which were sitting on all this exquisite material. The New York Béla Bartók estate and archives was for many years under the powerful direction of Victor Bator, who was once the personal legal adviser of Bartók but was not a musician and certainly not a scholarly man. Bator, who died in 1969, was brilliant about collecting material, yet he made terribly amateurish decisions when it came to keeping the original manuscripts safe and let dedicated musicologists such as Iván Waldbauer and John Vinton[11] leave the archive's staff. No wonder the planned thematic index could not be compiled, source analysis of the compositions ground to a standstill, and very few exemplary source studies were published. Bator's successor in the trusteeship, Benjamin Suchoff, whose policy was criticized by the musicological branch and partly by the heirs too, had practically closed the archives. Only the publication of a series of volumes devoted to the ethnomusicological works by Bartók, the personal ambition of the new trustee, went on energetically.[12]

The Bartók Archívum in Budapest, an institute of the Hungarian Academy of Sciences, had been established as a musicological workshop. Its first director (1961–1972), Denijs Dille, a Belgian priest, lyceum professor, and self-made music scholar, was sought out for this post by the composer Zoltán Kodály and by Bence Szabolcsi. His Bartók book, one of the earliest monographs, had been acknowledged by the composer himself. He established a new standard in source-oriented documentary studies, produced a superb survey of the juvenile compositions in the form of a thematic index, edited early compositions, and wrote basic studies on several issues, having a special interest in the works connected with critical moments in Bartók's life.[13] I began working with Dille in 1963 and became his successor at the archives in 1972. For several years I was thus the head of the only public Bartók collection — but without access to the American sources. Despite this impediment, members of our staff, Vera Lampert (Lampert-Deák) and Tibor Tallián, managed to accomplish crucial studies,[14] which were in turn complemented by the work of an even younger

11. For examples of their work, see Iván Waldbauer, "Bartók's First Piano Concerto: A Publication History," *MQ* 1965: 336ff.; John Vinton, "Toward a Chronology of the Mikrokosmos," *SM* 1966: 41ff.

12. Benjamin Suchoff edited *RFM*, 5 vols. (The Hague: Nijhoff, 1967–1975); *Turkish Folk Music from Asia Minor* (Princeton: Princeton University Press, 1976); *Yugoslav Folk Music*, 4 vols. (Albany: State University of New York Press, 1978); *The Hungarian Folk Song* (Albany: State University of New York Press, 1981). Suchoff also published a *Guide to Bartók's Mikrokosmos* (London: B&H, 1957), as well as several studies and editions, including Bartók's *Essays* (1976).

13. Dille/*1939*; *DocB/1–4*, ed. Denijs Dille (1964–1970); Dille/*Verzeichnis* (1974); Dille/*1990* (revised edition of Dille's selected essays).

14. Vera Lampert, "Vázlat Bartók II. vonósnégyesének utolsó tételéhez" [Sketch of the last movement of B's String Quartet no. 2], *Magyar Zene* (Budapest) 1972: 252ff. (also in *DocB/5*); and Lampert/*Quellenkatalog* (1981); Tibor Tallián, "Bartók opusz-számozásának kérdéséhez" [On B's opus numbers], *Muzsika* (Budapest) 1975: 17ff.; idem, *Bartók Béla* (Budapest: Gondolat, 1981; the English edition is Tallián/1988); and idem, "Die Cantata profana — ein Mythos des Übergangs," *SM* 1981: 135ff.

generation, my former pupils, who had been trained in the concept of complex Bartók studies.[15] The Budapest Bartók Archives is, however, still not authorized to let independent scholars, regardless of their nationality, make unlimited use of the sources in the collection. Although housed in the archive on permanent loan, a great many of these documents have been the property of Béla Bartók Jr.

As a consequence of such restrictions, in spite of a high standard in analytical work contributed from the late 1960s onward by János Kárpáti or Peter Petersen, Frank Michael or Ilkka Oramo,[16] to name a few, a complex study of the genesis of the compositions was regrettably missing in the majority of the new studies. Granted, there were exceptions in the 1960s and 1970s. György Kroó, one of the central figures in Bartók studies in Hungary,[17] was able to examine sources for the stage works in New York and collect data on Bartók's compositional plans,[18] while Günter Weiss (Weiss-Aigner) and Yves Lenoir obtained access to the Budapest Bartók material in order to write their dissertations.[19] Elliott Antokoletz, now a prominent figure in American Bartók studies, managed to consult photocopies of the New York manuscripts for his dissertation and his major analytical study, and Miklós Szabó, author of the basic book on Bartók's choruses, was able to see some sources.[20] Since the 1980s ambitious young musicologists have increasingly found

15. The work of the next generation includes András Wilheim, "Bartók's Exercises in Composition," *SM* 1981: 67ff.; idem, "Skizzen zu 'Mikrokosmos' Nr. 135 und Nr. 57," in *DocB/6*: 235ff.; Sándor Kovács, "Reexamining the Bartók/Serly Viola Concerto," *SM* 1981: 295ff.; idem, "Über die Vorbereitung der Publikation von Bartóks großer ungarischer Volksliedausgabe," *SM* 1982: 133ff.; Sándor Kovács and Ferenc Sebő, ed., *Bartók Béla: Magyar Népdalok. Egyetemes Gyűjtemény* I (Budapest: Akadémiai Kiadó, 1991; English edition: *Hungarian Folksongs. Complete Collection* I [Budapest: Akadémiai Kiadó, 1993]). See Klára Móricz's dissertation, "Bartók Béla: Concerto zenekarra" [Concerto for orchestra] (Liszt Ferenc Zeneművészeti Főiskola, Budapest, 1992); idem, "New Aspects of the Genesis of Béla Bartók's Concerto for Orchestra: Concepts of 'Finality' and 'Intention'," *SM* 1993–94: 181ff.; and László Vikárius, "Béla Bartók's Cantata Profana (1930): A Reading of the Sources," *SM* 1993–94: 249ff.

16. János Kárpáti, *Bartók vonósnégyesei* (Budapest: Zeneműkiadó, 1967), published in English as *Bartók's String Quartets* (Budapest: Corvina, 1975); idem, "Les gammes populaires et le système chromatique dans l'oeuvre de Béla Bartók," *SM* 1969: 227ff.; idem, *Bartók's Chamber Music* (Stuyvesant, N.Y.: Pendragon Press, 1994); Peter Petersen, *Die Tonalität im Instrumentalschaffen von Béla Bartók* (Hamburg: Wagner, 1971); idem, "Bartóks Sonata für Violine solo. Ein Appell an die Hüter der Autographen," in *Musik-Konzepte 22*, ed. H.-K. Metzger and R. Riehn (1981); Frank Michael, *Béla Bartóks Variationstechnik. Dargestellt im Rahmen einer Analyse seines 2. Violinkonzertes* (Regensburg: Bosse Verlag, 1976); Ilkka Oramo, "Marcia und Burletta. Zur Tradition der Rhapsodie in zwei Quartettsätzen Bartóks," *Die Musikforschung* 1977: 14ff.

17. György Kroó, "Duke Bluebeard's Castle," *SM* 1961: 251ff.; and idem, *Bartók színpadi művei* [Stage works] (Budapest: Zeneműkiadó, 1962).

18. György Kroó, "Bartók Béla megvalósulatlan kompozíciós terveiről," *Magyar Zene* (Budapest) 1969: 251ff., available in English as "Unrealized Plans and Ideas for Projects by Bartók," *SM* 1970: 11ff.; idem, "Adatok 'A kékszakállú herceg vára' keletkezéstörténetéhez," Ferenc Bónis, ed., *Magyar Zenetörténeti Tanumányok II* (Budapest: Zeneműkiadó, 1969), 333ff., published in English as "Data on the Genesis of Duke Bluebeard's Castle," *SM* 1981: 79ff.

19. Günter Weiss, *Die frühe Schaffensentwicklung Béla Bartóks im Lichte westlicher und östlicher Traditionen* (Erlangen-Nürnberg: Friedrich-Alexander Universität, 1970); Yves Lenoir, *Vie et oeuvre de Béla Bartók aux États-Unis d'Amérique (1940–1945)* (Louvain: Université Catholique de Louvain, 1976); idem, "Contribution à l'étude de la Sonate pour violon solo de Béla Bartók," *SM* 1981: 209ff.

20. Elliott Antokoletz, "Principles of Pitch Organization in Bartók's Fourth String Quartet" (Ph.D.

ways to conduct source research, visiting the material in North America and Hungary. Some, such as Jürgen Hunkemöller in Germany and Malcolm Gillies in Australia, whose works stand at the forefront of international Bartók scholarship, and to an even greater extent the youngest generation of Ph.D. candidates working on Bartók projects, have realized that one must learn Hungarian in order to be a full-scale Bartók scholar.[21] Yet even in these important studies the inspection of sketches and manuscripts primarily serves to illustrate previously crystallized analytical statements: source studies only complement the analysis, rather than motivating the scholarly work in the first place.

The prospects for the study of sources have dramatically changed in recent years. After the death of Bartók's widow (1982) and the following legal procedure, in 1987–1988 the original sources of the former New York Bartók estate and archives came de facto into the hands of the younger son of the composer, Peter Bartók, who keeps the collection in his private archive in Florida. With his assistants he is working on the revision of the printed editions of the compositions,[22] as well as on the publication of folksong collections thus far unavailable in print. But he also sent a full set of photocopies of the primary sources for the compositions to the Budapest Bartók Archives in 1988 in order to aid our work on the preparation of the complete critical edition of the music, and in 1989 he invited me to examine the original sources at his home in Homosassa, Florida. In addition, the biographical and documentary publications of the composer's elder son, Béla Bartók Jr., have brought to light several unknown facts about the compositions.[23]

---

diss., City University of New York, 1975); idem, *The Music of Béla Bartók: A Study of Tonality and Progression in Twentieth-Century Music* (Berkeley: University of California Press, 1984); Miklós Szabó, *Bartók Béla kórusművei* [B's choruses] (Budapest: EMB, 1985).

21. Jürgen Hunkemöller, "Béla Bartóks Musik für Saiteninstrumente," *Archiv für Musikwissenschaft* 1983: 147ff.; Malcolm Gillies, *Notation and Tonal Structure in Bartók's Later Works* (New York: Garland, 1989); idem, *Bartók in Britain* (Oxford: Oxford University Press, 1989); Gillies/*Remembered*.

22. After I had mostly completed the manuscript of this book, a series of revised editions appeared under the supervision of Peter Bartók. These include the following corrected reprints of original UE editions, all marked "New Edition [with year] / Revision: Peter Bartók" (listed here in the works' chronological order, with the year of the new edition given in parentheses): BB 63 *Allegro barbaro* (1992); BB 69 *Rumanian Folk Dances* (1993); BB 70 Suite, op. 14 (1992); BB 71 *Five Songs*, op. 15 (1991); BB 76 *Rumanian Folk Dances*, for orchestra (1991); BB 79 *Fifteen Hungarian Peasant Songs* (1994); BB 84 Sonata for Violin and Piano no. 1 (1991); BB 86b *Dance Suite*, for piano (1991); BB 87a *Five Village Scenes* (1994); BB 88 Sonata, for piano (1992); BB 89 *Out Doors*, vol. I (nos. 1–3, 1990); BB 91 Piano Concerto no. 1, 2-piano reduction (1992); BB 93 String Quartet no. 3, parts only (1992); BB 101 Piano Concerto no. 2, 2-piano reduction (1993); BB 104 Forty-Four Duets [Duos], for two violins (1992); BB 110 String Quartet no. 5, parts only (1992). Furthermore, some revised B&H editions, also produced under the supervision of Peter Bartók, are now available: BB 105 *Mikrokosmos*, vols. 1–6, "New Definitive Edition 1987" (EMB license edition also); BB 123 Concerto for Orchestra, "Revised Edition, 1993"; BB 124 Sonata for Solo Violin, "urtext edition," copyright 1994; BB 127 Piano Concerto no. 3, "Revised Edition, 1994."

23. B. Bartók Jr./*Apám* (1981); Bartók/*Családi levelek* (1981).

We are at a turning point. The Bartók interpretation, the younger generations of musicology, and the Bartók cult deserve better conditions, otherwise the fair chances of Bartók's oeuvre will inevitably lag behind that of the music of his contemporaries. A guide — a thematic catalogue of the works (which is already in progress) — is badly needed so that scholars can orient themselves in the confusing landscape of the many versions and editions of his music. Even more urgently needed, however, is a reliable edition of the whole oeuvre, the *Béla Bartók Complete Critical Edition* in progress, with all the relevant information about Bartók's notation and performance practice for the performers, and completed with the significant documents pertaining to the genesis of the individual compositions (sketches, the draft, old and corrected versions, etc.), for future Bartók studies.

Since the late 1960s a major part of my work — greater than the list of my publications would suggest — has been dedicated to the study of the compositional process lying behind Bartók's oeuvre. My concern was stimulated by my daily contact with the manuscripts, by the archivist's job, and by an analytical interest in the original sources. Soon it was also motivated by the systematic preparation of the critical edition, a *Gesamtausgabe* that would need to be different from the classical series of postwar complete critical editions, because the case of Bartók, as I recognized it and as this book will reveal, is fascinatingly different. Unfortunately, from the mid-1970s temporarily I had to postpone the realization of the plan of the critical edition. Yet in teaching and lecturing I concentrated on the training of future Bartók editors and began advocating new approaches to Bartók studies in methodologically varied essays and analyses. The study of source types and source chains,[24] the publication of facsimile editions with commentaries,[25] editions and analyses of sketches,[26] the collection and edition of Bartók's records,[27] special essays dedicated to characteristic features of his performance,[28] the study of the evolution of Bartók's notation,[29] complemented by different kinds of style analysis[30] and the investigation of the influence of peasant music[31] — all mark the trends in my work during these years.

My intention in this book is thus to summarize the results of nearly three decades of work for the benefit of future Bartók studies. I hope to place Bartók's compositional process in a new light, to guide young scholars toward the gaps in research that can now be filled, and to establish the reputation of scholarship on Bartók as just one of the ordinary topics in the study of the oeuvre of the great composers.

24. Somfai/*MS vs. Urtext* (1981); Somfai/*Exhibition* (1987).
25. *Two Rumanian Dances for Piano* (Budapest: EMB, 1974); *Sonata (1926), Piano Solo* (Budapest: EMB, 1980); and *Black Pocket-book: Sketches 1907–1922* (Budapest: EMB, 1987).
26. Somfai/*Vázlatok I–III* (1984–1986), also in Somfai/*Tizennyolc* (1981), 31–113.
27. *Centenary Edition* (1981).
28. Somfai/*Rubato-Stil* (1977); Somfai/*Allegro barbaro* (1981).
29. Somfai/*19th-Century Ideas* (1987).
30. Somfai/*Strategies* (1977); Somfai/*Piano Year* (1984), also in Somfai/*Tizennyolc*, 194–217.
31. Somfai/*Influence* (a study from 1981, published in 1990).

Currently it is my good fortune, as a Bartók specialist, to have what is probably more firsthand experience with the primary sources in Hungary, the United States, and other countries than any of my predecessors and colleagues. In addition, owing to my editorial work and my study of sketches, style, and performance practice in the course of my studies on eighteenth-century composers, perhaps I have the perspectives necessary at this crucial moment to place the study of Bartók in the wider context of historical musicology. If at times I refer to my own publications with what might seem immodest frequency, I beg the pardon both of my readers and my fellow Bartók scholars. I do so largely for the sake of brevity, to avoid page-long quotations from my own writings. I mean no disrespect to the enthusiasm and dedication of other Bartók scholars, many of whom have produced extremely relevant studies despite the obstacles to research outlined above. I sincerely believe that our goal should now be to do justice to Bartók, rather than to Bartók scholarship, for the disadvantages of the past.

2 · BARTÓK ON COMPOSITION, HIS CONCEPTS, AND WORKS

Béla Bartók did not like to speak or write about his music. And when he did, he was shy, his words were unsophisticated. Bartók's masterpieces and his verbal communications exhibit a remarkable contrast. The works reveal immense technical resources; the composer said little about his workshop. Many of his outstanding instrumental works (such as the string quartets, the 2-piano Sonata, the *Music for Strings, Percussion, and Celesta*) are very "systematic" compositions. Bartók himself, on the contrary, stubbornly claimed that he had no system, created no theories in advance. The contrast was even more striking when folk music was involved. As an ethnomusicologist, in his transcriptions and studies Bartók was extremely positive, accurate, unbiased; but as a composer — and indeed one who claimed that peasant music was the primary source of his own style — talking about his individual works, he was intentionally vague concerning the actual connections.

Nothing would be easier for us than, with the usual self-confident professionalism of modern musicology, to read, comment, and reinterpret Bartók's own words; to confront them with the scores and thus transfer the author's reserved remarks into sophisticated analytical explanations. This, however, is not my intention at all. We must respect Bartók's attitude. So let us consider first what he thought suitable to reveal about his concepts and works; let us try to understand his motivation for saying no more than he did; and let us base our interpretation of Bartók's compositional process on the detailed study of the musical sources.

Hints and evidence in several types of reliable sources from different periods of his life suggest that Bartók did not want to reveal and analyze the moment of creation. He intended to maintain the feeling of natural instinct and directness in his own composition. For this reason he declined to teach composition on a regular basis: evaluating a new piece of music — in order to correct it, to explain his criticism — involved an amount of conscientious and sophisticated brain-work that Bartók felt was artificial in discussing art. What he said in 1937 during a well-conducted interview with Denijs Dille reflects Bartók's general attitude:

> I must state that my entire music . . . is determined by instinct and sensibility; useless to ask me why did I write this or that, why so and why not so. I could not give an explanation, except that I felt this way, I wrote it down this way.[1]

The Harvard Lectures of 1943 offer the only occasion on which Bartók went into significant technical details about his style: "Now that the greatest part of my work has already been written, certain general tendencies appear — general formulas from which theories can be deduced." This account, however, was still full of observations about elements that "developed quite subconsciously and instinctively." Before he explained how he worked out his bi-modality and modal chromaticism, a main feature of his music, Bartók made a statement, with important negations and at the same time with cryptic messages:

> I never created new theories in advance, I hated such ideas. I had, of course, a very definite feeling about certain directions to take, but at the time of the work I did not care about the designations which would apply to those directions or to their sources. This attitude does not mean that I composed without prealably[2] set plans and without sufficient control. The plans were concerned with the spirit of the new work and with technical problems (for instance, formal structure involved by the spirit of the work), all more or less instinctively felt, but I never was concerned with general theories to be applied to the works I was going to write.[3]

Amid public discussions on systems and methods, Bartók strongly believed that intuition played a central role and that "the spontaneous expression of Genius is sometimes more complicated than a mechanical creation, and the simplest means sometimes appear as the most complex" (1938).[4]

Bartók hated labels. As a contemporary of Arnold Schoenberg and Igor Stravinsky, of course he had his share of being labeled. In a letter written June 21, 1926, to his second wife, Ditta, from his asylum in their Budapest flat where after much frustration he was able to write piano pieces again, there is a remarkable outburst:

---

1. The interview was in German; Denijs Dille published it in French in *La Sirène* (Brussels, March 1937); reprinted in Dille / 1990, 27–29.

2. This word — which Bartók anglicized from the French *préalable* [preliminary] — appears in Bartók's autograph draft of the text of the Harvard Lectures (Lecture A in Peter Bartók's collection) but not in the *Essays* volume.

3. *Essays*, 376.

4. *Essays*, 516.

To be frank, recently I have felt so stupid, so dazed, so empty-headed that I have truly doubted whether I am able to write anything new anymore. All the tangled chaos that the musical periodicals vomit thick and fast about the music of today has come to weigh heavily on me: the watchwords linear, horizontal, vertical, objective, impersonal, polyphonic, homophonic, tonal, polytonal, atonal, and the rest; even if one does not concern one's self with all of it, one still becomes quite dazed when they shout it in our ears so much. As a matter of fact it is best not to read anything at all, and just write, regardless of all these slogans.[5]

It is owing to a few frank family letters, always written to the beloved woman, that we have any idea of how intensively Bartók was engaged with the real meaning of musical composition, with the extramusical connotations, with the secret message of a masterwork. In one of his letters (February 4, 1909) to Márta, soon to become his first wife, Bartók not only discussed the emotional resources of modern music but admitted that biographical events directly influenced his work:

It is curious that in music until now only enthusiasm, love, grief, or at most, distress figured as motivating causes — that is the so-called exalted ideals. Whereas vengeance, caricature, sarcasm are only living or are going to live their musical lives in our times. For this reason, perhaps, in contrast to the idealism manifested in the previous age, present-day musical art might be termed realistic, which without selection will sincerely and truly include all human emotions among those expressible.

. . . I strongly believe and profess that every true art is produced through the influence of impressions we gather within ourselves from the outer world, of "experiences." He who paints a landscape only to paint a landscape, or writes a symphony just to write a symphony, is at best nothing but a craftsman. I am unable to imagine products of art otherwise than as manifestations of the creator's boundless enthusiasm, regret, fury, revenge, distorting ridicule, or sarcasm. In the past I did not believe, until I experienced it myself, that a man's works designate the events, the guiding passions of his life more exactly than his biography. We are speaking, of course, of real and genuine artists.[6]

In spite of the slightly magistral overtone of this Bartókian type of love letter, the message is uniquely direct. We should remember that the group of works written to Stefi Geyer, the nineteen-year-old violinist, expressing Bartók's feelings about this hopeless romantic affair — pieces containing a leitmotiv, further coded themes, and motivic references[7] — were composed in 1907 or 1908. Such manifestations were, however, extremely rare even in the family correspondence. The most personal

5. The original Hungarian in Bartók/*Családi levelek*, 381; English version in Tallián/1988, 140.
6. Original in Bartók/*Családi levelek*, 187–188; English in Tallián/1988, 76f., 88f.
7. The list includes Violin Concerto op. posth. (no. 1) dedicated to Stefi Geyer; *Bagatelles* nos. 13–14 with bitterness and sarcasm ("Elle est morte," "Ma mie qui danse"); the first elegy with the leitmotiv at the peak; String Quartet no. 1, which Bartók's closest friend Zoltán Kodály described as an "inner drama, a sort of *retour à la vie*, the return to life of a man who had reached the shores of nothingness." See the facsimile of the letters written to Stefi Geyer by Bartók in *Béla Bartók: Briefe an Stefi Geyer, 1907–1908*, with foreword by Paul Sacher (Basel: Privatdruck Paul Sacher Stiftung, 1979).

words written to an outsider — for instance to Frederick Delius, about his *Fourteen Bagatelles* and other new works from 1908–1909 — could be considered rather as a shy self-excuse, with the typical reference to folk-music influence:

> Since writing them [the *Bagatelles*, etc.] I have regained some inner "harmony," so that, today, I am not in need of the contradictory accumulation of dissonances which express that particular mood. This may be the consequence of allowing myself to become more and more influenced by folk music. (1910)[8]

In public Bartók characterized the importance of the *Fourteen Bagatelles* differently: in a neutral way he underlined rather what he did not do, instead of revealing the essence of this new style. But this of course was a retrospective explanation written in 1945 in the United States:

> In these, a new piano style appears as a reaction to the exuberance of the romantic piano music of the nineteenth century; a style stripped of all unessential decorative elements, deliberately using only the most restricted technical means. As later developments show, the Bagatelles inaugurate a new trend of piano writing in my career, which is consistently followed in almost all of my successive piano works, with more or less modifications. (1945)[9]

A genuine impediment to our proper understanding of Bartók's statements is the languages in which they occur. Of the above quotations the interview with Dille, a Flemish-Belgian scholar, was made in German but noted and printed in French; the 1938 text was drafted in French; the letter to the English composer Delius was written in German; the Harvard Lectures and the introduction to the piano works are Bartók's English texts, but edited and heavily revised; the rest had been written in Hungarian. In addition to selected editions of Bartók's writings in several languages, so far we have two collected single-volume editions of Bartók's essays, one in Hungarian and the other in English (both believed to be complete and scholarly editions, though neither is a genuine critical edition and neither is complete).[10] An eight-volume complete edition, basically in Hungarian but with unpublished variants in their original language, is now under way;[11] and his major ethnomusicological volumes are available in new (and partly controversial) parallel editions in Hungarian, German, and English.

---

8. See *BBLevelei*, 168, translated from German; quoted in English in Tallián/1988, 83.

9. *Essays*, 432.

10. *BÖI* = *Bartók Béla Összegyűjtött Írásai* [BB's collected writings], ed. András Szőllősy (Budapest: Zeneműkiadó, 1967); *Essays* = *Béla Bartók Essays*, ed. Benjamin Suchoff (London: Faber and Faber, 1976).

11. *BBI/1* = *Bartók Béla Írásai*, vol. 1: *Bartók Béla önmagáról, műveiről, az új magyar zenéről, műzene és népzene viszonyáról* [BB on his life, work, the new Hungarian music, the relation between art music and folk music], ed. Tibor Tallián (Budapest: EMB, 1989); vol. 5: *A magyar népdal* [The Hungarian folksong], ed. Dorrit Révész (Budapest: EMB, 1990).

The textual and linguistic confusion around Bartók's writings is the more unfortunate because the texts that he wrote without much enthusiasm on his methods of composition, on his style, or on the folk-music influence in his music are full of stereotypes and figurative speech. We must look between the lines of certain sentences for their meaning. For instance whenever Bartók speaks highly in general terms about his fellow-composer Zoltán Kodály, he actually makes a confession about his own music. And we must learn to recognize the repeatedly used terms and expressions, text "panels," within a given context (most often, on the influence of peasant music), or search for the plausible cause of certain emphatic accentuations within the text by sifting through the biography and chronology that underlie it.[12]

Had the decision to analyze his works been left to Bartók, he would probably never have written about his music in general, or about a new work in particular. His basic attitude was that the music had to speak for itself; that program notes and introductions, though conventionally required aids, only interfered with the natural direct link between the listener and the only relevant form of a piece of music, its performed "acoustic" form.

In some instances the draft of a program note contained technical details revealing significant aspects of the structure, which Bartók then deleted or rewrote in a stereotyped formulation. For him the easy flow and "gusto" of essays such as those Alban Berg wrote for music periodicals pointed toward undesirable exhibitionism. The majority of Bartók's texts either limited themselves to sheer technical descriptions (using traditional terminology of form, or replacing explanation with incipits of themes) or included extramusical information (the plot of a stage work, the circumstances of a commission, the history of the composition). These texts deliberately avoided giving out genuine workshop "secrets" or advance hints about sophisticated schemes, which might allow a moment of pleased *ah-ha!* recognition in the listener. In our time — in an age of overspecialized and embarrassingly technical explanations by composers, whose analysis often creates the image of a composition different from, or more interesting than, the performed form of the actual work — Bartók's reserved attitude may appear old-fashioned.

But in Bartók's silence about the essentials of the musical quality of a new score the sympathetic listener recognizes the composer's awareness that even the most detailed technical descriptions of structure, organization, fabric, and compositional patterns only revealed "technical problems," matters he "all more or less instinctively felt." No technical description would uncover the very individual "spirit of a new work," which Bartók believed he could express in words only at the risk of trivializing them or of seeming (or at least feeling) ridiculous. In most cases "the spirit" of

12. In a documentary essay, "The Liszt Influence on Bartók Reconsidered," *The New Hungarian Quarterly* 27, no. 102 (Summer 1986): 210–219, I attempt to explain the hidden motivation of passages inserted in the autobiography about the significance of Liszt's music, which was connected with contemporary views that the "atonal" path of Wagner and Schoenberg influenced Bartók.

his new work was incompatible with the artistic goals, concepts, and strategies of his Western contemporaries. Of course he had his secret sources, unusual inspirations, bold multilevel concepts of forms: we will uncover a few such typical Bartókian plans during the survey of Bartók's compositional process. For Bartók himself, even the attempt to put his very complex but vague ideas on musical structure into words seemed embarrassing.

All the same, the number of relevant Bartók texts is still considerable. Most of them are now available, at least for the Hungarian reader, in a reliable edition (*BBI/1*) that contains some forty shorter and longer essays, articles, lectures, introductions, program notes on the composer's life and works, the new Hungarian music, and the relationship between art music and folk music. This volume includes eighteen items on individual Bartók works. There are typical turn-of-the-century German-type program notes with incipits[13] as well as program notes without music examples;[14] there are *Formübersicht*-type descriptions written for the pocket-score edition,[15] and short statements or introductory texts.

The essays and lectures on the influence of folk music often reveal more about certain technical aspects of Bartók's compositions and about what he liked in contemporary music, for example, in Stravinsky's oeuvre, than do his work analyses proper. A vitally important text is the German study written in 1920 for *Melos*, Berlin ("Das Problem der neuen Musik"),[16] with Bartók's views on atonality, twelve-tone music, micro-intervals, and the future of music. The first notable "disguised" essays from the same time are "Der Einfluss der Volksmusik auf die heutige Kunstmusik" (1920), also for *Melos* (discussing Stravinsky's *Pribaoutki*), and "The Relation of Folk-Song to the Development of the Art Music of Our Time," written in 1921 for the English periodical *The Sackbut*.[17] Further disguised essays are the lecture-recital text for Bartók's first North American concert tour (1928–1929) published in *Pro Musica* under the title "The Folk Songs of Hungary,"[18] in which Bartók pointed out the origin of several of his favorite chord structures; the 1931 set of Budapest lectures that included "The Influence of Peasant Music on Modern Music,"[19] describing the three-level concept of how folk music fertilized his style;[20] and the 1932 Vienna lecture, "Volksmusik und ihre Bedeutung für die neuzeitliche

13. Notes on *Kossuth*, Rhapsody op. 1, Suites nos. 1–2; a more interesting later one on Piano Concerto no. 2.

14. Notes on the *Dance Suite*, Sonata for two Pianos and Percussion, Concerto for Orchestra.

15. For String Quartet no. 4, and for *Music for Strings, Percussion, and Celesta*.

16. See the preliminary form and the corrections of the draft in diplomatic edition in *DocB/5*, 23–32; English translation of the final version: *Essays*, 455ff.

17. Drafts in *DocB/5*, 48ff., 91ff.; see also *Essays*, 316–330.

18. The German draft in *BBI/1*, 232ff.; see also *Essays*, 331ff.

19. Variant forms in *BBI/1*, 138ff.; see also *Essays*, 340ff.

20. Folksong arrangement; folk music imitation; complete absorption of peasant music without quotation.

Komposition,"[21] exposing how clearly Bartók saw the ramification of his music and the development of twelve-tone music.

In addition to these indirect statements on his concept and style are two crucial sources, one small and one major, both involving problems. One concerns Edwin von der Nüll's book *Béla Bartók: Ein Beitrag zur Morphologie der neuen Musik* (1930). Von der Nüll asked the composer a number of clever questions. The original German letters with Bartók's answers disappeared during World War II but the book quoted from them several times.[22] For example, Bartók wrote about the Three Studies for piano (1918), his boldest tour de force in terms of the tonal organization: "Even in the Studies there are firmly held, prominent centers of sound (masses of sound at the same pitch),[23] as a consequence of which, regardless of anything else, an effect of tonality is evoked."

The other source is probably the most important one of all: the fragmentary text of the Harvard Lectures, planned as a series of eight informal lectures, actually weekly conferences on Bartók's music, between February and July 1943 that Bartók would give as Visiting Lecturer in Music under the Horatio Appleton Lamb Fund. The difficulty of this major source arises from the incompleteness of the draft (Bartók finished only three and one-half lectures before serious illness caused him to stop writing), and from the composer's partly cryptic Hungarian notes referring to the music examples he played and analyzed, several of which were misunderstood by the editor and represented with mistakenly chosen examples in the *Essays*.

Among the manuscript pages of the Harvard Lectures is a sketchy first plan with the topics of the lectures (actually nine instead of eight), which gives us insight into the most exciting unrealized second part of the series:

1. Revolution, evolution
2. Modes, polymodality (polytonality, atonality, twelve-tone music)
3. Chromaticism (very rare in folkmusic)
4. Rhythm, percussion effect
5. Form (every piece creates its own form)
6. Scoring (new effects on instruments), piano, violin as percussive instr.
   (Cowel[1])
   (*hegedű kellene* [violin would be needed])
7. Trend toward simplicity
8. Educational works
9. General spirit (connected with folkmusic)

We might consider the time and scene — the sixty-two-year-old great European composer, neglected in the United States, irritated by labels attached to his approach

---

21. The German draft in *BBI/1*, 250ff.; see also *Essays*, 345ff.
22. These excerpts are included in *Béla Bartók Briefe*, ed. János Demény (Budapest: Corvina Verlag, 1973), 2:70.
23. "Klangmassen in der selben Tonhöhe."

— as elements that influenced Bartók's preferences and special emphases. But we have no reason to doubt that these topics, these ideas indeed played a central role in his musical philosophy. The first lecture dealt, for instance, with a favorite topic: his passionate rejection of revolutionary oversimplicity ("minimal art," we would probably call it today): "Those composers who achieved most in the last decades were not demolishing revolutionaries; the development of their art is, on the contrary, based on a steady and continuous evolution. And similarly, evolution was the basic principle in the creation of the New Hungarian art music."[24]

In the second Harvard Lecture, explaining the musical background of "a few young Hungarian composers" (meaning primarily himself), Bartók stated:

> They first studied eagerly the classics, in order to acquire the necessary technique in composition. The German romantic styles of the XIXth century, however, were not very well suited to their feelings and to their purposes. . . . Much more impulse could be drawn from Liszt's original works the transparency of which was absolutely non-German; and then, of course, of the French impressionistic music. The innovations of these gave very valuable hints for future possibilities.
>
> . . . The Hungarians, however, had the far reaching vision to turn their attention to a not yet exploited source, absolutely unknown until then. . . . This source of tremendous importance is the Eastern European rural music, especially the Hungarian rural music.
>
> . . . So, the start for the creation of the New Hungarian art-music was given first: by a thorough knowledge of the devices of old and contemporary Western art-music; this for the technique of the composition. And second: by this newly discovered musical rural material of incomparable beauty and perfection; this for the spirit of our works to be created. Scores of aspects could be distinguished and quoted, by which this material exerted its influence on us; for instance tonal influence, melodic influence, and even structural influence.[25]

Here is the starting point — the first mention of how scales and modes and their natural combinations in peasant music helped Bartók to build up his own characteristic style, polymodality and polymodal chromaticism — of the most significant statements of the Harvard Lectures. And this is exactly the point where all the trouble with understanding Bartók started. From Theodor Wiesengrund-Adorno's reviews in the 1920s[26] to Stravinsky's sympathizing pity in his conversations with Robert Craft, the reaction was puzzlement and disbelief: why did Bartók, this great man, creator of so many genuine masterpieces, have an obsession about tying his reputation to the supposed inspiration of certain suspicious primitive sources? After all, folklorism was considered to be an outdated nineteenth-century phenomenon.

Indeed, Bartók knew well enough that his essays and lectures on the influence of folk music made him suspect, and foreign musicians could not hear much difference

---

24. *Essays*, 360–361.
25. *Essays*, 362–363.
26. János Breuer, "Theodor Wiesengrund-Adorno: Texte über Béla Bartók," *SM* 1981: 397–425.

between a folksong and some typical Bartók themes — one of the reasons he so often referred to this or that theme being an "original" theme or one of his own invention. He knew that musicians could not distinguish themes that came from his extraordinary knowledge of peasant music, based on fieldwork and on sophisticated classification and analysis, from tunes simply borrowed from a book, a practice Bartók despised.

Actually what Bartók valued was not folklorism in general but, among twentieth-century works drawn from folk material, only his own and Kodály's methods of composition, and perhaps those of Stravinsky's so-called Russian period inspired or influenced by a special kind of folk music. Bartók really meant that "folk music will become a source of inspiration for a country's music only if the transplantation of its motives is the work of a great creative talent" (1931).[27]

Being an incurably urban individual, Bartók was indeed enthusiastic about, sometimes even dazzled by the music of rural communities. As he confessed:

> Our reverence for the Eastern European strictly rural music was, so to speak, a new music-religious faith. We felt that this rural music, in those pieces which are intact, attains an unsurpassable degree of perfection and beauty to be found nowhere else except in the great works of the classics. (1944)[28]

Reading his often stereotyped praise of the powerful influence of peasant music (rural music, folk music), we would expect to get more hints, direct references, and explanations about individual Bartók compositions too. In the authorized published texts there are, however, very few self-revealing remarks; the composer even deleted most of those he had written in the first drafts of texts.

Let us take the case of the *Dance Suite* (1923), one of the modern music hits of the mid-1920s: an unusual *attacca* form built up on strong musical characters, probably national characters (or so we might guess). There is no assistance in the form of titles of the movements. Bartók's text from the program notes of the premiere simply described the number and succession of the movements, mentioned that all the themes were recapitulated in the finale, and in a half-sentence stated that the themes of the five dances were original Bartók themes, similar to folk music but not borrowed.[29] Drafting a Hungarian lecture in 1931,[30] Bartók offered important details about the *Dance Suite* — even if he withdrew them later by deleting the whole paragraph:

> The thematic material of all the movements is an imitation of peasant music. The aim of the whole work was to put together a kind of idealized peasant music — you could say

27. *Essays*, 347.
28. *Essays*, 393.
29. *BBI/1*, 66 (missing from the *Essays*).
30. See nos. 70–72 in the *Essays*.

an invented peasant music — in such a way that the individual movements of the work should introduce particular types of music. — Peasant music of all nationalities served as a model: Magyar [= Hungarian], Wallachian [= Rumanian], Slovak, and even Arabic. In fact, here and there is even a hybrid from these species. Thus, for example, the melody of the first subject of the first movement is reminiscent of primitive Arabic peasant music, whereas its rhythm is of East European folk music.[31]

During the Harvard Lectures Bartók identified the theme of Movement I as his first "chromatic" melody.[32] There was another Arab piece too, according to the deleted paragraph of the 1931 lecture:

The fourth movement is an imitation of quite complex Arabic music, perhaps of urban origin.

. . . The ritornello theme is such a faithful imitation of a certain kind of Hungarian folk melodies, that its derivation might puzzle even the most knowledgeable musical folklorists. . . . The second movement is Hungarian in character.

The Slovak character mentioned by Bartók is not part of the present form of the *Dance Suite*. It was meant for the third movement, fully composed in the short-score draft,[33] but omitted from the orchestrated form, making the original plan incomplete but improving the composition. The next (the present third) movement Bartók characterized as "alternately Hungarian and Wallachian."

Thus in the discarded explanatory text Bartók opened up about the outlines of the concept of the *Dance Suite*, about the composition with "idealized peasant music" — but not about how quixotic the message of this composition seemed in the early 1920s just after the Treaty of Versailles, which stopped Bartók from going to his beloved Rumanian, Slovak, and even Hungarian peasant villages outside the artificially drawn new state borders. And of course he did not explain that the assembling of the quasi-national themes in the finale meant more than a colorful round-dance: it offered the clear expression of one of his most personal human ideals in the structure of a musical composition:

My own idea . . . of which I have been fully conscious since I found myself as a composer — is the brotherhood of peoples, brotherhood in spite of all wars and conflicts. I try — to the best of my ability — to serve this idea in my music; therefore I don't reject any influence, be it Slovakian, Rumanian, Arabic or from any other source. The source must only be clean, fresh and healthy! (1931)[34]

31. The original draft is in *BBI/1*, 239ff., and the deleted paragraphs on 249; English translation from Tallián / 1988, 133.

32. *Essays*, 379.

33. See the theme in chapter 7, ex. 68.

34. Letter of January 10, 1931 (*Letters*, 201), written in German to Octavian Beu, a Rumanian writer deeply affected by the Rumanian element in Bartók's art, whose major essay enthusiastically claimed that Bartók was a *compositorul român*. Bartók, confessing that he felt himself primarily Hungarian in music too, acknowledged the influence of other peoples' rural music and concluded with the famous ideas quoted here.

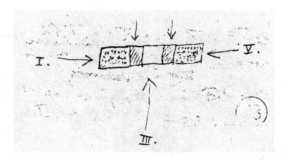

FIGURE 1   Symmetrical 5-movement form of String
Quartet no. 4, Bartók's drawing (BBA 3923).

A great idealist with unusual extramusical messages in his musical compositions, Bartók was unwilling to give his audience help in deciphering the message. Because music had to speak for itself.

Bartók was a shade less reserved in texts intended for performers. But in the short analytical texts written about the form of individual works, he still did not go into details or analyze his "system," either the specific procedures or the organization of the composition. Bartók willingly described the contours, named the major points of articulation of the form of the movement, and for this he used traditional terms that were understood by professional musicians. He readily pointed out the beginning of the themes, their appearance in the development section or in the recapitulation, and occasionally their reappearance in another movement of the cyclic form. Such information helped musicians to shape a well-proportioned performance and to emphasize the crucial thematic references.

In describing his multimovement instrumental forms, Bartók was not at all secretive about the symmetrical structures:[35] five-movement forms (such as String Quartets nos. 4–5) or five-part forms (Piano Concerto no. 2). He described this structure first in 1930, not yet calling it symmetrical, in connection with String Quartet no. 4. In the German draft, after a survey of the five movements, he formulated the following opening paragraph for the text (in the draft there is even a little drawing by Bartók, representing the symmetrical formation; see Fig. 1):[36]

The slow movement is the kernel of the work; the other movements are, as it were, arranged in layers around it. Movement IV is a free variation of II, and V and I have the

35. The analytical literature of the 1950s–1960s (Ernő Lendvai, etc.) called them "bridge-form" or "arch-form": the rounded-off view of the whole, with thematically related first and fifth, second and fourth movements as pillars of the "bridge" arching over the third movement. Or we might call the same structure "palindrome form": the thematic contents of the individual movements reach the central piece and return in reversed order but in fully reshaped, varied form, a relationship between corresponding movements that Bartók wished to display for the performing musicians.

36. The drawing is in BBA 3923.

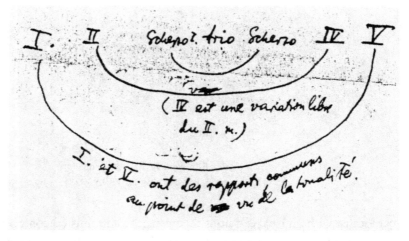

FIGURE 2 Symmetrical 5-movement form of String Quartet
no. 5, Bartók's drawing (BBA 3906).

same thematic material; that is around the kernel (Movement III), metaphorically
speaking, I and V are the outer, II and IV the inner layers.[37]

In the description of the form of String Quartet no. 5 (from a 1935 letter to the
impresario of the Pro Arte Quartet, written in French and rewritten in German),[38]
Bartók sketched out the five-movement overall plan (Fig. 2) and in particular the
sonata-form Movement I structured on the palindrome principle too. He stated that
in this movement the first theme, the transition, and the second theme are in B♭, C,
and D; the development section in E (that is, halfway between two B♭); then in the
recapitulation the themes return in reversed order and also inverted, through F♯ and
A♭ arriving to the home key of B♭. Perhaps Bartók did not disclose great secrets at all;
a music major student reading the score today can easily arrive at the same remarks,
and a lot more sophisticated ones too. But again, from the performer's point of view
(and thus indirectly, through the "acoustic form" of the work, for the listener who
meets Bartók's Fifth Quartet in the concert hall), Bartók's analytical remarks are not
banalities. They help string quartet players to concentrate on a clear tonal presentation of the strongly differentiated basic materials; to make a sensible differentiation
between a transition and a real theme; and to bring the characters of the inverted
form of the themes into relief—virtues often missing in present-day virtuoso rendi-
tions.

One of the most informative and concise texts Bartók ever wrote on his music is
the description of the four-movement structure of the *Music for Strings, Percussion,*

37. German original in the UE/W.Ph pocket-score edition; English in *Essays*, 412.
38. About the sources and differences between the versions, with the complete text of both, see
BBI/1, 76ff., 217ff.

and Celesta, a genuine chef-d'oeuvre of his music. He wrote it in 1937 (in German, in two versions, because the first was mailed to the wrong address)[39] for the UE/W.Ph. pocket-score edition.[40] Every single statement of this short text is significant. Several of Bartók's hints were developed into large-scale analytical theories after his death without any reference to this text. Yet here, for instance, he already used the word *Brückenform* (bridge form) for the ABCBA structure of Movement III. He outlined the basic relations of keys in the movements (which Ernő Lendvai later called Bartók's "axis system"): the first and last in A (with E♭, the "remotest key" to A at the climax of the fugue), with the second and third movements in C and F♯, respectively.

Other remarks of Bartók, however, have received little attention in the vast literature dealing with the *Music for Strings, Percussion, and Celesta*. For example, in his comments on Movement II in C (a sonata form, with the secondary subject in G), there are three statements by Bartók:

1. "in the development section the theme of Movement I, in altered form, appears too" (in a context of variation in European music, the German phrase, *in veränderter Gestalt*, may have broader meaning than just "altered form");
2. in the development section "also appears . . . an allusion to the first theme of Movement IV";
3. "in the recapitulation the 2/4 rhythm of the exposition is changed into 3/8," which is one of the basic rhythmic contrasts of "square" meter and rolling triple meter in Bartók's music, probably inherited from the Renaissance and Baroque *Proportz* tradition.

Another procedure that is central to his music is also mentioned first in the 1937 text in connection with the coda of the finale. "Section G brings the theme of the first movement, extending, however, the original chromatic form into a diatonic one." In the Harvard Lectures Bartók called this procedure the "extension in range" of a theme[41] and regarded it as one of his new devices, a procedure similar to rhythmic extension or compression, traditionally called augmentation and diminution. He liked this invention, because it changed "the character of the melody, sometimes to such a degree, that its relation to the original non-extended form will be scarcely recognizable." It gave variety, but the unity would remain undestroyed, because of

39. See the draft of the first version, and the printed German form of the second, in *BBI/1*, 223ff.

40. The 1937 English translation in the pocket score has a few oddities, e.g., "sidemovement" for secondary subject (from the German term *Seitensatz*). Incidentally the present English translation needs revision too; after all, inversion (*Umkehrung*) is not "contrary motion" as it appears in the *Essays*, 416, to name one of the translator's mistakes in terminology that those who do not read the composer's original text usually consider a sign of Bartók's illiteracy in musical terminology.

41. *Essays*, 381f.

the hidden relation between the two forms—a Bartókian expression of *Einheit und Mannigfaltigkeit* (unity and variety). And, so characteristically again, he added immediately that if others would object "that this new device is somewhat artificial," his only answer would be that "it is absolutely no more artificial than those old devices of augmentation, diminution, inversion, and cancrizans of themes."

But even this rationale was not enough for Bartók. He told his Harvard audience: "A rather surprising circumstance has been discovered in connection with the compression of diatonic melodies into chromatic melodies. I discovered it only six months ago [in 1942] when studying the Dalmatian chromatic style." And he related his great surprise at the discovery of the same phenomenon in rural music. "When I first used the device of extending chromatic melodies into diatonic form or vice-versa, I thought I invented something absolutely new, which never yet existed. And now I see that an absolutely identical principle exists in Dalmatia since Heaven knows how long a time, maybe for many centuries. This again proves, that nothing absolutely new in the world can be invented,"[42] said Bartók, returning to his evolution versus revolution idea, fully satisfied that once again the precedent for his own procedure was peasant music.

Can we follow Bartók's logic to broaden our understanding of his philosophy? Undoubtedly he was a singular individual. In the case of this "extension in range" of melodies, first he pointed out that his device was the logical extension of an old musical principle from the Western tradition. He was proud of his "invention." Then accidentally he discovered that at a remote spot on the map of Balkan folk music a similar phenomenon existed. Instead of concealing this fact—an absolutely irrelevant relationship, since he had introduced the device decades before he recognized the link—Bartók happily talked about it to his Harvard audience. Because the rural music, a "natural phenomenon," once again preceded the individual's intellect, and this fact, according to Bartók's philosophy, retrospectively justified the naturalness and vitality of his invention. A strange attitude indeed.

Yet we must not imagine that Bartók lost his judgment and gave up his personality simply because he let his creativity be influenced by different sorts of rural music that he happened to meet and absorb. Behind Bartók's interest in collecting, transcribing, classifying folk music again and again were purely musical reasons of a master of progressive music. One phenomenon that fascinated him most was the "micro-acoustic"—extremely detailed, exact, yet normal musical—notation of recorded folk-music items. As a composer he grew excited and even more creative as he made the notations. Indeed the written forms of his most mature and vigorously virtuoso transcriptions[43] look for all the world like a remarkably modern piece of

42. *Essays*, 382f.

43. In addition to the study of the printed material (e.g., *RFM*, vols. I–II; *Serbo-Croatian Folk Songs*, etc.), see the parallel edition of the records and Bartók's transcriptions in *Hungarian Folk Music Gramophone Records with Béla Bartók's Transcriptions*, ed. László Somfai (Budapest: Hungaroton, 1981), LPX 18058–60 (including two booklets).

music: with changing meter, highly complicated rhythm, micro-intervals, unusual vocal techniques. Bartók sincerely admired such a *gefundenes Objekt*, as only he was able to put it onto paper.

Listening to recordings and studying Bartók's microscopically detailed transcriptions, we can draw from them various provocative conclusions. One, that the rhythmic and other formulas, "invented" as he transcribed thousands of pieces of peasant music, directly quickened his compositional imagination. The other (for our understanding of Bartók, perhaps the more important one) is an aesthetic question. The composer had no doubt that before using such marvelously rich and complex items of folk music in a concert arrangement, he must first, unfortunately, simplify it radically to make it accessible to conservatory-trained professional musicians. Thus, contrary to the usual view that the composer's approach was to "embellish" the naive folk piece to rescue it and put it on stage, he had to simplify it first to the point that musicians could perceive it through the medium of written music (modern music; Western art music). To put it more crudely: classical music did not seem sophisticated enough for the proper reception of a tune of rural origin. For example, players who could perform Schoenberg's *Pierrot lunaire* or play complicated rhythms in Stravinsky's music could probably not reproduce rhythms at the speed they were written down in a Bartók transcription of a village fiddler's dance from Transylvania, themes he used in the two violin rhapsodies.

But who could, who would follow such highhanded ideas about the "shortcomings" of the highest level of art music? Bartók never expressed his deepest doubts and hesitations about the real values in classical music publicly. His best friend, Zoltán Kodály, certainly shared his fanaticism about the beauty of folk music, but he acknowledged Bartók's new path in composition less and less after 1920. Igor Stravinsky, whom Bartók himself considered his greatest contemporary, whose approach he long thought similar to or in a way complementary to his own, turned out to be an egoistic and uninterested partner in conversation during a personal meeting in Paris in April 1922.[44] (The genuine interest of Maurice Ravel and Darius Milhaud, the admiration of Francis Poulenc at the same visit could have been a consolation but not a compensation.) Bartók never had a composer's best audience for analytical discussions, students in a composition class, because he did not want to teach composition. Then who else would dare to ask him? to whom should he open up his thoughts? In the last decade in Hungary Professor Bartók was a highly respected but isolated man. In the last five years in the United States he was thought to be a strange man who did not want to do the obvious thing, that is, to live by teaching composition. The Harvard Lectures promised the only occasion for Bartók to speak about his concepts and analyze his works in technical detail.

44. See Bartók's letter of April 10, 1922, to Márta in Bartók/*Családi levelek*, 330–332, and a detailed description of Bartók's narration in Aladár Tóth's article in *Nyugat* 15, no. 12 (1922): 830ff., reprinted by János Demény in *Zenetudományi Tanulmányok*, ed. Bence Szabolcsi and Dénes Bartha (Budapest: Akadémiai Kiadó, 1959), 7:219–222.

It is indeed a pity that we will never know what Bartók intended to say and show about his forms ("every piece creates its own form"); the new effects on instruments; his "trend toward simplicity"; and about the "general spirit" of his works "connected with folk music."

To sum up, Béla Bartók — like many of his contemporaries — did not like to speak or write about his compositional workshop, his concepts, his works. Although he knew very well what he had accomplished and how he had done it, his attitude was not at all a pharisaical pose. According to his personal experiences, people either accepted a new musical composition because the music itself made a strong impression, or they did not. Words could hardly substitute for originality. If Bartók agreed to write about his individual works, he did it in a simple, objective way, preferably using traditional terminology. If he was willing to write or lecture on a broader subject, such as the influence of folk music on his composition, he often made general statements, was enthusiastic about the peasant music, and was rather noncommittal about his own accomplishment.

Bartók despised the image of the professional, easy-speaking, clever composer. For him musical composition was not primarily the product of regular intellectual work (such as one does every day, the paper work of which — sketches, notes, ideas — one dates and keeps in a reserve for further use) but a miracle. At least the beginning of the process was always unique and fresh: the birth of a concept, the finding of themes. He did not want to understand, and surely did not intend to tell other people, how his creative brain worked. The rest of the composition? the realization of the concepts? the usual procedures? his favorite chords and textures? the rhythmic patterns and else? For him these matters were mainly technique, workshop secrets of secondary importance.

Consequently, for a better understanding of Bartók's compositional process we have no choice but to undertake a serious, complex analysis of his manuscripts, the entire creative process from sketch to revised edition and recordings, looking not only for the direct meaning of the notes on the paper, but for Bartók's hidden concepts, for "the spirit of the work" as well.

3 · A SURVEY OF THE SOURCES

THE EXISTING SOURCES

Most of the primary sources of Bartók's oeuvre have survived and are not widely dispersed; thus the overwhelming majority of the crucial sources is available for our investigation.

By nature Bartók was a very thorough man who kept practically everything, particularly music paper, which was expensive in his youth. This helps us to a great extent, since the paper could be and actually was "recycled." Empty pages on bifolios with the transcription of recorded folk music were used for sketches; discarded pages of a composition could serve for a draft next time. The systematic nature of Bartók's everyday work — teaching days at the Liszt Academy and free days for home work; a surprisingly large amount of time for well-planned work on folk music (such as transcribing the new field collection; merging new data into the collection); dutifully answering letters — provides secondary information and a context for Bartók that helps to date his otherwise undated compositional activity.

How complete is the existing material? All in all the ratio of the available elements in the central body of primary sources (the draft; the manuscript of the final form, the engraver's copy; revised printed copies, Bartók's personal copies) for Bartók's mature work is very high: about 95 percent or more. The source material of many compositions is complete (except for corrected proof sheets of the first edition for the majority of the works). Of the rest only one or two links are missing and even those are at least registered. (In respect to the early compositions Bartók wrote before he left his mother's home at the age of eighteen, there are few of the drafts and sketches, mostly the final form alone survived, either in Bartók's or in his mother's handwriting. Many compositions that Bartók presented to school friends seem to be lost.)[1]

1. See details in Dille / *Verzeichnis*, and in the Appendix to the present volume.

What material is missing from Bartók's years of study in Budapest onward, and why? At this point we do not take into account copies (rarely original manuscripts) sent to the performer of a premiere or short *Albumblatt*-type autograph notations of a theme made after a concert: Bartók seldom let genuine "workshop"-form manuscripts out of his hand. There were exceptions though. Around 1903 and later Emma Gruber, a friend of Bartók's who later married Kodály, often got as a present, or perhaps simply took, scattered sketches and drafts from Bartók's desk. Occasionally other friends, former pupils, and musicians would receive a present of workshop forms or unpublished items. For instance, in 1922 Bartók gave two songs written in 1916[2] to M. D. Calvocoressi; the draft of the *Allegro barbaro* to a pediatrician, I. Péteri; sketches for the Violin Concerto (no. 2) to Tossy Spivakovsky; the draft of the *Fifteen Hungarian Peasant Songs* for piano to a friend in America, Agatha Fassett; the draft of Three Rondos (nos. 2–3) to his former pupil Wilhelmine Creel (later Creel-Driver). Performers also received autograph manuscripts: among them were Adila Arányi, Stefi Geyer, Joseph Szigeti, and Zoltán Székely.

In two special areas of the primary sources we have to reckon with considerable losses: sketches and corrected proof sheets. It seems to be an established fact that Bartók, continuing a nineteenth-century tradition among composers, destroyed sketches (and probably even sketchy drafts) up to the mid- or late 1910s; fortunately he changed his mind and kept later workshop material (see details in chapters 4 and 7). The other area of losses concerns the publisher's procedure of discarding corrected proof sheets, with the composer's autograph instructions, after the engraver had carried out the corrections. What has survived we owe to Bartók, who kept some of the sets of corrected proofs that the publisher no longer needed. From the proofs of approximately eighty Bartók works printed in his lifetime (more than one hundred with variant forms, not counting revised and rearranged editions), each checked and corrected in two or three subsequent proofs, no more than around thirty-five sets survived (see details in chapter 9).

From indirect evidence we surmise that from time to time, perhaps when he moved from one permanent home to another, Bartók arranged his manuscripts. A general sorting of the manuscripts of the compositions occurred immediately after the March 1938 *Anschluss* of Austria by the Nazis. Bartók decided to leave his publisher in Vienna, Universal Edition, to look for another publisher in a free country and, considering the unsettled future, to secure his manuscripts in Switzerland. He listed his lost or missing autographs;[3] he put aside the juvenile works, together with *Dolgozatok I–II* [Exercises I–II] from the time of his studies with Koessler and fragments, discarded pages, and other material under the heading *Különféle* [Miscellaneous]. These were left in Budapest and are housed today in the

2. See BB 71 / 1 and 73 in the Appendix.
3. See the list *Kéziratokból hiányzik* [Missing manuscripts] in Somfai / *MS vs. Urtext*, 40–41.

Budapest Bartók Archives (BBA),[4] and in Béla Bartók Jr.'s private collection in his home, respectively.

The manuscripts of the mature published works in Bartók's possession in 1938 were numbered 1–51 and forwarded to Switzerland (first mentioned in Bartók's letter of April 13, 1939).[5] Completed by the latest European works, this collection was forwarded via London to New York after Bartók arrived in the United States on October 30, 1940. After the composer's death in September 1945 this material, together with the manuscripts of the American works, formed the basis of the New York Béla Bartók estate and archives (which after the liquidation of the estate, following the death of Ditta Bartók in 1982, became Peter Bartók's collection and since 1988 is housed in his private archive in Homosassa, Florida).

The collection of major outside sources for the two archives occurred during the 1950s and 1960s. Victor Bator, trustee of the New York estate, in addition to making a considerable amount of minor acquisitions, succeeded in getting hold of the primary sources from the collections of the two largest publishers, Universal Edition (for Bartók's works between 1918–1938) and Boosey & Hawkes (from 1939). The Budapest archives obtained the existing material from Hungarian publishers (such as the former Rozsnyai and Rózsavölgyi) and manuscripts from other possessors, including Emma Kodály. At a rough estimate, more than 95 percent of the eminently important sources can be studied in the collections of the composer's two sons and in the Budapest Bartók Archives. Further important manuscripts are held in the Library of Congress, Washington, D.C.; the Pierpont Morgan Library, New York; the University of Pennsylvania, Philadelphia (moved from the Free Library); the British Library, London; the Paul Sacher Foundation, Basel; the Stadt- und Landesbibliothek and Österreichische Nationalbibliothek, Vienna; the Széchényi National Library and History Museum, Budapest; and in a few further public and private collections (for the present distribution of primary sources with reference to the former possessor, see Fig. 3).

Among the consequences of two wars, and particularly the separation of large territories from the former Hungary that followed the 1919 Treaty of Versailles — breaking off all the towns where Bartók had lived before he came to Budapest, including Pozsony (Pressburg; now Bratislava) — and the migration of various populations, we must include the displacement and loss of material possessions such as manuscripts. From those lost or given to family members, friends, and musicians, several are irreplaceable. Curiously enough, none of the publisher's archives are intact. Of the Hungarian material (from Bárd, Rozsnyai, Rózsavölgyi, and Magyar Kórus), about a dozen autograph or revised manuscripts seem to be missing altogether or in part; from the Universal Edition collection some six works; from the

4. Manuscripts with a BH number are permanent deposits by Béla Bartók Jr.
5. See *BBLevelei*, 621.

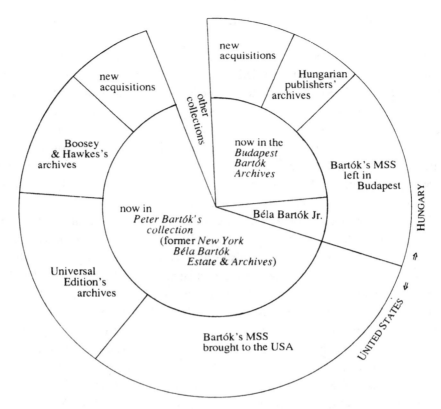

FIGURE 3   Distribution of the primary sources (former possessor:
outer circle; present location: inner circle).

Boosey & Hawkes collection three engraver's copies (lists and details are discussed in chapters 7–9).

THE FUNCTION OF DIFFERENT TYPES
OF MANUSCRIPTS

The physical evidence of the creative process, the chain of manuscripts and versions, may vary in each case; and Bartók's extemporization at the piano, which leaves no document, is a white hole in the formation of many of his works. But a classification of the source types will further our analysis. I see the theoretical model of Bartók's composition proceeding in four phases: the primary creative process (source types 1–2); the fixing, testing, and preparation for publication (types 3–4); the editing process (types 5–6); and the post-publication phase (types 7–8, and again eventually type-6 sources; see Fig. 4):

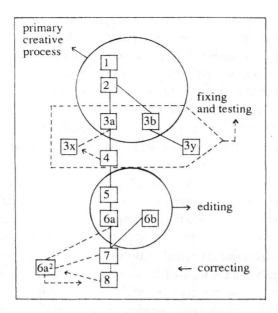

FIGURE 4   Theoretical model of the source types
related to the phases of the compositional
process.

1. thematic memos, preliminary sketches;[6]
2. draft(s);
3. autograph final copy or fair copy on ordinary music paper (3a), or on
   Lichtpause masters (3b); preliminary facsimile prints (3x) of full
   movements or sample pages; working copies (3y) of (3b);
4. copyist's copy written by a family member or a professional copyist, with
   Bartók's corrections;
5. corrected proof sheets;
6. authorized first edition (6a), or facsimile first edition based on Bartók's
   tissue masters (6b);
7. corrected copies, Bartók's personal copy or *Handexemplar*, alternative
   corrections;
8. recording(s) played by Bartók.

For several works, links in this chain of sources are missing — either because they
never existed or have been lost. In other cases some of the sources may exist in more
than one version. At times Bartók wrote quickly and found it easy to finish the

6. See the discussion of side sketches and partial sketches in chapter 4.

composition, but he also had "graphomaniac" periods when he wrote out three full autographed copies with few changes before he considered a piece ready for publication. Or he needed one copy for the publisher and one for his own performance (a problem that for some time he solved by having large-size photocopies made from his manuscript, and later by having contact copies or lithographs made from *Licht-pausen* of it).

It is not so much the outside appearance that classifies the source types but their function. There are drafts in neat handwriting as well as autograph copies with many corrections; but a draft does not include performing instructions, while a final copy does. Quite often autograph manuscripts had two functions and could therefore be classified under two types: a draft (2) in a next step with additional performing instructions could be turned into the final copy (3), which was sent to the publisher as the engraver's copy. The engraver's or printer's copy might be an autograph, a corrected copy, or a corrected printed edition. Or it might combine several types (3–4), because a member of the family (the composer's mother, or his wife, or even his first and his second wife together) worked side by side with Bartók.

In spite of such irregularities and borderline cases I prefer to use the terms listed above. To define a source implies a proper examination of its contents. This is not exactly the same as modern musical text criticism's use of the stemma, which involves a refined analysis of the musical text to trace the filiation of mostly secondary sources. The connection of the Bartók sources in general is evident but quite often needs minute procedures of comparative textual analysis. The ramifications of the versions are mostly restricted to two phenomena: in several cases the revision or correction produced two independent branches of the written text; with the printed and the recorded forms Bartók sometimes moved into different directions. We need to recognize the function of a document as a basic tool in reconstructing the chain of primary sources and thus deciding whether the documentation is complete.

RECONSTRUCTING THE CHAIN OF SOURCES

Within Bartók's oeuvre we can distinguish six patterns in the chain of sources, depending on the composer's age, working style, and relations with publishers (Fig. 5; dotted-line boxes indicate that the source seldom survived).

(a) The source chain of the juvenile works is short and incomplete: in most cases we have only the copy written by Bartók's mother or (after he was seventeen) by the composer himself. The rare sketchy drafts were written in pencil, the copies in ink.

(b) From 1899 to 1903, while he studied with Koessler, Bartók carried out his exercises and free compositions in a two-step process: a draft in pencil, and a final copy in ink. The output of the following years — the romantic years of the young

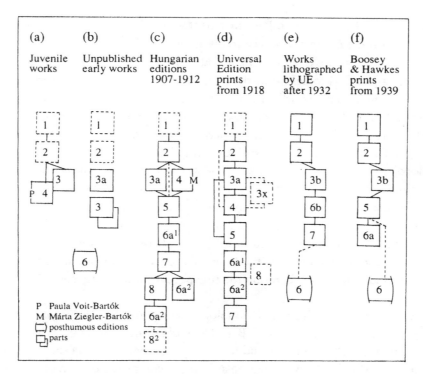

FIGURE 5   Typical source chains in Bartók's composition.

composer — suffered most from his destruction of sketches: some large-scale works written between 1903–1907 exist only in the autograph full score (and occasionally in autograph parts too). After his graduation, he rarely used pencil in composition.

(c) The year 1908 marks not only the beginning of a new style but a new situation as well: after some casual printed editions Bartók's music was now regularly published in Budapest. In this period he gave his autograph manuscript (often the revised draft), or a revised copy (written by professional copyists) to the engraver. From 1909–1910 Bartók had a dedicated helper, his first wife, Márta, who was able to read and interpret his abbreviations, and who made the copies under his supervision. The text of the first editions of these years needed considerable revision later, either for the original publisher or for another in the United States during the 1940s; the printed music many times differed from the version recorded by Bartók. Thus the chain, including the corrected versions, in many cases is long.

(d–e) Bartók's working procedure changed little in the first years with his new publisher, UE Vienna. When Bartók remarried in 1923 he lost, however, the perfect family copyist. For a time his second wife, Ditta, a pianist pupil, made copies but Bartók soon decided to write an extra copy (a "fair copy") for the publisher in his own hand (1926) or to use glossy photoprints of the autograph with handwritten additions (1928–1929) — both inconvenient solutions, though. In 1929 he became familiar with the *Lichtpause* procedure, writing the fair copy on onionskin (transparent tissue), in a calligraphic style in india ink. From this he could make several intermediary or final copies for working purposes, sending one to the performer and the publisher or keeping one as his own concert copy. A few scores were even printed in facsimile directly from Bartók's *Lichtpause* masters under the label of UE.

(f) During the Boosey & Hawkes period, from 1939 onward Bartók also used india-ink fair copies on *Lichtpausen*, sometimes with several, differently corrected, copies of the tissue master. Occasionally he still wrote the full score on normal music paper and returned to use pencil in drafts when he was in Saranac Lake or Asheville, away from his normal working environment that included a piano. A serious problem of the B&H period is the posthumous publication of several new scores and revised versions: some were still proofread by Bartók but printed only posthumously; some were edited on the basis of a good source but without Bartók's consent (and with wrong dates on the title pages); others were compiled posthumously.

We must always look at the chronology and the special circumstances of each composition. During his lifetime Bartók's working habits changed considerably, depending not only on his age and increasing experience, but on the material circumstances (whether he was working at home in complete isolation or sketching a new piece while he was on a trip); on the genre he was going to write; on his dependence on a trusted copyist; on his relations with his publisher and the printing process.

Because of the unusual richness of the sources, chronology-sensitive methods in our source studies are relatively easy to develop. They allow us to assess the completeness or the incompleteness of the chain of sources for individual works.

Another fact to recognize at the first steps in Bartók source studies is that the crucial "sources" of a composition do not end with the autograph manuscripts but include corrected copies and printed editions and, whenever they exist, Bartók's recordings of his own music. And we should know that this quasi-oral transmission of the work, an absolutely authentic form of transmission, opens up alarming problems. Despite the author's aim to chisel the perfect *Fassung letzter Hand* version — the final version — in so many stages, with so much care and invention, it does not tell us how much of the intended real acoustic (performed) form of the individual composition has been fixed or indeed could be fixed unambiguously in the printed form.

We have to survey the stages of the compositional process one by one, before we face this ultimate question of musical composition.

4 · SKETCHES AND THE PLAN OF A WORK

TERMINOLOGY

Bartók seldom wrote a descriptive tag on the cover of a manuscript. He did so, however, when in 1938 he surveyed his manuscripts and decided what to store in Budapest and what to transfer from Hungary to a safer country. Thus Bartók numbered and titled works before he packed and mailed them to Annie Müller-Widmann in Switzerland.[1] At the preliminary survey for manuscripts he left in Budapest he used Hungarian terms, calling them *vázlat* [sketch] or *fogalmazás, fogalmazvány* [draft] with no obvious attempt at differentiating among the terms or being consistent.[2] For those he sent off, Bartók used German or French terms to similar effect: *Skizzen* or *Konzept* or *brouillon* designated a sketchy draft, except that a score draft or vocal-score-form draft was usually not called *Skizzen* but rather *Konzept* or *brouillon*. The next manuscript — the final copy or fair copy, or simply the orchestration — became *Partitur, Reinschrift,* or *Lichtpausreinschrift* if written on transparent tissue.

This book introduces a more elaborate terminology for the study of Bartók's sketches and drafts that is not automatically compatible with terms used in sketch studies with a long tradition for composers such as Mozart, Beethoven, and Schoenberg. But if our interpretation of Bartók's compositional process — with its routine procedures and occasional irregularities — is valid, this terminology will help us to designate the nature of a source or place it in the composition's source chain. The basic terms used here are the following (set out in Fig. 6 too):

Preliminary memo: notation of individual (mostly short) musical ideas during the preparation for a new work.

---

1. See Bartók's letters for 1938: April 13, May 24 and 29, June 6 and 14.
2. E.g., *Különféle* [Miscellaneous] heading for fragments (BBA BH46/1–27); *Dolgozatok I* and *II* [Exercises] for compositional studies under Koessler (BBA BH47–48).

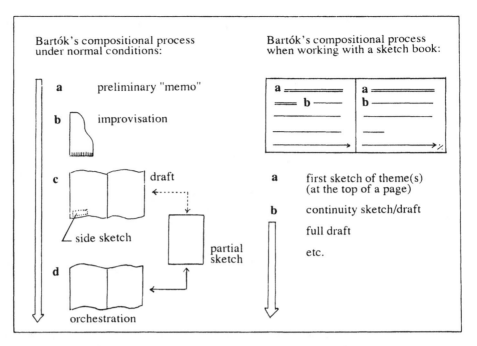

FIGURE 6   Bartók's compositional process and the terminology of sketches.

Side sketch: quick notation of related ideas within a work's context (on the
same page, in the margin, etc.) either simultaneously with the writing or
when working again with it (e.g., preparing the fair copy or the
orchestration).

Partial sketch: quick elaboration of contrapuntal, harmonic, textural, and
most often scoring ideas on a separate paper during the creation of a draft
or an orchestration.

Sketch-book: a rare phenomenon in Bartók's compositional process; pocket-
sized book with 10-staff paper (which he regularly used in folksong
collecting) in which he wrote down shorter or longer sketches when he
was far from his home and piano.

Sketch vs. *continuity draft*: often subsequent steps of the same process on the
same page, i.e., originally thematic sketches continued and drafted at
length as a next step or at some later point.

There are two less frequent types of sketches, actually "pseudo sketches" only: an
Albumblatt with the composer's notation of a theme or motive,[3] and an autograph

3. E.g., in the BBA collection: *1904.jan.28. Albumblatt* with a theme from *Kossuth* (BBA 468),
1936.márc.3. with the Trio theme of Mov. III of String Quartet no. 5 (photocopy: BBA 291/2).

shorthand copy for himself to serve occasional performing purposes (like the transposition of the piano accompaniment of a folksong arrangement, or a shorthand notation of his piano part written down from memory).[4]

DESTROYED AND LOST SKETCHES OR NO SKETCHES?

Trustworthy recollections,[5] a survey of the origin and first possessors of the existing sketches, and above all a thorough study of internal evidence of the complete existing source material verify the old suspicion among Bartók scholars that Bartók in his early years made no effort to keep sketches or scattered pages but deliberately destroyed them.[6] He surely knew of earlier composers' belief, probably shared by his professors, that embryonic ideas, imperfect forms did not belong to posterity. Presumably when he became acquainted with Beethoven facsimile editions,[7] Bartók changed his mind and recognized that succeeding generations had the right to study the manuscripts and sketches of a major composer. But on this subject we can only guess; Bartók never discussed it.

Why do we think that sketches must be missing? The investigation of the extended sketch material of large-scale compositions might be illuminating. Let us pick up the surprisingly rich sketch material of Suite no. 2 for orchestra (written in 1905, the finale in 1907) and the early Violin Concerto op. posth. (begun in July 1907). The orchestration of the two works followed in late summer 1907 and December 1907 to February 1908, respectively. If we compare the scores of the works with preliminary memos as well as shorter and longer continuity sketches on separate pages and in the *Black Pocket-book*,[8] we see that the ratio (in measures) of known sketched sections to those without existing sketches is not shockingly different (197:202 in the concerto, 376:500 in Movements I–II & IV of the suite). Yet the Violin Concerto sketches probably cover all the material necessary to draft a violin-and-piano-reduction-type short score. In contrast, the Suite no. 2 material is undoubtedly incomplete: at least the beginning of Movement I and II had to exist in

4. Among the sources, see BB 47 *Eight Hungarian Folksongs* in the Appendix; and read F. László, *Bartók Béla: Tanulmányok és tanúságok* [BB: Studies and testimonies] (Bucharest: Kriterion, 1980), 77–92.

5. Zoltán Kodály remembered that around the end of the 1910s in Rákoskeresztúr Bartók burned his manuscripts (private communication from Denijs Dille).

6. He must have done so sometime between 1918, the last year of the war, and spring 1920, when the Bartók family moved from Rákoskeresztúr to Budapest.

7. Bartók acquired the first Beethoven facsimile edition (Piano Sonata in A-flat, op. 26, Bonn 1895) for his library in 1909; the direct cause of Bartók's interest around 1918–1920 in preserving his sketches has not yet been discovered. In the early 1930s he was a member of a special committee of the League of Nations and (as Otto Erich Deutsch counseled) became an ardent advocate of printing facsimile and urtext editions (see my commentaries to the facsimile edition of *Two Rumanian Dances*, Budapest 1974).

8. See the sources of Suite no. 2: PB 12FSS1ID1, BBA 2002a; the sources of the Violin Concerto: BBA BH39, BH206, also in PB 12FSS1ID1.

sketches (if so much of the continuation was written down), before Bartók started to write the complete short score (now lost).

		total measures
Violin Concerto (1907–1908)		
Mov. I	sketch: 1–30, 34–40, 48–61, 77–80	55
	no sketch:	49
Mov. II	sketch: 1–47, 58–60, 79–83, 91–95, 103–148, 153–166,	
	182–196	142
	no sketch:	153
Suite no. 2 (1905–1907)		
Mov. I	sketch: 172–182, 188–198, 203–216	36
	no sketch:	188
Mov. II	sketch: 139–352	214
	no sketch:	229
Mov. III	(no surviving sketch)	
Mov. IV	sketch: 30–70, 99–128, 151–175	126
	no sketch:	83

To assess the extent of lost or destroyed first autograph notation of Bartók, it is essential (1) to deal with each work individually, and (2) to consider sketch and continuity sketch/draft, or a first full draft score, as eventually complementary links in the compositional process. In many cases we cannot even guess whether there were any preliminary memo notes or not. But with Bartók we can usually be quite sure if the whole drafting stage is missing from the manuscript material that survived.

Of the symphonic works, stage works, and concertos — except for minor losses and pages missing here and there — the short-score (piano *particella*)-like full draft is certainly missing (see the survey of missing drafts in chapter 7, p. 114) for *Kossuth* and for Suites nos. 1 and 2 (though some memos or other sketches of these three works do exist); a violin-and-piano-reduction-type full draft is missing for Movement I of the Violin Concerto op. posth. Furthermore, we might suspect that considerable sketches preceded the existing (vocal-score-like) draft of *Duke Blue-beard's Castle*; that parts of the two-piano draft of *Four Orchestral Pieces* might be preceded by an amount of continuity sketches; that yet more sketches might exist for the draft score of Piano Concerto no. 2, of *Music for Strings, Percussion, and Celesta,* and of the Divertimento.

In contrast, we seem to have a complete written legacy of the sketching and drafting process in the available sources of Violin Concerto (no. 2), Concerto for Orchestra, Piano Concerto no. 3, and Viola Concerto; except for missing sketch pages here and there, probably the complete preliminary written documentation of *The Wooden Prince, The Miraculous Mandarin,* Piano Concerto no. 1, and *Cantata profana* has also survived.

Of solo and chamber music from 1903 onward, probably less was destroyed. Nevertheless, there had to be a considerable amount of sketches for the Sonata for Violin and Piano of 1903, for the Piano Quintet, and for the solo-piano original version of Rhapsody op. 1. Furthermore, more sketches might have been written for String Quartets nos. 1 and 2. Within Bartók's mature piano work, we can only speculate on discrepancies in the sketch material. For instance, why did Bartók sketch nos. 1 and 3 of *Four Dirges* in the *Black Pocket-book* but not the two other pieces? Was it because these were written during a trip and those at home, with the piano at hand for developing the piece up to a nearly finished form by improvisation? In the case of the *Dirges* this may be a correct explanation. But was Bartók always in the mood and able to concentrate and shape a whole piano piece at the piano, before he sat down at his desk to write out the more or less full continuity draft? To take an example from the year 1926: from the number of sources — collected in the draft complex of the Sonata and *Out Doors*[9] — and the visible signs of elaboration and revision of the individual movements, we might guess that the manuscripts of piano solo pieces written in summer 1926 are fully preserved. Yet this firm expert opinion was shaken when a 1926 letter to his wife that held a one-page sketch with the very first ideas of the exposition of Movement I from the Piano Sonata of 1926 came to light in 1982 within Ditta Bartók's estate.[10] Bartók might indeed have made several similar memo notes for other movements, ones that he threw away or presented to somebody. Or this one-page sketch may in fact be an exception: after all this was the only sonata-form opening movement among the solo piano pieces of summer 1926 and, if our reconstruction of the micro-chronology is correct, it was the very first piece written after a long silence.[11]

To sum up, in several cases we can safely claim that the first link of the source chain is missing. But in many cases we can only guess whether there were any lost or destroyed sketches.

SEPARATE PRELIMINARY MEMOS

To differentiate between preliminary memos that are separate and those in the context of another manuscript is not an arbitrary procedure but has value as we study the so precious first written sources. Since it was not Bartók's habit to record the circumstances of how he began the compositional process (by giving the date or place on a sketch[12] or in a diary), it is essential to separate at least those few sketches

9. PB 55–56PS1.
10. BBA BH214.
11. See further comments about chronology in chapter 7, p. 178.
12. The exceptions usually marked significant biographical events; for instance, he dated the sketch of Bagatelle no. 14 on *1908.márc.20.* (see facsimile in *DocB/2*, 158), in a bitter mood after the break with Stefi Geyer.

EXAMPLE 1   Anagram motives for the Piano Sonata 1898.

F. A.   = FrAEnCl   = FrEnCl ACost

that, appearing on a specific spot of another Bartók manuscript, presumably in process just then, may arrest the moment of inspiration and be understood in context.

The separate preliminary memos most typically come into sight on individual pages: leftover or discarded pages from another score, single sheets, often a half-page or a slip of paper only, sometimes recycled papers (from folksong transcriptions, etc.). But such memos also appear on pages of the rare sketch-books, in a small booklet of papers with printed or hand-ruled staves, or in schoolbooks from Bartók's Pozsony years.

To begin with the last group, we can approximate the date of sketches from his youth by themes noted on the margin of schoolbooks because we know the curriculum of a *Gymnasium* (high school) student in Pozsony in the 1890s. Still these are not memos in (musical) context. At best we learn that young Bartók, instead of concentrating on his homework, got musical ideas that he quickly fixed on paper nearest at hand. One example involves seven such memos written between January and March 1898 in Hinter's Greek textbook, the *Odyssey*, and in a volume of *Herodoti Epitome*; they represent the basic themes of all four movements of Piano Sonata BB 12, a large-scale work preserved in an autograph dedication copy (thought lost until recently)[13] that Bartók presented to a schoolmate's sister. In Movement IV there is an anagram reference to the friend of the young lady, a certain Fränzl Ágost (August Fränzl) violinist. In addition to the seven sketches, extra sketches to anagram motives appear in the Herodotus schoolbook experimenting with just the initials in the Hungarian word order *F A*, or the full name, including the *ae* representation of German *ä*, then *e* for *ä*, with the Hungarian spelling *c* for the pronunciation of German *z* (Ex. 1). Further sketches in the same textbook can be found for Sonata for Violin and Piano, *Scherzo oder Fantasie*, and Piano Quartet.

Genuine thematic memos from Bartók's years of study with Koessler (1899–1903) and the following years of his large-scale national and romantic compositions (*Kossuth*, Violin Sonata [1903], Piano Quintet, Scherzo for Orchestra and Piano, Rhapsody [op. 1], Suites nos. 1–2) are extremely scarce. An early typical page with memos dates from 1907.[14] On one side, written in pencil, three thematic ideas of the Violin Concerto appear (Ex. 2), probably the very earliest ones inspired by the

13. Somfai, "Újabb Bartók 'opusz 1'?" [A new 'op. 1' by Bartók?], in *Muzsika* 29, no. 6 (May 1986): 3–5.
14. BBA BH39; facsimile in *DocB/2*, 158.

EXAMPLE 2   Thematic memos for the Violin Concerto op. posth.

happy days spent with Stefi Geyer's family in late June 1907 in Jászberény. None are opening themes: Ex. 2a is the theme of the middle part of Movement I in the final key, already *dolce* but with a different tempo marking;[15] Ex. 2b is the secondary subject of Movement II (mm. 58ff.) in the final key but in a slightly different metric and harmonic context; Ex. 2c is a short form of the Tempo I (*quieto*) bass theme following the secondary subject area (mm. 91ff.) in the final key, with Hungarian words probably suggesting a programmatic background: *vastagon, morgósan* [= thick, grumbling] and a series of *bumm!* [bang!] for the pesante notes. Actually the memos of the opening themes of the two movements can be found elsewhere, on fol. 1r of the *Black Pocket-book* (Mov. I, mm. 1–12) and on a 24-staff music paper (Mov. II, 34 measures).[16]

On the back of the page with the Violin Concerto memos, written later and in ink, four thematic ideas for String Quartet no. 1 appear (Ex. 3). Again none of them are opening themes in the final form: Ex. 3a is now a transitional motive to the theme proper of Movement II (mm. 4–7); Ex. 3b, upper staves, is the secondary subject of Movement II first in the exposition (mm. 73–78) and then, lower staves, marked *vagy így* [or so], in the development section (mm. 118–123); Ex. 3c is the Adagio contrast theme of Movement III (mm. 94–96); Ex. 3d is the second motive in the primary theme group of Movement III (mm. 17, 20–21). There are further preliminary memos in the *Black Pocket-book* (Ex. 4) as well as partial-sketch-type continuity sketches (on fol. 32v).

The identification of preliminary musical ideas by reference to the measures in the final form is naturally misleading. What finally became the continuation might have

15. In the final form, Poco meno sostenuto in the Andante sostenuto movement.
16. Together with sketches of Suite no. 2: p. 76 in PB 12FSS1ID1.

EXAMPLE 3   Thematic memos for String Quartet no. 1.

been planned as an opening. Can we guess the original meaning of the Roman numerals I and II in Exx. 3a and 3b? The first and second movements? Or the first and the second themes in an Andante movement, but in which movement? an opening movement? Had the Adagio theme originally been intended for the same movement or not? Had the beginning of a new line indicated different movements (in this case: an Andante, an Adagio, and a third movement) or just different characters?

Compared to the coherent notation of sketches for String Quartet no. 1 on the bifolio from around 1907 (Ex. 3), the memos in the *Black Pocket-book* (Ex. 4) are widely scattered and were probably written at different times in 1908. The sketch in Ex. 4a on fol. 31ᵛ (see the ostinato bass motive in Mov. III, mm. 185–186) may have been noted down first; Ex. 4b is at the top of fol. 12ʳ and represents the germ of the *molto appassionato* theme of the middle part in Movement I (mm. 33–34); Ex. 4c is a more elaborate form of the same on staves 6–7 on fol. 9ʳ (as in Facsimile 2); Ex. 4d on staff 1 of the same page is a six-note sketch (compare it with the motive in Mov. III, mm. 44–45, and the longer sketch on this very same page); Ex. 4e on the

EXAMPLE 4   Thematic memos in the *Black Pocket-book* for String
Quartet no. 1.

top of fol. 11ʳ (also in Facsimile 3, below) is a second sketch of the Adagio contrast
theme of Movement III, here two measures longer than in Ex. 3c.

Folios 8ᵛ–9ʳ in the *Black Pocket-book* (Facsimiles 1–2) contain several memo
sketches. These two opposite pages give an unusual, nervous impression. Bartók,
who habitually set everything, even his sketches, so clearly down on the music paper,
here filled all the corners and empty spots on the page by cramming memos for
different pieces together. The scribble alone (fol. 9ʳ top left corner) is not atypical.
When he got stuck as he was writing a draft, Bartók used to scrawl unintelligible
drawings or childish figures (for instance, a little pig drawn with square lines).[17] But
he seldom packed so many independent musical ideas onto the same page while the
pocket-book still had dozens of blank pages, even if the neighboring pages had been
used. The layers of the handwriting of these two pages are reconstructed in Ex. 5.

First, Bartók wrote a 17-measure piece, a fragment (for piano), in the style of the
Fourteen Bagatelles (fol. 8ᵛ st. 1–10; see the diplomatic transcription in Ex. 5a).
Later he sketched *Bagatelle* no. 13 (fol. 8ᵛ from the middle of st. 9–10, continued in
st. 9–10 of fol. 9ʳ; see mm. 2–10 of the final form; Ex. 5b). Next, he noted the
memo for *Bagatelle* no. 8, mm. 1–2 (fol. 9ʳ from the middle of st. 9–10; Ex. 5c) or
perhaps the one-staff memo for *Bagatelle* no. 9 (mm. 1–5 in the empty right-hand

17. See again the facsimile on *DocB/2*, 158 and 162 (substituting for his signature); his first wife,
Márta, used to draw similarly childish figures in her copies of Bartók's drafts, see *DocB/4*, 47.

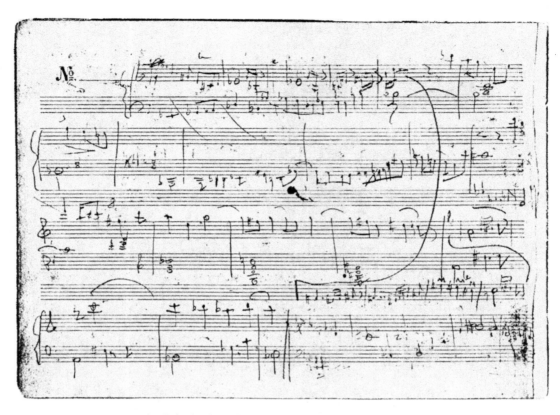

FACSIMILE 1 Folio 8ᵛ of the *Black Pocket-book* (BBA BH206), sketches from 1908 (see Ex. 5a–b, d).

measures on fol. 8ᵛ st. 1, mm. 6–7 in the second half of st. 8, mm. 11–14 in st. 6 and st. 5; Ex. 5d). As for the balance of the second page, fol. 9ʳ, we must assume that the two short memos for String Quartet no. 1 in st. 1 in pencil and in st. 5–7 in ink (see again Exx. 4c and 4d) were already on the page when Bartók continued the sketch of *Bagatelle* no. 13 in the bottom staves. The longer sketch in st. 1–2, 4–5, 7–8, now mm. 60–69 in Movement I of the quartet, might or might not have been on the paper at that time. More important, we do not know whether this is a partial sketch from the time when Bartók worked on the draft score of String Quartet no. 1 (ca. fall 1908) or whether it is rather a preliminary memo of a four-part progression, maybe without a clear concept of the present opening movement (and thus one he sketched in spring 1908?), inspired by the six-note motive in staff 1. The second suggestion seems more plausible.

Postponing discussion of other unrealized compositions and fragments and of the page complexes typical of working with a sketch-book (which we discuss later in this chapter), we see that the *Black Pocket-book* includes a variety of preliminary memos not really in context. There are one-staff melody sketches as well as sketches

FACSIMILE 2   Folio 9ʳ of the *Black Pocket-book* (BBA BH206), sketches from 1908 (see Ex. 4c–d, Ex. 5b–c).

in two staves. There are opening themes (such as *Three Burlesques* no. 1 on fol. 10ᵛ), characteristic internal themes of a complex form (such as the English horn theme from *Bluebeard* on fol. 12ᵛ);[18] themes for both movements of *Two Pictures* on fol. 12ᵛ–13ʳ; sketches for the development, recapitulation, and coda of Movement I of String Quartet no. 2 (on fol. 13ᵛ); simpler chord progressions (e.g., for *Two Elegies* no. 1 on fol. 8ʳ); and a collection of first ideas of a longer composition (the planned curtain music [?], the Princess's theme, the Dance of the Trees in *The Wooden Prince* on fol. 13ᵛ–14ᵛ) alike. There are even continuity-sketch-like notations for nos. 1 and 3 of *Four Dirges* (fol. 11ʳ and 12ʳ).

Both sketches for the *Dirges* are incomplete but in different ways, although in both cases the missing part of the form has a similar function: it would provide a "diminuendo" after the climax of the short piece. Why is it missing from these first sketches? Probably because it meant rather a technical problem for Bartók. The sketch of the *First Dirge* (Facsimile 3 and Ex. 6) contains the skeleton notation of

18. Perhaps this theme belonged to ideas for the 1910 *Two Pictures*; see the sketches around it.

EXAMPLE 5 Sketches in the *Black Pocket-book* for the *Fourteen Bagatelles* and an unrealized composition (a).

mm. 1–17 of the 28-measure piece with minor but significant differences from the final version (enharmonic notation and the correction of the right-hand melody in mm. 11–13). The sketch of the *Third Dirge* (Ex. 7), all together about 21 + 2 measures of the 33-measure piece, builds up the climax, starts the fragmentation, and, clearly not as a direct continuation, sketches the two closing measures. Bartók's next manuscript, the draft of the *Third Dirge*, not only fills the gap but revises the climax considerably by additions, making it longer, more effective, and for the coda clearly choosing the minor mode with G in the right hand.

FACSIMILE 3   Folio 11ʳ of the *Black Pocket-book* (BBA BH206), sketches from 1908 (see Ex. 4e and Ex. 6; in staves 3–5 two unused themes with a variant version).

EXAMPLE 6   Sketch of no. 1 of *Four Dirges*.

EXAMPLE 7   Sketch of no. 3 of *Four Dirges*.

FACSIMILE 4   Sketches for *The Wooden Prince* (BBA 2016b).

Interesting memos survive from the compositional process of *The Wooden Prince,* surely only a small fragment of similar sketches. On a bifolio,[19] partly filled with transcriptions of Rumanian folk music that Bartók had recorded, he sketched several things on the blank pages or spaces. On one half-empty page (practically continuing the play from that point where the musical memos on fol. 14[v] of the *Black Pocket-book* end) there is an outline — a text in Hungarian — of the Third Dance with the intended tempi, a very rare phenomenon among Bartók's sketches and plans. On the opposite page (Facsimile 4) typical memos line up: the motive of the waiting (after rehearsal no. 67); the Prince lifts the puppet up (at no. 73); themes to the Dance of the Wooden Prince (after no. 75); unused musical ideas (in staves 10, 13, 16); and, in the bottom staves, the Prince's despair (at no. 123). On a third half-empty page of the same bifolio appear two-staff sketches for the coronation scene (at nos. 136–141).

A next larger group of separate memos dates from the so-called piano year 1926. From June to September, having sent the family to relatives for a longer stay in the country, Bartók sketched/drafted some twenty solo piano movements (Sonata; *Out Doors; Nine Little Piano Pieces;* nos. 81, 137, 146 of *Mikrokosmos*), and finally Piano Concerto no. 1. The major part of the solo pieces was apparently sketched and drafted between June 1–30; the sketching of the concerto was postponed to August.

Two pages with sketches for the Sonata bear witness to the feverish and unusually productive work at the beginning of this period so vividly represented in Bartók's letter of June 21, 1926, to his wife (quoted in chapter 2; see p. 11). On one page, a cut-out piece of 20-staff music paper folded and mailed in a letter to Ditta,[20] we can identify the full basic thematic material of Movement I. The 64-measure sketch corresponds to the exposition and the beginning of the development section of the final form, which is 168 measures long. Although this sketch is made up of four (coherently written) progressions with unwritten measures in between (mm. 1–33; 34–41; 42–56; 57–64), our diplomatic transcription (Ex. 8), in which the disposition of the notation on the music paper agrees with the original, has a continuous numbering of the measures. Here is a concordance with the content of the final form:

1–27	2–37	(Theme I)
28–33	44–49	(Theme II)
34–41	55–67	(Theme III, considerably different)
42–56	68–115	(Theme IV)
57–64	116–137	(Theme V and the development section)

The deviations between these first memos and the final version are worth studying in detail.[21] It is certainly significant that the (printed) first measure with the

19. BBA 2016a–b.
20. BBA BH214; the date of the letter that contained this music is not known.
21. Somfai/*Vázlatok II.*

EXAMPLE 8   Sketch of Movement I of the Piano Sonata 1926.

dissonant major-plus-lydian fourth is missing yet; that the right-hand drumming (printed mm. 8–13) is shorter, and the 4/4 vs. 3/8 polymetric texture (mm. 22–37) is less crystallized; that Theme III in the sketch outlines a quasi stanza, a genuine contrast theme rather than an organically developed variant (as in the final version); that for Themes IV and V only motivic elements are present without the shape of a Bartókian theme. Finally, from the tonal point of view it is not without interest that Bartók, who had absolute pitch and as a habit immediately fixed the final key when he sketched musical ideas, here decided on the transposition from m. 42 on, as a second thought. Yet his Hungarian note did not fix the new key but indicated only, "rather in another key" or "rather at another pitch level" (*inkább más magasságba*).

The other Piano Sonata memo page belongs to the finale (Facsimile 5).[22] In addition to unused thematic ideas in staves 1–8, probably memos for the planned

22. Page 33b in PB 58PPS1.

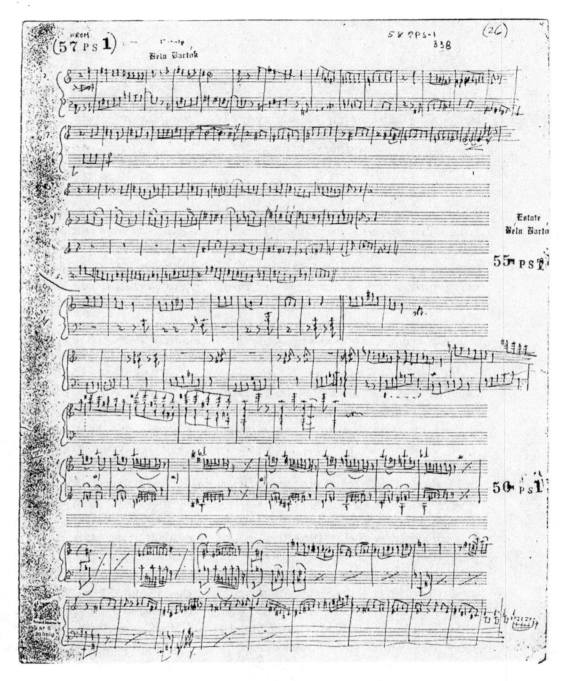

FACSIMILE 5   Sketch page from 1926 (PB 58PPS1, p. 33b) with unused thematic ideas probably for Piano Concerto no. 1 (staves 1–8) and the themes of the finale of the Piano Sonata (st. 9–21).

EXAMPLE 9   Sketch for no. 4 of *Out Doors*.

piano concerto, the rest of the page contains ideas for the urform (long form) of the finale with a *Musettes* as an episode.[23] Thus Bartók sketched the rondo theme (st. 9–10),[24] with a memo for one type of possible variation (see st. 9; *stb.* [= etc.]); the contrast motive (st. 11–12), and the closing scale motive (st. 11–12 & 13–14) of the ritornello block; another theme (st. 15–16), which was first an episode of the finale but became the first theme of no. 3 of *Out Doors*, with an additional theme for the same bagpipe material (st. 18–19 & 20–21).

Let us examine two more sketches for piano solo from 1926, one representing minute work and the other extreme haste. On the bottom of a leftover music paper[25] Bartók set down the "peasant flute"-style third theme of "The Night's Music" (*Out Doors* no. 4; Ex. 9). The variants above and below the main line look very much like Bartók's folk-music transcriptions. We may assume that he considered these possible variant forms rather than corrections, as the notes in parentheses suggest.

The first sketch of "Ostinato" (*Mikrokosmos* no. 146)[26] is an extreme example of Bartók's fastest notation (Facsimile 6). The musical ideas recognizably belong to the well known piano piece, yet not much of it was finally used in the same form or the same key. A rough comparison: in staves 1–2 the opening theme (at least sketch mm. 1–2 = print mm. 9–10 in the same key) and another motive appear in a different key (mm. 6–9 ≈ 106–109); in st. 3–4 a variant of the theme still in D (mm. 12–19 ≈ 96–103); in st. 5–6 and 7–8 (sketch mm. 22–35) unused material and the embryonic form of the second bagpipe theme (mm. 36–38 ≈ 32–34, in another key); in st. 9 the Meno vivo theme a step down (mm. 42–50 ≈ 81–89) with a continuation in st. 9 and 10–11, which Bartók used in a different context (mm. 51–53 and 54–58 ≈ 118ff. or ca. 105 and 108ff.); and finally, after the double bar (mm. 59–69), further development of the sketched ideas that in this form, however, point to "Marcia delle Bestie" (*Nine Little Piano Pieces* no. 7) no less

23. See Somfai/*Influence*, 546ff.
24. Still starting with note E, see in chapter 7, p. 180.
25. Page 37 of PB 58PPS1.
26. Page 2 of PB 57PS1.

FACSIMILE 6   Sketch from 1926 (PB 57PS1, p. 2), the first notation of the "Ostinato" (*Mikrokosmos* no. 146).

FACSIMILE 7   Sketches from 1926 (PB 58PPS1, p. 33a), unused ideas for Piano Concerto no. 1 (staves 1–10) and the beginning of Movement III (staves 12–19).

than to the Ostinato. No wonder that years later when Bartók started working on the *Mikrokosmos* intensively, he made a new sketchy draft.[27]

The preliminary memo material of Piano Concerto no. 1 written in 1926 is rich. In addition to the unused themes already mentioned and partly illustrated in facsimile are three more pages with separate memos. On one page[28] the basic themes of Movement II are noted: the piano theme from rehearsal no. 3 to three measures before no. 6, and the middle part from about four measures after no. 11 — with several preliminary notes in Hungarian about the special use of drums, sticks, and the like. Another page (Facsimile 7)[29] contains both realized and unrealized sketches. The first six and one-half measures in 9/8 meter, with the 3rd staff used for a percussion rhythm without pitch, obviously refer to the concerto in preparation — but which movement? The next 9-measure sketch in one-staff notation might have been planned for the first movement as well as the finale. The 5-measure memo in 3/4 time in st. 9–10 is an enigma: which movement of the planned concerto, if it is a concerto sketch at all? On the lower part of the same page Bartók outlined the theme that became the Allegro molto opening theme of Movement III. The first 16 + 13 measures correspond to mm. 1–37 in the final version; the music in the last brace (15 measures), although a direct continuation of the sketch in the brace above, does not appear in this form. The end of the sketch (6 measures) goes over to the third page; we present the facsimile of this third page in another context: among the fragments (see Facsimile 18 in chapter 5).

Separate memos are scarce from the next decade and a half — side sketches, memos in context, sketch-like discarded pages dominate. Fine exceptions are two pages of the Violin Concerto source material with the first notation of the opening themes of Movements I and II and the "twelve-tone theme" (incidentally a ten-note motive first) of Movement I (I dealt with these sketches in detail;[30] see also chapter 7, pp. 158ff.). Side sketches or themes outside the context of a sketch-book or draft are scarce during the American years. Page 95 of the Turkish field-book (the central source of the Concerto for Orchestra sketches) is, however, a typical collection of separate memos (see Ex. 10).[31] The first theme and its inversion (the only sketch written in ink on this page) may remind us of the 1944 Sonata for Solo Violin fugue theme, but since it is on the top of the page, it preceded the Concerto for Orchestra sketches from (or the latest from) 1943: Ex. 10d is from Movement I, m. 272; Ex. 10e from Movement IV, m. 43; Ex. 10f from Movement IV, m. 21; Ex. 10g from Movement IV, m. 5 or IV, m. 33. In other words, Exx. 10a and 10b were probably

---

27. On pp. 35–36 of PB 59PS1.

28. Page 34 of PB 58PPS1.

29. Page 33A of PB 58PPS1.

30. Somfai, "Drei Themenentwürfe zu dem Violinkonzert aus den Jahren 1936–37," in *DocB/6*, 247–255.

31. Page 95 in PB 80FSS1.

EXAMPLE 10   Sketches on p. 95 of the Turkish field-book, including themes for the Concerto for Orchestra.

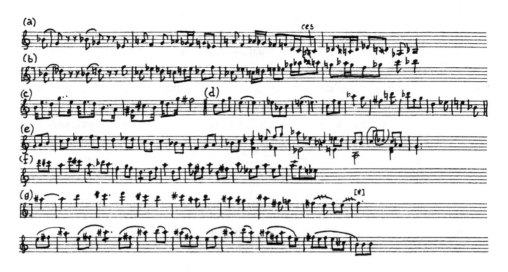

EXAMPLE 11   Thematic memo for Piano Concerto no. 3.

also originally planned for the Concerto for Orchestra. The theme in Ex. 10c with the double-dotted rhythm seems to be another idea matured only later (1945: Piano Concerto no. 3, first theme).

The actual memo of the Piano Concerto no. 3 opening motive appears in the Arab field-book (the exclusive source of sketches for the Sonata for Solo Violin), all but the last five notes in a matured form (Ex. 11). There are two more documents that seem to belong to this complex. The first is a small piece of tissue paper with Bartók's handwriting in india ink and pencil (Facsimile 8). The six "themes" must be birdsongs.[32] The only one of them with a number and title, no. 6, *Parting in peace,* is identical, even in pitch, to the piano motive in mm. 60–63 of the Adagio religioso. This is a sensational document and an enigma at the same time. What is the meaning of the number and title? Did Bartók himself collect these birdsongs and plan to make a collection with numbers, designating the assumed meaning of the bird's call? Or did he copy it from a book?[33] The other document, a rhythm noted at the bottom of

32. Among the quasi texts see *Té vu-ti-te tru tru* or *rrrrrr.*

33. Peter Bartók remembers that he saw the birdsong theme of the piano concerto in a pocket-book of his father's; when I discovered this small tissue paper in his collection among miscellanies, he thought it was another notation.

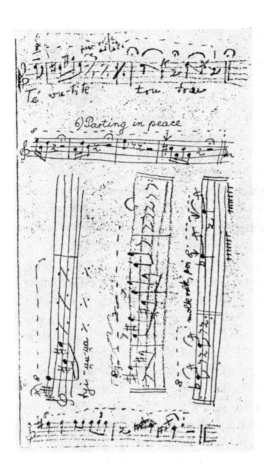

FACSIMILE 8   Bartók's handwriting with six birdsongs (PB Misc.C-27/55b); no. 6 used in Movement II of Piano Concerto no. 3.

EXAMPLE 12   Notation of a rhythm in the Turkish field-book.

pp. 65–66 of the Turkish field-book in pencil (Ex. 12), is not connected with the drum-rhythm introduction to Movement II of the Concerto for Orchestra.[34] The asymmetrical "measures" probably fix the actual rhythm of a birdsong, though the meaning of the upside-down stems is not quite clear.

34. The introductory drum solo (mm. 1–7) was added to the already drafted full score as a second thought (see p. 22 in PB 80FSID1).

PRELIMINARY MEMOS IN CONTEXT

Some of the already discussed separate memos could be interpreted as sketches in context in a wider sense, that is, from the viewpoint of chronology. The English horn theme from *Duke Bluebeard's Castle* on fol. 12ᵛ of the *Black Pocket-book,* to take an example, is surrounded by sketches for the *Two Pictures,* a score finished in 1910; thus this theme preceded the actual composition of the opera (1911). In fact one type of Bartók's preliminary memos in context is the sketch in chronological context proper: the location of the sketch may indicate the approximate time (or year) when Bartók noted it or can pinpoint his preoccupation when the new idea occurred to him. The second group — certainly an arbitrary collection of mine — selects from all the source material those sketches in context that seem to reveal the direct ignition of the creation of a new musical idea, usually a new variant of a Bartókian theme.

An exact or even an approximate dating of the memo sketch in context is often impossible yet offers chronological significance. A case in point (Ex. 13) concerns one page of the extra sheets kept together with the *Mandarin* draft.[35] Among the inserts and corrections to the autograph piano 4-hand reduction of the pantomime[36] there appears a penciled memo, Ex. 13a, that is very probably the direct forerunner of the *Dance Suite*'s Ritornello theme (13b). To the *Mandarin* inserts kept on the same page Bartók added his typical preparatory notes for the orchestration also in pencil (number of staves needed in the score, name of the instruments, and so forth). The 4-hand reduction existed in spring 1921 (with or without the corrections);[37] the *Dance Suite* was drafted in April–August 1923 (see the date on the score); and Bartók did not start writing the full score of the *Mandarin* until April 1924.[38] Thus the memo with the preparatory notes for the *Mandarin* orchestration had to be written between 1921 and spring 1923. This dating of the *Dance Suite* theme may not be very accurate but is our only source of useful information about Bartók's preparation for the belated scoring of the *Mandarin.*

More typical is the case of ideas occurring to Bartók while copying music (e.g., writing the autograph fair copy from the draft). He would immediately put down the idea in the empty staves of the draft, which was usually a recycled piece of paper, a private document for his eyes only. So for instance Bartók sketched sometime in mid-June 1926 on empty staves between the drafts of *Out Doors* nos. 1–2[39] sixteen measures (Ex. 14) that he used during August, when the Piano Concerto no. 1 was gradually taking shape, for the "Stravinsky-style" central part of the development

35. Page 48 of PB 49FS1.

36. PB 49TPPS1.

37. According to Bartók's letter of April 7, 1921, to Universal Edition, he could not get the 4-hand *Klavierauszug* back from H. Scherchen.

38. According to Bartók's letters to Universal Edition, he planned to start the scoring in April 1924 (letter of March 19) but just began the work in June (letter of June 5).

39. On p. 10 of PB 55–56PS1.

EXAMPLE 13   Memo of a theme (a) related to the Ritornello theme of the
              Dance Suite (b).

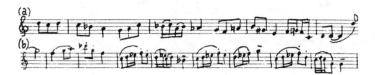

EXAMPLE 14   Sketch for Movement I of Piano Concerto no. 1.

EXAMPLE 15   Sketch for no. 5 of *Nine Little Piano Pieces*.

section of Movement I (Allegro moderato at no. 29). It was in fact a new theme rather than the development of the themes of the exposition.[40] Furthermore, in the next staff Bartók sketched the first twenty measures of the "Menuetto," no. 5 in *Nine Little Piano Pieces* (Ex. 15), both in the final key.

A similar working pattern explains the appearance of sketches for two themes of *Cantata profana* (finished September 8, 1930) at the bottom of a page with corrections to the *Four Hungarian Folksongs* for mixed choir, a score completed in early May 1930. The first sketch (Ex. 16a) is the descant of the choir in mm. 27–35, the first genuine melody of *Cantata profana*; the second (Ex. 16b) is the preliminary form of the hunting fugue theme at m. 74 in diminished rhythm, with a slightly different melody that followed the prosody of the original Rumanian words.

A collection of sketches for the Divertimento is an extremely interesting source for studying Bartók's creative process. The page itself (Facsimile 9) was used for correc-

40. A few thoughts about the form of Movement I are in Somfai/*Piano Year*, 48–58.

EXAMPLE 16   Two themes sketched for the *Cantata profana*.

tions to the first page of the draft of Movement I too. The sketches are in pencil in staves 1–9 and belong to all three movements of the Divertimento. When did Bartók write them down? A careful analysis of the micro-chronology of the sketch results in a series of fairly well founded conclusions:

1. The 2/4 variant forms of themes in Movement III in st. 1–3, varying the original shape in Movement I, were sketched while Bartók still worked on the development section of Movement I; see st. 4–8 (= Mov. I, m. 96 with sharps in the sketch and flats in the final form): the notation in st. 4 (the curved tie) goes around the triplet figure that belongs to st. 3;

2. following the thematic memos for Movement III and the partial sketches to the imitation in Movement I, in st. 9 Bartók wrote preliminary memos for the slow movement, in fact first only two short pieces (2 + 5 measures); as the arrow indicates, the continuation of m. 2 after the second double bar came later;

3. in between the first two variants Bartók probably inserted the four measures in bass clef in the middle of st. 8 (= Mov. II, 33ff.).

Incidentally the Movement II memos are not in the final key — a phenomenon that is quite rare among Bartók's sketches. Here is a rough list of the contents on the nine staves:

st. 1: III, mm. 14–19, 26–30, 36–39 + 44–46;
st. 2: III, mm. 47–48, 65–67 plus 5 measures, 184–191 (in another key);
st. 3: III, mm. 103–117 + 132, 133–135, 139 (above it: *többször* [several times]), 146–148;
st. 4–8: I, mm. 95–97 (98) and 101–103;
st. 8, from the middle of the staff: II, mm. 33–34 (in augmented rhythm);

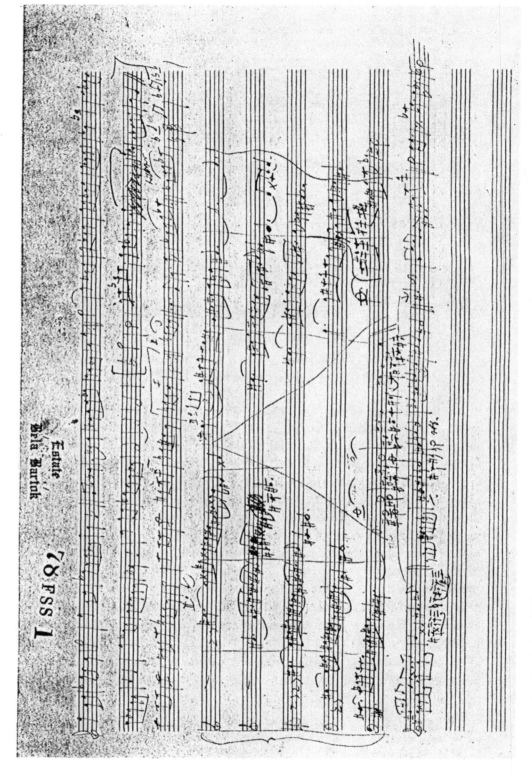

FACSIMILE 9   Sketches from 1939 for Movements III, I, and II of the Divertimento (PB 78FSS1, p. 2).

EXAMPLE 17   Thematic memos for String Quartet no. 6.

EXAMPLE 18   Thematic memo for the *Contrasts*.

st. 9: II, mm. 11–12, 1 and 6–9 (*stb.* [etc.]), 12 (with *stb.*) plus one measure
(see m. 18), 20–21 (in augmented rhythm).

On the last page of the Divertimento draft (finished and dated *Saanen, 1939.
aug.2–17*), which actually is the end of Movement II,[41] in four staves there are
sketches for String Quartet no. 6 (Ex. 17), the next composition by Bartók (dated
Saanen–Budapest, 1939.VIII–XI). The embryonic form of the later motto theme
appears here in two transpositions (Exx. 17a, 17c), none of them in the key used in
the final form; Ex. 17b is the actual opening Vivace theme as Bartók originally
drafted the beginning of Movement I, without the slow introduction, in the same
key;[42] Ex. 17d is the theme of the "Marcia" (Mov. II, mm. 66–70); Ex. 17e was the
second theme of the planned fast finale. We might well wonder whether the typical
Bartókian polymodal chromaticism (his term in the Harvard Lectures) of the motto
theme was not directly inspired by the chromatic motive in the last measures of the
Divertimento draft (Mov. II, 66–70). (N.B. We discuss the next stages of the
evolution of the motto theme in another context; see Facsimile 22 in chapter 6,
p. 108.)

I would not hesitate, however, to assert a direct motivic interrelationship between the descant melody in the last measures of Movement II of the Violin Con-

41. Bartók drafted the movements of the Divertimento in the sequence I-III-II. (Throughout, italics
are used to signal all remarks in Bartók's hand: words, short instructions, and — as here — dates.)
42. On the first recto in PB 79FSS1, arbitrarily paginated as p. 2 (see Figure 13 in chapter 6).

certo and the Trio theme in Movement III of *Contrasts* (mm. 134ff.). The beautiful folksong-like theme[43] (Ex. 18) came to Bartók's mind while he was scoring the last measures of Movement II of the concerto, using the already prepared lithographed copy of the violin-piano form.[44] This is an exceptional moment of inspiration caught "in the act."

SIDE SKETCHES IN DRAFTS

Almost every Bartók draft contains some marginalia: sketched notations above and under the staves, in empty staves between two braces and at the bottom of the page, or in hand-ruled staves. Most of these marginalia came from immediate correction during the primary drafting process; some emerged from revisions at a next reading, perhaps before Bartók or a family member made the copy. In orchestral pieces a great amount of small musical notes belong to the preparation for the scoring. The phenomenon at issue here, the side sketch, usually belongs to the first stage of the drafting process. While he was writing a new work, Bartók sometimes got ideas related to the continuation of the composition — to the shape of a later part of the movement or another movement of the same work — which he noted immediately. Instead of a chronological survey of selected examples, here an ordered set of examples may lead to a better understanding of Bartók's compositional process.

(A) *Variant form of a theme for later use.* In the violin-piano draft of the Violin Concerto,[45] sketched in the empty staff under the solo part,[46] Bartók immediately added a 3/4 meter variant form too (Facsimile 10). He applied this new form, after the completion of the here missing mm. 5–6, as the first theme of the finale. A whole complex of side sketches (Ex. 19) occurs at the bottom of the first page of the sketches of String Quartet no. 4[47] with the beginning of Movement I.[48] On this page appears the theme of the transition (mm. 16f. in the final form; Ex. 19a) in its final form, which ignited the following versions sketched in the bottom staff: the theme in the same key but starting on the beat, with the note *tükörkép is* [inversion too],[49] with a melodic extension to upper C (Ex. 19b); the sketch of the contrast theme of the finale (see Mov. V, mm. 156–165, in another key; Ex. 19c); and in the hand-ruled extra staff the opening theme of the finale (Mov. V, mm. 15–18 plus 32–34;

43. The rhythm has a Bulgarian asymmetry and at the same time gives the impression of a slightly rubato performance of a very clearly Hungarian melody inspired by folksongs from the Old Style.

44. BBA 4091, p. 21.

45. PB 76VPS1.

46. It was Bartók's habit to leave an empty staff between the solo string part and the upper staff (piano right hand) of the symphonic texture to allow for eventual corrections or simply for the high notes.

47. Page 30 in PB 62FSS1 (reproduced in Antokoletz/1983, facsimile 6).

48. See p. 155 in chapter 7.

49. See mm. 24–26 in the printed form.

FACSIMILE 10   First page of the draft of the Violin Concerto (no. 2), 1937, with a side sketch in staff 2 for the first theme of Movement III (PB 76VPS1).

EXAMPLE 19   Side sketches in the draft of String Quartet no. 4.

EXAMPLE 20   Side sketch in the draft of String Quartet no. 4.

Ex. 19d). Thus the idea of the finale featuring variations of certain themes from the opening movement probably occurred to Bartók while he made these side sketches. He made similar side sketches on the first page (p. 9 of the same MS) of the Presto con sordino Movement II too, although this time not at the bottom but between the 4-staff braces of the score-form sketchy draft. Directly under the cello theme (mm. 1ff.) Bartók made a note of the form introducing the coda (Ex. 20 = II, mm. 213–220); between braces 2–3 and 3–4 he continuously sketched 24 measures that he used in the draft of the coda (p. 14 in the MS) but strongly revised and rewrote later.[50]

(B) *Side sketches for the continuation of a movement.* A typical case seems to be the side sketch (Ex. 21) in the draft of the finale of Piano Concerto no. 1. On the first page (p. 21, the draft from m. 1 to rehearsal no. 6) in the bottom staff the oboe-clarinet theme (m. 4 after no. 11) is sketched (Ex. 21a); on the next page under the trombone theme (at no. 10), as a variant form, the piano theme at no. 16ff. is noted in a slightly different rhythm (Ex. 21b) and, above the bottom brace, the horn theme (at no. 25) appears (Ex. 21c).

The Piano Concerto no. 3 draft is extremely rich in side sketches. One of the most informative pages is the one with the beginning of Movement I including the

50. Another fascinating side sketch occurs at the bottom of p. 1 of the full-score-form draft of *Music for Strings, Percussion, and Celesta* (PB 74FSS1): the "extended in range" version of the fugue theme (see Mov. IV, mm. 203ff.), here still in A, the key of the original "narrow" form in the fugue.

EXAMPLE 21   Side sketches in the draft of Piano Concerto no. 1.

EXAMPLE 22   Side sketch in the draft of the *Contrasts*.

2-piano draft of mm. 1–26 (Facsimile 11).[51] Between the four-staff braces, the subsequent themes of the sonata-form exposition are all sketched here. Bartók wrote the side sketches presumably in this order: first 4 measures in staff 12 (I, mm. 44–47); next in st. 5–6 the third theme (I, mm. 54–62), continued in st. 12 (I, mm. 63–65) and st. 24 (I, mm. 66–67 plus 68–69), thus ending with the closing motive.

(C) *Side sketches for a later scene of a stage work*. A striking example can be found at the bottom of the first page of the draft of *The Miraculous Mandarin*,[52] which contains the music from m. 1 to m. 2 before no. 3. In a one-staff melody sketch, the second "decoy game" (from no. 22 to no. 24) is noted in ink. Whether Bartók immediately planned it as the second of the three decoy games or just as the so characteristic melody of the recurring scenes (the clarinet starting with note A, C, and E, respectively), cannot be decided.

(D) *Themes for another movement*. Another typical phenomenon of the side sketches in Bartók's drafts: rather than take a new page for the by and large crystallized beginning of the next movement, he often fixed the rough idea as a side sketch on the page that occupied him. So he sketched the embryonic form of the opening theme of Movement II of *Contrasts*, a piece subsequently added to the slow-fast rhapsody-form original plan suggested by Joseph Szigeti[53] (Ex. 22). Or, drafting the finale of the Divertimento, Bartók sketched ideas for Movement II (Ex. 23 =

51. Page 1 in PB 84FSS1. About the sequence of the pages and the pagination see Figure 16 in chapter 6, p. 107.
52. PB 49PS1.
53. See Szigeti's letter of Aug. 11, 1938 (*DocB/3*, 226ff.).

FACSIMILE 11   First page of Movement I of the draft of Piano Concerto no. 3, 1945 (PB 84FSS1, p.
1), with side sketches in staves 5–6, 12, and 24.

EXAMPLE 23   Side sketches in the draft of the Divertimento.

mm. 17–18 and 22–24) at the bottom of p. 19 of the draft,[54] at that moment working on the measures ca. 301–311 of Movement III with the same ink.

An extraordinary side sketch survived on p. 31 of the draft of Piano Concerto no. 2[55] (Facsimile 12). As a relatively rare phenomenon, this work was composed directly in full-score-form draft. There may or may not have been a considerable number of preliminary sketches written for all three movements. The only existing one is, however, the two-part thematic outline of the fifth-chord contrary motion string music of the first Adagio of Movement II noted on the empty spots of the page with the last measures of Movement I. The sketch starts in staves 24–25 (= II, mm. 1–13) and continues in a column after the double bar of the full score in st. 9–10 (with immediate corrections in three steps; see II, mm. 14–17 of the final form), then in st. 14–15 with the end of the first part (II, mm. 18–22). The two shorter string music entries (II, mm. 30–38 and 54–61) are sketched in st. 16–21 in the approximately final form except for the cadence (D–A ending instead of C–G). In addition to minor corrections — presumably to avoid undesirable chords resulting from the rigid fifth-chord mixture of the outer voices (see, e.g., the F–E♭–D♭–C–D–E bass of mm. 4–5 in the sketch) — Bartók considerably revised what finally became mm. 11–15. In Ex. 24 I attempt to reconstruct the correcting process.

(E) *Side sketches for the revision of a piece.* A special form of side sketches, not to be confused with the routine correction in the original layer of every draft by Bartók, belongs to the preparation of the revision of a piece. One such case was connected with Zoltán Kodály's criticism. Sometime in the 1910s Bartók showed him the 2-piano-form draft of *Four Orchestral Pieces* (sketched 1912, scored 1921). On the last page of the "Marcia funebre"[56] (see Facsimile 24 in chapter 7 and the notes to it on p. 124) Kodály made two significant suggestions in pencil, both seriously considered by Bartók. The one concerned the last five measures of the work; here Bartók sketched two new ideas but finally returned to a shortened form of the original idea.

54. PB 78FSS1.
55. PB 68FSS1.
56. PB 31TPPS1.

FACSIMILE 12   Sketches for Movement II in the draft score of Piano Concerto no. 2, written on the
page with the end of Movement I, 1930 or 1931 (PB 68FSS1, p. 31).

EXAMPLE 24   The layers and corrections of mm. 11–20 of the sketches for
Movement II of Piano Concerto no. 2 (see Facsimile 12).

EXAMPLE 25   Old and revised form in the draft of Movement IV of the *Four Orchestral Pieces*.

The other was a note by Kodály referring to the measure at rehearsal no. 7 of the
printed score, suggesting *hosszabban* [longer, make it longer]. In Ex. 25 I present
the criticized version in a condensed form (Ex. 25a) along with Bartók's side sketch
written on the previous page (Ex. 25b).

MEMOS EXTENDED INTO CONTINUITY SKETCHES

Not even the terminology specified in this chapter in connection with Bartók's
sketches can bypass problems in dealing with unusual (atypical) cases, or even less

with the frequent phenomenon of typical thematic memos that Bartók continued in a next step and thus turned into a continuity sketch or continuity draft. This happens in the greater part of Bartók's sketch-books (discussed in the next subchapter in detail). In addition, dozens of first drafts of shorter movements that Bartók conceived in one sitting (when writing pieces for the *Mikrokosmos,* Forty-Four Duos, folksong arrangements for piano or for voice and piano) represent borderline cases between a genuine memo soon extended into a full piece, and a sketchily noted complete continuity draft. A minute study of the writing act of Bartók's drafts considering the color of the ink, the size of the notation, and the angle of stems or other linear characteristics of the handwriting may result in a nuanced interpretation of the chronological layers of the manuscript, a better understanding of what may have been a memo in a first step.

There are a few striking examples of extended memos. One is the fascinating sketch of Movement III of String Quartet no. 2, in facsimile and diplomatic transcription published by Vera Lampert.[57] This page, which Emma Kodály picked up from Bartók's desk and kept,[58] is similar to a working score by Beethoven: the four-staff sketchy notation has several layers with a great many corrected versions. It was not at all typical that here in the original layer (written in ink) Bartók left empty measures that he later filled in in pencil.[59] Another unusual feature of the manuscript is that Bartók sketched the piece in diminished rhythm; the 55 measures of the continuity sketch cover about mm. 1–111 of the 141-measure Lento. We take up the draft of String Quartet no. 3[60] in chapter 6 (see p. 144), but one feature of it actually belongs here. As a first step, on the top of two separate pages Bartók wrote down the beginning of the fast and the slower movement, that is, the later Seconda parte and Prima parte. The extension of the fast movement immediately grew into a draft and, figuratively speaking, circumscribed the spot with the other memo on the next page. For the draft of Prima parte Bartók noted the primary theme again on another page. All these memos have structural significance that we discuss in another context in chapter 6.

WORKING WITH A SKETCH-BOOK

The three major sources that we may call "sketch-books," a term Bartók himself never used, belong to two different periods of his life and therefore, and because of the special circumstances, form two considerably different types. The *Black Pocket-*

---

57. V. Lampert, "Bartóks Skizzen zum III. Satz des Steichquartetts Nr. 2," in *DocB/5*, 179–189 and facsimiles 21–23.

58. BBA 494.

59. A similar place, in connection with contrapuntal elaboration, occurs in the draft of the 2-piano Sonata; see Facsimile 37 in chapter 7, p. 137.

60. PB 60FSS1.

book, although originally meant to be a folksong-collecting fieldwork sketch-book, became Bartók's compositional pocket-book that he repeatedly used between 1907 and 1922 — with interruptions and evidently alongside a multitude of other sketches — when he was on a collecting trip or spent his summer holidays with his family, far from home and his piano.[61] The two other pocket-books, the "Turkish field-book" and the "Arab field-book," were collecting pocket-books that contained still un-published folksong material, therefore Bartók took them to the United States. As a coincidence, being away from New York City and working on ethnomusicological and compositional projects side by side, during 1943 in Saranac Lake, N.Y., he wrote down the major part of the Concerto for Orchestra sketches on empty or half-empty pages of the Turkish field-book,[62] and during 1944 in Asheville, N.C., wrote the full sketches of the Sonata for Solo Violin in the Arab field-book.[63] Although these two sketch-books contain further memos (see again Exx. 10–11), in them Bartók typically extended the first thematic ideas into a complete continuity draft that directly served for writing the autograph copy or, after the usual preparatory notes, for making the orchestration.

Compared to the concentrated work in the sketch-books in the United States, even the most coherent sketches of a longer composition in the *Black Pocket-book* can pass for continuity "sketches" only, always followed by a rough manuscript: a draft of the full form. Four longer compositions are represented among the extensive sketches in the *Black Pocket-book.* For the Violin Concerto op. posth. (1907–1908) Bartók sketched coherent sections, presumably at different times (using ink and pencil alike) in quite different layouts (like 2- or 3- or 4-staff score, 2-st. short score, 1 + 2 st. violin-piano-form sketches). The sequence of the sections does not always correspond to the final form.[64] The continuity sketches for *The Miraculous Mandarin* occupy some twenty pages in the pocket-book and cover a good half of the pantomime from the "pursuit" scene to the end. The work had to be in progress for rather a long time (the portions are sometimes clearly distinguishable from the handwriting in ink or pencil), and the layout varies (mostly 2-st. short score, occasionally with 1- or 3- or 4-st. sections, depending on the texture). Yet everything here reveals tremendous concentration, conviction, and inspiration along with a low rate of correction. Nevertheless Bartók wrote a full draft short-score as a next step.

61. Bartók did not note down compositional sketches in the pocket-sized field-books used on folksong collecting trips between 1906 and 1918, of which sixteen are kept in the BBA. An interesting exception is the sketch on page 51 (= fol. 34^r) of the mixed-content *III.t.*, i.e., the 3rd Slovak pocket-book (actually more than half its contents are Rumanian). In the bottom staves 9–10, surrounded by Rumanian folksong notations from January 1912, Bartók sketched two ideas in pencil. Although both are in 2/4 and not in 3/4, they seem to belong to Movement II of *Four Orchestral Pieces* (drafted 1912): the first, a theme, closely related to the trumpet-horn-woodwinds theme at no. 22 (with E♭ repetition); the second, a chordal progression, only slightly resembling the chords at no. 9 or 49.

62. PB 80FSS1.

63. PB 81FSS1.

64. E.g., among the sketches of Movement II on fol. 4^r–8^r those to the development section precede a sketch to the exposition (see the analysis of the content on xiv–xv of the facsimile edition).

We see a third compositional process in the sketches of the two violin sonatas in the *Black Pocket-book*. These thirteen small oblong pages belong to the most instructive sketches of the existing source material of the music of Béla Bartók. Their significance lies above all in the disclosure of the way Bartók first noted basic ideas of a multi-movement composition on the top of different pages, thus fixing the starting point of complex forms, and next turned these memos (first in shorter, then in longer sections) into continuity sketches. The exact location of the musical ideas on a page and the precise reconstruction of the sequence of the continuation is the necessary first step for the musical analysis of such sketches, as the case of the six-page sketches of the three-movement Sonata for Violin and Piano no. 1 (1921) reveals.[65] Sketches of the Sonata for Violin and Piano no. 2 (1922), representing the last use of the *Black Pocket-book,* occupy seven pages. The first layer of the handwriting on its opening two-page spread (see Facsimiles 13–14, with inserted letters *a* to *h* and short identification of the themes) includes the basic themes of the two-movement *attacca* form, implying contrasting and developmental ideas alike. In my reading, these sketches already show the following:

The work starts with a violin theme in the improvisational style of a
  Rumanian *hora lungă* (*a*);[66]
opposing it is an independent piano theme involving mirror motion of the
  two hands (*f*);
the theme of the contrasting (fast) dance movement builds on the pitch
  collection of the *hora lungă* (*b*) and proceeds into variant folkdance-like
  forms (*c–d*);
a bagpipe-imitation fiddler episode (*g*) is to appear somewhere.

The next four pages forecast furthermore that a lament-style episode will appear in the first movement (fol. 28ᵛ–29ʳ) and there will be a montage formed from the lament and from some material of the fast movement (fol. 29ᵛ–30ʳ). The sketches do not reveal, however, that the *hora lungă* theme will develop in several steps into a quasi-strophic final form (i.e., in the course of the two-movement composition the improvisation-like melody, as it were, arrives at a higher-level closed form, representing a later phase in the evolution of peasant music); that the fast second movement also has an independent piano theme with variant forms; that the second movement is written in an unorthodox sonata form. Fig. 7 gives a survey of the two-movement form, marking the place of the *Black Pocket-book* sketches in the final form (arrows in the shaded areas indicate continuity sketches; curved lines connect the returns of the *hora lungă* theme).

65. In detail in Somfai / *Vázlatok II*.
66. The *hora lungă* or *cântec lung* melody type, as Bartók discovered it first in nonceremonial songs in villages of the Rumanian territories in Transylvania, was one of his major discoveries as an ethnomusicologist and at the same time one of the latent sources of his inspiration as a composer (see Somfai / *Influence*, 542–543).

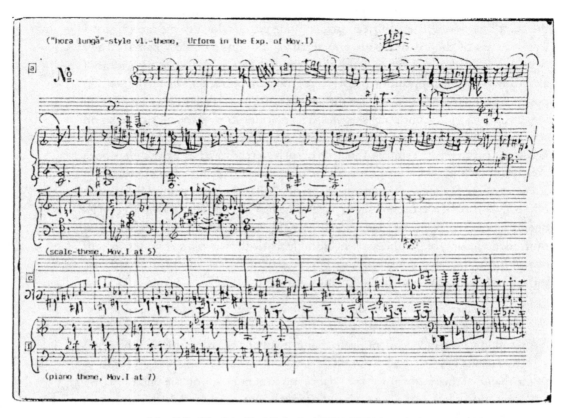

FACSIMILE 13 Folio 27ᵛ of the *Black Pocket-book* (BBA BH206) with sketches for the Sonata for Violin and Piano no. 2, 1922 (letters and notes inserted for the identification of the themes).

The description of the first sketch-book used during the American years for the Concerto for Orchestra would need a whole chapter. Of the 95 numbered pages of the oblong booklet pp. 2–74 were more or less filled with folksong notation and related notes during the 1936 field trip to the nomadic Yürük tribes in Anatolia, Asia Minor. Therefore the very first sketches for the Concerto, written in ink, appear on the top of the next six pages (pp. 75–80). On p. 75 the first theme, on p. 76 the *dolce* secondary theme of the Allegro vivace sonata-form first movement are sketched in the final key but not in the final form (I, mm. 76–110, with later revision and continuation in pencil, and I, mm. 174–ca. 188). For the rest of these preliminary memos, on p. 77 there is a theme that, although it reminds us of certain passages in Movement II, has not been realized (Ex. 26a);[67] on p. 78 is the opening fanfare of Movement V but in G instead of F (Ex. 26b); at the top of p. 79 seems to be a planned finale first theme with related thematic ideas on the same page (Ex. 26c);

67. The meter is an enigma: 10/16 meter? quintuplet 16th notes? triplet-duplet combination in 2/4?

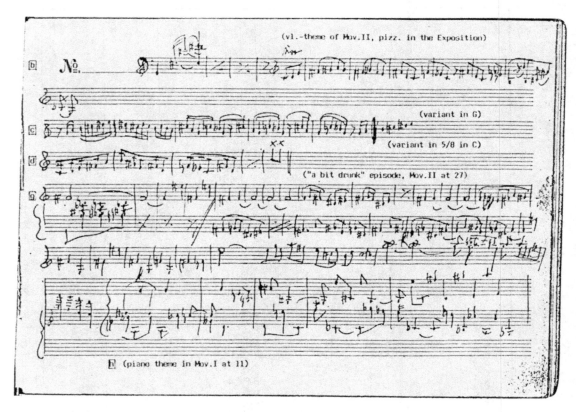

FACSIMILE 14 Folio 28ʳ of the *Black Pocket-book* (BBA BH206) with the continuation of the sketches for the Sonata for Violin and Piano no. 2.

Ex. 26d written in pencil and Ex. 26e from the original layer in ink are probably the nearest to motives of the present finale; Ex. 26f on p. 80 may also have been planned for the finale but was not used in this form.

The continuity sketches of the five movements written in pencil probably followed in this order: Movement I on pp. 75–80 and 89–94 (the slow introduction only as a later addition); Movement II on pp. 81–84, 62, 58, 46–45–44 (working backwards on half-empty pages too, but the notation on pp. 81–84 could have preceded the elaboration of Movement I on pp. 75–80); Movement III on pp. 10–16 and 20–22; Movement IV on pp. 18–34; mm. 1–285 of Movement V are sketched on pp. 36–42, 74 and 96–97, whereas mm. 286–606 are on standard-size extra music papers.[68] In addition to the most typical 2- and 3-staff short-score sketches we find a great variety of partial sketches and insertions; the whole continuity sketch was prepared for scoring in a next step.

68. PB 80FSS2.

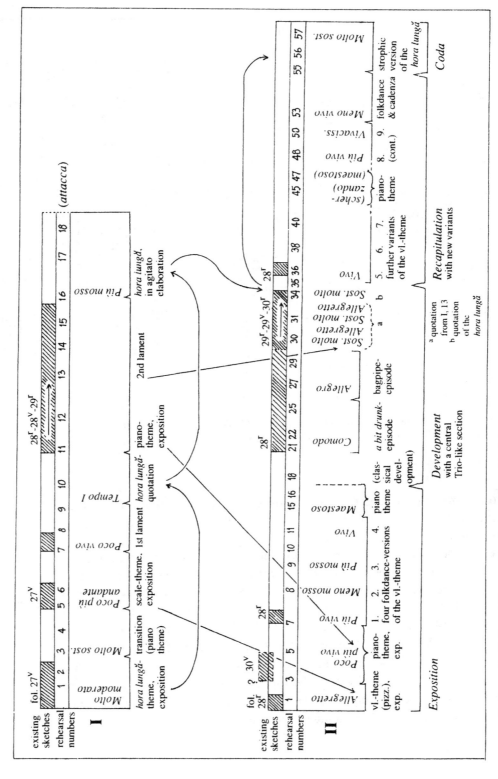

FIGURE 7 Sonata for Violin and Piano no. 2: an interpretation of the 2-movement *attacca* form with the affiliation of the existing sketches.

EXAMPLE 26   Preliminary memos in the Turkish field-book together with the sketches of the Concerto for Orchestra.

The other sketch-book used in the United States, the Arab field-book, had more empty pages; thus Bartók could work on the Sonata for Solo Violin in a less complicated way. The blank pages started with p. 38 on which Bartók sketched the first idea of the Ciaccona theme in pencil in staff 1 (Ex. 27a), but mostly ideas for the Melodia in an extremely crowded form: the opening theme in G, written in ink in st. 2, 4, 6, 8 (27b); a new version of the opening theme already in B♭, written in pencil in st. 10 (the beginning: 27c), continued in st. 1, then st. 3; the inversion (the beginning: 27d) is sketched in the next stage in several forms. In Fig. 8 I survey the contents of pp. 37–64 of the Arab field-book and summarize here the chronology of the composition of the four movements. First, after preliminary memos and some work on the Melodia (pp. 38, 37), on two opposite pages Bartók began the Ciaccona and the Fuga (pp. 39–40). From these first he continued the Fuga (pp. 41–42), then, presumably adding in parallel to the one and the other alike, proceeded and finished first the Fuga, then the Ciaccona. After completing the Melodia (and rewriting the first 29 measures in a clear form), Bartók began writing the finale. Thorough study of pp. 56–57 shows us that the Presto in its original conception started with the dance-style *forte* theme (i.e., the first episode of the rondo form, IV, mm. 100ff.) and that the famous quarter-tone *pianissimo* beginning formed the first episode. What a difference it would have been! In terms of Bartók's aesthetics, the reconsideration is crucial: the rustic folk dance as a symbol does not represent an organic finale for such a serious multi-movement work but rather a dramatic contrast to it.

Facsimile 15 is a characteristic sample of the working process in this sketch-book. Normally Bartók filled staves 1, 3, 5, and so on, using the other staves for correction

EXAMPLE 27   Sketches for Movement III of the Sonata for Solo Violin.

or side sketches. This page (p. 40) represents the first steps of the composition of the Fuga.[69] Measures 1–17 are written in ink in st. 1, 3, 5, 7, with a sketchy continuation of mm. 17–21 in pencil; there are side sketches of planned forms of the inversion in the hand-ruled staff at the top of the page and in st. 2 and 10 of which the sketches in the top left corner come nearest to the final form (see II, mm. 45–49 in the printed version). There are significant little corrections, like the rhythm of the last quarter in m. 2, probably decided when Bartók wrote down m. 7; and there are interesting performing instructions in the original layer of the handwriting, like the bowing indications and *leg.* (= *legato*) in st. 3. In contrast, the down-bow marks and some slurs in st. 5 and 7, in turn, written in india ink, were added when Bartók checked the manuscript as a preparation for completing the india ink fair copy on onionskin; thus these represent a later revision.

69. A more detailed description in Somfai, "Diplomatic Transcription versus Facsimile with Commentaries: Methodology of the Bartók Edition," in Wolfgang Gratzer and Andrea Lindmayr, eds., *De editione Musices: Festschrift Gerhard Croll* (Laaber: Laaber Verlag, 1992), 95–97.

Ciaccona	Fuga	Arab field-book	Melodia	Presto
mm. 1-150	mm. 1-107		mm. 1-68	mm. 1-418
		p. 37	17-26	
(theme)		p. 38	(theme), 1-29	
1-14		p. 39		
	1-21	p. 40		
	22-37	p. 41		
	37-55	p. 42		
15-32		p. 43		
	56-76	p. 44		
32-54		p. 45		
	77-80, 85-92	p. 46		
54-74		p. 47		
75-90		p. 48		
91-93[a]		p. 49		
	93-107 ‖	p. 50		
94-116		p. 51		
117-143		p. 52		
144-150 ‖	80-84	p. 53	30-42	
		p. 54	43-53	
		p. 55	1-29[b], 49-51[b]	
		p. 56	63-68 ‖	100-123, 269-275[c]
		p. 57		124-148, 1-24[d]
		p. 58		25-87
		p. 59		88-99, 149-199
		p. 60		200-270
		p. 61		271-328
		p. 62		329-383
		p. 63		384-418 ‖
		p. 64		(alternatives)

[a] And discarded version of I, 75-79 plus ca. 6 measures
[b] Newly written form
[c] IV, 100-123 probably sketched as an opening theme of the finale
[d] Probably an episode in the original concept of the form

FIGURE 8 Sonata for Solo Violin: distribution of the sketches and the draft in the Arab field-book.

FACSIMILE 15   Draft with sketches of Movement II of the Sonata for Solo Violin in the Arab field-book, 1944 (PB 81VS1, p. 40).

PARTIAL SKETCHES FOR THE FINAL TEXTURE OR THE INSTRUMENTATION

The "partial sketch" — the elaboration of contrapuntal, harmonic, textural, and most often scoring problems on a separate piece of paper — is a common phenomenon in Bartók's manuscripts. Hundreds of such short sketches exist in drafts or in the short scores of orchestral works. Whereas the sketches we studied up to this point represent crucial documents of the primary stage of composition, the physical traces of a new art work's creation, the partial sketch is a secondary document. It points to certain aspects of the compositional technique in which Bartók often needed some cool brain-work and the help of an extra piece of paper.

Partial sketches that survive on extra music papers are not very numerous, but nothing indicates that Bartók distinguished such sketches from others. A typical scoring problem was solved on the *Kossuth* sketch page preserved by Emma Kodály.[70]

70. BBA 3344; see facsimile 14 in *DocB/1*.

FACSIMILE 16   Partial sketches to the score of the *Dance Suite*, 1923 (BBA BH213); at the bottom
of the page, two lines in Ditta's handwriting.

Two partial sketches with a harmonic progression and the elaboration of a contrapuntal place in Suite no. 2 for orchestra were hiding on a bifolio that Bartók used as a title-
page cover for the Piano Quintet autograph.[71] From the time when he put aside all of
his manuscripts, such sketches usually were placed at the end of the draft or short

71. BBA 2002a; see facsimiles 1–2 in Somfai/*MS vs. Urtext*, 28.

score. So is p. 15 after the short score of the *Dance Suite*,[72] containing sketches for the tinkling ten measures between nos. 31–32 of Movement III (originally missing in the draft). This is a first sketch immediately developed into a partial sketch of the harmonics in the strings. Curiously enough, there is another page (Facsimile 16) devoted to the same place; after using it, Bartók sent the page to Ditta in a letter of Aug. 14, 1923.[73] Here the stretto of the orchestral score is already elaborated in the 4-hand piano part but the countersubject in the harp and the string harmonics are only sketched; in addition Bartók made a plan of the number of staves needed for this page in the full score.

Bartók wrote partial sketches in later works mostly for a first elaboration of contrapuntal textures. Such interesting extra pages survived with the vocal-score draft of *Cantata profana*;[74] among the discarded pages of the score draft of String Quartet no. 5[75] and of *Music for Strings, Percussion, and Celesta*;[76] and on standard-size sketch pages, with the continuation of the finale sketches, in the material of Concerto for Orchestra.[77] It has to be mentioned that Bartók, who preferred sketching in ink, on such pages often switched to pencil, or rather wrote certain voices in ink first and later added the missing voices or measures in pencil. But even in cautious work like this, erasure was not at all frequent. Incidentally, in contrapuntal sections of a full draft the ink-and-pencil mixed notation also appears.[78]

In chapter 8 we will study further examples of partial sketches closely related to the preparation of the scoring.

"PLANS" AND "CALCULATIONS"?

Hundreds of little arithmetic calculations and groups of numbers in Bartók's handwriting occur at the back of folk-music notebooks, in the margin of a draft of an article, on music paper with or without music on it, on scrap papers. They deal with simple computations and clearly reveal their purpose. For instance,[79] Bartók computed how much a folksong collecting trip had cost; how many hours and days the collecting and transcription took; how many words he had written for a dictionary; how much he was supposed to spend during the 1927–1928 American tour; what was the percentage of certain types of melodies in a folksong collection. The tran-

72. PB 53PS1.
73. BBA BH213, with Ditta's note about the date of the letter in which Bartók sent it to her.
74. See pp. 26–27 in PB 67VoSS1.
75. See pp. 52, 59–60 in PB 71FSS1.
76. E.g., pp. 78–79 and 81 in PB 74FSS1.
77. E.g., pp. 1–2 and 8 in PB 80FSS2.
78. E.g., pp. 17–18 of the draft of Sonata for two Pianos and Percussion (PB 75FSS1), the fugato in Movement I.
79. A collection of such "calculations" is itemized in the catalogue Somfai/*Exhibition*, 11–12; see facsimile on 13.

scription of recorded folk music frequently involved calculation. Most typically, if it was a rigid *giusto*-rhythm dance song, Bartók computed the precise metronome (MM) number from the length of the performance (in seconds) and the length of the notation (in measures or shorter rhythmic units). In this way he arrived at such absurd MM numbers as a sixteenth-note = 356 in a folk dance in 17/16 meter,[80] or MM numbers that do not exist on a metronome, or abstract short rhythmic units and speeds that a metronome cannot measure. Incidentally the meter, as irregular as it may be in a Bartók transcription of Rumanian or Turkish or other folk music, was not the result of Bartók's "exact metrical plan for the transcription," as Roy Howat states in discussing a set of numbers in the Turkish field-book,[81] since the metrical arrangement (the barring) in folk music objectively followed the beat, the accent in the actual performance — and Bartók was not only careful but highly experienced in this respect. Thus Howat's conclusion in this case (the only irritating mistake of an otherwise so important study), that "the song's metrical organization is analyzed wholly in terms of the Lucas sequence numbers," is irrelevant and misleading.

Additions in Bartók's drafts and other manuscripts of the compositions are usually related to the timing at the end of a movement or the whole composition. Numbers are quite frequent in short scores prepared for the orchestration, indicating the number of staves needed in a brace, the number of measures in a line, etc. Sometimes Bartók planned the page and staff arrangement of the remaining part of the full score.[82] And at least in one case he made a "diagram," a drawing with different length of lines with numbers: it was his plan for the cutting and rearrangement of the tissue master of *Cantata profana* that was first used for the facsimile edition of the full score, then (after the cut-out vocal parts were added to the piano reduction) for the facsimile print of the vocal score.[83]

To summarize this survey of computations in the complete existing source material of Bartók's compositions as well as manuscripts of folk-music transcriptions, drafts of articles, and scattered scrap papers in the Hungarian and American estate: there are lots of numbers and little calculations in Bartók's hand, but not a single calculation of the proportions of a composition — with Fibonacci or other numbers — has been discovered. We observe, on the one hand, the composer's notorious lifelong habit of keeping and recycling every bit of paper and, on the other, the absence of preconceived calculations of proportions for any composition. This is solid evidence against the widespread assumption that the fascinating Golden Section proportions found in several of Bartók's works by Ernő Lendvai and others must necessarily have been deliberately planned by the composer. Even if, as we have

80. See the facsimile mentioned in fn. 79.
81. Roy Howat, "Review-article: Bartók, Lendvai, and the Principles of Proportional Analysis," in *Music Analysis* 2, no. 1 (March 1983); see facsimile on 86.
82. For instance, in the case of Suite no. 1 for orchestra, on a discarded page originally intended as the cover for the MS of Rhapsody op. 1 (BBA 484).
83. This plan is among the varia of BH in BBA.

observed, Bartók destroyed sketches in his early years, some "calculations" or "plans" should have survived, the more so considering that the chief examples analyzed by Lendvai were written at a later time when the composer carefully preserved his sketches. Even supposing that Bartók for some reason wanted to obliterate the traces of such plans, and only such plans, the drafts still should have revealed dozens of indirect clues: pre-planned barring, insertions or cuts of significant length, and the like. We will see in chapter 7 that no such secondary indication of calculated proportions exists. Even in the draft of the Sonata for two Pianos and Percussion we will find contrary evidence. At present, then, we must content ourselves with the perhaps less satisfying conclusion that in the process of composition Bartók followed his instinct for balance and proportion — an extraordinarily acute instinct, at that.

5 · FRAGMENTS, UNREALIZED PLANS

Before the logical next step in the study of the Bartók sources — the examination of drafts immediately after sketches — we survey the complex of the fragments. After all in Bartók's working process a fragment is typically an unfinished or unrealized work that survived as a sketch.

Fragments and unrealized compositional plans represent two extremes of a chain of evidence. A fragment, on the one hand, is physical proof of the beginning of compositional work, but often without the remotest indication of what the piece was to become. A plan, on the other hand — outlined, for instance, in Bartók's correspondence with the publisher — may clearly formulate the general intention of a planned work (the genre and often the approximate length too); all the same, this may not be enough to connect it with specific sketches or fragments. Further problems arise from a close study and a classification of the existing fragments and related forms. In addition to the fragment proper — a fragmentary form either of an unidentified piece by Bartók or a recorded but not completed work of his — there are borderline cases as well as problematic related forms. In sketch complexes for a longer work or group of works (e.g., sketches from summer 1926), the borderline cases may be called sketches: either preliminary ideas for realized works, if they seem sufficiently similar to the final forms; or, if they are considerably different, sketches for unrealized compositions — genuine fragments. Other problematic cases are represented by forms of works from Bartók's mature years that were not published in his lifetime and remain unfinished or not fully matured, that is, "fragmentary" forms. In this sense not only the Viola Concerto but also such works as the *Three Ukrainian Folksongs* and the *Goat Song* (1945), "Krutí Tono vretena" (1916), the *Nine Rumanian Folksongs* (ca. 1912) and the *Two Rumanian Folksongs* (ca. 1909), not to mention other sets and individual pieces published posthumously, can be considered fragments.[1] Complete movements written at the same time as published movements of a cyclic composition but omitted from the final set might also be considered fragments of a sort. A special study focusing on dropped pieces of this kind might help us toward a better understanding of Bartók's aesthetic criteria. Here is the list of omitted movements, starting from 1906:

Hungarian Folksongs (published with Kodály): two pieces;[2]
For Children: three pieces;[3]
Rumanian Folk Dances: an opening movement;[4]
Suite op. 14: an Andante as Movement II;[5]
Fifteen Hungarian Peasant Songs: six pieces;[6]
Dance Suite: the discarded Movement III;[7]
Forty-Four Duos: one piece;[8]
Mikrokosmos: four completed pieces and two fragments.[9]

A survey of the existing fragments in a narrower sense, however, has to be preceded by a survey of unrealized compositional plans. Two major groups of this kind have been studied for a long time: unrealized stage works, plans, and libretti in Bartók's documentary legacy,[10] and compositional plans (including further stage works) discussed in Bartók's correspondence with his two major publishers, Universal Edition and Boosey & Hawkes.[11] In this context we may ignore the majority of Bartók's preliminary considerations of stage works: except for the planned "Ballet Symphonique" none of them came to the point of Bartók's sketching musical ideas. Also leaving out his plans that obviously refer to soon-to-be-completed items, we must keep the following projects in mind when we attempt to link plans and existing fragments:

a. 1918: six or seven concert studies for piano, long and very difficult (Bartók's letters to UE, April 11 and 28, 1918); by July 11, 1918, three studies were finished;

1. Of works written after 1904 see, e.g., BB 37–38, 41, 43–44, 45a, 46, 97.
2. Pieces marked as nos. III and VI in PB 13VoPS1; no. III in the BBA 485 manuscript too (see p. 9 of the facsimile edition: Denijs Dille, ed., *Béla Bartók–Zoltán Kodály: Hungarian Folksongs for song with piano* [Budapest: Editio Musica, 1970]).
3. See pp. 24, 33, 35 in PB 22PI.ID1.
4. See in chapter 7, pp. 190–91.
5. See in chapter 7, pp. 140 and 194.
6. See in chapter 7, p. 191.
7. See in chapter 7, p. 190.
8. See p. 19 in PB 69VVS1.
9. See pp. 20, 28, 44, 48, 50 in PB 59PS1.
10. Somfai, "Nichtvertonte Libretti im Nachlass und andere Bühnenpläne Bartóks," in *DocB/2* (1965), 28–52.
11. György Kroó, "Unrealized Plans and Ideas for Projects by Bartók," in *SM* 1970: 11–27.

b. 1920: easy folksong àrrangements for piano (Hungarian,[12] Slovak, Rumanian, German), or piano 4-hand pieces (Bartók to UE, January 21, 1920);

c. 1931: orchestral work based on piano pieces from *Out Doors* and *Nine Little Piano Pieces,* ca. 15 minutes;

d. 1931: string symphony based upon String Quartet no. 4;

e. 1931: new choruses "with simple accompaniment" (three 1931 items from UE's protocol after the December 17, 1931, meeting with Bartók);

f. 1932: cantata cycle (*Cantata profana* and 2 or 3 further cantatas) (Bartók, October 12, 1932, to UE, and letters ca. October–November 1932 and March 17, 1933, to Sándor Albrecht);

g. 1936: orchestral work for normal double scoring, a series of short pieces (Bartók, July 24, 1936);[13]

h. 1939: long orchestral work: a "Ballet Symphonique" (Ralph Hawkes, March 6, 1939; Bartók, April 19, 1939: "Must be postponed for summer 1940 or 1941");

i. 1939: "Studies for orchestra" (12–15 minutes): Bulgarian Dances, "but also some other pieces from the *Mikrokosmos*" (Bartók to Hawkes, April 17, 1939; the scoring of the Bulgarian Dances mentioned already in Hawkes's letter, April 6, 1939);[14]

j. 1939: "very easy suite for string orchestra, for students . . . either based on folk-tunes or on original themes" (Bartók, April 17, 1939);

k. 1942: series of concertos in the style of the Brandenburg Concertos by Bach (Hawkes suggests, April 17, 1942; Bartók replies, August 3, 1942: "Just before my illness I began some composition work, and just the kind you suggested");[15]

l. 1944: choruses (Hans Heinsheimer suggests, February 28, 1944; Bartók replies, March 18, 1944: "I have a certain idea");

m. 1945: prelude for orchestra for *Genesis,* Nathaniel Shilkret's project[16] (requested in 1944, considered by Bartók in July 1945);[17]

12. One may speculate whether one or two pieces of the *Improvisations* on which Bartók worked were not meant as easy arrangements.

13. I discussed the probability that this plan had been turned into the music of Mov. II of the Violin Concerto, in Somfai/*Strategics*, 162.

14. Tibor Serly's scoring of *Mikrokosmos* pieces in 1942 seems to be in connection with this plan.

15. Although there is no hard evidence to link this 1942 idea to Movement II of the Concerto for Orchestra, I conclude that Bartók nurtured for some time the ideas that allowed him to compose the concerto in 1943 fairly quickly.

16. Stravinsky wrote his *Babel* in 1944 for the same project, as did Schoenberg the Prelude op. 44 in 1945.

17. See Bartók's letters to Heinsheimer (July 14 and 23, 1945) and to Shilkret (July 28, 1945).

EXAMPLE 28   The opening theme of a fragment for violoncello and strings.

n.   1945: String Quartet no. 7 (commissioned by Hawkes, £250 as the purchase of the copyright remitted to Bartók in February 1945);[18]

o.   1945: concerto for two pianos (requested from Bartók who rejected the idea, see letters to Peter Bartók, February 8 and 21, 1945);

p.   1945: *Rumanian Folk Dances*: "a (new) transcription for normal orchestra"[19] (refused commission from Eugene Ormandy in summer 1943 but agreed in principle two years later; see letter July 14, 1945).

And now we may survey the existing significant fragments. There are, quite naturally, fragmentary pieces from Bartók's early years (described in detail in Dille's thematic index of the juvenile compositions) as well as what appear to be "fragmentary" exercises from the time of Bartók's compositional studies under Koessler (see Dille again who as a matter of fact did not always make a clear distinction between composition and exercise, between deliberately fragmentary exercise and compositional fragment or sketch). These juvenile fragments are not included in the following summary that lists in approximate chronological order the significant unidentified sketches and fragments from Bartók's mature years.

(1) Slow piece for violoncello solo and strings,[20] ca. 50 measures on two opposite pages of an oblong bifolio (fol. 1ʳ and 2ᵛ blank), written ca. 1906–1907 (?), kept by Bartók in the file *Különféle* [Miscellany].[21] Short score in 1 to 4 staves. The music paper is rare among Bartók's manuscripts. The suggested dating is based on the handwriting, on stylistic considerations, and references in Bartók's unpublished letters written to Emma Gruber from his concert tour with Ferenc Vecsey in Spain and Portugal, March to May 1906, according to which he planned a concerto for violoncello. The musical concept seems to be very much similar to the beginning of that of the Violin Concerto op. posth. (1907–1908), Movement I (which is the "Ideal" portrait): a monologue of a solo string instrument, here 26 measures (in-

18. Hawkes's letter to Westminster Bank (Feb. 8, 1945) and to Bartók (May 23, 1945), according to which Hawkes hoped to present the premiere of the seventh Bartók quartet in October or November in Wigmore Hall.

19. Instead of the 1917 scoring for small orchestra, BB 76.

20. See BB 129c in the Appendix.

21. Facsimile of the first page in Somfai/*MS vs. Urtext*, 31.

EXAMPLE 29   Sketches of a Fuga, (a) and (c), based on the opening
theme of Movement II of the Violin Concerto op. posth., (b).

cipit: Ex. 28), gradually growing into a rich, free polyphonic texture without strict thematic entries.

(2) Fugue, ca. 17 measures, March 1908 (Ex. 29). A fugue theme (Ex. 29a) — the grotesque variant of the first theme of Movement II of the Violin Concerto op. posth. (Ex. 29b) — sketched together with *Bagatelle* no. 14, dated March 20, 1908.[22] Based on a pianistic version of the same theme (Ex. 29c), on fol. 9ᵛ–10ʳ of the *Black Pocket-book* Bartók sketched a by and large full fugue exposition.

(3) Piano piece, 17 measures, ca. 1908 spring, on fol. 8ᵛ of the *Black Pocket-book*, quasi in the style of the *Bagatelles* (see chapter 4, Facsimile 1; Ex. 5a).

(4) Piano piece, 8 measures, ca. 1908–1910, on fol. 11ᵛ of the *Black Pocket-book*, perhaps from about the time of *Seven Sketches*.[23]

(5) Difficult piano piece, 31 measures, ca. 1918, one full page (Facsimile 17; the back of the page is blank; PB Miscellaneous Box C-26/6). Since the paper and the ink are identical with those used in the draft of Three Studies nos. 2–3,[24] we may assume that this is one of the planned six or seven concert studies; see (a) of the listed plans. Even if Bartók gave up this fragment, he clearly used elements of it in the opening scene of *The Miraculous Mandarin,* his next composition.

22. See facsimile in *DocB/2*, 158.
23. This fragment and other sketches in the *Black Pocket-book* are transcribed and discussed in detail in Somfai / *Vázlatok III*.
24. PB 48PS1.

FACSIMILE 17   One-page fragment of a piano piece, ca. 1918 (PB Misc.C-26/6).

EXAMPLE 30   Fragment of a piece for piano.

(6) Difficult piano piece, 11 measures (Ex. 30), ca. 1917–1918 (?), written on the top of a page (PB 42FSS1, p. 53) in ink. The page is part of a bifolio that was used as a cover to the autograph complex of String Quartet no. 2. The earliest date could be 1917, the very latest 1920, because in the next staves Bartók sketched 13 measures of *Improvisations* no. 1 in pencil. I would suggest that this is another piece planned for the six or seven concert studies set and the year 1918 seems to be the probable date.

(7) Piano piece, 31 measures (reduced to 24), summer 1926, on a page which belongs to the sketches of Piano Concerto no. 1[25] (Facsimile 18). In staves 1–2 there are sketches for the finale of the piano concerto (the direct continuation of our Facs. 7), on the back of the page sketches for "The Night's Music" (see Ex. 9). The fragment, as it starts in st. 3–4, might be a planned solo piano piece as well as a first idea of the slow movement of the piano concerto.

25. PB 58PPS1.

FACSIMILE 18 Fragment of a piano piece (in staves 3–19) among the sketches for Piano Concerto no. 1 (PB 58PPS1, p. 36).

EXAMPLE 31   Fragment of a piece in the draft of String Quartet no. 3.

(8) Two Hungarian folksong arrangements for piano, the first complete (33 measures), the second a fragment (21 measures), ca. 1926 (?), kept in the *Különféle* file (BBA BH46/5; the back of the page blank; see the facsimile of the page in Somfai/*Exhibition*, 34). This type of small paper was used by Bartók in 1926–1933 but the arrangements do not fit into any known compositional project.

(9) Piano (?) piece, 30 measures, summer 1928, written upside down on a page of the draft of String Quartet no. 3 (PB 60FSS1, p. 17). At this point Bartók was working on the passage preceding the end of the Seconda parte. He interrupted the string quartet draft, crossed the page; the rewritten form starts on another bifolio. The two-part fragment (Ex. 31), written, as I think, during the intermission, is stylistically related to the "Four Dialogues" (*Nine Little Piano Pieces* nos. 1–4, 1926) as well as some *Mikrokosmos* pieces (written from 1932 on), but in 1928 Bartók is not known to have been working on a solo piano composition.

(10) Orchestration of "With Drums and Pipes" (*Out Doors* no. 1), 31 measures, ca. 1932, on the first two pages of a bifolio kept in the *Különféle* file (BBA BH46/17; the rest of the bifolio blank). This is a rare case of a fragment with clarified background: it is the only existing notation of an orchestral work based on piano music promised to UE in December 1931; see above under (c). The drumming bass of mm. 1–4 is scored for 2 timpani, and gran cassa; the right-hand theme in mm. 5–12 is given to the bassoon, and double bassoon, in mm. 13–20 to the trombone. From m. 22 onward the scoring is fragmentary.

(11) Slow movement presumably for orchestra in piano short-score form (see Facsimile 19), 12 measures, ca. 1943, on p. 85 of the Turkish field-book, which is the main source of the Concerto for Orchestra (PB 80FSS1). The fragment is sandwiched between sketches for the Concerto: for Movement II on the pages before, partial sketches for Movement I from p. 87 on (p. 86 was left blank). We

FACSIMILE 19   Fragment in the Turkish field-book (PB 80FSS1, p. 85), 1943, among the sketches and the draft of the Concerto for Orchestra.

might speculate whether this was meant as a first idea of a slow movement for the Concerto for Orchestra. The demonstratively Hungarian style of the opening measures would fit the general concept of the Concerto, and the music seems to be written for orchestra (for strings perhaps). Note that while the opening measures would fit a piano solo too, the following progressions of the crossing voices are more idiomatic for orchestra than for piano.

(12) An orchestral fragment, 103 measures (sketch plus a short score, without preparation of the scoring), ca. 1943 (?); in the American estate kept together with the Concerto for Orchestra manuscript (PB 80FSS3) and traditionally considered an unrealized plan for the Concerto. A close examination of the musical content and the notation — see the first page of the short score (Facsimile 20) with one-sharp key signature that changes after eight measures, or the rhythmic-motivic retransition into G at the end (on the back of the page) — proves that this is not the beginning but rather an episode of a piece. And it does not belong to the Concerto. The motives of the mentioned retransition refer to Bartók's chorus "Hussar" (from the Twenty-Seven Choruses), originally a cappella (1936), with school orchestra accompaniment too (1937), which he revised and slightly re-scored for B&H in the

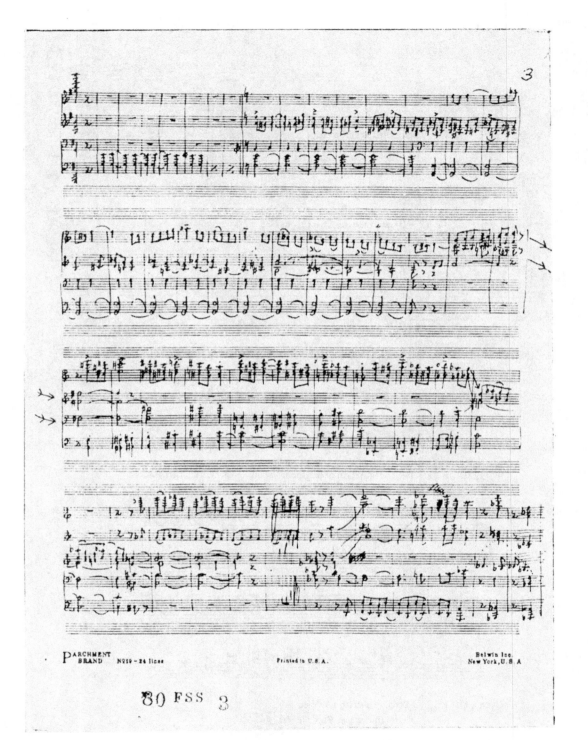

PARCHMENT BRAND   Nº19 – 24 lines   Printed in U.S.A.   Belwin Inc.
New York, U.S.A

80 FSS 3

FACSIMILE 20   Orchestral fragment ca. 1943 (?) (PB 80FSS3, p. 3), planned as an episode for the orchestrated version of the chorus "Hussar."

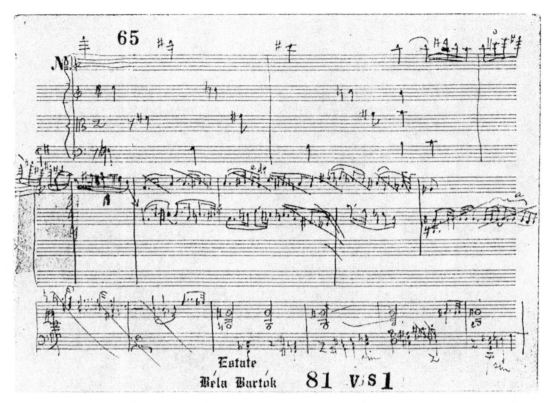

FACSIMILE 21   Fragment perhaps for String Quartet no. 7 (?) in the Arab field-book (PB 81FSS1, p. 65), 1944 or 1945.

EXAMPLE 32   The continuation of fragment Facsimile 21, written perhaps for a seventh string quartet.

EXAMPLE 33   Sketch of a rhythm related to the fragment (see Facsimile 21).

United States (1941). These 103 measures, an oversized episode probably between two stanzas, were not incorporated into the revised version. As a matter of fact, the date of the fragment cannot be decided: Bartók used similar music papers from 1941 to 1945.

(13) Slow piece (for string quartet?), including the crossed measures all together ca. 26 measures, 1944 or 1945; on pp. 65–66–67 of the Arab field-book (PB 81FSS1), which contains the Sonata for Solo Violin sketches. The last sketches of the Sonata are on p. 64; thus the earliest probable date of the fragment is April 1944, but Bartók could have used the pocket-book any time later. (The sketch of the first theme of Piano Concerto no. 3, see Ex. 11, is on p. 69; it gives the ante quem date for our fragment, but of course Bartók could have sketched it later in 1944 or, at the latest, in summer 1945.) The first page (Facsimile 21) shows that the beginning of the fragment looks like a string quartet texture. The continuation in two or three staves is more sketchy (transcription of pp. 66–67: Ex. 32). I presume that this sketch belongs to String Quartet no. 7 commissioned by Ralph Hawkes in February 1945; see this item (n) among the compositional plans. But it might be virtually anything: an orchestral work, a concerto, a prelude for the *Genesis*; see (m), etc. The music itself, as Bartók put it in a shorthand notation on paper, outlines a powerful beginning of a composition. Note that the double-dotted motive in the first measure of the bottom brace is similar to the beginning of fragment (11). The rhythm marked with letter *a* in the last measure of the second brace was also sketched by Bartók, without pitch, at the end of the Turkish field-book mostly used in 1943 (PB 81FSS1, p. 98; see Ex. 33).

To sum up, aside from discarded pieces and movements written for longer sets, except for the Viola Concerto, no sketch or fragment survived that could be reconstructed as a satisfactorily authentic complete work or significant individual movement.

6 · PAPER STUDIES AND THE MICRO-CHRONOLOGY OF THE COMPOSITION

For the study of the drafts another preliminary survey also seems essential: a look at the various music papers Bartók used and his typical procedures with bifolios.

The mass-produced music paper of Bartók's time had no significant individual watermarks. Therefore we are left with the examination of the printed ruling of the paper. Apart from a few exceptions — tiny pieces of paper that Bartók picked up on the spur of the moment to scribble on or leftover pages hand-ruled for folk-music transcription — Bartók used music paper with printed staves. The quality of the paper, the variety of the number or size or density of the staves (or even the ready-made braces for piano, for different types of chamber music, for orchestra) made them the most practical choice. Larger music publishers and shops produced music paper with various numbers of staves and their own trademark (the *Schutzmarke*) printed on them, usually with a number identifying the type, and another number referring to the number of staves (e.g., *18 linig*). Since music paper was expensive and Bartók was habitually economical, he used it carefully and recycled the leftover pages.

More than fifty types of music paper exist among Bartók's manuscripts (classified in Fig. 9, except for his juvenile compositions), but before the composer moved to the United States he usually chose the assortment delivered by Eberle, Vienna, marked *J. E. & C°* or *J. E.* Some of the paper types that Bartók used infrequently can help us to date manuscripts, just as watermark and multi-staff *rastrum* do for seventeenth- and eighteenth-century sources; in contrast, music papers without trademark, mostly cheaper and of bad quality, are hard to identify and classify.

The starting point in paper studies with Bartók is the bifolio (one folded sheet that equals four pages). Apart from the *Lichtpausen* or tissue masters (see paper types 8, 11, 12 in Fig. 9), which are single sheets written on one side only, all the

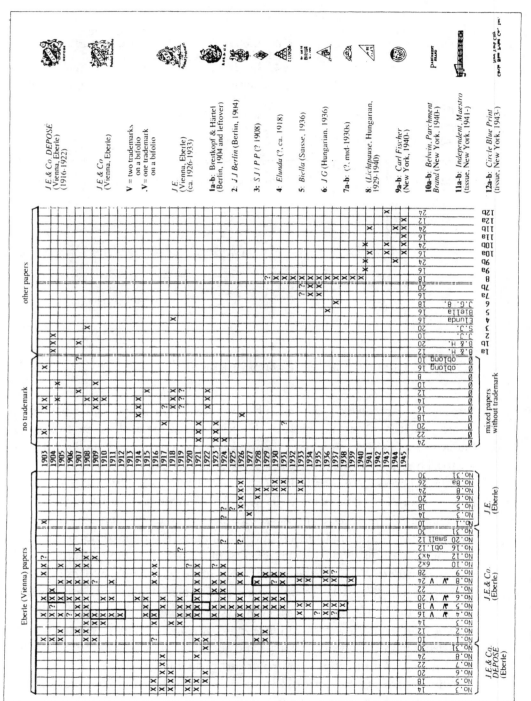

FIGURE 9   Chronological survey of music-paper types Bartók used in 1903–1945.

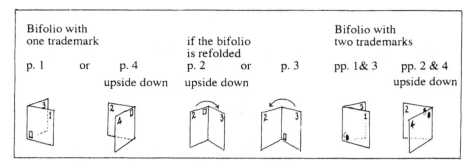

FIGURE 10   Position of the trademark in different foldings of a bifolio.

FIGURE 11   Bartók's habit of using bifolios.

listed music papers were produced in bifolios usually joined and sold in gatherings of ten or twelve. As to the place of the printed trademark, there are two kinds: bifolios with one trademark in the bottom left corner on p. 1; and bifolios with two identical trademarks, one on p. 1 and another on p. 3. Note, however, that among the Eberle papers were certain bifolios (*J. E. & C°* 16-, 18-, 20-, and 24-staff papers) of which both kinds were available to Bartók in the same year (see the framed fields in Fig. 9). Since the composer sometimes started to write on a bifolio turned around (i.e., with the trademark upside-down in the top right corner on p. 4 and none on p. 1) or for certain reasons refolded the bifolio (changing the original p. 1 with trademark to p. 3), a longer Bartók manuscript may contain bifolios in six different positions (Fig. 10). To be familiar with these foldings and positions is as essential in the Bartók paper studies as the recognition of the mold side and the felt side, or mold A and B watermarks in seventeenth- and eighteenth-century papers. Experience with the possible foldings and sequences allows us to reconstruct the original order of the bifolios in the major part of the autograph sources.

    Why is a reconstruction necessary in any case? Has the original form of Bartók's manuscripts — the bifolios, gatherings, fascicles — disintegrated? Unfortunately, for the major part a reconstruction is indeed unavoidable. The present physical condition of the two major collections of Bartók manuscripts reflects different philosophies. In the Budapest Bartók Archives the original form of the manuscripts was carefully preserved: bifolios, single sheets, stitched fascicles are kept in the same form (large scores that Bartók had bound were restored and rebound), with only the minimum stamping but no librarian's pagination with ink or print. Through careful restoration, most of the pages that were stuck together have been opened and the smaller corrections pasted over the original layer of writing have been loosened. Where the condition of the paper was poor, individual pages were laminated.

By contrast, in the one-time New York Béla Bartók Archives and Estate — now Peter Bartók's collection in Homosassa, Florida — scandalous decisions were made decades ago. Through a misconception of preservation, the bifolios were cut or rather torn apart into single sheets; the sheets were put into old-style plastic folders that prevented the airing of the paper and accelerated chemical reactions;[1] before that, a pagination was stamped or rather printed on the pages with a so-called numbering machine, not in their original sequence but in an arbitrary sequence set by the archivist in the New York Estate who "analyzed" the content (starting with the first page of the first movement according to the final form in the source, ending with sketches and discarded pages, i.e., pages belonging to an earlier layer of the source).[2] Moreover, the manuscripts were photographed in this arbitrary order of the pages,[3] and only such photocopies, with the misleading pagination, were given to scholars for decades; no restoration project was done, and thus most of the music under the stuck and pasted pages and slips of pages was unavailable for study.

Examining the originals in Peter Bartók's collection in 1989, I made an effort to piece the matching halves of the bifolios together — thousands of bifolios — on the evidence of the visible irregularities along the cutting or torn lines.[4] With 85 to 90 percent of the bifolios I was successful.

In spite of the difficulties, paper studies can become an important tool in the investigation of the micro-chronology of Bartók's compositional process, in part because of Bartók's sparing use of music paper and his methodical way of working. It was his habit to fill a page, a bifolio, before taking the next one; to add a hand-ruled staff at the bottom, if he could gain one more brace on the page; to use a single sheet, a leftover, if it was enough for the rest of the piece. When Bartók drafted a longer new work, he would take one bifolio after another and fill each one (see Fig. 11).

1. I was present in 1989 when Peter Bartók took out the precious pages from the plastic folders, which smelled of acid, and put them between acid-free blank paper sheets; one hopes that the chemical reaction could be stopped in time.

2. As a result of this arbitrary analysis of the content of a MS source, consecutive recto and verso pages often got quite different page numbers.

3. Actually they were photographed before the pagination with the numbering machine, with a provisional handmade pagination that often differs from the printed pagination; in this book references will be to the final pagination printed with the numbering machine.

4. Unfortunately the edges of the paper sheets forced into the plastic folders often became distorted, thus making a perfect matching impossible.

But when he copied the already drafted work, or made the instrumentation, he could already calculate the approximate amount of pages and thus assemble a neat gathering (*Heft*) from bifolios in advance. After all, one or two fascicles were easier to handle than a bunch of loose bifolios and pages. Even if there are exceptions, the reconstruction of the original paper composite of an autograph manuscript, as the first step of the analysis of the micro-chronology, is a good starting point for further examination.

What does the paper structure tell us about the micro-chronology? One example, and probably the most fascinating "workshop secret" revealed by the paper studies, is this: Bartók originally meant String Quartet no. 4 to be a four-movement rather than a symmetrical five-movement composition. The idea of the present Movement IV and thus the realization of his first multi-movement arch form (symmetrical form, palindrome form) was an afterthought, when Bartók had already finished the fair copy of the four-movement version. Evidence to support this fact comes from the physical form of the autograph fair copy (PB 63FSFC1). Inside the cover bifolio with the title page, in Bartók's own pagination from pp. 1 to 39, there is an original layer including Movements I, II, III, and V, with an insertion containing Movement IV. The original layer is on 18-staff paper, a gathering of 9 bifolios[5] (but the last sheet, 2 empty pages, was cut down). Note on Fig. 12 that Movement III ends on a recto and Movement V starts on the verso of the same page. The inserted Movement IV is on 20-staff paper and could physically be "inserted" only between pages 29 and 30. Bartók's subsequent pagination then clarified the order of the movements.

A close look at the sketch and draft complex of String Quartet no. 4 (PB 62FSS1) gives more detail about the micro-chronology of the composition (see the left column of Fig. 12). Independent of the arbitrary pagination of the New York archivist, if we put the torn-apart bifolios back together and analyze their contents, we can separate the different stages of the notation. After Bartók made the preliminary sketches for Movements I and III, he first elaborated Movements I and II on 2 bifolios each, then Movement V on another sort of paper; empty pages at the end of these continuity drafts contain versions of Movement III. Movement IV (originally planned in another key) appears on a separate bifolio plus a folio of a third type of paper.[6]

The case of String Quartet no. 4 has a lesson for Bartók research. Prominent American Bartók experts had seen the manuscript sources or had at least studied photocopies of the autograph. And yet, until my paper studies suggested that Movement IV was an insertion, not even the idea had occurred that in this instance the overanalyzed symmetrical structure could have been only an afterthought on the

5. The manuscript bifolios were torn apart in the New York Archive, but the connection of the sheets is sure.

6. See the more detailed discussion in Somfai, "Bartók and the Paper-Studies: The Case of String Quartet No. 4," in *Hungarian Music Quarterly* 1, no. 1 (1989): 6–13.

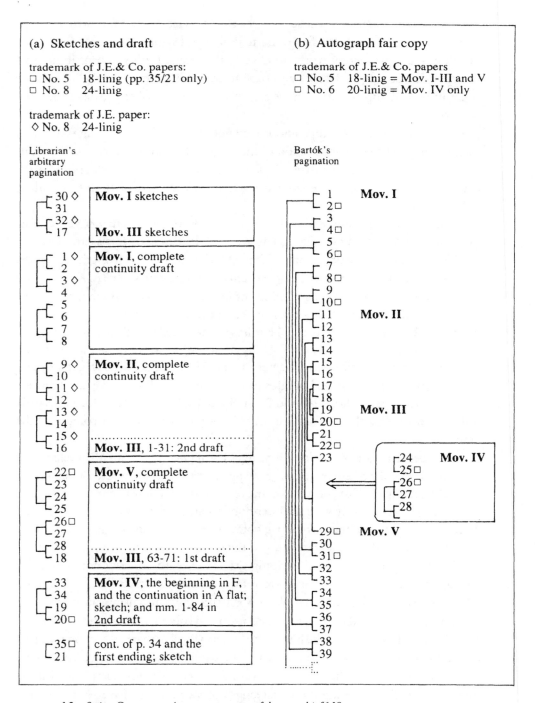

FIGURE 12   String Quartet no. 4: paper structure of the two chief MS sources.

composer's part. All this of course does not alter the fact that the authorized version of String Quartet no. 4 — the first of Bartók's five-part symmetrical large-form compositions — is a pioneering work. To observe the idea at birth still contributes to a better understanding of Bartók's approach to composing. It reveals the importance of intuition and improvisation in his art, even for the overall structure of the composition.

Other drafts of major compositions may not reveal such astonishing facts about their genesis. Yet the reconstruction of the original bifolio structure usually points toward interesting details of the sequence of the work, or interruptions in the composition, or revision of certain parts — some of which are obvious facts, others only hypotheses.

To begin with the example of the Divertimento, the three movements were drafted in the order I, III, and II (see Fig. 13), just as Bartók mentioned in his letter (August 15, 1939) to Ditta. The draft score of Piano Concerto no. 2 — a work the composer dated in the facsimile edition as being written *Budapest, 1930.X., 1931.IX.X.* — is not on successive bifolios but on gatherings of bifolios. We may assume that the first gathering contains the 1930 part of the composition (Mov. I, mm. 1–ca. 185), written on 20-staff *J. E. & C°* paper, 5 bifolios in one fascicle (with an additional page with corrections, 18-staff). The rest of the composition, as we think the 1931 part, includes the recapitulation of Movement I, and Movements II–III. Here a thicker gathering was formed: inside 4 bifolios (24- and 26-staff *J. E. & C°* papers) there is a series of successive bifolios (24- and 26-staff *J. E.* papers) inserted. Because Bartók still needed paper, a thin fascicle with 2 bifolios plus a single sheet completed the draft.

The paper structure of the draft of String Quartet no. 3 (PB 60FSS1) tells more. First, at the top of two empty pages (now pp. 4 and 5) Bartók wrote a score sketch for the beginning of a fast and a slower movement, the opening of the Seconda parte and Prima parte, probably with the intention of starting the composition with a fast piece. Then (on p. 1 of the current pagination) he began drafting the present form: he completed the Prima parte, continued the sketch of the Seconda parte (on p. 4, and, on the top of p. 5, circumscribing the sketch with the new notation), and arrived on p. 17 to the "disintegration" of the themes (which is the music around rehearsal nos. 44–45). Here Bartók stopped and only later, using another sort of paper, wrote the revised form of this page again and completed the *attacca* form (pp. 10–15). The significance of the interruption lies in the fact that this section is indeed the dramatically problematic point of the *attacca* form: it had to be a convincing return to the themes of the opening slower movement. The four-part overall structure — or rather, considering the actual length of the parts, its *A B a' b'* form — has aesthetic implications. Here as elsewhere in Bartók's works, if I may thus formulate, the contrasting points of the dramaturgy are the "ego" and the "community" in a most Bartókian sense. It is not the simple juxtaposition of the sensitive, lyrical

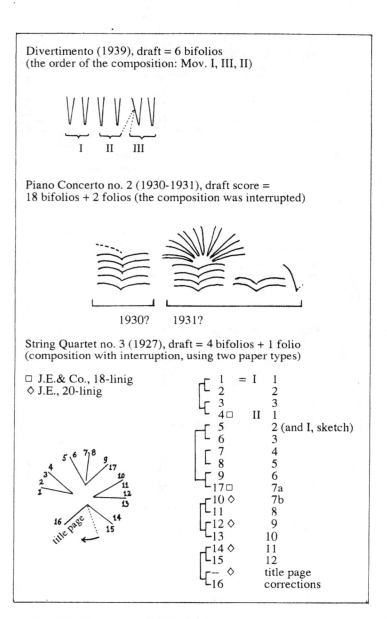

Divertimento (1939), draft = 6 bifolios
(the order of the composition: Mov. I, III, II)

I   II   III

Piano Concerto no. 2 (1930-1931), draft score =
18 bifolios + 2 folios (the composition was interrupted)

1930?   1931?

String Quartet no. 3 (1927), draft = 4 bifolios + 1 folio
(composition with interruption, using two paper types)

□ J.E.& Co., 18-linig
◇ J.E., 20-linig

1	= I	1
2		2
3		3
4□	II	1
5		2 (and I, sketch)
6		3
7		4
8		5
9		6
17□		7a
10 ◇		7b
11		8
12 ◇		9
13		10
14 ◇		11
15		12
— ◇		title page
16		corrections

FIGURE 13   Paper structure of three draft scores.

element (here: the Prima parte) to the rustic, dancelike one (Seconda parte) but a
more complex dramaturgy. After the exposition and development both parts open
up: there is a search for charismatic feeling. For Bartók the preparation of the return
to a strongly modified form of the lyrical movement was not without difficulties, as
the interruption of the draft proves. He may have been hesitating at this point in the

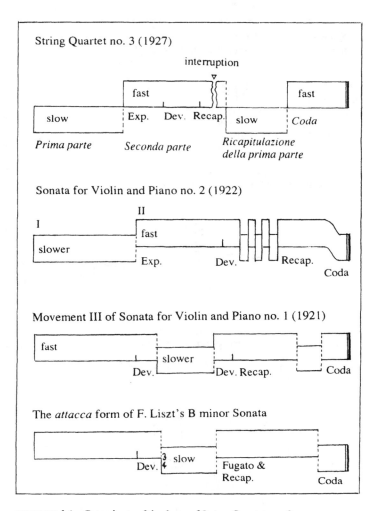

FIGURE 14   Precedents of the form of String Quartet no. 3.

composition as to how to end the *attacca* form: with a return of the slow material alone, or with a double return of both characters. Not that here Bartók worked with an unfamiliar structure. The form of String Quartet no. 3 (see Fig. 14) had its origins in the more complex *attacca* structure of Sonata for Violin and Piano no. 2 or, in a single movement, in the finale of Sonata for Violin and Piano no. 1 with a pattern that can be linked to Beethoven's sonata rondo with a long coda or, more specifically, to the *attacca* form of Liszt's B minor Sonata, one of the great experiences of the young pianist-composer Bartók.[7]

7. Read his memoir of his struggle to understand Liszt's Sonata (*Essays*, 453–454); see also Somfai/ *Liszt's Influence*, 212ff.

Music for Strings, Percussion, and Celesta was directly drafted as a full score. Working against the pressure of time for the premiere that Paul Sacher was to conduct, Bartók revised and sent this draft to UE in Vienna (with German instructions to the copyist).[8] Because of the multifunctional character of the score draft — including pages with considerable sketches, heavily corrected pages with half-page size or smaller corrections pasted up, fully rewritten pages that looked like a copy — a description of the paper structure (Fig. 15) is an essential precondition to any analysis of the compositional process. Along with the main body of the score (in Bartók's pagination pp. 1–71) that Bartók got back from UE, he kept the discarded pages too (pp. 72–83, in the arbitrary later pagination). During the composition he proceeded with the routine use of bifolios in a draft, that is, filling one bifolio after the other. At the beginning he used 18-staff Hungarian paper; from p. 17 of the original layer, 24-staff Eberle paper; from p. 47 on, 26-staff Eberle paper. The rewritten pages 5–6 and 17–24 are on similar 26-staff bifolios. In the present form (PB 74FSS1) the pasted up corrections and the folios that were stuck together (pp. 25–26 and 69–70) have not yet been opened up and restored; therefore we must guess at their contents. We can, however, study the two major areas of the revision. Bartók rewrote the last two pages of the opening fugue movement that was sketchy in the first notation and did not have a celesta part yet. And he strongly revised the last section of the exposition and the first part of the development section in Movement II (ca. mm. 110–263).

It is essential to note that the lack of homogeneous scoring in the final form of the four movements (genuine double-choir notation of the strings in Movs. II–III–IV only) shows even more clearly in the score draft. In the original layer of Movement I Bartók scored purely string music in 5-staff braces. The addition of percussion parts on pp. 3 and 4 appears on 26-staff paper, that is, as an afterthought from the time of the last revision of the finished score draft. He did, however, not bother to eliminate the contradiction originating in the double-choir seating of the strings, whereas in Movement I with negligible exceptions viola 1 & 2 and violoncello 1 & 2 play in unison. The seating concept developed simultaneously with the concept of the composition: an opening movement for normal string orchestra followed by spectacularly scored "stereophonic" movements.

For our paper study the compositional process of String Quartet no. 6 is a clear case (Fig. 16, left column) that contains interesting hints about Bartók's reshaping of the overall form. He wrote the four movements in their final order, according to the original plan with a fast finale preceded by a slow introduction (mm. 1–45 of the present Mov. IV), as Benjamin Suchoff described it,[9] but on the same last bifolio Bartók drafted the slow ending too. In spite of the arbitrary pagination in the

8. See also pp. 117–18 and 129 in chapter 7.
9. Benjamin Suchoff, "Structure and Concept in Bartók's Sixth Quartet," in *Tempo*, no. 83 (1967–1968): 2–11.

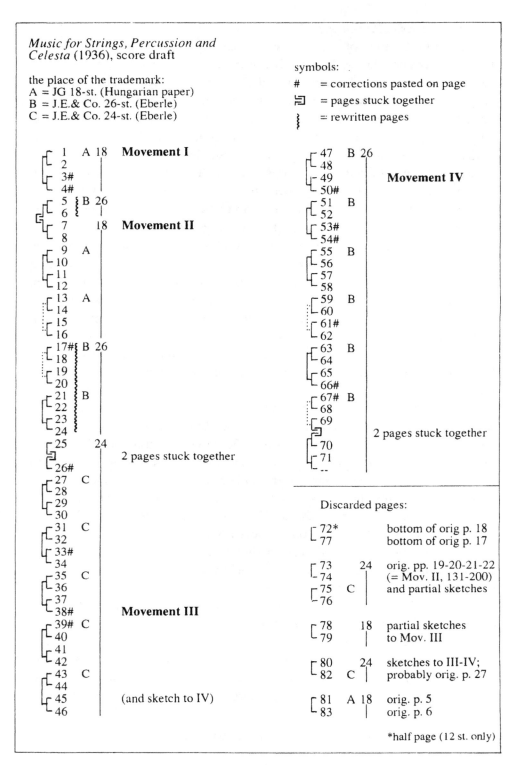

FIGURE 15   Paper structure of the draft score of *Music for Strings, Percussion, and Celesta*.

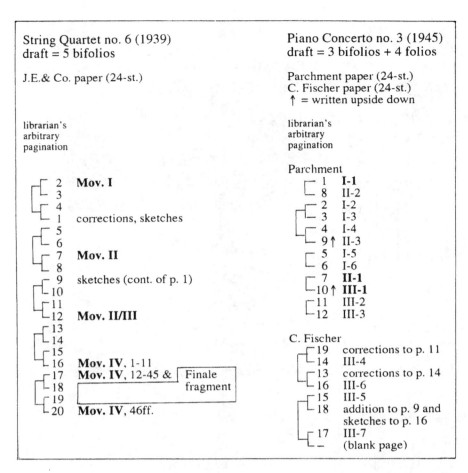

FIGURE 16   Paper structure of two draft scores.

present form of the manuscript (PB 79FSS1), Bartók clearly began drafting the first movement on p. 2 (= first page of the bifolio) with the leggero primary subject of the sonata-form opening movement (= I, mm. 24–); that is, originally there was neither a Mesto solo melody for the viola nor a pesante tutti announcing the leggero theme. Bartók was already working on the third page (= p. 4, ca. m. 186) when on the yet empty next page, the last page of the bifolio (= p. 1; see Facsimile 22) he started to note corrections and new ideas. In st. 1–4 *A.* is a correction, a rewritten section (I, mm. 39–46) belonging to page 1 [*1. lapra*]. In st. 6–9, in a four-staff brace, first Bartók wrote five Lento measures, designed as the beginning [*eleje*] (I, 19–23). Probably as a next step he added five more measures in score and, with an arrow, transferred the Lento measures after these ones. Next Bartók wrote another insertion in st. 10–14, 16–19, and the beginning of st. 21–24, a replacement for *B.* on the third page (= p. 4; I, mm. 186–208).

FACSIMILE 22 Corrections and sketches for the beginning of Movement I on "page 1" in the draft of String Quartet no. 6 (PB 79FSS1, p. 1), 1939.

A sketch of the chromatic ritornello theme, however, could not yet get on this page at this stage of the composition. Although Bartók sketched an embryonic form of the melody, together with other preliminary ideas of the planned new quartet, on the last page of the draft of the Divertimento (see our Ex. 17), originally the ritornello theme was not planned to play a role before Movement I. When did Bartók actually decide that Movements I–II–III–IV would be introduced by versions of the ritornello theme in 1-, 2-, 3-, and 4-part elaboration? Before we come up with a sound hypothesis, let us survey the versions of the ritornello theme on the correction page (= p. 1), with reference to the numbered staves on Facsimile 22. First (st. 5) Bartók wrote an 8-measure version of the theme for viola, ending on E, which he corrected (in st. 6–7) into a 12-measure form, ending on F. In a next step Bartók rewrote the whole theme (in st. 21–22, with corrections in st. 20 and 23), arriving at a by and large final form, ending on E♭ (with an alternative ending, in st. 22 between the question marks). Bartók also sketched the new beginning of the unison (I, mm. 14–16) and, as a consequence he once again revised the opening measures marked *eleje* in st. 6–9; thus the beginning of Movement I was ready. In addition to these sketches, in st. 23–24 Bartók began the sketch of a 2-part elaboration of the ritornello theme. He continued it on the top of the first page of another bifolio that is now p. 9. Although still in a rather rough form, this became the ritornello leading to Movement II ("Marcia"). Also on p. 9 Bartók sketched the inversion of the same 2-part elaboration, an idea that he discarded. The rest of p. 9 contains the draft of "Marcia," from m. 70 onward, a direct continuation of the draft on pp. 7–8.

When did Bartók sketch these things on p. 1 and p. 9? When did he decide the presence of the ritornelli? Based on the fact that he used the same ink and a very similar hand motion to write these ritornello-theme sketches on the two pages mentioned above, and furthermore that the rest of the music on the new bifolio (p. 9) is not the continuation of Movement I but of Movement II, it seems to follow that Bartók sketched the ritornelli to Movements I and II while he was working on "Marcia." At any rate the 3-part ritornello leading to Movement III ("Burletta") was already part of the original layer of the notation (pp. 12–13). As to the general character and the implicit narrative of the whole composition, it is indeed the recurrences of the ritornello that so dramatically show the colorful "pictures" or "scenes" (Movs. I, II, III) to be memories of the past in contrast to the overwhelming pessimism of the present, Bartók's view of life in autumn 1939.[10]

The paper structure of the draft of Piano Concerto no. 3 is another source of significant observations and conjectures on the course of the composition. The librarian's printed pagination of the autograph manuscript (see Fig. 16, right column) is very misleading. In three instances the original bifolio unit can satisfactorily

10. His mother, Paula Voit, was at death's door; the political scene in Europe and in Hungary was hopelessly bitter, so Bartók soon decided to leave his country.

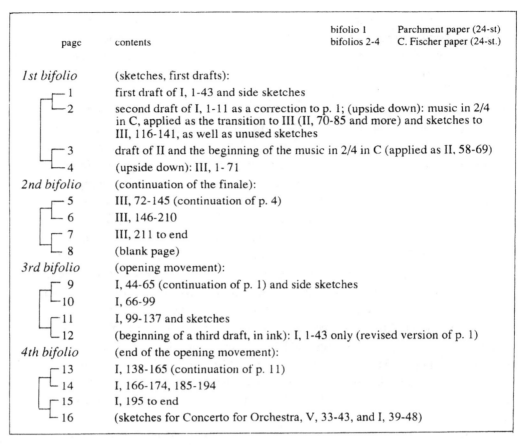

	page	contents	bifolio 1	Parchment paper (24-st)
			bifolios 2-4	C. Fischer paper (24-st.)

1st bifolio   (sketches, first drafts):

1   first draft of I, 1-43 and side sketches

2   second draft of I, 1-11 as a correction to p. 1; (upside down): music in 2/4 in C, applied as the transition to III (II, 70-85 and more) and sketches to III, 116-141, as well as unused sketches

3   draft of II and the beginning of the music in 2/4 in C (applied as II, 58-69)

4   (upside down): III, 1-71

2nd bifolio   (continuation of the finale):

5   III, 72-145 (continuation of p. 4)

6   III, 146-210

7   III, 211 to end

8   (blank page)

3rd bifolio   (opening movement):

9   I, 44-65 (continuation of p. 1) and side sketches

10   I, 66-99

11   I, 99-137 and sketches

12   (beginning of a third draft, in ink): I, 1-43 only (revised version of p. 1)

4th bifolio   (end of the opening movement):

13   I, 138-165 (continuation of p. 11)

14   I, 166-174, 185-194

15   I, 195 to end

16   (sketches for Concerto for Orchestra, V, 33-43, and I, 39-48)

FIGURE 17   Paper structure of the Viola Concerto draft.

be reconstructed; the rest probably was leftover pages that Bartók had on hand at Saranac Lake. In the first phase of the composition (up to ca. m. 480 in Mov. III) Bartók wrote on Parchment Brand papers produced by Belwin Inc., New York, whereas for the rest of the draft he used papers by C. Fischer, Inc., New York. Without going into a detailed musical analysis of the contents of the individual pages at this point, we can summarize the crucial facts as follows.

As a first step Bartók sketched-drafted the beginning of all three movements, practically at the same time, but very probably in this sequence. First, the Adagio material of Movement II on one sheet (= p. 7). Second, the beginning of Movement I, on another sheet (= p. 1). Third, upside-down on the back of the first sheet (= p. 10), the beginning of Movement III. Fourth, continuing the sketching of Movement II on p. 7, he filled the back of the other sheet (= p. 8) with the Più mosso middle part of Movement II. Fifth, by taking an empty bifolio, on the first page (= p. 9) Bartók finished the rough continuity sketch of Movement II. Thus he completed Movement II first, albeit in a rather sketchy form.

Next followed the elaboration of Movement I. When p. 1 had been filled, Bartók turned the bifolio upside down and started to write from the other "first page" (= pp. 2–3–4) and ended the movement on another sheet (= pp. 5–6).

Movement III he wrote in an unusually nervous way: several correcting pages refer back to already filled draft pages. Bartók had considerable struggle with this form that was neither a sonata form nor a simple rondo. Page 18 seems to prove that he began revising the already completed movements and making preparations for the scoring before he finished Movement III. On the top of this page he sketched the short score of the wind "chorale" of the Adagio return in Movement II (note that on p. 9 Bartók sketched the piano part only); on the rest of the page he wrote down sketches for Movement III mm. 644–ca. 695 (see p. 16), probably after August 30, 1945, when he returned from Saranac Lake to New York City.

As a last example of the information value of the description of the paper structure, here is the case of the Viola Concerto as I see it. All together four bifolios contain the complete existing draft; two pages are blank. (Serly's attempts at reconstructing the pagination are misleading; my suggested pagination in Fig. 17 is not a straight reconstruction of the sequence of the composition but simply an identification of the pages in the facsimile edition.)[11] The 1st bifolio, certainly the very first of the four, is Parchment paper, the sort Bartók had used in the first phase of Piano Concerto no. 3, while the three other bifolios are C. Fischer papers, like those for Movement III of the Piano Concerto.

We may characterize the 1st bifolio as the preparation for the composition, probably from the stage when Bartók still planned a 4-movement work described in his letter to William Primrose on August 5, 1945:

> However embryonic the state of the work still is, the general plan and ideas are already fixed. So I can tell you that it will be in 4 movements: a serious Allegro, a Scherzo, a (rather short) slow movement, and a finale beginning Allegretto and developing the tempo to an Allegro molto. Each movement, or at least 3 of them will [be] preceded by a (short) recurring introduction (mostly solo of the viola), a kind of a ritornello.[12]

One must presume that some of these ideas were elaborated only in Bartók's mind. After all, the 1st bifolio does not seem to contain enough material for a fourth movement (the Scherzo),[13] and there are no grounds for believing that either Bartók discarded or Serly lost a whole bifolio or sheet with further sketches. The probable micro-chronology of the 1st bifolio is the following: (1) the first draft of the beginning of Movement I on the first page; (2) the second notation of the first

---

11. Béla Bartók, *Viola Concerto*. Facsimile Edition of the Autograph Draft with a Commentary by László Somfai and Fair Copy of the Draft with Notes Prepared by Nelson Dellamaggiore (Homosassa, Fla.: Bartók Records, 1995).

12. Fragmentary letter to Primrose, probably not mailed (BBA 186/21).

13. Unless the 2/4 music in C (used as the transition to Mov. III) and related sketches on p. 2 were meant as a scherzo second movement: see S. Kovács, "Reexamining the Bartók/Serly Viola Concerto," *SM* 1981: 302–304; and Somfai/*Viola Concerto*.

measures of the opening theme on the second page; (3) the continuity sketch of the "(rather short) slow movement" on the third page. We cannot even guess whether the composer wrote the rest — the upside-down notation on the second page and the beginning of the finale on the fourth page — immediately following the notation of (1)(2)(3), or later. Therefore the chronology of the three other bifolios is also hypothetical: Bartók either finished drafting the finale first (2nd bifolio) or worked first on Movement I (3rd and 4th bifolios) and only later on the finale. Or he worked in parallel on the two movements as he presumably did on Piano Concerto no. 3 too. He even started to write a copy of the beginning in ink (p. 12), which he did not continue.

For the sake of clarity, without going into a detailed analysis of Tibor Serly's reconstruction, scoring, and editing, note that the Viola Concerto draft was left in a preliminary form compared to the draft of Piano Concerto no. 3 or any other draft that Bartók himself orchestrated. In this case he did not have time to revise the music as he habitually did while preparing the draft for scoring.

7 · THE KEY MANUSCRIPT: THE DRAFT

GENERAL CHARACTERISTICS

In Bartók's working process the draft is the first complete form of a work. It does not have a uniform appearance: there are mixed forms (bi-functional manuscripts) in both directions of the source chain. In certain cases the two-step process of writing down sketches first and a draft next was replaced by a gradual process of turning memos and continuity sketches into a full continuity draft in the same sketch-book (e.g., Concerto for Orchestra, Sonata for Solo Violin; see chapter 4, pp. 72–78). In a next step Bartók occasionally revised the original layer of the notation of his draft and applied the performing instructions so that he could send it, as the engraver's copy, to his publisher[1] or use the draft for making preparations for the orchestration (see chapter 8). However, under normal conditions there is a typical form of a Bartók draft, written in ink, in full notation rather than shorthand (although abbreviations, words, and notes are common); but usually it is only the rough form of the work, without the elaboration of the performing instructions; and the draft of the stage works, symphonic music, concertos, and major choral works is, with a few exceptions, only a short score — a *particella* or (in the case of the choral works) a vocal-score-like short score.

Before about 1918 Bartók probably destroyed not only sketches (see chapter 4, p. 35) but many of his autograph drafts or short scores written up to 1907, and occasionally later ones too. In addition, a few drafts that served as engraver's copy, or that were given away as gifts, seem also to be lost. The list of works and primary sources in the Appendix gives detailed information about the existing and missing drafts. From Bartók's juvenile output genuine drafts are rare.[2] The losses of the next

---

1. See, for example, the facsimile edition of the autograph manuscript of *Two Rumanian Dances* for piano (EMB, 1974).

2. In the Appendix see BB 1, 7, 18.

period (up to 1907) are also considerable. Our impression is that in these years the production of the orchestration or, if not a symphonic work, the existence of a fair copy usually led to the obliteration of the short score or the draft. We cannot even guess how many such pages are missing, maybe several hundred.

Aside from juvenile compositions and works written during Bartók's studies with Koessler, as well as lost works,[3] and occasional missing pages from longer manuscripts,[4] here is a list of missing drafts from 1902 onward. The existence of the items marked with an asterisk is only an assumption based on my analysis of the writing of the existing autograph sources.

1902	Four Songs (Pósa) for voice and piano
1903	*Four Piano Pieces*: nos. 3–4
1903	*Sonata for Violin and Piano: I–II[5]
1903	*Evening*, for voice and piano
1903	*Kossuth*, symphonic poem: short score (and the draft of "Marche funèbre" for piano solo)
1903–1904	Piano Quintet
1904	*Székely Folksong* for voice and piano
1904	*Scherzo for Orchestra and Piano, op. 2: draft short score
1904	Rhapsody, op. 1, for piano solo
1905	Suite no. 1 for orchestra: short score
1905–1907	Suite no. 2 for orchestra: short score[6]
1907	*Three Hungarian Folktunes from Csík*, for piano
1907–1917	*Eight Hungarian Folksongs* for voice and piano: nos. 2–3
1907–1908	*Violin Concerto, op. posth. (no. 1): the violin-and-piano-form draft of Mov. I[7]
1908	*Ten Easy Piano Pieces:* no. 3
1909–1910	*Seven Sketches:* nos. 1–2
1909–1911	*Three Burlesques* for piano: nos. 2–3
1910	*Two Pictures* for orchestra: short score[8]
1911	*Duke Bluebeard's Castle*, opera: the first draft in vocal-score (?) form[9]
1913	Piano pieces for the Piano Method (Bartók–Reschofsky)
1916–	Three Rondos for piano: no. 1[10]
1932	*Székely Folksongs* for male choir

3. BB 7, 9, 32, 46/2.

4. E.g., pp. 1–6 of *The Wooden Prince* piano short-score-form draft; but see the Appendix.

5. There exists a draft for Movement III though.

6. Between the continuity sketches discussed in chapter 4, p. 35 (preserved fragmentarily) and the autogr. full score there had to be a full draft.

7. The case of Mov. II clearly shows that between the continuity sketches known from the *Black Pocketbook* (fragments only) and the orchestration, Bartók needed a violin-and-piano-form full draft.

8. The mixed-form autogr. MS (PB 27TPS1) is neither a full draft (from [the second] p. 4 up to the end, p. 17, it is not the actual draft but rather a piano reduction made after the full score was finished) nor a complete printer's copy of the piano reduction (because pp. 1–4, the major part of Mov. I, were not engraved from this MS, pp. 1–4 of which seem to belong to the draft proper of the work).

9. Most probably the Budapest MS, in many ways an unusually neat script, was preceded by a rough continuity draft that Bartók discarded.

10. The autograph of the three independent Slovak folksong arrangements written ca. 1916 (and

The extent of the existing drafts, especially when Bartók's dense notation is taken into account, is very impressive. The following survey, in five chronological chapters, brings approximate numbers of the manuscript pages, which I sort into three columns:

(a) *drafts* of piano works, chamber music, works for voice(s) and piano, choruses — genres that Bartók used to draft in the final layout;

(b) *short-score*-form or vocal-score-form drafts of works that he orchestrated in a next step;

(c) *full scores*, a mixed group including (1) genuine draft scores (Piano Concerto no. 2; *Music for Strings, Percussion, and Celesta;* all together 146 pp.) and two other types discussed in the next chapter, namely (2) regular autograph full scores, orchestrated from short-score-form drafts, and (3) full scores directly orchestrated in a quasi fair-copy handwriting on tissue masters (in Bartók's *Lichtpause* period; all together some 190 pp.).

	(a) draft	(b) short score	(c) full score	(a + b + c) total pages
1890–1901	80	—	20	100
1902–1907	87	52	366	505
1908–1918	339	148	422	909
1919–1931	345	139	605	1,089
1932–1945	385	170	445	1,000
total pages	1,236	509	1,858	3,603

Some 1,891 of these 3,603 pages — the drafts, the short scores, and the two draft full scores from column (c) — are primary documents of the creative process, the genesis of Bartók's works.

Draft proper. Bartók's choice of immediately writing the draft as a full score, or drafting a short score first, reflected certain working habits that were quite typical among composers around the turn of the century and were probably taught in Koessler's class.[11] While the sketches usually occur in condensed form (e.g., 1-staff and 2-staff sketches of String Quartet no. 1 and Sonatas for Violin and Piano nos. 1–2 in the *Black Pocket-book*), the draft of a work in the following genres was usually in the final layout:

---

copied about that time by Márta; see the original layer of the mixed-form MS PB 45PFC2), rearranged in the present form probably around 1927 or later, is lost.

11. In the manuscript complexes of *Dolgozatok* [Exercises, see BB 19] submitted to and corrected by Koessler is ample evidence that from a first rough elaboration in pencil, clearly a document for himself alone, Bartók prepared a copy in ink and brought it to Professor Koessler's class. But Bartók said nothing about destroying immature forms of a work.

piano solo in 2 staves (Facsimiles 30, 32, 40; occasionally in 3 or 4 staves too);

violin and piano in 1 + 2 staves;

voice and piano in 1 + 2 staves;

chorus in full score (one staff for each voice, as in Facsimile 34), except the condensed 2-st. draft of the *Four Old Hungarian Folksongs*;

string quartet in 4 staves (see Facsimiles 33, 35–36, 41);

trio or quartet special ensembles: *Contrasts* in 1 + 1 + 2 staves (Facsimile 39), Sonata for two Pianos and Percussion in 2 + 2 + 2 staves, with additional single lines (Facsimiles 37–38);

chamber orchestra: Divertimento in 5 staves (occasionally 4 or 6).

Short score or vocal-score-form short score. Quite logically there are no extra short scores of arrangements for (or with the accompaniment of) orchestra (Rhapsody op. 1 for piano and orchestra; *Two Portraits,* Movement II; *Rumanian Dance* 1911; *Rumanian Folk Dances* 1917; *Three Village Scenes;* Violin Rhapsodies nos. 1–2; *Dances from Transylvania; Hungarian Sketches; Hungarian Peasant Songs;* five plus two choruses from Twenty-Seven Choruses; Concerto for two Pianos and Orchestra). Of the original compositions for/with orchestra, aside from continuity-sketch-like fragmentary drafts (Suite no. 2, Violin Concerto op. posth.), two problematic cases discussed above (*Two Pictures:* piano reduction rather than short score; *Bluebeard's Castle:* vocal-score-like second notation rather than actual draft), and the works written in Koessler's class (dances, scherzo, symphony), this group contains ten works that we can put into five categories:

traditional short score in 2–3 (sometimes more) staves: *The Wooden Prince* (Facsimile 23), *Dance Suite,* Concerto for Orchestra;

short score of a symphonic work in a 2-piano or 4-hand layout: *Four Orchestral Pieces* (2-piano layout, but note that while Movements III and IV seem to belong to the draft proper, Movements I and II might be a second notation;[12] Mov. IV: Facsimile 24); *The Miraculous Mandarin* (a 2-piano-like beginning, followed by sketchier pages with 2–3–4-staff draft, finally turned into a more or less piano 4-hand draft in 4 staves);[13]

concertos with solo string instrument: Violin Concerto (no. 2) and Viola

12. The study of the paper structure of the draft (PB 31TPPS1) indicates that on the back of the last page of the draft of Mov. IV Bartók started writing Mov. I, as I believe, in a second draft using the (later destroyed?) rough draft; and that the present form of the draft (also a second draft?) of Mov. II ends on a recto page with blank verso, the only such empty page in the MS. The graphic style of Movs. I & II is not very different from Movs. III & IV, but I believe that the first two represent a second draft while "Intermezzo" and "Marcia funebre" are genuine first drafts. For details see Somfai, "Béla Bartók's Draft of *Four Pieces for Orchestra,*" in *Sundry Sorts of Music Books: Essays on the British Library Collections, Presented to O. W. Neighbour on His 70th Birthday,* ed. Chris Banks, Arthur Searle, and Malcolm Turner (London: The British Library, 1993), 309–318.

13. From (stamped) p. 39 of the autogr. MS (PB 49PS1) already in a 4-hand layout.

Concerto, in 1 + 2 (occasionally 1 + 3 or more) staves (see Facsimiles 25–
   26);
piano concertos in a 2-piano-form draft: Piano Concerto no. 1, Piano
   Concerto no. 3, in 2 + 2 (occasionally 2 + 3) staves (Facsimiles 11, 27),
   here and there with single lines for percussion;
vocal-score-like draft: *Cantata profana*, in max. 8 + 2 (3) staves, or fewer,
   depending on the texture (double-choir setting, just the choir, with or
   without the soloists, etc.).

Full score draft. Aside from the orchestral song *Tiefblaue Veilchen*,[14] there are two
major compositions that, with the help of a certain amount of sketches, seem to be
drafted immediately in full score: Piano Concerto no. 2, 1930–1931, and *Music for
Strings, Percussion, and Celesta*, 1936 (Facsimile 29). Why did Bartók draft these two
scores in an unorthodox way? In composing the piano concerto he seemingly was
not in a hurry. The date *Budapest, 1930.X., 1931.IX.X.* reveals that Bartók postponed
part of the composition to the next year, since he could not finish the whole work in
October 1930.[15] (We know that from the mid-1920s onward he rarely did major
compositional work while he was teaching and concertizing.) Therefore Bartók's
decision might have been connected with the unusual concept: in the opening
movement of the new concerto, as he certainly decided in advance,[16] he used only
winds, percussion, and piano in a dominantly linear/contrapuntal style, a texture
clearer in full-score-form draft than in short score.

   The case of the draft score of *Music for Strings, Percussion, and Celesta*, one would
guess, did indeed involve the pressure of a deadline. On June 23, 1936, Paul Sacher
asked Bartók to write a new work for the January 21, 1937, jubilee concert of the
Basel Chamber Orchestra. We know that Bartók finished drafting the score in early
September (*Budapest, 1936.szept.7*), so that the copy of the score and parts could be
produced by UE for Sacher in time.[17] But the case is not that simple. When Sacher's
letter reached Bartók, he must already have written a considerable part of the draft of
the new work. He not only accepted the commission immediately (June 27, 1936)
but went into specifics. He offered a *Werk für Saiten- und Schlaginstrumente*, in

   14. There is a draft full score written in pencil, but a sketchy continuity draft, now missing, must have
preceded it.
   15. As I analyze the paper structure of the MS (PB 68FSS1), the 1930 portion of the composition
probably ended around m. 185 of Mov. I, which is the recapitulation of the first theme (see chapter 6,
p. 103).
   16. Bartók's 1939 notes on Piano Concerto no. 2 (in *Essays*, 419ff.) reveal that he "wanted to produce
a piece which would contrast with the first," and that here the role of the orchestra rather than the piano
was an important factor. Suggestions of a prominent role for wood and brass sections, or of alternation
between strings and wood-plus-brass, was already present in the concept of Piano Concerto no. 1. Based
on his experience about the performance of the first concerto, he surely made decisions in advance to
produce a texture "which would be less bristling with difficulties for the orchestra and whose thematic
material would be more pleasing" (ibid., 419).
   17. Bartók's letter to UE, Sept. 1, 1936.

addition to the strings with piano, celesta, harp, xylophone, and percussion. The paper structure of the manuscript (chapter 6, p. 106) shows us that Movement I was originally drafted in 5 staves for strings alone, and the double string orchestra plus additional instruments were a second thought only, from Movement II on. In other words, when Bartók received Sacher's letter, he was already thinking about a revision of the concept. If it was not lack of time that led him to draft in full-score form, then the cause, although irregular, seems obvious. He continued the usual full-score notation of a string (chamber orchestra) texture from Movement II on, for a larger body of instruments, in a similar layout. In mid-September, at this stage already really under the pressure of time, Bartók "edited" this rough, heavily corrected manuscript, inserting some ten newly written pages and lots of pasted additions (half pages, etc.), so that the Vienna copyist, carefully following Bartók's special instructions, was able to produce a decent full score.[18]

Place and date of composition. Incidentally, the place and date of composition, as given by Bartók and printed at the end of a work, is a confusing matter. It gives more or less precise data about the "composition," whatever that means. But what exactly does it mean? Did Bartók refer to the actual period (or closing date) of writing the draft? Or the end of the period resulting in the production of the full score, or a fair copy, or in later years the *Lichtpause* fair copy? Unfortunately Bartók was neither uniform nor consistent nor even always reliable in dating his scores. Several major scores[19] and many of his piano works, folksong arrangements, and so forth, were not dated at all.[20] The form of the date, when given, can vary: some scores give a from-and-to date, others just the closing date; the year only, or year and month(s), or year, month, and day; with or without the place. The time and place of recording the date may also vary: there are dates immediately written down in a sketch or in a draft (though rarely), in the final copy or the full score (often), or introduced subsequently in the proofs of the first edition (often). As to the crucial question of whether the date concerns the stage of drafting or the moment of finishing a work, a few samples are revealing:

> Violin Concerto op. posth. (no. 1): *1907.dec.24. (reggel 5 órakor)* [at 5 A.M.] (at the end of Mov. II, violin-and-piano-form manuscript) = end of drafting; *Jászberény 1907.jul.1–Budapest 1908.febr.5* (end of autogr. full score) = total period of composition, including the instrumentation;

18. Bartók's letter to UE, with *Anweisungen* for the engraver, dated Sept. 14, 1936.

19. Including Scherzo op. 2 (1904) and the concerto version of Rhapsody op. 1 (1905).

20. Or the dating is indirect: Bartók gave the year of the composition in one of his worklists made, corrected, or authorized by himself, such as the *Table chronologique* 1921 (in *La Revue Musicale*, 2e année, no. 5, 1 March 1921: 218; Bartók's personal copy with his corrections in BBA); a worklist in the UE Bartók leaflet (n.d.); the *Lijst der Werken* 1938 in Dille/1939 (a facsimile of the worklist with Bartók's 1938 corrections in Dille/1990, p. 289).

The Wooden Prince: Rákoskeresztur, 1914–1916 (end of short score) = period
   of drafting; *Rákoskeresztur, 1914.IV.–1917.I.* (end of full score) = total
   period of composition, including the instrumentation;

the dates probably span the whole period of drafting and writing the full
   score: *Duke Bluebeard's Castle* (on the first and last page of the autogr. full
   score): *(1911.febr.), 1911.szept.20.;*[21] Violin Concerto (no. 2, *Lichtpausen* of
   the vl.-piano reduction and the full score): *Budapest, 1937.aug.–
   1938.dec.31.;*[22]

Four Orchestral Pieces: the date specifies the year of the short-score-form draft
   (although the date is on the copy of the full score): *1912* (N.B., Bartók
   orchestrated it only in 1921);

Piano Concerto no. 1: the date undoubtedly specifies the end of the drafting
   process (last page of the 2-piano-form short score): *1926.nov.12.* (but
   Budapest, 1926.VIII.,XI. in the engraver's copies of the full score and the
   2-piano reduction);[23]

the date specifies the end of the orchestration: Suite no. 2 (on the last page of
   the autogr. full score and in Bartók's own edition): *Bécs* [Vienna],
   1905.nov.–Rákospalota, 1907.szept.1.[24] (in the UE 2nd edition, revised by
   Bartók, specifying the composition of the individual movements with the
   year only: *I.II.III: Bécs, 1905; IV: Rákospalota, 1907*); *Dance Suite* (on the
   last page of the autogr. full score): *Radvány, 1923.aug.19.* (on August 3
   Márta was already working on the copy of the score);[25]

the date very probably specifies the time of writing or finishing the draft full
   score in the chamber music works (String Quartets nos. 1–6; 2-piano
   Sonata; *Contrasts;* Divertimento) and the two unorthodox draft full scores
   (Piano Concerto no. 2; *Music*), in these cases the fair copy or the *Lichtpause*
   copy was finished at a later time;

but at least in one case the date seems to specify the production of the
   Lichtpause fair copy: Sonata for Solo Violin (on the last page of the tissue
   master): *1944.márc.14.,*[26] certainly an irregular case, because the continuity
   sketches were directly written into the final form on *Lichtpause;*

21. The vocal-score-form autogr. MS was ready by July 8, before Bartók went to Paris, and was left
with Márta who made the copy of it (see letter July 22 in Bartók/*Családi levelek*).

22. Bartók probably started to work on the concerto, at least considering concepts and perhaps
making preliminary memo sketches, as early as August 1936 (see fn. 3 in Somfai/*Strategics*). The date
August 1937 seems to refer to the beginning of the drafting process.

23. Since Bartók almost never dated the draft short score (which he did not let out of his hands, so
that a date here was a note for himself alone), this must fix the day when he finished working on the draft.
The exact time of the orchestration has not yet been settled.

24. See Bartók's letter of July 30 about working on the scoring in Transylvania in inns, in a boot-
maker's workroom, and in the open air (*BBLevelei*, 119).

25. See Bartók/*Családi levelek*, 343.

26. See B. Bartók Jr./*Apám*, 455: Bartók sent the tissues in two letters (March 9 and 16) from Ashe-

in addition, there are cases open to further research (such as *Cantata profana, Budapest, 1930.szept.8.:* finishing of the vocal-score-form draft or the first full score?);[27] dates that may indicate a shorter period than the actual composition including preliminary memos (Concerto for Orchestra, at the end of the autogr. full score: *1943.okt.8.;* in the B&H full score, after the first ending: *1943.aug.15–okt.8;* this was perhaps the crucial period of writing continuity sketches and maybe even part of the full score, but considerable sketches — at least thematic memos — could have existed from the year before);[28]

furthermore, confusing datings occur, as with the *Two Rumanian Dances* for piano: in the authenticated worklists 1910[29] and 1909–1910[30] appear; in the Rózsavölgyi 1st edition at the end of the second dance "1910.III." was printed, but in the autogr. draft, which was the printer's copy, the date *1910.márc.* is still at the end of the first dance[31] (based on a close look at the sources I believe that the first dance was written in 1909 — on March 12, 15, and 19, 1910, Bartók was already playing it in Paris as well as in Budapest — and the second in 1910);

and finally, some dates, written in Hungarian as usual, are misleading, since *okt.31-re* or *okt.31.-ére* means "for October 31," which was the birthday of Bartók's second wife, Ditta; pieces positively not written on this day are *Nine Little Piano Pieces* nos. 1 and 9; "Lánycsúfoló" from the Twenty-Seven Choruses[32] (N.B. the Piano Sonata 1926, originally marked *Dittának, Budapesten, 1926.jun.* [for Ditta, Budapest, June 1926], in a printed copy prepared in America for a revised edition was marked *Dittának, Budapesten, 1926.okt.31-re,* i.e., stressing her birthday rather than the month of the composition).

Summing up the complex of Bartók's dating (which in the printed edition usually appears after the last measure), we must acknowledge that each case might be

---

ville to New York. One can only speculate whether he actually finished drafting Mov. IV as late as March 14 and, since the *Lichtpause* of Movs. I–III was ready, made the fair copy of it in the next day or two.

27. According to László Vikárius's studies, this was the date of finishing the first draft score (PB 67FSS1); the date may indicate that Bartók planned to send the score to the publisher, in which case its dating would have been his usual practice; he probably decided only in 1932 to write a *Lichtpause* fair copy for the facsimile production of the UE lithographed edition.

28. Probably the thematic ideas written in ink on pp. 75–80 of the sketch-book (the Turkish field-book, PB 80FSS1) belong to this initial stage of the composition. A detailed analysis of the sources is in Klára Móricz's dissertation, "Bartók: Concerto zenekarra. Genezis, analízis, recepció" [Bartók: Concerto for Orchestra. Genesis, analysis, reception] (F. Liszt Academy of Music, Budapest, 1992), and in her recent study cited above, chapter 1, n. 15.

29. According to the 1921 worklist (see above in note 20): 1910.

30. In the typescript of the 1938 Dille worklist (also see in note 20) Bartók corrected 1910 to 1909–1910.

31. See p. 8 in the 1974 EMB facsimile edition, and my commentaries, p. 25.

32. An autogr. dedication copy, with the text *1935.okt.31-re* was in Ditta's estate (BBA BH216).

different, and that cautious investigation is needed to clear up the actual meaning of each date.

After these necessary detours about the layout and dating, we return to the general characteristics of Bartók's drafts: the method and style of writing and correcting; special graphic signs he used; verbal notes and abbreviations. As a starting point we compare two autograph pages: the first page of the draft (Facsimile 30)[33] and that of the first autograph copy (Facsimile 31)[34] of Sonata 1926. Both were written in June 1926, on the same brand of paper, with the same fountain pen and ink. By the way, these are not the only autograph sources of the opening movement. Considerable sketches preceded the draft (see Ex. 8), and a second autograph copy was submitted to UE as the engraver's copy.[35]

The amount of music on the pages of the draft and the copy is by and large the same. The disposition of seven braces on 20-staff paper, leaving blank staves for corrections or for extremely high and low notes, is identical. The size of the notes and the neat rhythmic arrangement of the measures do not differ from draft notation to copy. The amount of dot-virgule-dot ∠ repeat signs (e.g., in m. 3, both hands) is very similar; the rules of proper notation (e.g., direction of stems, correct part-writing) are already evident in the draft. Crossed-out measures, as a result of revision, and extra measures on the margin, as an addition, occur in both manuscripts.

Of course this first copy is not a mechanical copy at all but rather a newly written version, incorporating new textural ideas (as in brace V, mm. 6–7, l.h., vs. the last measures in brace VII of the draft). If Bartók had shaped the final form already in the draft, which in this case would have meant complicated insertions and cancellations, after the necessary revision as well as the addition of performing signs, he could have used the draft as the final manuscript ready for the publisher. But the amount of immediate and subsequent corrections is considerably greater in the draft than in the copy. And, as a determining feature, the draft has no performing instructions beyond scattered slurs, while the copy is fully furnished with dynamics and tempo marks, even some fingering (see brace VII, m. 1, r.h., above notes 2–3: 5 5).[36]

Here are typical graphic features, abbreviations, and other characteristics of Bartók's drafts selected from the facsimile pages in this chapter (Facsimiles 23–41):

  a. repeat sign for one measure (e.g., Facsimiles 23, 25, 27, 29, 32, 37–39, 41) or double repeat sign for repeating two figures (Facsimile 25), two or more measures (Facsimile 32);

33. PB 55PS1.
34. Budapest OSZK Ms.Mus.998, deposited in BBA; see also the 1980 facsimile edition.
35. PB 55PFC2.
36. Bartók very likely practiced the Sonata and played its first performances in Budapest in fall 1926 from this MS.

b. repeat of measures or figures indicated by letters *a) b) c),* etc. (Facsimile 30 brace IV, Facsimile 32); occasionally insertion of measures was also identified by letters (Facsimile 27);

c. repeat indicated by worded notes, in combination with a horizontal brace: *bis* (Facsimile 32); *3szor, 2szer* [= 3 times, 2 times] (Facsimile 23); *többször* [several times, repeatedly] (Facsimiles 38–39), etc.; in combination with a V-shaped interpolation sign: *még egy ütem* [one more measure] (Facsimile 37);

d. interpolation marked by large V-shaped signs, or circle around the additional music and reference to the proper place (Facsimiles 23–24, 26, 30, 32–33);

e. insertion noted on the margin (Facsimiles 28, 30, 34, 38), sometimes with V- or O-shaped figures crossed once, twice, etc. (Facsimiles 33, 39), or at the lower part of the page (Facsimiles 32, 39), or on another page, referred to by using capital letters or other signs (Facsimile 33; see *A*, the interpolation on Facsimile 22 in chapter 6, p. 108);

f. change indicated by S-shaped wavy line for sequence of neighboring notes (Facsimiles 25, 27, 37), or for voices (Facsimile 41; here also by U-shaped sign in brace I for shift of two measures from vl. 2 to vl. 1);

g. corrected pitch of notes confirmed by letters, in Hungarian (or German) form, as in Facsimile 25 brace II: *b cis g dis* [= B♭, C♯, G, D♯]; sometimes in a writing barely intelligible for the non-Hungarian, as in Facsimile 26 brace III, solo viola, mm. 1–2, in addition to the letters *a) b) c),* meaning repeat, the Hungarian word *vissza* [back] after the first upward figure, *de g♮-vel* [but with G♮], *alsó* [lower] *a♭, alsó g♮*; Facsimile 33 brace III, vl. 1, m. 8: *c*; Facsimile 40 brace IV, m. 8: *cisis* [C𝄪];

h. words referring to transposition (in Facsimile 34, above Andante: *1 egész hanggal feljebb* [one whole tone higher]),[37] or enharmonic notation (as in Facsimile 28 brace II, m. 3: ♯-*re* [to ♯]; Facsimile 41 brace III, vlc. m. 2: ♯-*kel* [with sharps]); or octave doubling (Facsimile 39, under staff 17, twice: *oktávban* [in octave]).

For immediate or subsequent corrections and cancellation Bartók frequently crossed out material (but sometimes changed his mind; see *marad* ["stet"] in Facsimile 39 brace III, m. 6, piano r.h.). In a draft proper erasing is less frequent (but see Facsimile 28: the two first and the last but one measures), whereas in a bifunctional draft such as the draft of *Music,* annotated for a professional copyist (Facsimile 29), for the sake of clarity it occurs often. Also characteristic is the way

---

37. The transposition was motivated by practical considerations: the tessitura of children's voices.

FACSIMILE 23   *The Wooden Prince,* p. 31 of the draft, ca. 1916 (PB 33PS1), with later additions by
Bartók and by Márta.

FACSIMILE 24 *Four Orchestral Pieces*, the last page of Movement IV in the draft, ca. 1912 (PB 31TPPS1), with notes by Zoltán Kodály (staves 6, 16) and Bartók's side sketches and notes for the orchestration.

FACSIMILE 25 Violin Concerto (no. 2), p. 4 of the draft, 1937 (PB 76VPS1).

FACSIMILE 26   Viola Concerto, p. 1 of the draft, 1945 (PB 85FSS1), with side sketches in staves 23–24.

FACSIMILE 27   Piano Concerto no. 3, p. 7 of the draft (PB 84FSS1), with preparatory notes for the
orchestration; the note *2nd mov.?* in the top left corner by alien hand.

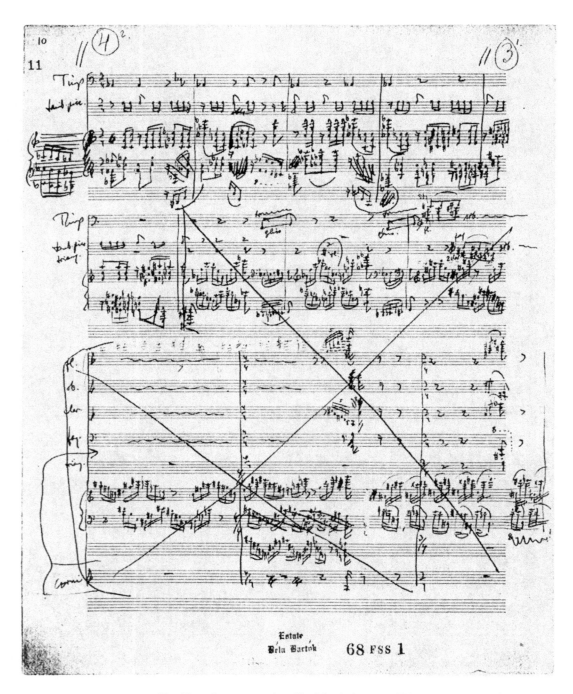

FACSIMILE 28   Piano Concerto no. 2, p. 11 of the draft score, 1930 (PB 68FSS1), with a deletion.

FACSIMILE 29   *Music for Strings, Percussion, and Celesta,* p. 40 of the draft score, 1936 (PB 74FSS1), with later corrections and notes for the copyist.

FACSIMILE 30 Piano Sonata 1926, the beginning of Movement I in the draft (PB 55–56PS1, p. 21).

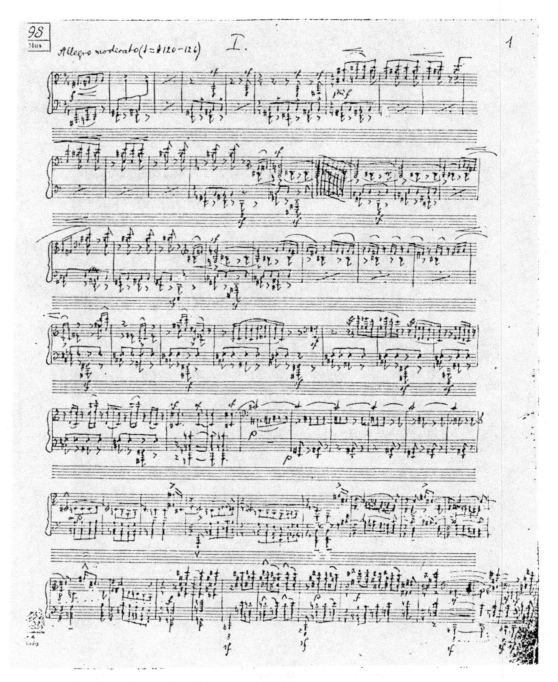

FACSIMILE 31   Piano Sonata 1926, the beginning of Movement I in the first autograph copy
(OSZK Ms.Mus.998, deposited in BBA).

FACSIMILE 32 Draft of "Bagpipe" (*Mikrokosmos* no. 138), ca. 1937 (PB 59PS1, p. 72), with the
duration of five pieces; *no. 138* by alien hand.

79 FSS 1ª

FACSIMILE 33   String Quartet no. 6, the first page of the draft, 1939 (PB 79FSS1, p. 2); see the
insertion to *A* in facsimile 22.

FACSIMILE 34   Draft of "Wandering," from Twenty-Seven Choruses, 1935 or 1936 (PB 72SAS1, p. 3), *1 egész hanggal feljebb* = 1 whole tone upwards; in staves 1–2 a sketch for *Mikrokosmos* no. 98.

FACSIMILE 35   String Quartet no. 5, the beginning of Movement II in the draft, 1934 (PB 71FSS1, p. 13).

FACSIMILE 36 String Quartet no. 1, p. 3 (Movement I) of the draft, 1908–1909 (PB 20FSS1), with cuts and preparations for the copyist's work.

75 FSS 1

FACSIMILE 37   Sonata for two Pianos and Percussion, a sketchy page of the draft, with later
additions in pencil, 1937 (PB 75FSS1, p. 18); *még egy ütem csak II.z. és gr.c.* = one
more measure, only II.P[iano] and gr[an] c[assa].

FACSIMILE 38   Sonata for two Pianos and Percussion, p. 35 of the draft (PB 75FSS1), with notes in pencil for the layout of the *Lichtpause* copy; *többször* = several times; *utoljára* = for the last time.

FACSIMILE 39   *Contrasts*, for violin, clarinet, and piano, the end of Movement III in the draft, 1938
(PB 77FSS1, p. 13), with a side sketch for Movement II; *többször* = several times;
oktávban = in octave.

FACSIMILE 40   Suite op. 14, for piano, the discarded original Movement II in the draft, 1916 (PB 43PS1, p. 19).

FACSIMILE 41   String Quartet no. 5, the beginning of the first version of Movement III in the draft, 1934 (PB 71FSS1, p. 63).

that Bartók turned white note-heads into black and vice versa, or shifted a note one step up or down by making it bigger; big notes are mostly corrected notes. For the rearrangement of meter and rhythm, or for changes in the synchronization of the voices, as a second thought, curved or wavy bars occur (e.g., Facsimiles 26, 33, 37). Rather seldom we find question marks (e.g., Facsimile 26 brace III, where Bartók considered leaving out the bass and in a next step did so)[38] or, less rarely, alternative versions not yet decided. Indecisiveness, however, was not characteristic of Bartók. No question that during the drafting process (actually much more intensively than in the sketches) he constantly revised the music, often to and fro, but with conviction. Incidentally his draft notation was so regular, quick, and well arranged that graphic image, color of ink, size of notation, angle of stems, and similar details barely show the beginning of a new day's work on a longer composition. There are drafts obviously written with greater speed and self-assurance (e.g., Facsimiles 28, 34, 38), and others written with hesitation and a great many immediate corrections (e.g., Facsimiles 26, 33, 37, the latter with blank parts for later elaboration that he filled in in pencil), or written at great speed but with lots of corrections (e.g., Facsimiles 32, 41).

A draft is, however, often a bi-functional manuscript, with later layer(s) of writing: preparatory notes for the orchestration; revision and completion for the copyist (eventually for Bartók himself); and a draft occasionally with notes written by an alien hand. Regarding our selection of facsimile pages note the following additions:

Facsimile 23, *The Wooden Prince*: tempo and dynamic marks, rehearsal numbers added later by Bartók, or copied by Márta at a next stage of the composition (from the autograph full score or from the manuscript of the piano reduction), with scattered preparatory notes for the orchestration, as in m. 2 after no. 171.

Facsimile 24, *Four Orchestral Pieces,* end of Movement IV: additional preparatory notes for the orchestration, throughout in pencil. There are notes in pencil by Kodály who read the draft and advised Bartók to make the music of the second brace somewhat longer[39] and to reconsider the end of the piece[40] (see in chapter 4, p. 66).

Facsimile 27, Piano Concerto no. 3, Movement II. (N.B. This page is a very much mixed-form autograph: braces I–III represent the first sketch of the choral theme of the piano, followed by the draft of the prelude, interludes, and postlude of the orchestra, some in two versions; only the last six

---

38. On the second page of the 2nd bifolio (see Fig. 17 in chapter 6, p. 110), i.e., in the continuity draft of Viola Concerto Mov. III, written in ink.

39. Bartók followed Kodály's advice and at the bottom of the previous page sketched the new version; see Ex. 25b in chapter 4.

40. In the bottom left corner of the page, in the last two staves, there are two new sketches that show Bartók trying to implement Kodály's suggestion.

measures of the page represent a typical continuity draft.) Bartók made the orchestration from this sketchy form directly onto *Lichtpausen*. Oblique double lines with a number (e.g., *6* ‖ above staff 1) indicate the arrangement of the number of staves (here, 6 staves) and the length of a line (here, from the beginning of the piano chorale, including the insertion marked *b*: 12 measures) in a system (brace) of the full score. Numbers and instrument names also sketch the plan of the page (e.g., under the bottom line: *2 zong.* [= piano, i.e., two staves for the piano], *3 von.* [str.], *ob., clar., fl., tromb.*, all together 9 staves; see number *9* above the last bar at the end of the page, where the word *lap* [page] indicates that this will be the end of a page in the full score).

Facsimile 28, Piano Concerto no. 2, Movement I: above staff 1 Bartók's plan of the layout of the *Lichtpause* fair-copy full score. The large circled number represents the staves needed in the brace, the small number marks that the 4-st. brace will be the second brace on the page, the 3-st. brace the first on the next page.

Facsimile 29, *Music for Strings, Percussion, and Celesta,* Movement III: with additional expression marks, with German instructions to the copyist about the sequence of the instruments, and, from a later time when Bartók (in connection with a rehearsal or performance?) checked it again, marked with red pencil as a further change — *vált.* [oztatás] — the correction of three *p* signs into *pp*.

Facsimile 32, *Mikrokosmos* no. 138: timing (*1'10"*) at the end of the piece, and the length of a 5-piece group of *Mikrokosmos* pieces (bottom left corner).

Facsimile 34, "Bolyongás" (Wandering), from Twenty-Seven Choruses: in a second step, Bartók edited the draft by adding performing instructions so that Jenő Deutsch could make the *Lichtpause* fair copy. (On the top of the page: sketch for *Mikrokosmos* no. 98.)

Facsimile 36, String Quartet no. 1, Movement I: the draft full score was given to a professional copyist;[41] therefore in a next step Bartók filled it in with performing instructions, added rehearsal numbers, but above all profoundly revised the music (see, e.g., the deleted measures). Notes in pencil (e.g., *cresc.* under the bottom staff) probably date from the time of rehearsals for the first performance.

Facsimile 39, *Contrasts,* Movement III, last page: in the top right corner Bartók's notes about the duration of Movements I and III (i.e., he measured the length of the sections before the work was written into fair copy). (In the bottom staff: sketch to Mov. II, written after Mov. III was drafted.)

41. Copyist X who produced the original layer of the printer's copy.

In a broader context the secondary use of a draft is not connected at all with the notational character of the manuscript. Heavily corrected and neatly written drafts were equally used in a next step or were left untouched. The draft of Suite op. 14 for piano (see Facsimile 40) for instance has a well-arranged notation, which could easily have been furnished with tempo and expression marks and sent to the publisher. But in the late 1910s Márta was on hand to make a fair copy that Bartók then revised and edited, adding expression marks.

FORMATION OF A WORK

For the genesis of a work, the draft undoubtedly contains the greatest amount of information on Bartók's compositional method and practice. This information is, however, of varying documentary value: unambiguous facts directly gathered from the notation; well-founded assumptions based on a close reading of the draft, considering the first intention, the changes, corrections, layers in the autograph text; and, last but not least, observations based on the analytical interpretation of Bartók's probable motivation in doing exactly what he did.

The central task of this book, to survey such information, presents a rather awkward problem. The main experiences of a three-decade systematic examination of the manuscripts can of course easily be summarized. But to what extent can these experiences be documented and shown to others? Since the reader does not have access to a vast amount of original sources, with so few complete facsimile editions at hand[42] we could either focus on one single work (giving the full draft in facsimile and/or in diplomatic transcription) or take short samples of a fair range of drafts, representing different genres, styles, and problems. As no single work represents the "typical" Bartók and no single Bartók draft demonstrates all the significant features of his compositional process, even the deepest possible analysis of one single work seems to me an unacceptable limitation. Therefore we are going to visit and examine a selection of examples, more as an introduction to further individual studies in the genesis of major works, a much needed special field in future Bartók research.

String Quartet no. 3, Ricapitulazione della prima parte

As a launching point, let us take a close look at a draft of considerable length, actually a whole movement of an *attacca* form: the third part of the 4-part structure of String

42. Aside from short movements and minor compositions, there are five crucial editions: Denijs Dille, ed., Bartók–Kodály, *Hungarian Folksongs for song with piano* [1906] (Budapest: EMB, 1970); László Somfai, ed., *Two Rumanian Dances for Piano* (Budapest: EMB, 1974); idem, ed., *Sonata (1926) Piano Solo*, (Budapest: EMB, 1980); idem, ed., *Black Pocket-book: Sketches 1907–1922* (Budapest: EMB, 1987); Peter Bartók and Nelson Dellamaggiore, ed., with commentaries by László Somfai, *Viola Concerto* (Homosassa, Fla.: Bartók Records, 1995).

Quartet no. 3 (1927) in the final printed version titled Ricapitulazione della prima parte. In six braces, from the bottom of p. 10 to the top of p. 12 of the draft full score,[43] the 70-measure music represents a notation that we may call typical: written in ink with considerable fluency, but not without immediate and later corrections. The diplomatic transcription (Ex. 34) includes the original and the corrected notes, crossed-out notes, deleted measures, inserted notes and measures, interpolations, verbal notes (see *marad cis* [remains C♯] in m. 46). I have numbered the measures of the draft. Notes marked ⸢?⸣ represent questionable readings, as in m. 22; clefs, time signatures, accidentals in square brackets are additions; spots circled with a dotted line, as in mm. 69–70, refer to scratched corrections where the original is unintelligible. Bartók used pencil, probably at a first revision, for example in mm. 38–50, mostly finalized later in ink (e.g., in the revised vl. 1 part in mm. 38–46, but not in mm. 47–50, which are rewritten in ink in a 2-staff brace). Preliminary notes:

before m. 1, vlc.: the last three measures of the transition leading to m. 1 belong to the first layer (later revised on p. 16 of the manuscript);

m. 3: inserted measure;

m. 8: the correction in the vlc. in pencil;

m. 16: first in 3/4; the 16th tremolo second beat is an insertion, parallel to the cancellation of m. 18;

mm. 19–20: C♯–C♯ glissando corrected to C♮–D♯;

m. 29: only the chord on the second beat is crossed out;

mm. 35–37, vl. 1–2: in spite of the S-shaped wavy line, in the final version Bartók kept the original sequence of the notes;

mm. 47–50: the short-score-form correction is written at the bottom of the page;

m. 54, vl. 1: correction in pencil.

The music here seems to be very much *in statu nascendi*. Dozens of little changes in pitch, rhythm, chordal structure, voice leading, and phrase length obviously improve the piece. Each seems to be significant and worth studying. Here follows a personal selection for a short discussion, arranged by topics rather than the course of measures.

Pitch, chord. In m. 5 (vla.) D is better than G, probably not because of the pitch organization, but to prevent the exact repetition of motive A–C–G in mm. 4–5 and 6–7. Corrections in m. 8 are closely connected with the preference of certain intervals (Ex. 35). Version 35a has a chain of semitones (A/A♯, D♯/D, F♯/G). In version 35b on the first and second beat (in enharmonic reading) there are two major thirds in minor third distance outlining a major/minor chord, one of Bartók's

43. PB 60FFS1; see also Fig. 14.

EXAMPLE 34a–c   Diplomatic transcription of the draft of the *Ricapitulazione della prima parte* of String Quartet no. 3.

EXAMPLE 34c

EXAMPLE 35   String Quartet no. 3, Ricapitulazione:
             corrections of m. 8.

EXAMPLE 36   String Quartet no. 3, Ricapitulazione: corrections of mm. 31–33.

EXAMPLE 37   String Quartet no. 3, Ricapitulazione:
corrections of mm. 21–23.

favorite chords. He still changed the vlc., and as a consequence, to get the same intervals, the rhythm of the viola had to be corrected. Why did Bartók modify the vlc. part in m. 8? He liked the "extension in range" of the scale (mode) system of a melody, as a special form of variation, discussed in the Harvard Lectures.[44] The four cello motives in mm. 4–11 show an extension of the frame (i.e., the interval between the 1st and 4th notes, in semitones): 14, 15, 16, 19.

The formation of mm. 31–34 happened in three steps (Ex. 36). Following the F major/minor portato chord progression (see m. 30), Bartók first led the bass line stepwise down (E–D) in m. 31, joined by an F major/minor complex (m. 32) and a similar separated chord. His second thought was an E pedal note in the cello, with the necessary slight rearrangement of the voice leading in m. 32, plus the cancellation of the chord in m. 33. Finally he transposed the chords to A♭ major/minor. So curiously enough, the lovely pentatonic motive E–B–C♯ in the cello, marked espressivo with a cresc.–dim. swell in the final form, was born after considerable hesitation too.

The correction of the entries in mm. 21–22, delaying the F–B tritone to the beat by changing the cello part, seems to be primarily a harmonic improvement (Ex. 37).

Rhythm, articulation. The change to make a single note, a chord, a repeated figure, a progression longer — rarely shorter — is characteristic of Bartók's drafts. Studying hundreds of such corrections, we get the impression that during the composition Bartók checked their effect in actual performance again and again. (He did not necessarily play it at his instrument but considered the imaginary performance in real tempo.) Such minor adjustments of the length, whether they concerned one note or a progression, rarely changed the essence of the rhythmic development but certainly improved the gesture, the performance. The insertion of m. 3, a quasi *corona* on the opening note, is typical. The deletion of the chord in m. 29 (actually the repetition of the previous one in m. 28) makes the gesture more concise, achieving the gradual slowdown in one coherent motion. The extension of mm. 58–60, and 62, although it is not just a repetition but involves significant recomposition, arises from the same feeling: considering the tension created before, Bartók was not satisfied with the length and power of these measures. Even the reorganization of

44. *Essays*, 381.

mm. 16–18 seems to originate with the revision of the gesture. In the original version, in 3/4, m. 16 offered a strong articulation, followed by another stop soon in m. 18, with its quivering chords. This actually separated the two-note slurred motive of m. 17 from its fragmentation and reverberation in m. 19. Bartók, however, definitely wanted to keep the chord repetition (a reference to the *sul ponticello* motive in Prima parte, 2nd measure after no. 4). Thus he transferred it to m. 16, and the deletion of m. 18 brought the reappearance of the two-note slurred motive (a reference to m. 4 after no. 4 in Prima parte), and its reverberation in m. 19 next to each other.

Form, motivic concept. In motivic references to the opening movement, it is amazing that not the slightest hesitation occurs in the outline of the form, or in the number and sequence of the varied and transformed recalls of motives from the Prima parte. Bartók must have been very sure about the narrative of this unusual shortened recapitulation and about the nature of the recomposition of the original themes. Probably two minor, nevertheless quite important modifications should, however, be mentioned. The correction of the vl. 1 motive in m. 54 helps the listener to recognize the music it refers to (Prima parte m. 3 after no. 10). On the contrary, in mm. 58ff. Bartók avoids the direct quotation of the repeated notes (Prima parte m. 6 after no. 10), holding it back to mm. 62–63, and first offers a development, a climax of the two-note slurred figure.

Melodic invention, elaboration, contrapuntal texture. The density of corrections shows that the only major problem zone for Bartók in this movement was the developmental texture of mm. 35–53. He decided to build up a climax from the three-note pentatonic motive (C–G–A, etc.) and the emblematic broken chord so typical of Bartók (here: E–C♯–G♯–E♮), both introduced in the previous measures. Already the first version produced considerable tension, typical Bartókian dissonances, and ample driving force. The descant, however, was rather flat, bringing the emblematic major/minor broken chord twice (mm. 39–40, 45–46). Characteristically, Bartók concentrated on improving the melody by writing a new vl. 1 part. It is a simple, vocal-style melody with different sizes of circling motion. All together probably not very original; perhaps much too close to certain melodic formulae of Bartók's much loved folk-music sources — but this certainly had not worried him at all. Since he frequently used such melodies, I risk a general observation: despite his powerful imaginative creation of highly original themes and motives, in the course of the more or less routine compositional process of filling out the full texture, Bartók was not always at ease in shaping the melodic/polyphonic fabric. In such cases the correction usually aimed at an emotionally persuasive rephrasing of the progression, focusing on a melodic climax or a dramatic gesture in rhythm, even if it meant a simplification of the polyphony.

Piano Sonata, the Beginning of Movement I

Compared to the one-manuscript drafting process of String Quartet no. 3, my next example, the ca. 60 opening measures of Piano Sonata 1926, represents the opposite working procedure. It was written during one of Bartók's periods of quasi "graphomania": in addition to considerable sketches, he wrote no fewer than three autograph versions without major changes before he considered the piece ready for publication. As an integral part of our analysis of the primary drafting process, we must compare three manuscripts: the sketch for the ca. 60 opening measures, which is a genuine continuity sketch (full transcription in chapter 4, Ex. 8); the draft proper (see Facsimile 30); and the first autograph copy, which we might call the second draft (see Facsimile 31), specifically as regards Movement III. This example is an eminent case study in Bartókian rhythm. Rhythmic drive, strictly even speed, rattling motion, unexpected and cruel beats seldom create in Bartók's music such high tension. Given the length of the piece, the sonata-form opening movement is an absolute rarity in his output. Not a single rallentando or rit.–a tempo articulates the form; slightly slower or faster tempi assigned to different themes, otherwise so natural in Bartók's longer movements, are fully missing here. Only after 253 measures of strict tempo, in the coda, appear three completely unprepared changes in the tempo: a Più mosso, an abrupt Tempo I interpolation, and a similarly abrupt return to Più mosso.

While drafting this movement, Bartók's main concern was to bring the rhythm to perfection: the duration of a given motion; the number of repeated notes or groups of notes; the interpolation of enlarged or compressed measures into the pulsation of a steady 2/4 meter; unexpected beats set against the regular beat of the meter; polymetric interactions such as 3/8 motion against 2/4.

After he had developed the ascending terraces of the primary theme in mm. 1–6[45] and added the all-important head motive of m. 1 (missing from the sketch), Bartók met with difficulties in mm. 4–6. The question was, how many "blows" (percussive beats with the right hand at the lower limit of the keyboard) should prepare, should urge the thematic entry in m. 7, and in what rhythm? The first version in the sketch (see Ex. 38 upper brace) was already very effective: a first blow on the 6th beat of the ostinato motion, followed by three subsequent beats in accelerando, with only one F♯ (a quasi dominant) as the last one. The second version, the original layer of the draft, containing five percussive beats with a monotonous B–F♯–B–F♯ progression at the end, was an improvement and a weaker version at the same time. Realizing that, Bartók canceled the original m. 6, inserted a new one, returned to the directionality of the four-blow B–B–B–F♯ concept, with the exciting rhythm. Mean-

45. I refer to measures of the printed score. Since Bartók and his publishers did not number the measures in his piano music, a useful first step for the comparative study of sources and versions is to number a personal copy.

EXAMPLE 38   Piano Sonata, Movement I: the beginning.

EXAMPLE 39   Piano Sonata, Movement I: correction of mm. 7–13.

while he also corrected the pitch collection of the left-hand motion, turning the F♮ into F♯, creating a scale he often favored.[46]

The next terrace with E *repercussio* (mm. 7–13) changed the progression from the 6–1–3–5–1–1 eighth notes each separated by eighth rests in the sketch into the revised 8–5–3–1–1–1–1 concept in the draft: from an irregular agitation to an organized one, a directional rhythmic process. Numbers 8–5–3 naturally remind us of the Fibonacci series. But before we take it as proof of Bartók's manipulations with the famous numbers, note that the set is imperfect, because not 2 but 1 comes after 3; besides, with the rest after the repeated E notes the actual length is rather 9–6–4–2–2–2–2 eighth note values (Ex. 39).

The third terrace, reaching G, needed extensive correction. The first section of it (mm. 14–20, Ex. 40), in the sketch only 4 measures, in the draft 8, was finally (in the next manuscript; see Facsimile 31) reduced to 7. This change reflects Bartók's hesitation about the ideal length of a *corona*, the first quasi rubato gesture in the so tense rhythmic style. The following measures (mm. 21–28, Ex. 41) were crucially revised. In the sketch the right-hand motives just started to break up the 2/4 meter,

46. C D E F♮ G♯ A♯ B pitch collection in the sketch, C D E F♯ G♯ A♯ B in the draft, which is a mode in *heptatonia tertia* (Lajos Bárdos's term; see Somfai/*Strategics*, 169–170).

EXAMPLE 40   Piano Sonata, Movement I: correction of mm. 14–20.

EXAMPLE 41   Piano Sonata, Movement I: correction of mm. 21–28.

with a single place suggesting 3/8 pulsation (the later mm. 27–28). In the draft Bartók fully realized the polymetric play with great ingenuity.[47]

The climax of the primary theme area (mm. 29–35; see Ex. 42) matured in three stages: the short form in the sketch (see again Ex. 8, mm. 23–27); the original layer of the draft, crossed out and partly erased (reconstruction: Ex. 42a); and the corrected form in the draft, written above the old layer in empty staves and in the margin (Ex. 42b). From one stage to the next the improvement is incredible indeed. For the rhythm, the embryonic form of the sketch first developed into a well-proportioned transition with changing pitch levels of the left-hand chord (G and D repetition) and with a rich variety of larger or smaller motivic circles in the right hand, not yet surpassing the compass D^2. The rewritten form has a magnificent gesture when reaching the peak and then fragmenting the r.h. motion. More important is, however, the basic correction of the tonal context. Bartók extended the tessitura up to E♭–F. With the G–C–E♭ frame this leads to a Bartókian modulation, actually to the fulfillment of the tonal action started with the E lydian/major beginning, with G♯–B, C♯–E, E–G thematic entrances, leading from the G♯–B–E–G (= E major/minor) complex to the related E–G–C–E♭ (= C major/minor) complex (see Ex. 43).

Measures 36–37, the 2-measure new version of the arrival to A–C–C♯, the key of the second theme, is written in brace VI, clearly not as a continuation of the measure before. The sequence of the steps in composition seems to be the following. First Bartók proceeded with the original layer till m. 4 in brace VI. Next he recomposed the climax in braces IV–VI (Ex. 42b) and, as the end of the new version, added these two rephrased measures. Then, with mm. 7–9 of brace VI, naturally using his

47. See in detail in Somfai/*Piano Year*, 32–33.

EXAMPLE 42   Piano Sonata, Movement I: correction of mm. 29–37.

mm. 29-37

(a) draft, ground layer

(b) draft, after correction

EXAMPLE 43   Piano Sonata: pitch collection of the beginning of Movement I.

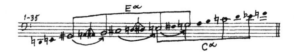

preliminary sketches (Ex. 8), Bartók went ahead. But after m. 5 of brace VII he stopped again and, as a second thought, inserted 6 more measures with the quotation of the primary theme as a stronger articulation before the second theme. Incidentally, in this movement Bartók showed great concern about the interpolation of the head motive of the movement as a forceful signal for the articulation of the form. As a later correction in the first autograph copy,[48] at the beginning of the development section (m. 135), he added this motive to the clockwork texture (m. 137, etc.).[49]

48. See the facsimile edition of the Budapest MS, top of p. 3.
49. Somfai/*Piano Year*, 45–48.

EXAMPLE 44   String Quartet no. 4, Movement I: formation of mm. 1–4.

String Quartet no. 4, the Beginning of Movement I

The third example, the formation of the opening measures of String Quartet no. 4 (1928), is also dedicated to metric/rhythmic complications that Bartók faced when drafting this music. In the rough draft score,[50] without marking time signature, he conceived the beginning in changing meter, with immediate revision of the bars. The final notation of String Quartet no. 4 is extremely rare in Bartók's music in that although the music of all five movements is unusually rich in metric changes, asymmetrical phrases, and polymetric textures, in the notation itself there is not a single change of meter. (The 6/8 vs. 2/4 phenomenon in Movement II is not to be considered as changing meter.) Bartók put down the music in a fixed framework of 4/4 (Movs. I & III), 6/8 (Mov. II), or 2/4 (Mov. V). However, the actual beats, accents, stresses, deviant from the natural beats in the meter, are clearly indicated with expression marks.

The primary form of the 4/4 meter "rock-hard" rhythm opening statement (mm. 1–4; see Ex. 44) was in 3/4. In spite of the quasi-hocket (or in Bartókian terms, *komplementär*) rhythm, this urform had a bit of a valse swing. Whether immediately or at a next reading, Bartók corrected the first version by adding quarter rests to mm.

50. The oldest layer of 62FSS1 in Peter Bartók's collection, p. 30, reproduced in facsimile in Antokoletz/1984, illustration 6 after p. 77.

EXAMPLE 45   String Quartet no. 4, Movement I:

formation of mm. 5–7.

2 and 4 (and rearranging the bar between mm. 3–4), creating changing meters. In the final version, already in the second (full) draft,[51] he extended mm. 1 and 4 to get a steady 4/4 motion.

The next section (mm. 5–7, Ex. 45) in the urform showed a 5/4–3/4–5/8 compression of the meter. The cello entry on E♭ was positioned on an offbeat, the second eighth of the measure—as if Bartók wanted to suggest an abstractly even performance, one without the natural feeling of any beat; this actually seems to be the very essence of the music in these measures. But the real performance of an intricate polyphonic texture starting with an entry on the second eighth was more than risky. So Bartók rearranged the bar between mm. 4–5, offering an upbeat entry to the cello, by this making the job of the three other musicians considerably easier. Besides, he elongated m. 7. Note that the so characteristic first presentation of the six-note emblem motive of the cello in m. 7 was still missing. This motive came to

51. On p. 1 of 62FSS1.

EXAMPLE 46   String Quartet no. 4, Movement I: formation of mm. 8ff.

Bartók's mind while he was writing the first draft at around m. 83 (in the printed form). Thus in the second draft the six-note emblem was already part of the form concept. (See m. 7 in the bottom line of Ex. 45.)

The third section of the primary theme area (mm. 8–13 in the printed form) suffered considerable changes too. Bartók knew exactly which notes, which textures he wanted to present here. But he was not so sure about the rhythmic arrangement, especially the placement of the bars. As I read the first barring and the erased bars in the rough draft, Bartók's first notation (see the continuous bars in Ex. 46) had a changing-meter concept. This arrangement, however, did not correspond to the differently asymmetrical articulation of the texture. As a second thought he corrected the rhythm of the first measure and made a new barring (see the bars between the staves, i.e., the 5/4–3/4–4/4–4/4 arrangement). The final version in the uniform 4/4 notation resulted in still another barring. More importantly, however, Bartók inserted a short but powerful contrapuntal elaboration of the six-note emblem motive.

What lesson can we learn from this case? The crucial matter is that the much analyzed pitch content of the beginning of String Quartet no. 4 came without hesitation in the very first rough draft, while Bartók had to work hard on the proper rhythmic/metric notation of the characteristic textures. We might wonder whether the transformation of the 3/4 swing of the opening into the well-known 4/4 rhythm was an unambiguous improvement of its character or not. Such criticism may be justified by the assumption that the switch from the exciting changing-meter concept to a uniform 4/4 probably involved a compromise in Bartók's concept. Yet the aesthetic evaluation and comparison of the two versions, as equal variant forms, has no solid ground. Bartók withdrew the first form at an embryonic stage of the composition. He rephrased the original idea, made it a forceful statement in a new rhythmic/metric context. And we should add that the presentation of the six-note emblem in these introductory measures (mm. 7, 11–13), although a second thought, is indeed a great improvement: this motive functions as the goal of the process, as the first crystallized thematic idea born from the creation act of the first measures.

Violin Concerto, the 12-tone Melody

A fourth example concerns an eminent case of pitch organization. The calmo lyric contrast theme of Movement I (mm. 73–95, etc.) of the Violin Concerto (no. 2) achieved a certain reputation, not so much in the analytical literature as among musicians, of being Bartók's only twelve-tone melody. Allegedly this was some kind of coquetry on Bartók's part.[52] In this case the comparative study of the sketch and the short score is indispensable. The sketch was presented by Bartók to the violinist Tossy Spivakovsky[53] in a letter of November 26, 1943: "Finally I found those first sketches to the violin concerto I mentioned to you, so I am sending them enclosed. They are hurriedly written just as they came to my mind: the 1st theme of the Ist and IInd movement, and various tentative forms of the 2nd theme of the Ist movement (some of them never used)."

Actually the variation theme of Movement II is on a small piece of paper with hand-ruled staves (probably sketched as early as 1936),[54] the rest on one side of a sheet of standard music paper (presumably sketched with or just after the Sonata for two Pianos and Percussion, July–August 1937), containing mm. 7–22, the opening solo theme, in a 2-staff-form sketch, and in staves 8–11 and st. 13–14 the "tentative forms" of what Bartók called the second theme (see Ex. 47: a diplomatic transcription with Roman numerals of the six staves, and numbers of measures [measure "0" is a later addition]; small notes are additions in pencil; parentheses[55] in staff VI originate with Bartók).

52. According to Zoltán Székely (personal communication), during their rehearsals Bartók asked him whether he noticed the *Zwölfton* theme. (Note that when I wrote the present study, Claude Kenneson's *Székely and Bartók: The Story of a Friendship* [Portland: Amadeus Press, 1994] had not yet appeared.) Bartók also asked Yehudi Menuhin in America about this passage and said, "I wanted to show Schoenberg that one can use all twelve tones and still remain tonal" (reprinted in Gillies/*Bartók Remembered*, 185).

53. *As a souvenir to Mr. Tossy Spivakovsky of his memorable performance on Oct. 14, 15, 17, 1943, in New York*; in the collection of Mr. Spivakovsky.

54. Somfai/*Strategics*, 162.

55. Actually written as square brackets (see facs. 15 in *DocB/6*), which I changed because I use square brackets for editorial additions.

EXAMPLE 47   Violin Concerto, Movement I: sketches of the "twelve-tone" theme.

In my reading of the layers, the steps of notation of the sketch, and thus the genesis of the "twelve-tone" theme, can be summed up as follows:

1. Bartók wrote measures I, 1–3 and II, 1–3, actually a ten-tone theme with clear tonal ending on A as the 11th note, together with a fourth transposition (or fifth down, treating it as if it were in the key of the recapitulation).

2. Next he formed a free inversion of the ten-tone theme with characteristically different rhythm of the beginning, again with a transposition, in III, mm. 1–3 and IV, 1–3. N.B. The sequence of notes 7–8 was later changed in III, m. 2 and consequently Bartók also changed I, m. 2 and II, m. 2.

3. In addition, taking the set of III, 1–3 Bartók sketched two further thematic variant forms by placing certain notes an octave higher or lower; see measures I, 4–6 and III, 4–6 with a full and a partial transposition in II, 4–6 and IV, 4. These three sets produced useful melodic variants of the same row not so much in the spirit of the Schoenbergian twelve-tone technique as in Bartók's way of creating variants (Ex. 48).

4. As a next step Bartók extended the theme into a twelve-tone melody, keeping even in this form the tonally so crucial 13th note; see the additional measures and inserted notes in I–IV (mm. 0 and 4). Unfortunately, the addition of the four eighth notes meant that the two characteristic head-rhythms had to vanish. At this point Bartók put the thematic elaboration aside and worked in a rather abstract quarter-note

EXAMPLE 48   Violin Concerto, Movement I:
melodic variants of the twelve-tone row.

rhythm on the still missing *R* (retrograde) (= V, mm. 1–4) and *RI* (retrograde inversion) (= V, mm. 5–8). Here too he added a melodic variant to each, with pseudo-inversion contours (= VI, mm. 1–4 and 5–8).

To sum up the compositional ideas documented on the sketch page: Bartók invented a ten-tone tonal theme that he later extended into a twelve-tone form. In addition, he not only complemented the orthodox *I*, *R*, and *RI* forms but composed melodic variants partly with pseudo-inversion contours. During this process, presumably looking for a better motivic shape, he changed notes in the original set.

From here onward we study the corresponding page of the draft (see Facsimile 25). It is indeed striking to observe how many times Bartók changed the sequence of the notes. To revise the order so extensively was not typical of him at all. The reorganization or addition of notes must have been connected with his choice from the sets sketched on the extra page. Which set or sets did Bartók use in the original layer of the draft? A close look at the first solo entry (end of brace I on Facsimile 25) and the first tutti (brace II, from the second measure) (Ex. 49) reveals that he intended the 10-tone melody with the characteristic rhythm for the solo violin, and the 12-tone even-motion form for the orchestra. Exactly which versions of the 10- and the 12-note series did he put into action first? As Ex. 50 shows, he began by picking out the original 10-note series (with the urform E–C sequence), and the extended 12-note series (with C–E as the 9th and 10th notes), and, as a next step, the transposition of both by a fourth (see mm. 5–10 in brace II).

The remaining three entries (solo violin, tutti, solo violin) consist of another melodic variant of the original 10-note series with the original rhythm, its transposition by a fourth, and the one and only inversion (see III, mm. 0–3 in Ex. 47).

Bartók, however, was not satisfied with the music in the original layer notation of the draft. On the one hand, he had extended the first two solo entries into a 12-tone form, making the 3-note upbeat more effective and changing notes in the two phrases differently, in order to achieve variety and independent melodic contours.

EXAMPLE 49   Violin Concerto, Movement I: correction of mm. 73ff. and 77ff.

EXAMPLE 50   Violin Concerto, Movement I: 10- and 12-note series.

He had also varied the notes in the two orchestral answers. On the other hand, he still liked the following 10-note theme and its transpositions — the initial form as it came to his mind. Some final touch was needed, however, to make the *I* form fit as the closing phrase of the calmo theme.

In terms of twelve-tone manipulations, we can describe the permutation of the 12 notes of the ground series as follows (see numbers in Ex. 50; superscript means transposition, italics mean inversion):

mm. 73–75	solo	1	3	2	4	6	5	7	8	9	10	11	12	(1)
mm. 76–78	tutti	1	3	2	6	4	5	7	8	9	10	11	12	(1)
mm. 79–81	solo	^{1}	^{3}	^{2}	^{4}	^{5}	^{6}	^{7}	^{9}	^{8}	^{10}	^{12}	^{11}	(^{1})
mm. 82–84	tutti	^{1}	^{2}	^{4}	^{3}	^{5}	^{6}	^{8}	^{7}	^{9}	^{11}	^{10}	^{12}	(^{1})
mm. 85–86	solo	1			4	5	6	7	8	10	9	11	12	(1)
mm. 87–88	tutti	^{1}			4	5	6	7	8	9	10	11	12	(^{1})
mm. 89–91	solo	*1*	*2*	*3*	*9*	*6*	*5*	*7*	*4*	*8*	*10*	*11*	*12*	

Note, however, how absurd such an analysis is: none of the sets of numbers is identical with the final version in the sketch; each of the seven sets is different; and the notes' change of place was obviously connected neither with an a priori theory nor with a permutational scheme but was motivated by sheer musical considerations like directionality vs. oscillation in the melody, singing character and rhythmic drive vs. standstill in the interludes.

In addition to the seven sets (five 12-tone and two 10-tone) in the exposition, the recapitulation of the sonata form brings six more sets, actually seven in Bartók's first concept. Here the draft includes two independent variant forms in connection

EXAMPLE 51   Violin Concerto, Movement I: seven sets in
the recapitulation.

with the changing strategies of the recapitulation. According to the first strategy Bartók brought new material but kept the original sequence of the basic themes. Thus in the first version the transitory passages (mm. 220–227 in the printed form) were followed by a contrapuntal development of the first two measures of the opening theme (ca. 15 mm., with the participation of the solo violin);[56] a free recapitulation of the risoluto theme (ca. 20–22 mm.);[57] and some virtuoso passage-work (ca. 20 mm.),[58] leading to the lyric 12-tone theme area. In this first version seven sets appeared, very much in the style of the exposition, changing solo and tutti entries, the characteristic rhythm of the first two solo presentations alternating with even-motion tutti, then two 10-tone forms of the set, and a last solo entry serving as a means of slowing down. While the exposition presented *O* forms and one *I*, here the seven sets (in a way closing a circle) bring *R, RI, I* and *O* (Ex. 51). Unlike the reorganization of the notes of the series in the exposition, here in the first layer of the draft Bartók simply kept the basic order of the notes.

56. The bottom half of p. 10 (PB 76VPS1), under the later half-page paste-over containing the orchestral passage as it is now known.
57. From the end of p. 10 on p. 11 without the pasteups.
58. On p. 12, crossed out.

He made slight changes, however, in the sequence of the notes, in the general contour of the theme (turning an ascending melody into a descending shape; see staff 2 in Ex. 51), and in rhythm, in addition to canceling the first orchestral passage, when he rewrote a considerable part of the recapitulation (mm. 228–279 in the printed score). According to the second strategy, after the transitional passage came a splendid stretto (mm. 228–247),[59] a powerful recomposing of the original idea, followed in turn by a montage alternating recapitulation of the risoluto theme and the lyric twelve-tone calmo theme (mm. 248–279). In the dramaturgy of this montage, the risoluto loses power while the calmo interruptions become longer and longer (3, 6, 9 measures). As a consequence of this new strategy, the first calmo entry is just a violin solo; Bartók discarded the even-motion tutti answer. Other minor corrections resulted from the context: he gave a quiet descending contour to the first solo entry (m. 255) and (m. 261) a genuine calmo rhythm to the second.

Although strict twelve-tone technique was obviously not in Bartók's line, he carefully considered the exploitation of the four shapes (O, I, R, RI). As a general strategy in this sonata-form movement, themes in the recapitulation return both in inversion (usually with a different character) and in the original form. In the section we are discussing, the three risoluto passages differ in this respect. In the first passage (m. 248) both the leading voice (solo violin) and the canon-like entries with the opening motive present the I form. The second passage (m. 258) juxtaposes O in the violin solo and I in the pseudo-canon motion. In the third passage (m. 267), a genuine three-part canon texture appears with the O shape alone. Thus the theme gradually returns from the counterpole to the primary shape. The calmo theme, thanks to the twelve-tone technique, involves not a bipolar but a circular connection:

$$I$$
$$O \quad RI$$
$$R$$

In the exposition of the calmo theme Bartók moved from O toward I; he dealt with two shapes. Here in the recapitulation he visits R, RI, I, O shapes, thus closing the circle. Probably it was Bartók's acute sense of balance that came into play. Corresponding to the alteration of the other themes in recapitulation vis-à-vis the exposition (two shapes vs. one), with the calmo theme a ratio of four to two seemed right.

Recapitulation Strategies in Piano Concerto no. 2, Movement I

Among Bartók's recapitulation strategies in sonata-form head movements, the Violin Concerto seems to represent a refined variant of an already matured concept. In

59. On the half-page paste-over on p. 10.

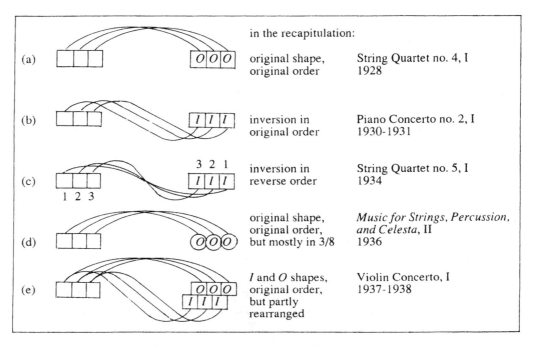

FIGURE 18 Bartók strategies in the recapitulation of themes in sonata form — a theoretical model.

connection with mostly symmetrical (bridge or palindromic form) multi-movement compositions from String Quartet no. 4 onward, he explored several ideas and step by step developed his concept (see Fig. 18). The sequence and shape of the themes in the recapitulation, to put it in a clearly simplified way (but after all, precompositional decisions usually are simple and abstract), show a trend to move from the traditional form (i.e., themes in the original shape and order of the exposition, as in String Quartet no. 4, I) toward more twisted schemes. In the next major sonata-form head movement (Piano Concerto no. 2, I) Bartók kept the order of the themes but used inversion; we will soon return to the irregularities and the special function of the "motto" motive.

As a logical next step in Movement I of String Quartet no. 5, the *I* shapes of the themes are recapitulated in a reverse order — probably the most daring concept of a palindromic structure of a sonata-form movement in Bartók's realm. After all, for him a strict *hin und zurück* form — going to-and-fro note by note — in a long piece with strong thematic characters was simply unthinkable. Already the strategy of this opening movement involved danger. If Theme I (mm. 1–14) after a transition (14–24) leads to Theme II (24–44),[60] which leads to Theme III (44–58), as a dramatic

60. Bartók's analysis (*Essays*, 414) calls the transition an "appendix to 1st theme" and the 2nd theme a "transitional section"; as an exception in this case I do not follow Bartók's terms, because the genuinely thematic profile of the *sempre f* music at m. 25 has no transitional character at all.

series of actions, how could the reverse order of these themes be "natural"? To minimize the danger, in this movement Bartók reconsidered the usual dramaturgy of the exposition. Instead of a continuous growth of the musical scenes welded together, here he presented three thematic blocks very different in character, heavily punctuated by fragments of the first theme. Therefore dramatic contrast rather than organic development is the key word, and so the reverse order of the thematic blocks in the recapitulation is less artificial. Nonetheless Bartók badly needed a genuine dramatic development leading to a climax, and easing the tension. In this irregular sonata-form structure he realized this eminently in the development section and the powerful coda — through a very Beethovenian concept.

After the exploration of the three hard-core variant forms Bartók was looking for less systematic, though musically no less fascinating irregular variants. The first one was based on a rhythmic/metric idea: square-meter tense themes in the recapitulation reappear in relaxed, dance-like rolling triple time (*Music for Strings, Percussion, and Celesta,* Mov. II).[61] Incidentally he raised and tested this idea in the first and last movements of a palindromic structure: in the rondo finale of Piano Concerto no. 2, between the 2/4 blocks of the ritornello, the themes from the first movement reappear in triplet motion. (And of course, as a simpler case, in the Violin Concerto 4/4 themes of the first movement come back in 3/4 in Mov. III.)

The other irregular variant of a recapitulation occurs in Movement I of the Violin Concerto. As we have seen, Bartók drafted this recapitulation not without hesitation and correction. The drafts of the four other recapitulations surveyed here, on the contrary, show no significant correction of the overall strategy. Was the case of the Violin Concerto more complex than the others? In a way it was. For instance, the length, the natural beauty, and singing quality of the opening theme were not suited to inversion. Bartók did compose a fanciful piano con calore inversion (mm. 194–203), broken off in the middle of the four-phrase arch of the original theme, soon followed by a piano tranquillo quotation from the original shape in the high octave (213–219), again referring to the beginning of the theme. He had not yet recapitulated the climax of this great violin theme (m. 15). But he would not omit it altogether. Bartók held back the heroic momentum up to the beginning of the coda after the cadenza (mm. 354–359) as if to recapitulate the opening theme. Thus, at least with one theme, he incorporated the reversed-order recapitulation scheme into the narrative of this irregular sonata form.

In the above survey I simplified the case of the opening movement of Piano Concerto no. 2. The primary theme of the piano, together with a countersubject played

61. This technique is not unlike the *proportio* praxis of Baroque dance music, a phenomenon certainly known to Bartók.

EXAMPLE 52   Piano Concerto no. 2, Movement I:
             motivic relationship between three subjects.

EXAMPLE 53   Piano Concerto no. 2, Movement I:
             transformation of the motto theme.

by the woodwinds (mm. 4–24), in fact returns in *I* shape though in fragmentary form only (180–199), foreshadowing the Violin Concerto. But the second theme (the piano figuration and a woodwind motive, mm. 32–57), returns in a combined *I* & *O*-shape form (mm. 200–211), again reminding us of the Violin Concerto's form. The sonata-form structure, however, is ingeniously combined with a rondo-like superstructure,[62] a typical Bartókian idea. The quasi ritornello is the short trumpet theme (see the *O* shape in Ex. 53), the first six notes of which are a quotation of a Stravinsky theme from the *Firebird*, which Bartók believed to be an original folksong. The organic motivic connection between this theme — I will call it "motto" — and the piano primary theme on the one hand (see Ex. 52 bottom staff) and the woodwind countersubject of the piano theme on the other (top staff), is obvious, as is its intricate rhythmic interaction.

The short motto theme offered Bartók more than two shapes (*O* & *I*). As a matter of fact, one of his inspirations was the discovery of the otherwise so neutral (emphatically non-Hungarian) theme turning in retrograde inversion into a warm, pathetic Hungarian phrase with the emblematic dotted-rhythm Hungarian cadence. So Bartók could create a well-planned but not mechanical schedule for the develop-

62. According to Bartók's analysis (traditionally printed with serious mistakes, even in the *Essays*; see Somfai, "The Rondo-like Sonata Form Exposition in the First Movement of the Piano Concerto No 2," in *The New Hungarian Quarterly* 22, no. 84 [Winter 1981]), "the exposition of the 1st movement resembles, however, a section of a rondo form."

ment and variation of this motto theme.[63] The steps of the elaboration of the motto are as follows:

(mm. 2–3) the motto as a trumpet solo;

(mm. 25–31) in canon;

(mm. 68–73) canon on descending fifth (end of the exposition);

(mm. 128–135) free melodic variants in the development section;

(mm. 169–179) as a retransition: *I* shape in canon, stretto;

(mm. 182–187) together with the *I*-shape recapitulation of the piano theme: *I* shape in canon;

(mm. 211–221) after the second theme, as a transition to the cadenza: *RI* shape in solo and in dux-comes stretto;

(mm. 222–253) cadenza from *O* and *I* shapes of the motto;

(mm. 285–307) the second half of the coda: *O* and *I* shapes in character variation, mirror canon, leading to a trumpet melody (mm. 295–305) which is the triumphant singing Hungarian-style conclusion of the development of the motto theme.

Thus, in contrast to the *O–I* scheme of other themes in the exposition–recapitulation, the motto theme underwent a transformation of *O, I, RI, I* & *O* shapes. One of the four possible forms (see Ex. 53), the retrograde shape, Bartók rejected. It might have been useful for other composers, but it was simply useless for him: his goal was not the systematic elaboration of the four shapes of a theme. He used the transformation to underline the directionality of dramatic changes in this complex piece — to lead us from the objective outside world into his innermost subjective world, from the neutral contemporary-music form to a more idiomatic version (the *I* shape, with Bartók's favorite polymodal chromaticism; see mm. 174–177), and even further to his Hungarian confession (the *RI* climax on the brass). After all of these, for him the *R* shape had no value. Thus with a typical Bartókian stepping back he ended the movement returning to the *O*- and *I*-shape forms.

Development Section Strategies

Among the intriguing aspects of Bartók's planning a form — making preliminary decisions about the size, contours, arrangement, proportions, and the intended narrative of a longer section of the structure — the development section of sonata-form movements deserves special attention. As a broad generalization we may say that for Bartók the development section, in contrast to the building up of an exposi-

---

63. The existing autograph draft score no longer retains any sign of working on or with this motive at a preliminary stage.

tion or finding the appropriate variant form in the recapitulation, presented fewer problems. Perhaps he visualized this section for himself as a whole in two or three large blocks, coherent in texture and style. These blocks do not necessarily focus on the elaboration of the musical ideas of the exposition but rather on creating vigorous contrasts. In the draft the so-called development section of the sonata form usually occurs in a determined notation with a low rate of conceptual changes. There are returning patterns of variants of the same plan. As a selection I give the simplified description of three significant strategies with a few examples.

The first strategy involves interrupted thematic development with inserted scenes, with traditional elaboration of themes of the exposition at the beginning and the end, but the central part forming a scene (or scenes) highly original in sound and texture. This in a way is an episode interrupting the regular process of the form, even if the new material, as analysis can point out, has motivic connections with themes of the exposition. Two examples:

Sonata for Violin and Piano no. 2 (1922), Movement II
    from no. 19: elaboration of the closing theme of the piano;
    from no. 21: first scene, in "a bit drunk"[64] character;
    from no. 27: second scene, a quasi-bagpipe-music imitation on the violin;[65]
    from no. 29: quotations from Movement I and continuation of the
        traditional elaboration of themes (see Fig. 7 in chapter 4, p. 74).

Sonata for 2 Pianos and Percussion (1937), Movement I[66]
    mm. 133–194: elaboration of the closing theme, the tranquillo theme (from
        m. 161), and the transition (from m. 175);
    mm. 195–261: the central scene, in ternary contours: the first ostinato
        (195–), the fortissimo middle part (217–), and the second ostinato
        (232–);
    mm. 262–273: retransition from material of the primary theme.[67]

The second strategy takes in a two-plus-one part development section with metric/rhythmic elaboration in the first, motivic/melodic elaboration in the second, and contrapuntal texture in the third part (retransition). Two examples:

Piano Sonata (1926), Movement I
    mm. 135–154: rhythmic clockwork motion, based on the polymetric
        composition of six motives of different length; dominating touch:
        staccato–non legato;[68]

64. I refer to no. 2 of *Three Burlesques*, "Kicsit ázottan" [A bit drunk].
65. Bagpipe-music imitation on violin (or on Jew's harp) was a folk-music phenomenon that occupied Bartók throughout his ethnomusicological work (see, e.g., *Maramureş*/1975, 24).
66. Here we survey the development section in the final revised form (see p. 198).
67. See the discussion of the original form of the retransition on pp. 196ff.
68. Details in Somfai/*Piano Year*, 45ff.

mm. 155–175: extending and shortening of phrase length of the second theme, melodic development; dominating touch: tenuto;

mm. 176–186: retransition with fragmentation of the opening theme (*fausse reprise* character), with short stretto of the head motive.

Music for Strings, Percussion, and Celesta (1936), Movement II

mm. 186–242: polymetric clockwork texture combined with the rhythmic variant of the fugue theme of Mov. I; pizzicato, Bartók-pizzicato, secco;

mm. 243–309: new theme (the theme of Mov. IV)[69] with melodic development including extension and shortening of the phrase length, inversion, etc.; pizzicato;

mm. 310–372: retransition, a fugato from the primary theme; legato, con sordino, then senza sordino.

The third strategy concerns a symmetrically outlined development section with a great many variant forms, partly related to our first strategy too. Two significant examples both represent Bartók's tribute to Stravinsky in one way or another:

Piano Concerto no. 1 (1926), Movement I, 4-part development

from no. 19: classical development: elaboration of the scale theme with interruptions (piano cadenzas);

from m. 6 after no. 22: a first ostinato (still interrupted by the piano at the beginning) in a neoclassical style; tempo beginning MM 92, end MM 130;

from no. 29: a second Stravinsky-style ostinato, with accelerando from MM 100 to 160;

from m. 4 before no. 35: continuation of the classical development: contrapuntal, etc., elaboration of the Allegro primary theme with retransition to the recapitulation (no. 39).

Piano Concerto no. 2 (1930–1931), Movement I, 3-part development

mm. 74–118: a Bartókian ostinato in the piano combined with the elaboration of the secondary theme, including a fugato;

mm. 119–135: traditional motivic elaboration of the motto motive and the primary theme;

mm. 136–179: above a Stravinsky-style ostinato, motivic elaboration of the motto and related motives, including Bach-style techniques, stretto, etc.

I stress that these are only simplified descriptions of patterns, observed in a way perhaps not alien to Bartók's planning, although he certainly did not formulate them in technical terms. However, for the study of Bartók's compositional process the

69. In his concise analysis of the form for the W.Ph.V. pocket score edition Bartók found it worth mentioning that in the development section there is "eine Anspielung auf das Hauptthema des IV. Satzes" ("an allusion to the first theme of Movement IV") (see *Essays*, 416).

recognition of such patterns is of considerable importance. Writing the development section of a large sonata-form movement, he experienced more freedom than while working on the exposition or recapitulation. In this section Bartók more easily reached the highest level of individuality, originality, and, we may assume, the pleasure of creation.

Formation of the Coda in Piano Sonata, Movement I

In sonata-form movements as well as in other structures, the end of a piece, the coda of a complex movement used to be a problem zone with Bartók. The Bartók literature has already pointed out that the satisfactory ending of several major works, eminently of the stage works but often the ending of shorter pieces too, entailed difficulty for Bartók. He was satisfied with the third *Bluebeard* ending only;[70] the second ending of *Mandarin* was already printed and the score performed in this form when in 1931 Bartók decided to shape a third end. In several cases he was able to draft almost the whole piece — e.g., a piano piece ("With Drums and Pipes," no. 1 of *Out Doors*, 1926) — in one act, except the end.[71] He could not immediately find either the proper gesture, the ideal length, or just the style of an effective coda. In several other cases he drafted the bare notes of the ending but then began struggling with the performing details — tempo, dynamics, piano texture, orchestration, or proper length — that often led to further insertions or rewriting.

The proportion of revised/rewritten measures for the end of a work (a movement) is considerably higher than for any other section of his forms. It forces us to acknowledge that Bartók was frequently unsure about the ideal ending of his compositions. A critical survey of his basic finale types,[72] his self-chosen limitations, reveals his preference for either a Beethovenian triumphant/exalting finale, or a "brotherhood of nations"-type dance finale, or, as an opposite, a tragic slow ending. The general mood, the character of the coda, the way the piece echoes in the listener's memory when the performance comes to an end shows, contrasted to the music of Stravinsky, a very limited variety of the acceptable endings. First, Bartók was probably conservative in this respect. Second, being such an experienced concert pianist, he probably cared too much about the ending gesture of a new composition as he wanted to be sure that, at least at the end, the message of his new work was fully understood. Thus Bartók changed and corrected, during the primary compositional process and after he had already finished the score, and sometimes presented alternative endings too. Whether this is a weakness of Bartók's music or not, depends on one's personal judgment. However, for the scholar the phenomenon

70. György Kroó, "Data on the Genesis of Duke Bluebeard's Castle," *SM* 1981: 79ff.
71. See the facsimile in Somfai/*Tizennyolc*, 74.
72. Somfai, "'Per finire': Some Aspects of the Finale in Bartók's Cyclic Form," *SM* 1969: 391–408.

gives highly interesting material to study, and for the editor of the critical edition and for the performer it is a challenge.

Here is a survey of the famous cases of variant endings:

(a) = ending(s) rewritten during composition
(b) = alternative endings, printed together
(c) = old vs. new ending, printed in subsequent editions

Duke Bluebeard's Castle (1911)
three forms of the ending (two 1911, one 1917)   (a)

The Wooden Prince (1914–1917)
new ending for the short suite version   (b)

The Miraculous Mandarin (1918–1919)
1/ concert ending (for the concert suite version)   (b)
2/ three forms of the ending of the pantomime, the third written
in 1931   (a)(c)

Violin Rhapsody no. 1 (1928)
1/ original ending (in G):[73] three forms in the manuscript of the
vl.-piano version (two forms in the manuscript of the vl.-orch.
version)   (a)(b)
2/ alternative ending (in E):[74] two forms in the manuscript   (a)
(N.B. only form 1/ in the vlc.-piano version)

Violin Rhapsody no. 2 (1928)
1928 ending (= 1929 UE ed.); several preliminary forms in the
manuscript   (a)
1936 ending (= B&H rev. ed.)   (c)

Violin Concerto (1937/38)
two endings: the first without, the second with vl. solo   (b)

Concerto for Orchestra (1943)
two endings: the first (1943) premiered under Koussevitzky, the
second (1945), the longer form, an optional ending   (b)

In the last part of this chapter, in connection with the reorganization of the form, I will discuss some cases of the variant endings. Here we return to the primary compositional process and Bartók's struggle with the coda gesture of a piece. For practical reasons — because at least one of the autograph manuscripts is available in facsimile edition — I chose as a sample case the coda of Movement I of the Piano Sonata

73. When the two movements are played together.
74. Intended only for the performance of the *Friss* movement alone but generally favored by violinists, including Joseph Szigeti, who recorded the Rhapsody with Bartók in this anachronistic form; see later in this chapter.

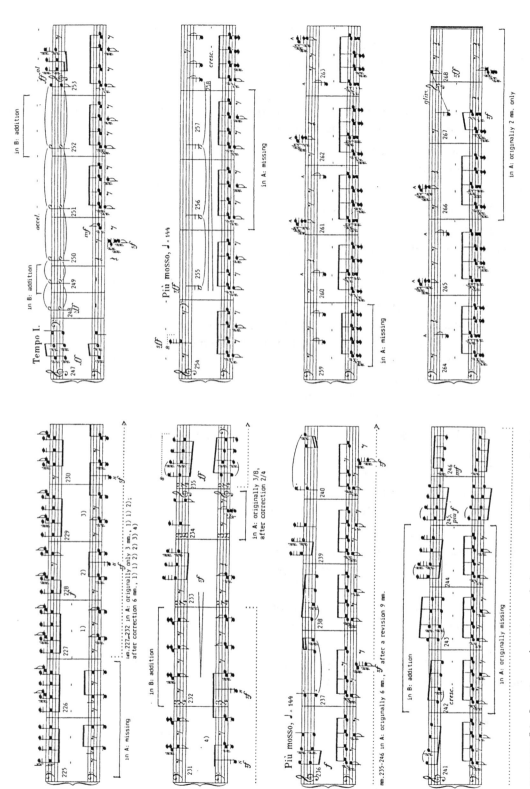

EXAMPLE 54   Insertions and revision on the last two pages of Movement I of the Piano Sonata.

(1926). Ex. 54 presents an annotated version of the last two pages of the final printed form (A = the autograph draft;[75] B = the second draft, the so-called Budapest manuscript [see the 1980 facsimile edition]; brackets refer to insertions, dotted-line brackets to revised/rewritten measures).

The gradual lengthening of the music is quite obvious. The 44 measures on these two printed pages can be seen as four distinct sections:

mm. 225–232 (= 8): the crescendo ostinato, leading to
mm. 233–246 (= 14): the closing theme, from the 4th measure onward Più mosso, leading to
mm. 247–254 (= 8): the fortissimo cadence and the accelerando, leading to
mm. 255–268 (= 14): the Più mosso closing ostinato.

The length of these four sections in the two autograph drafts, considering the original layer as well as the corrected form, is as follows:

A	original layer	$4 + 7 + 4 + 10 = 25$
	after correction	$6 + 11 + 6 + 11 = 34$
B	original layer	$7 + 11 + 6 + 14 = 38$
	after correction	$8 + 14 + 8 + 14 = 44$

Looking behind the bare numbers of the measures, we note that the changes and corrections differ considerably in type and importance. Some belong to the final refinement of, as we may call it, the pianist's agogics in an effective performance: for example, the elongation of the *sff* beat (m. 248) by the addition of one tied measure (m. 249 in B; see Bartók's typical insertion in the facsimile edition), or the insertion of one additional measure of repetition soon after this place (m. 252). The prolongation of an ostinato motion in diminuendo (mm. 256–257) or crescendo (m. 259) in some cases is still primarily a change for performance and not for structural reasons. Although the strongly, repeatedly revised first crescendo (mm. 225–232), with the shortening phrases of the right-hand hammering and the built-in brake of a 3/4 measure, belongs to the correction of the middle-ground articulation of the form.

Crucial revision occurred, by contrast, in the closing-theme area (mm. 233ff.). Bartók's first idea was, if we read the rather confusing notation of source A properly, a very dynamic motion in changing meter — astonishing in the metric context of Movement I (Ex. 55). The second version, still in manuscript A, restored the steady 2/4 beat, and returned to a recognizable form of the closing theme (Ex. 56), which Bartók took over into manuscript B too except that in manuscript B he returned to the 3/8 form of m. 234. In a next step he inserted mm. 242–244, added not only slurs and dynamics but (in manuscript B only, with pencil) the somewhat strange Più

75. PB 55PS1.

EXAMPLE 55   Piano Sonata, Movement I: the first version of mm. 233ff.

EXAMPLE 56   Piano Sonata, Movement I: the second version of mm. 233ff.

mosso in m. 236 as well, to the second bar of a 3-measure phrase-structure theme, thus giving an upbeat-downbeat-like 1 + 2 swing to the otherwise Hungarian-style music. Compared to Bartók's first idea, this is indeed a significant change. Curiously enough even so the whole closing theme area is still the relatively weak spot of the movement, as many live and recorded performances of the Sonata seem to prove; pianists usually struggle to find a convincing interpretation of the abrupt Più mosso gear shift.

As to the very end of the Piano Sonata, the last three measures of the final form originally were only two (Ex. 57), which Bartók corrected during the primary writing. In the light of other small changes of length, this might be considered as a minor correction similar to those that refine the agogics, the gesture, or the proper length of an ostinato-like motion. The three-and-a-half octave glissando cannot be executed properly within an eighth note value; thus Bartók allowed more time for it. But a close look at the rhythmic/metric composition of the Più mosso last measures reveals this to be a conceptual correction as well. Ex. 58 summarizes the rhythmic action according to the final form, considering the rhythm of the left-hand chords, the right-hand jumps upward and downward, and the additional accent signs. I marked the beginning of the "meter-breaking 3 + 3 + 2" cycle (as I call it),[76] a rhythmic phenomenon that, similar to the role of hemiola in 3/4 time in Baroque music or works by Mozart or Brahms, was Bartók's favorite means to break the steady pulsation of 2/4 time and so prepare a cadence. The 3 + 3 + 2 cycle — following the syncopation of the previous measures — starts on the second eighth, shifting the beat. Two such 3 + 3 + 2 cycles make up a phrase (in mm. 260^2–264^1); a second phrase also starts, but Bartók disrupts it with a 4-eighth subphrase and a 3-eighth glissando, arriving at the final super-beat a fraction of a second early but on

76. See Somfai/*Piano Year*, 23ff.

EXAMPLE 57 Piano Sonata, Movement I: two versions of the ending.

EXAMPLE 58 Piano Sonata, Movement I: the rhythmic action of the ending.

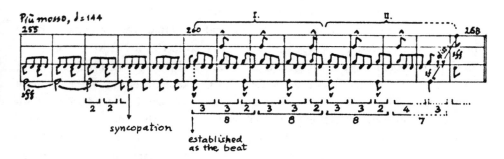

the beat of 2/4 time again, with an impatient and triumphant gesture. The creator deactivated the man-made machine. Supposing that such a rhythmic gesture was indeed Bartók's intention, the original version was too short, abrupt; its effect was weak — it had to be corrected.

Draft Complex of Piano Pieces from 1926

The first draft of the Piano Sonata 1926 belongs to an autograph draft complex, a special phenomenon: piano pieces that later became movements of two sets — the Sonata and *Out Doors* — here appear in a yet undecided order, as if in the haste of inspiration and search for piano concerto ideas Bartók wrote down solo piano pieces without a settled concept of their final arrangement. The phenomenon is not unparalleled. In 1908–1910 he wrote piano pieces without set plans for their final cyclic arrangement.[77] In 1915 he wrote the three piano sets based on Rumanian folk songs and dances (*Christmas Songs, Rumanian Dances,* Sonatina) on pages of another draft complex. (Larger volumes of folksong arrangements in general matured in one draft complex for a while, as *For Children, Fifteen Hungarian Peasant Songs,* 44 Duos.) And of course *Mikrokosmos* is a chief example of composition in a draft complex through several years, although here only the number of the pieces and the sequence was an open question but not their belonging together.

77. E.g., BB 50, 54 and 58 in the list of sources.

The connection between the 1926 draft complex and Piano Concerto no. 1, the central composition of the year 1926, is extremely complex. In addition to the general approach of building up a percussive new piano style for solo and concerto alike, there are such hidden links as key and meter. Movements I and III of Piano Concerto no. 1 are in E, either in dominating 2/4 time or a mixture of 2/4 and changing meter. Movements I and III of the Piano Sonata are also in E, one in 2/4 and the other in changing meter; in addition, no. 1 of *Out Doors* ("With Drums and Pipes") is also in E and 2/4 time.

Now turning to the draft complex, we notice that in the final form the two sets are considerably different in style and structural concept. The Piano Sonata is a genuine sonata with a sonata-form head movement, and a complex monothematic rondo finale — originally much too long, so Bartók decided to cut out its longest episode, which he rewrote in turn as an independent piece and used in the other set (no. 3, "Musettes").[78] The pieces collected in *Out Doors* he kept either in a simpler ternary form (nos. 1–2) or in a more complex but not sonata-form-like structure (nos. 4–5).[79] This, however, reflects only the final distribution of the piano pieces. Can we reconstruct the actual sequence of the composition of the seven movements and thus understand the creative process? Can we fix the approximate date of these pieces within the month of June 1926 when they were composed?

The exact reconstruction is practically impossible and this fact alone throws light on the complexity of Bartók's working method. The documents to consider are the following:

(1) Four undated sketches: (a) the themes of Movement I of the Piano Sonata (see Ex. 8 in chapter 4); (b) themes for Movement III of the Sonata (see Facsimile 5, also in chapter 4, p. 49) — N.B. (a) and (b) are together with unused sketches, all in connection with the piano concerto plans; (c) a sketchy fragmentary draft of no. 1 of *Out Doors* together with a short sketch to no. 2 of *Out Doors*;[80] (d) a partial sketch of no. 4 of *Out Doors*. The sequence of these four items is uncertain but (c) was probably written on June 1; see below.

(2) The autograph draft complex,[81] containing the seven movements, written on 20-staff Eberle paper in three units; see (A)(B)(C) in Fig. 19. Without any date on them, the chronological sequence of these three units cannot be decided. It might be useful to note that both (B) and (C) have blank page at the end, thus Bartók could have written the beginning of the Sonata's Movement I after the draft of Movement II, if he had not already drafted it on another bifolio. It is a fact, however, that nos. 1–2 of *Out Doors* and Movements III and II of the Sonata were written in this order and that nos. 4–5 of *Out Doors* were also drafted together, whereas the Sonata's

78. See the facsimile edition of the Sonata MS (with the commentaries) and Somfai/*Influence*, 546ff. and Fig. 1.
79. About the form and/or narrative of these two pieces see Somfai/*Piano Year*, 5–17.
80. See the facsimile of (c) in Somfai/*Tizennyolc*, 73–74.
81. PB 55–56PS1.

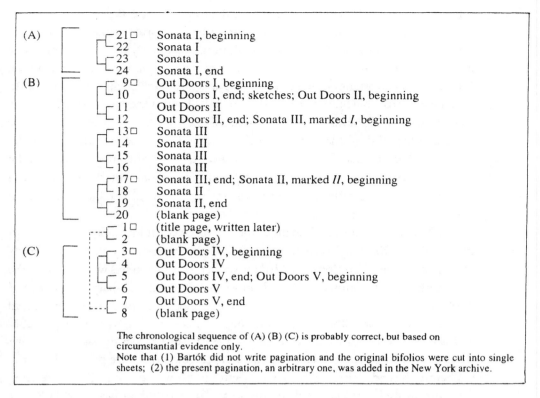

(A)		21 □	Sonata I, beginning
		22	Sonata I
		23	Sonata I
		24	Sonata I, end
(B)		9 □	Out Doors I, beginning
		10	Out Doors I, end; sketches; Out Doors II, beginning
		11	Out Doors II
		12	Out Doors II, end; Sonata III, marked *I*, beginning
		13 □	Sonata III
		14	Sonata III
		15	Sonata III
		16	Sonata III
		17 □	Sonata III, end; Sonata II, marked *II*, beginning
		18	Sonata II
		19	Sonata II, end
		20	(blank page)
		1 □	(title page, written later)
		2	(blank page)
(C)		3 □	Out Doors IV, beginning
		4	Out Doors IV
		5	Out Doors IV, end; Out Doors V, beginning
		6	Out Doors V
		7	Out Doors V, end
		8	(blank page)

The chronological sequence of (A) (B) (C) is probably correct, but based on circumstantial evidence only.

Note that (1) Bartók did not write pagination and the original bifolios were cut into single sheets; (2) the present pagination, an arbitrary one, was added in the New York archive.

FIGURE 19   Paper structure of the 1926 draft complex containing Piano Sonata and *Out Doors*.

Movement I was written on an independent bifolio. A further interesting fact is that at a certain point Bartók added Roman numeral *I* (for Mov. I?) to the draft of the present finale of the Sonata[82] and marked the second movement as *II*,[83] perhaps as a temporary plan of movements I–II of a set, not necessarily a Sonata yet.

(3) Two references in Bartók's letters in June 1926 written to his wife Ditta in Hungarian, with partly identifiable hints, the first in his letter of June 17: "So far I started to make some 5 piano pieces, 2 are finished already, the rest — we will see. What I send here is the thing which I began on June 1. Right at that time I wrote this sketch: can you find your way in it? At present this is in progress, perhaps I finish it by tomorrow." The folded music paper was the fragment of no. 1 of *Out Doors* plus the sketch of no. 2, (c) above in paragraph (1). The second hint comes in the famous letter of June 21 about his feverish work (quoted on p. 11): "Now here I write down a little oddity," and Bartók, on hand-ruled staves, quoted 9 measures from Movement III of the Sonata with the title "Musette," still in the original

82. On the top of p. 14, the third page of the draft of the movement; there seems to be no explanation why this number is not on p. 12.

83. On p. 17 above the bottom brace in which the draft of Mov. II starts.

form.[84] From these hints we conclude that the fragment plus sketch of nos. 1–2 of *Out Doors* had been done on June 1; on June 17 Bartók started to elaborate no. 1 (as we guess, writing the draft described above) but had already drafted two pieces or movements (nos. 4–5 of *Out Doors*, the only two-piece unit of the draft?); and on June 21 he was working on an episode of what is now Movement III of the Sonata (i.e., he had probably finished the draft of nos. 1–2 and started to work on the next piece in unit B of the draft between June 17–21). Note that these pieces make altogether five. If the Sonata finale was also among the five pieces mentioned in the first letter, Movements II and I of the Sonata were the latest compositions. But the sketch of Movement I—the sonata-form head movement—could also have been one of the five pieces Bartók referred to; in this case considerable time elapsed between sketch and draft.[85]

(4) The second autograph manuscript—a mixed-form manuscript, already furnished with performing instructions but full of corrections, not yet a fair copy ready to send to Universal Edition—divided the seven pieces in two sets without titles: the 11-page Budapest manuscript of the Piano Sonata[86] and the 11-page manuscript of the 4-movement form of the later *Out Doors* set[87] (nos. 1–2 and 4–5 here numbered I–II–III and the last without number). The two manuscripts were written probably in this sequence, because both are on 20-st. Eberle paper except the last bifolio with the end of "The Chase," which is on 16-st. paper. And both were presumably written before the end of June. (Cf. Bartók's letter to his wife on June 28, announcing that on June 30 he would travel and meet her: "A vast amount has to be written: I must copy 13 pages of music till Wednesday evening, or perhaps even more.") The date on the printed edition of the two works gives little new information. At the end of the Sonata: *Dittának, Budapesten, 1926.jun.*; at the end of the one-volume original edition of *Out Doors: Budapest, 1926.VI.VIII*, August being the date of the revision of the Sonata finale and thus the elaboration of the independent form of "Musettes."

Thus the exact chronology of the group composition could not be reconstructed. Bartók's creativity seems to have been warmed up by an intensive period of improvisation, with some memo sketches. Then in mid June he began writing the full draft of seven pieces, partly as pairs of movements (as they are in the final set too), partly as yet undecided movements of further sets. By the end of June the Piano Sonata and the urform of *Out Doors* were copied (= the second draft). Maybe a few

84. See the facsimile in Bartók/*Családi levelek*, 382.
85. Iván Waldbauer, who worked on the micro-chronology of this draft complex for a planned facsimile edition, believes that Mov. I of the Sonata forms the latest part of the manuscript. Based on a close look at the original MS I suggest, as Fig. 19 indicates, that pp. 21–24 of the manuscript (remember that the pagination has nothing to do with Bartók!) actually form the oldest part of the MS.
86. When in 1928 the Magyar Nemzeti Múzeum [Hungarian National Museum], whose library later became independent as the Széchényi National Library, asked Bartók to present a manuscript to the national collection, Bartók selected this MS of the Sonata as a representative item.
87. PB 56PFC1.

more pieces were also sketched/drafted with them (on 16-st. paper, soon incorporated into *Nine Little Piano Pieces* or put aside and used later in *Mikrokosmos*).[88]

Corrections in the Draft of String Quartet no. 6, Movements III & I, and String Quartet no. 5, Movements III & II

As a special subject of the study of the formation of a work, I would like to draw attention to certain types of corrections in Bartók's drafts that may have a sobering effect on the stereotyped use of established analytical approaches. We have already seen examples of considerable reshaping of *meter* and *rhythm*, often connected with the revision of phrase length too. Here follow a few thought-provoking examples of reshaping the pitch content and the melody.

First discourse: *Pitch* and tonal relationship of successive ideas. The point at issue here is not the change of single notes, notes in a chord, notes in a contrapuntal texture, and so on — hundreds of such changes occur in Bartók's drafts — but a special phenomenon: the shift of a section to another pitch level without modulatory corrections, as if the first and the revised pitch levels had represented substitute versions in a broader context, although the new one was beyond doubt an improved version of course. Or else the exact pitch of certain gestures in a complex piece was of secondary importance for Bartók.

To illustrate this phenomenon I take very simple examples from one score, the draft of String Quartet no. 6,[89] and only corrections indicated by (Hungarian) words or phrases in the autograph. The case of the second measure of the "Burletta" (III, m. 22; see Ex. 59) sets out the phenomenon. Between two statements of the opening burletta head-motive (III, mm. 21, 23) in F, which is the key of Movement III, as a second thought Bartók shifted the Db–Eb "whoop" motive a fourth up. In respect to the pitch content we can analyze this shift in different ways, but the likeliest Bartókian motivation may have been that in this context Gb/Ab sounds more tense. Besides after the F major chord Bartók preferred the emphasis on the minor third rather than the original form. The fourth measure (see the second half of Ex. 59) in the original form used Ab repercussion in vl. 2 with F# in the viola, that is, the pitches of the corrected second measure. Bartók had intended to transpose it a fifth up, keeping the vl. 2 unchanged, but on reflection rewrote the three lower parts.

88. In the first draft (PB 57PS1) eight of the nine pieces (without no. 8, and no. 9 still as a sketch) plus sketches for *Mikrokosmos* no. 146 ("Ostinato") and no. 137 ("Unison") can be found. In the second draft (57PID1) the nine pieces plus *Mikrokosmos* no. 81 ("Wandering") were written down in an intermediate sequence, joining the following pieces though (i.e., on the same page: end of the one and the beginning of the other): nos. 1 and 9; nos. 7–3–2–4; nos. 6–5; *Mikrokosmos* no. 81 and no. 8 of the *Nine Little Piano Pieces*.
89. PB 79FSS1.

EXAMPLE 59   String Quartet no. 6, Movement III: transposition in the draft.

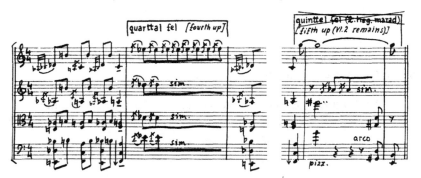

Soon after these corrections, a longer tonal shift occurs in the draft. The passage from m. 33 to the first note in m. 41, otherwise exactly the same as we know it now, was originally written a tone lower (by the way, vl. 2 in m. 33 not with flats but with sharps). Bartók had already passed this point in writing the draft when he reconsidered the whole progression and simply shifted eight measures without correcting the connecting measure. He just made a note for himself: *egész hanggal fel egészen $-ig* [one whole tone up till $].

A chain of similar corrections occurs in String Quartet no. 6 Movement I, mm. 126–143, where the growing tension of the canon-motion sequence leads to the Tempo I climax (m. 137) followed by the calming down. In the original layer of the draft the climax had been prepared by 9 measures (as opposed to the 11 in the final form), starting on B♭ (high D in the final form). Here Bartók made more than one note for himself: *innen egész hanggal feljebb* [from here one tone up], *még egyszer feljebb* [once more up], *nagy terccel feljebb* [major third up]. A common feature of this correction with those in Movement III is that the direct continuation — the actual end of the sonata-form exposition closing in F — could after the shifted section remain in the original key.

Another fascinating tonal shift takes place in the draft of the present finale of Piano Sonata 1926. In the first sketch (see staves 9–10 on Facsimile 5 in chapter 4, p. 49) the movement in E started on E in the right hand, leading to A above a D fourth chord. In the first draft[90] Bartók began to elaborate the same form. He had already written down 38 measures when he recognized being in the "wrong key": in D instead of E. So he crossed the last measures out, continued the draft one tone higher and in the next manuscript (in the so-called Budapest manuscript) the finale already starts with F♯ in the right hand leading to a cadence in E.[91]

90. On p. 12 of PB55PS1.
91. About the tonal "shift" in this folksong-like theme see Somfai/*Influence*, 546–547 and Ex. 1.

Second discourse: *Pitch* and the tonal relationship of simultaneous ideas. There are ample examples in Bartók's drafts confirming the fact that for him, at least in certain contexts, the leading voice (the theme) and the texture around it (the chords, the counterpoint, etc.) were not equally important, did not get equal treatment. A theme could eventually combine with considerably different textures or harmonies. A remarkable case is that of the urform of the Trio in Movement III (Scherzo Alla bulgarese) of String Quartet no. 5. The draft[92] on two crossed-out pages (pp. 18 and 67 in the arbitrary pagination of the manuscript) contains some 49 measures, including the $3+2+2+3/8$ violin motive (see m. 1 in Ex. 60) also known from the printed version, and the pizzicato motive (m. 3), but with a different melody. Disregarding the question of the basic key of the Trio — G in the urform, F in the printed form[93] — the urform actually has two versions: as Bartók wrote it down first (with immediate changes such as transferring the beginning of entries: mm. 3 and 31; correcting the melody: m. 23; cutting: mm. 17 and 19 respectively), and as he rearranged the harmonic context with verbal references to transposition: *½ hanggal lejjebb* [semitone down], *1 hanggal lejjebb* [one tone down], *kis terccel lejjebb* [minor third down], *nagy terccel lejjebb* [major third down], etc., *innen rendesen* [from here properly (i.e., as written)]. N.B. the word *sokszor* [many times] is a shorthand note for a later decision of the actual length of the crescendo-diminuendo swell formed from the music of m. 42.

Summarizing the differences between the two urform versions (Ex. 61), we can state: according to the original intention there was an immobile harmonic background (staves 2 & 3) of the D^3–G^2 fifth, filled chromatically by the violin motive, which was extended downward by adding G^2–C^2 (inverted motive), F^1–B♭ (inverted motive), and finally C^2–F^1 (original). In the revised version (now read staff 3 together with staff 1) Bartók adopted the concept of a mobile chord mixture. The two versions produce very different effects. The immobile background is unquestionably stiff but leads to considerable tension between melody and harmony. The mixture motion of the chord in the second version builds up tonal connection between the tune and the accompaniment, although the outcome is not very exciting.

A comparison with the printed version gives us insight into the further development of the concept. Bartók maintained the idea of transposing the violin motive as the main carrier of the background harmony but instead of a descending-ascending pattern now he preferred gradual rise with tritone motives between the regular ones

92. PB 71FSS1.

93. Bartók's analysis (sketchy draft in French and German versions, both in a diplomatic transcription in *BBI/1*, 217–222; English translation from the German version in *Essays*, 414–415) designates the key of the Scherzo as C♯ and the key of the Trio as E (the latter only in the German version). With all due respect to his text (if E is not a simple misprint for F), I still think that F is the key of the Trio that is clearly presented at the beginning (mm. 1–10) and at the end (the viola figures in mm. 54–65).

EXAMPLE 60   String Quartet no. 5, Movement III: the original form of the Trio.

EXAMPLE 61   String Quartet no. 5, Movement III: the revision
of the harmonic background in the original form of the Trio.

EXAMPLE 62   String Quartet no. 5,
Movement III, Trio: the harmonic
background in the final form.

with a fifth frame (Ex. 62), reserving the inverted motives until the final extension of the fifth.

It is, however, more important that Bartók invented a new *melody* too. What makes the theme of the final version of the Trio better than the theme of the urform? After all both have a similar rhythmic drive (which, although written in a so-called Bulgarian meter, actually is an agitating Hungarian rubato with a bit longer and shorter syllables); both unfold in a rough three-part form that resembles three stanzas, some of them very much like Bartókian folksong stanzas indeed. Is the melodic line of the new version more original? has it a better balance? does it include more of the ingredients of Bartók's style? We must ask ourselves whether questions,

EXAMPLE 63   String Quartet no. 5, Movement III, Trio: the "melody" in the original form and the
final form.

comparisons, descriptions formulated according to established style-analytical methods would in this case be illuminating on their own.

Based not only on a careful comparison of the two Bartók themes (Ex. 63) but on
a study of similar revisions of the thematic material in other drafts too, I strongly
believe that it was the miniature narrative of the three stanzas in the urform that, at a
second thought, worried Bartók most. The first and the second stanza had solid
tonal framework with a somewhat unclear and irregular "3-line structure" (a term of
the folklorist Bartók), whereas the third stanza arrived to a clear-cut "4-line" (i.e.,
regular) folksong-like form. But this third stanza was not the result of a folk-music-
like "evolution," for instance from an archaic type to a new-style melody: it is just a
more melodious tune than the ones before. The narrative of the printed version is
more like Bartók's normal procedure. A coherent 4-line stanza is the first, followed
by a freer stanza-like formation that gets louder and decomposed, then falls apart
totally — all together a miniature drama leading from a lyric song to a Bartókian
explosion.

Reshaping the melody to a lesser degree was a usual procedure in Bartók's drafts.
A typical example is the formation of the melodic countersubject to the quasi-choral
chordal progression in Movement II of String Quartet no. 5 (see Facsimile 35,

EXAMPLE 64 String Quartet no. 5, Movement II: the correction of
mm. 46ff.

braces 2–3, on p. 135). Of the six short phrases of vl. 1, compared to the printed score, phrases 2–3 and 5 needed no correction: these perfectly fitted Bartók's favorite procedure of a *komplementär* melody. The fourth phrase (D–B♭–B♮–F♯–G♯) he replaced by a slightly changed shape keeping the peak tone for the next phrase and correcting the orthography (B♮–B♭–B♮–G♭–A♭). The sixth phrase — originally two phrases in the draft — needed condensation and correction: a reshaping of the original triads at the end of the melody besides the correction of the chordal cadence. Interesting is the case of the first phrase. Bartók as a first thought wrote D♭–E♭–F–F♯–C, which happens to be the final version, but next he tried out F♯–D♭–E♭–B♭–C as an alternative. The pitch content of the two are basically the same for Bartók. Why did he delete the second version? We can only assume that the second sounded static as an opening phrase, whereas the original version ignited a set of similar but varied motives in a rising pattern from D♭, E, F, building up the climax of the melody.

Incidentally, the extremely condensed recapitulation of the chorale in Movement II (mm. 46ff.), with the hesitant, isolated beautiful B♭ and high A♭ tenuto tones substituting for a whole melody, is also a corrected version. Bartók immediately found the form of the condensed chord progression, but the memories of the melody, as he first formulated it (Ex. 64), had a distinct Hungarian style with dotted rhythm and special ornamental figures. The con sordino and tenuto sublime form was Bartók's second thought.

REORGANIZATION OF THE FORM

Major changes or cuts powerful enough to affect the form as a whole or at least the character of the conclusion of the work occur only in a relatively small number of Bartók's compositions. However, they are connected with various stages of the formation:

in the primary act of writing the draft (see, e.g., below, the case of the Alla
bulgarese Scherzo in String Quartet no. 5);

before the finalization of the form (e.g., the rewritten finale of the Piano
Sonata; Three Rondos no. 2; discarded movements in the *Rumanian Folk
Dances*, Suite op. 14, *Fifteen Hungarian Peasant Songs, Dance Suite*; new
endings for Violin Rhapsody no. 1 and Violin Concerto);

before the printing of the already premiered final form (new retransition for
Movement I of Sonata for two Pianos and Percussion; variant endings for
Concerto for Orchestra, etc.);

after the publication of a first printed form (in addition to the new version of
For Children, etc., the new ending for the *Mandarin*; Suite no. 2 in two
subsequent revisions; Seconda parte of Violin Rhapsody no. 2).

String Quartet no. 5, Scherzo

Movement III of String Quartet no. 5 seems to be a seminal case, an introduction to
the discussion of selected examples, because the revision fundamentally changed the
original structure and concept. (See Fig. 20; note that the pagination is arbitrary
and extremely confusing and that therefore I have had to reconstruct the paper
structure of this part of the manuscript.) On six pages of the rough manuscript
Bartók drafted the first version of the complete Scherzo and Trio plus 36 measures of
the Scherzo da capo, before he broke off the composition. As a second attempt,
mostly on fresh sheets of paper (only keeping 17 measures from the end of the
Scherzo on p. 18), he rewrote the movement according to a revised concept of the
form. To help readers follow the changes, I have labeled the thematic material as
Theme I (from m. 3 in the printed score), Theme IIA (mm. 24ff.), IIB (mm.
30ff.), and IIC (mm. 36ff.). Bartók composed these themes more or less in the
spirit of folk music — only the rhythm, by the way, is in Bulgarian style. The first
theme has the least direct connection with actual folk music: while the quasi four-
line stanza structure with a melodic arch is folk-like, sublime Bartókian originality
emerges in the pitch content and the triadic arpeggiando of the leading voice as well
as the contrapuntal nature of mm. 2, 4, 6 (and so on) in the countersubject. Yet
Themes IIA and IIB are striking dance tunes, three-measure outbursts in a rustic
peasant-fiddler-style ending on a long note, interwoven with motives of Theme I
throughout. Theme IIC, played by the cello, has a motivic drive not unlike that of
instrumental improvisation in folk music.

The reorganization of Movement III's scherzo form (Fig. 21) seems to be closely
connected with the conceptual question of how the original forms (*O*) of the
themes and their inversions (*I*) could build up an effective dramaturgy in the first
Scherzo and its varied restatement in the Scherzo da capo. The deleted first page of
the first version (Facsimile 41, p. 141) shows that the *O* form of Theme I was

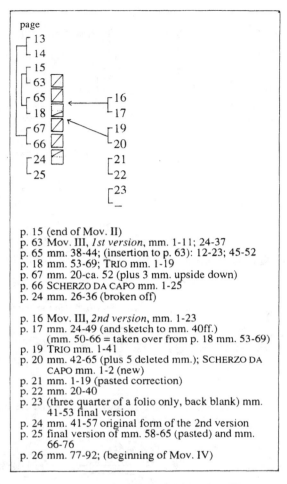

page

- 13
- 14
- 15
- 63
- 65 → 16
- 18 17
- 67 19
- 66 20
- 24 21
- 25 22
   23

p. 15 (end of Mov. II)
p. 63 Mov. III, *1st version*, mm. 1-11; 24-37
p. 65 mm. 38-44; (insertion to p. 63): 12-23; 45-52
p. 18 mm. 53-69; TRIO mm. 1-19
p. 67 mm. 20-ca. 52 (plus 3 mm. upside down)
p. 66 SCHERZO DA CAPO mm. 1-25
p. 24 mm. 26-36 (broken off)

p. 16 Mov. III, *2nd version*, mm. 1-23
p. 17 mm. 24-49 (and sketch to mm. 40ff.)
      (mm. 50-66 = taken over from p. 18 mm. 53-69)
p. 19 TRIO mm. 1-41
p. 20 mm. 42-65 (plus 5 deleted mm.); SCHERZO DA
      CAPO mm. 1-2 (new)
p. 21 mm. 1-19 (pasted correction)
p. 22 mm. 20-40
p. 23 (three quarter of a folio only, back blank) mm.
      41-53 final version
p. 24 mm. 41-57 original form of the 2nd version
p. 25 final version of mm. 58-65 (pasted) and mm.
      66-76
p. 26 mm. 77-92; (beginning of Mov. IV)

FIGURE 20   String Quartet no. 5, Movement III:
            distribution of the two versions on the pages
            of the draft.

directly followed by the *O* form of Theme IIA and a later discarded *I* form of it.
Bartók continued with Theme IIB (bottom of the page) and wrote a few measures
on the top of the next page when he interrupted the notation and — as a second
thought, an insertion to the place marked with a crossed circle on the first page —
added the *I* form of Theme I. After the *O* + *I* of Theme I and *O* + *I* of Theme IIA,
however, the continuation was different. Instead of an *I* form of Theme IIB Bartók
used a melodic variant (Theme IIB^var; see Ex. 65) and ended the Scherzo with a
rephrased version of Theme I that in itself presented *O* and *I* (convex- and concave-
curving) phrases in alternation (see Ex. 66). Note that the opening form in mm. 3ff.
already contained the germ of the inversion in the form of the fourth phrase, i.e., the

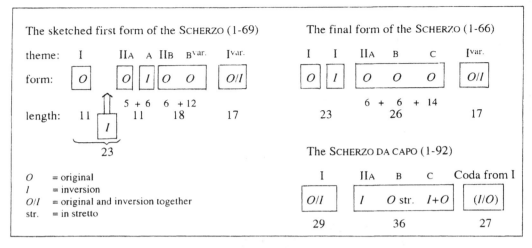

The sketched first form of the SCHERZO (1-69)   The final form of the SCHERZO (1-66)

theme: I   IIA   A   IIB   B^var.   I^var.   I   I   IIA   B   C   I^var.

form: | *O* | | *O*   *I*   *O*   *O* | | *O/I* | | *O* | | *I* | | *O*   *O*   *O* | | *O/I* |

                         5 + 6   6 + 12   6 + 6 + 14

length: 11   11   18   17   23   26   17

           | *I* |

              23

The SCHERZO DA CAPO (1-92)

O   = original   I   IIA   B   C   Coda from I
I   = inversion
O/I   = original and inversion together | *O/I* | | *I*   *O* str.   *I+O* | | *(I/O)* |
str.   = in stretto

                                      29   36   27

FIGURE 21   String Quartet no. 5, Movement III: survey of the form of the Scherzo.

EXAMPLE 65   String Quartet no. 5, Movement III: Theme IIB^var in the first form of the Scherzo.

EXAMPLE 66   String Quartet no. 5, Movement III: convex- and concave-curving phrases of the theme in mm. 3ff. and 50ff.

EXAMPLE 67   String Quartet no. 5, Movement III: versions of Theme IIA.

O–O–O–I-phrased opening theme got an *O–I–O–I*-variant form at the end, which also entailed significant changes in the pitch content.

Such inconsistencies in the thematic process as the discontinuation of the *O + I* principle with Theme IIB (see Fig. 21) must have been all too obvious to Bartók. He must have felt, moreover, that the *I* form of so natural a Hungarian folk-dance-style melody as Theme IIA in the first version (top line in Ex. 67) was artificial or at least a bit strange in context.[94] Nevertheless it was not until he got entangled in the excessively extended recapitulation of Theme I in the Scherzo da capo (using *O-* and *I*-shape phrases successively, combined with imitation and stretto textures) that Bartók broke off the notation and decided to revise the first Scherzo. He kept the *O* and *I* stanzas of the primary theme but discarded the original *I* form of Theme IIA, and for the IIB[var] cello theme he substituted another cello theme (IIC) that made similar gestures. As a result the final version of the Scherzo gained a well-proportioned (23 + 26 + 17) ternary form with piano–forte–piano contours, and Bartók still had the option of a considerably varied form for the Scherzo da capo.

In the da capo he maintained the *O/I* combination form of the primary theme (though not without significant corrections pasted over the original layer of the notation of the 2nd version). The da capo of the forte middle part offers three different variation techniques for the three thematic constituents (Themes IIA–B–C): inversion in the case of IIA but enlarged into an arch form resembling a stanza of new-style Hungarian folk music[95] (see the bottom line in Ex. 67); a compact stretto for IIB; and a slightly varied version of IIC first in inversion, then in its original form. The stretto combination of IIB and IIC in Agitato leads to the coda containing the essence of Theme I, *I*- and *O*-shape phrases alike. This is altogether a masterpiece of Bartókian *veränderte Reprise* combining systematic thinking in the planning phase with a strong pragmatic/musical control during the actual composition — all in the crucial primary act of writing the rough draft.

Deleted Movements and Episodes

Equally interesting reorganizations could occur during the next stage of the formation of a work, that is, before Bartók finalized the form (wrote the fair copy, or made the orchestration, or revised the copy before sending it to the publisher). An extremely illuminating example is the revision of the finale of Piano Sonata 1926, which can be studied in the facsimile edition of the second autograph manuscript[96]

94. This is not the place to discuss in detail how Bartók's folk-music experience affected his own technique. But anybody familiar with Hungarian folk music recognizes that the exact inversion of the first two measures of theme IIA, which sound very much like a song of the old style with descending fifth structure, is technically possible but strange — to say the least.

95. A A⁵ B A and A A⁵ A⁵ A are common stanza structures of Hungarian folk music; the inversion of Theme IIA in the da capo is certainly closely connected to such an arch form.

96. Ed. by László Somfai (EMB, 1980).

EXAMPLE 68   *Dance Suite*: the theme of the discarded Movement III.

EXAMPLE 69   *Rumanian Folk Dances*: the beginning of the
discarded opening movement.

and which I have discussed in another essay.[97] In the course of shortening a 416-measure monothematic rondo to 281 measures, Bartók sacrificed a planned full "catalogue" of ethnomusicological genres — the piece's "secret program" — for the sake of a more effective and compact form. But as compensation, in the revised version he introduced further, even more sophisticated peasant-music principles into the variation technique.[98]

Another fascinating revision of the original narrative of a major composition occurs in the *Dance Suite* (1923). According to Bartók's text, quoted in chapter 2 (see p. 17), his original concept called for a Slovak piece to be included among the standard national characters. It is missing from the orchestrated final version, but the piano-score-type draft[99] contains it between the present Movements II and III, in the form of a 66-measure movement with an additional Ritornello (10 mm.). This discarded movement is relatively short compared to the neighboring movements (Mov. I: 120 plus 25 mm. Ritornello; Mov. II: 93 plus 19 mm. Ritornello; the present Mov. III: 156 mm.). Moreover, while it may have satisfied the musical criteria — the major mode and later the lydian motives (Ex. 68) — of a quasi Slovak scene as planned, it is a relatively weak piece in context. Bartók removed it, we may assume, for purely musical reasons, rendering the original plan incomplete but improving the composition as a whole.[100]

97. Somfai/*Influence*, 545–555.
98. Bartók turned stanza-form reprises of the theme into an open-form motivic elaboration, one that surprisingly corresponds with the *shifted rhythm* style of motivic variation studied by Bartók in Rumanian peasant-fiddler and bagpipe dances.
99. PB 53PS1.
100. See also Tibor Tallián, "Quellenschichten der Tanz-Suite Bartóks," *SM* 1983: 211ff.

Considerations of musical quality were apparently the chief reason to discard the first of the original *Rumanian Folk Dances* too (intended to precede the current no. 1). Its autograph is located on p. 5 of the 1915 draft complex of Rumanian arrangements for piano, a manuscript containing the first series of *Rumanian Christmas Songs,* the *Rumanian Folk Dances,* Movements II–III–I of Sonatina, and the second series of *Christmas Songs*, presumably written in this sequence[101] and originally planned for publication more or less as the continuation of *For Children* using Rumanian folk music.[102] The discarded piano arrangement and the one following it (the current no. 1) are dances in the same key (in A); both dances were played in this sequence by the same village gypsies in Mureş, as recorded by Bartók in 1912 on the same cylinder (MF 2040a–b). Based on the 2-violin *învârtita*, an exquisite folklore item (see no. 240 in *RFM*, vol. I), the 26-measure piano arrangement (Ex. 69) is much too close a copy of the original — for which reason, perhaps, Bartók finally decided to leave it out.

Reorganization of a longer set of folksong arrangements, also connected with a draft complex, is represented by the case of *Fifteen Hungarian Peasant Songs* for piano, dated 1914–1918 and printed by UE in 1920. Bartók wrote 24 such arrangements in all, in two distinct groups (see Fig. 22) of which only the nine "Old Dance Tunes" (nos. 7–15) were conceived as a well-planned series. Recent research[103] has disclosed that by 1914 Bartók had already arranged 15 *Ungarische Bauernlieder* (based on 16 pieces) for Rózsavölgyi into a planned volume that could not be realized in the war years. This initial form contained 12 pieces of the final set and had a similar ternary contour: four old sorrowful songs *attacca,* two contrasting pieces, and the *attacca* chain of old dance tunes. When in the late summer of 1918 Bartók felt like writing eight new arrangements based on brand-new items in his collection, he considered three of the eight to be so good that he replaced nos. 1, 5, and 6 of the 1914 set by new pieces for another project (*Fifteen Hungarian Peasant Songs*) for his new publisher (UE in Vienna), including the "Scherzo" and the "Ballade (tema con variazioni)," based on a tune in 7/8 meter. The harmonic language of the 1918 movements is more advanced, but Bartók considered the quality of the music more important than uniformity of style. The nine arrangements from the draft complex left unpublished formed a reserve: in addition to a facsimile reprint of one piece in 1925 (see BB 80a), its revised form and two more tunes were Bartók's contribution to the 1942 "Homage to Paderewski" album (BB 80b *Three Hungarian Folktunes*); the remaining six are still unpublished.

Involving peasant tunes but in a more sophisticated Bartókian structure, the second of the Three Rondos is a fascinating case of reorganization of the form that

101. PB 36–37–38PS1.

102. According to Károly Rozsnyai's letter of April 22, 1915, to Bartók, the composer and his publisher discussed the publication of new Rumanian piano arrangements.

103. Somfai, "Problems of the Chronological Organization of the Béla Bartók Thematic Index in Preparation," *SM* 34: 345–366.

1914 layer

paper	content	note	folksong
1	**7**	**7-15** originally	1907-12
2	**8, 9, 10**	numbered *1-9*	
3	**11, 12**		
4	**13, 14**		
5	**15-**		
6	**-15-**		
7	**-15, +1**	**+1** orig. no. *10*	1912
8	**+2, 4**	**4** orig. no. *4*	1912
9	**I, +3, 2-**	**I** orig. no. *4* then *I*	1914
10	**-2**	**+3** = no. *6*, **2** = no. *2*	
17	**3**		1914
–	(blank page)		

1918 layer

paper	content	folksong
11	**II, 5-**	1918
12	**-5, 1-**	1918
13	**-1, +4**	1918
14	**III**	1918
15	**6-**	1918
16	**-6, +5, +6**	1918

The planned 1914 form for Rózsavölgyi, *Ungarische Bauernlieder / Chansons paysannes hongroises* (or *Chants des paysans hongrois*):

> *Régi keserves énekek / Alte Trauenlieder / Vieilles chansons funèbres*: no. 1 "Leszállott a páva" (= **I**), nos. 2-4 (= **2-4**)
> *Ujabb dal / Neuere Melodie / Mélodie nouvelle*: no. 5 "Jó estét, jó estét Csáki bíró lánya" (= **+1**)
> *Játékdal / Spiellied / Chanson de jeu*: no. 6 "Viszik már, viszik már Danikáné lányát" (= **+3**)
> *Régi táncdalok / Tanzlieder / Airs à danser*: nos. 7-15 (= **7-15**)

1, 2, etc. = final no. in *Fifteen Hungarian Peasant Songs*
I, II, III = number in *Three Hungarian Folktunes* (published 1942)
+1, +2, etc. = six unpublished arrangements
no. *1, 2* etc. = original numbering in the 1914 layer

FIGURE 22 *Fifteen Hungarian Peasant Songs* for piano: contents of the two layers of the draft.

would repay detailed analysis.[104] Dating in all probability from 1927, nos. 2–3 of the Rondos testify to Bartók's renewed interest in the symmetrical (palindromic) structure that soon led to the symmetrical multi-movement form of String Quartet no. 4. According to the original draft that the composer presented in December 1943 to his former pupil Wilhelmine Creel,[105] he cast no. I of the two "small rhapsodies"[106] (the present Rondo no. 3) with little hesitation in a perfect symmetrical form with the palindromic key sequence F–C–G; A; G–C–F, based on a simple percussive Bartók motive and two Slovak folksongs. But no. II (the present second Rondo) underwent major changes. In the (deleted) first and in the second

104. The Budapest Bartók Archives contains several documentary essays on the genesis of Rondo no. 2: by Halsey Stevens and Barry Wiener (both unpublished); and by Gábor Kiss (*Magyar Zene* 33, no. 2 [June 1992]: 213–224); here I summarize my own observations.

105. See *BBLevelei*, 698. The MS is now in New York in the Pierpont Morgan Library's R. O. Lehman Deposit.

106. Bartók's Hungarian title on the draft; he premiered the three rondos (Nov. 29, 1927, Budapest, played from MS) as *Három kis rapszódia népdalok fölött* [Three small rhapsodies on folk tunes].

draft, based on three Slovak folksongs (for descriptive purposes I shall call them
A,[107] B, C) and a motivic development of the second tune (b), it had a structure that
was less prominently rondo-like and certainly not palindromic but rather a "small
rhapsody" with the sectional contour A–B–b–B–C–A^var–B–b, starting in the key of
D and ending in the key of A. Only after additions and major cuts, deleting folksong
A entirely, did Bartók arrive at the final form: b–B–b–C–b–B–b (or marking the
motivic framing material as x: x–A–x–B–x–A–x), now both starting and ending in
the key of D. As Bartók wrote to Miss Creel, commenting on the difficult birth of the
piece in typical, laconic fashion: "I had much trouble with the second rondo, I
wanted first to include a 3rd theme which later proved to be impracticable."

A less crucial revision of a no less irregular form based on folklore material took
place between the drafted form and the finalization of the Seconda parte of the
Violin Rhapsody no. 1. In its primary form with the original ending first scored for
violin and piano,[108] it was intended to be a chain form, a series of scenes with dances
without a recapitulation of the opening theme, because the opening "verbunkos"
theme of the *Lassú* first movement was to end the *Friss* movement. (The idea of
returning to the opening theme of the *Friss* arose with the conception of the second
ending only.) In this chain-form Seconda parte a major cut was made: instead of the
two measures before rehearsal no. 12, for a time there had been a 39-measure
Allegretto scherzando grazioso including an additional dance tune (no. 376a in
RFM, vol. I; see Ex. 70).[109] This episode interrupted a more extensive presentation
of the Allegro dance, 22 measures long in the final version (between nos. 10–14 of
the printed score), in D♯ aeolian in piano con sordino, then in B aeolian in forte
senza sordino with harmonics. In the draft the con sordino stanza (at that time in
the key of B) was followed by the pianist's presentation of the theme with *düvő*[110]
double stops in the violin, then the 18 measures of the later discarded scherzando
dance, and a return to the Allegretto theme, first on the piano with pizzicato accom-

107. For the folksong in the deleted parts of the rondo see no. 678 in Bartók/*SP* vol. 2.
108. PB 61VPS1.
109. On pp. 7–9 of the draft.
110. Typical rhythm of accompaniment in Hungarian instrumental folk music with repeated notes
played on string instrument, by giving accent to the 2nd and 4th beats in a 1–2 3–4 two-note bowing.

paniment, and finally on the violin in the version with harmonics. Bartók, after some transposition and revision, included this quite long scene in the fair copy of the violin and piano version, in the orchestrated form, and the violoncello-piano adaptation, with an elaborate tempo scheme: beginning with MM 120 accel. 152; 100 for the Allegretto scherzando; a tempo, accel. 152, Più mosso 160 for the stanza in harmonics. But before the premiere he reconsidered and reorganized the form. Whether it was the excessively varied tempo structure or the musical quality of the scherzando dance or the excessively heavy presence of the piano or the phenomenon of a thematic return (the A–B–A form of these 39 measures) that motivated the revision, one can only agree with Bartók's sharp criticism.

Before turning to the problem of the end of this movement, let us mention another deletion, this time in an original composition. The four-movement Suite op. 14 for piano (February 1916) originally included, as has been known since 1955,[111] a fifth movement placed between Movements I and II. This 47-measure piece of which we present the autograph draft (Facsimile 40, p. 140; in the fair copy Bartók numbered it *2* and marked it *Andante*)[112] is not only a good and characteristic composition by Bartók but an important constituent of the 5-movement key plan (I: B♭, II: F♯, III: B♭, IV: D, V: B♭). For one or two years, at the time without a publisher, Bartók considered the Andante an appropriate piece of music: he had Márta copy the draft and even let a pupil copy and study it.[113] Yet by the time he offered the score to UE (letter February 4, 1918) Bartók described it as "eine kleine Suite für Klavier in 4 Sätzen." The motivation of his criticism can only be guessed. In addition to the overall quality and style, Bartók may have considered a structural point, namely the tempo structure of the multi-movement form. The medium–fast–faster–slow pattern seems to be a second thought. In the original layer of the fair copy it was preceded (first without metronome markings) by an Allegretto, Andante, Allegro, Allegro, Sostenuto pattern. The title Scherzo (for the present Mov. II) as well as the additional molto (Mov. III) are corrections.[114]

Endings for the Violin Rhapsody no. 1 and the Violin Concerto

It is a well-known fact that the performer of the Seconda parte of the Violin Rhapsody no. 1 has a choice between two printed endings: the first (the originally intended) form leading back to the key (G) and the opening theme of the Prima parte, thus rounding off the slow–fast rhapsody form; and the second, composed later, ending in the key of the Seconda parte (E), meant as an attractive variant

111. *Új Zenei Szemle* 1955/10, 3–4.
112. PB 43PFC2.
113. Irén Egri's copy: BBA 5412.
114. The gradual quickening of the MM numbers of Movements I–III as known from the present edition (I: 120, II: 122, III: 124) appeared in the 1927 rev. UE edition first. The 1st edition contained MM numbers 140, 152, 114; Mov. I in the printer's copy originally had MM 152.

EXÁMPLE 71   Rhapsody no. 1 for violin
and piano: the original ending
with an ad libitum cadenza.

ending if the performer played only the fast Seconda parte. This variant ending became, however, the absolute favorite among violinists, including Joseph Szigeti (the dedicatee of the score).[115] Several pages (pp. 12–18) in the draft complex show that Bartók struggled with the proper formulation of both endings, if he fully succeeded at all.

There is a special issue related to the first ending of Rhapsody no. 1: the gesture of the very end of the piece with or without a quasi cadenza. As a first stage Bartók intended to leave the elaboration of an ad libitum cadenza to the violinist (see Ex. 71, taken from the autograph version as given to Szigeti). In his copy Szigeti sketched a short violin cadenza in pencil,[116] which did not seem to be satisfactory. As a next step Bartók sketched a short cadenza (incompletely preserved on p. 12 of the draft), then wrote another one, a voluminous attempt with lots of action on the part of the pianist too (in the draft: the full p. 18, still incomplete). Finally (on p. 13) he drafted the version we know, which he then added to the fair copy and saw printed. This is a medium-sized cadenza with a good final effect, although still a relatively weak point in the composition.[117] The same cadenza was subsequently inserted into the orchestrated form,[118] but interestingly enough Bartók did not add it to the violoncello-piano version.

---

115. Szigeti already had the first ending when in July 1929 he received the second ending (see *DocB/3*, 143), which he liked very much; he and Bartók played this version both in the studio recording and the live concert recorded at the Library of Congress in 1940 (see in the reissued CD collection, László Somfai and Zoltán Kocsis, eds., *Bartók at the Piano*, Hungaroton HCD 12326–31). For Bartók this ending must have been a compromise and not his choice. Zoltán Székely (who also played the first Rhapsody with Bartók) chose the first ending for his recording in the Hungaroton Complete Edition (SLPX 11357).

116. See p. 15 in PB 61VPFC1.

117. Isaac Stern, who played the first Rhapsody for the composer in the United States, remembers his own complaint about the very end of the violin part that, from the violinist's point of view, did not have a genuine ending effect. According to Stern (private communication) Bartók suggested a better final formula that Stern then played.

118. See pp. 34–35 (Bartók's pagination) in PB 61TFSS1.

The two alternative endings of the Violin Concerto 1937–1938 bear witness to a slightly different configuration of Bartók's search for the ideal closing of a large-scale work. The draft and the preparatory notes for the orchestration[119] prove between them that his original intention was a triumphant orchestral close as we know it from the second ending in the printed score, with unusual instrumental effects for the brasses (glissandi on the trombones and then on the trumpets and horns). According to a private communication with Zoltán Székely, who commissioned the concerto and had some insight into the development of the composition, he asked Bartók to write another ending in which the soloist would take part in the final measures. Bartók accepted this suggestion and rewrote the solo ending (six measures longer, basically with the same progression) as the main text, complemented — as he worded it[120] — by a *2.fine (ad libitum)*, which was chronologically the earlier of the two and his favored version. Naturally one cannot blame violinists nowadays for favoring the solo ending.[121] Yet one might wish that conductors, at least as a refreshing surprise, would occasionally urge a hearing for the tutti ending.

New Retransition in the 2-piano Sonata

Of the significant recompositions or changes that happened after the premiere but before the publication of a composition, two examples require little explanation: the new retransition in Movement I of the Sonata for two Pianos and Percussion, and the alternative ending for Concerto for Orchestra. In both cases Bartók's second thought is unquestionably an improvement.

Bartók composed the last 45 measures (229–273 in the printed score) of the 141-measure development section (133–273) of the sonata-form opening movement of the 2-piano Sonata subsequently to replace 50 measures in the former version that was elaborated, written in fair copy, and duplicated from the *Lichtpause* originals. What is more, Bartók and Ditta played the Sonata some ten times in this earlier version, from the January 16, 1938, Basel premiere to ca. summer 1939, before he composed the new version of the end of the development section.[122] In 1940 the new version already existed: the additional manuscript sections written for the Concerto version of the Sonata use the new bar numbers[123] and the recorded New York radio performance (November 10, 1940) presented the final form of the

119. The draft: PB 76VPS1; the preparation of the orchestration in BBA 4091 (except Mov. III, prepared in the draft).

120. In the *Lichtpause* fair copy of the vl.-piano version (p. 35) as well as in the full score (p. 97).

121. The soloist of the Hungarian premiere, Péter Szervánszky, played the tutti ending (a phono-amateur recording of the Jan. 5, 1944, Budapest performance exists). Frankly he had no choice: the *Lichtpause* copy available for the conductor János Ferencsik lacked the soloist ending.

122. There exists a *Lichtpause* copy still in the old form with a dedication by the Bartók couple dated June 18, 1939 (present owner: Prof. János Sólyom, Stockholm).

123. PPB 75TFSS1.

EXAMPLE 72   Sonata for two Pianos and Percussion, Movement I: the original form of the retransition.

2-piano Sonata.[124] What did motivate Bartók to rewrite these 50 measures? Discarding the unlikely idea that the correction was imperative for the sake of exact Fibonacci numbers,[125] we should look for the typical Bartókian self-criticism: what did not work in performance according to his expectations?

124. The percussion parts produced in America (PB 70DID3) follow the new version.
125. Theoretically, to subtract 5 measures may correct the overall proportions of a whole movement — the length of the "positive" and the "negative" section, using Lendvai's term — but destroy all the exact middle- and small-dimension internal proportions in these sections, if there were such.

A detailed comparison of the two versions reveals that in the first half of the rewritten section Bartók was content to revise the urform by cutting here and adding there (note that the characteristic rhythm in mm. 229ff. and the piano ma intenso passage from m. 248 were such additions), whereas the second half needed more basic correction. The explicitly Hungarian pianissimo climax (old mm. 233ff.;[126] see Ex. 72) was beautiful music but appeared somewhat unprepared; and the 6-measure staccato retransition, even if Bartók took part in the performance, could hardly lead from this solitude to the loud recapitulation of the main theme in a natural way.

	old form*				new form
	198–202	(5)	≈	(3)	229–231 reshaped simpler version
	203–209	(7)	=	(7)	232–238
	210–211	(2)	≈	(3)	239–241 extended version
	212–213	(2)	=	(2)	242–243
	214–215	(2)	≈	(4)	244–247 extended version
	216–224	(9)	≠	(8)	248–255 new thematic elaboration
	225–228	(4)	≈	(4)	256–259 similar, in transposition
pianissimo climax and	229–232	(4)	≠	(2)	260–261
staccato retransition	233–247	(15)	≠	(12)	262–273 un poco tranquillo stretto retransition

*In the MS of the old form the *Allegro molto*, after the 31-measure-long *Assai lento*, began with m. 1 again; therefore m. 198 of the old form is identical with m. 229 of the new form.

Endings for the Concerto for Orchestra and the Violin Rhapsody no. 2

The so-called alternative ending of Movement V of the Concerto for Orchestra — 24 measures in place of the last 5 measures of the original version — seems to be a self-critical second thought by Bartók. He finished the work October 8, 1943, with the short ending and with it Serge Koussevitzky premiered the score on December 1–2, 1944, in Boston, repeated it on December 29–30 (the December 30 performance has been recorded), and again on January 10 and 13, 1945, in New York at Carnegie Hall. (Incidentally the piano reduction[127] that Bartók made in January 1944 also contained only the short ending.) The composer was present at the premiere and although a printer's copy of the full score had already been sent to Boosey & Hawkes in London, he decided to introduce some changes. The most important was the addition of the longer ending, which he drafted in early 1945. The publisher's New York manager Hans Heinsheimer informed Bartók (letter of March 15, 1945) how happy Koussevitzky was about "the new ending." From the musical point of view there is hardly any doubt that the new ending is more idiomatic and with its broad gestures fits better into the al fresco symphonic style of the triumphant finale. Con-

126. This page (p. 14) is reproduced in facsimile in Somfai/*Exhibition*, 28.
127. PB 80TPFC1.

ductors today do not hesitate to take the longer version, because it is a successful ending. In spite of all these, the original short ending has an unmistakable Bartókian gesture, resolving the tension with an abrupt passage that only Bartók perhaps could do convincingly at his piano. I believe that someone should at least try to recreate an adequate performance with the orchestra and occasionally play the original short ending.

Finally, from among the revisions that Bartók carried out after a first printed edition had appeared, here I raise only the question of the Seconda parte of Violin Rhapsody no. 2 and discuss other cases at some length in chapter 9.

The problem of the *Friss* movement of the Second Rhapsody naturally goes far beyond the two different printed versions (UE 1929; B&H revised edition copyright 1947). There are two aspects of the multistage reorganization of the movement that require extensive study: changes throughout the form as the movement gradually developed in the violin-piano draft and in later manuscript sources; and the formation of the ending(s).

The concept of the movement is an extraordinary one even among Bartók's unusual compositions based on folklore material; its problems relate only to its continuity and balance. It is probably the boldest of the four movements in the two rhapsodies. For it Bartók selected seven dances played by village gypsy fiddlers in Transylvania,[128] mostly longer dances improvised in an open form using a few motives,[129] in a wild virtuoso style that in its full rhythmic and ornamental richness, as recorded and transcribed by Bartók, could not fit into the framework of a regular concert piece. However, Bartók made an effort to keep as many of the peculiarities of these fantastic dances as he could. With the exception of the first dance[130] he kept the original key (or, if the gypsy fiddler had happened to tune the instrument in a lower or higher pitch, the original hand position and stops on the strings). And he recreated the natural mood of the individual dances as if he were the fiddler improvising, expanding or shortening the recorded form according to the nature of such Transylvanian dances rather than equalizing/elaborating it according to the rules of his own music. Actually the direct composition in the violin part is minimal: 4 measures before no. 8 and two further passages, from no. 36 to 37 and from no. 43 to the end (referring to the longer version in the UE edition).

The dances in this scheme are not closed numbers played *attacca* but form an uninterrupted dance cycle in which one dance improvisation leads to the next one. The ideal length of the sections was not governed by the normal rules of concert

128. See the transcription in its rudimentary form in the 1920s and data about the sources in Lampert/*Quellenkatalog*, 117–123.

129. See Bartók's description of the phenomenon in *RFM* I, 50ff.

130. Beginning in G in the Rhapsody; originally played in (written) D (see *RFM* I, no. 661), but because the violin was tuned lower, it actually sounded closer to B♭ (see Lampert/*Quellenkatalog*, no. 231).

	draft, original layer	draft, revised	fair copy, original layer	fair copy, revised	UE edition	B&H edition	length of the phonographed folk dance	source
Allegro moderato	66	66 >	64 >	48	48 >	47	32	*RFM* I, no. 661
Molto moderato, pesante	20 <	30 >	24	24	24 >	20	95	*RFM* I, no. 669
Più mosso	36 ≠	36	36	36	36 >	25	40	*RFM* I, no. 653b
Presto; meno vivo	55	55	55	55	55 >	35	29ff.	*RFM* I, no. 652
Allegro non troppo	133	133<	145>	142	142>	134	73	Ruthenian F 353a
Allegro mosso	47	47	47	47	47	47	28	*RFM* I, no. 414
Meno mosso	26 <	45 <	48 <	64	64 ∥	67	12	*Mar.* no. 151a
total length:	383	412	419	416	416	375		

FIGURE 23 Rhapsody no. 2, Seconda parte: changing length of the sections during the composition and the revisions.

music. The transition passage to the next dance or its equivalent in this scheme was not an organic or logical progress but a sequence of convincing or less convincing gestures. Indeed Bartók fought with the proportions (the actual length of certain dances), with the transitional gestures, and above all with the conclusion of his chain form as a whole. The changing length of the sections at the different stages of the composition and revision alone (see Fig. 23) does not tell much about Bartók's compositional problems but at least points toward the problem zones of the form. The shortest of all versions is the *Fassung letzter Hand* (the B&H edition), the longest is the first finished form (as Székely premiered it);[131] the UE first edition (after cuts in the first two sections but an expansion at the end) represents another long version.[132]

The ending of the Violin Rhapsody no. 2 suffered particularly heavy changes. In the final analysis we can speak of three versions: the Rhapsody as played by Székely in 1928 from the manuscript; the UE first edition as printed in 1929 (and this form of the ending was also used in the orchestrated version); and the B&H "revision 1945" version as printed in 1947—revised, however, no later than 1935 (i.e., not in the United States but still in Europe).[133] The second ending is an extended and improved version of the first ending, but the third ending is basically new music in a softer, lighter, more appealing style; we can indeed question whether this is a gen-

131. The first known performance: Zoltán Székely with Géza Frid, Nov. 19, 1928, Amsterdam.

132. UE received the printer's copy only on August 12, 1929.

133. Bartók sent the final *Änderungen* to the vl.-piano and the vl.-orchestra versions to UE July 6, 1935; several sets of *Lichtpause* copy of these changes existed, which Bartók cut up and pasted in copies of the UE edition or kept for later use.

EXAMPLE 73   Rhapsody no. 2 for violin and piano: the 1a ending.

uine improvement or just an alternative suggestion in a more popular style for the solution of a compositional dilemma. (According to Zoltán Székely's recollection Bartók thought that the original ending, i.e., the first and the second, was much too similar to the end of the Sonata for Violin and Piano no. 1. As the two works were sometimes played together in the same recital, he preferred to make a new ending for the Rhapsody no. 2.)

In reality the manuscripts of the Rhapsody no. 2 include perhaps ten versions or stages in the gradual maturation of the first, second, and third endings. Even if the process cannot be analyzed without the sources, the sheer amount of work Bartók devoted to this composition already alerts us to his occasional problems with the "formal structure involved by the spirit of the work," as he formulated it in the Harvard Lectures. Here is a quick survey (with reference to the manuscripts for those who have access to them).

1a ending = 24 mm., sketchy draft (on p. 12 and on a fragment of a page in the manuscript PB 63VPS1). *1b ending* = 45 mm., an extension of *1a*, sketchy draft (ibid., plus p. 15). *1c ending* = 44 mm., a revision of *1b*, still in 2/4 throughout (p. 15 revised). *1d ending* = 48 mm., the copy and revision of *1c*, already with changing meter; see the last measures in Ex. 73 (pp. 17–18 in the fair copy 63VPFC2);[134] I presume that Székely played the Rhapsody with this ending at the first performance.

2nd ending = 64 mm. (45 measures from *1d* and 19 new ones), drafted by Bartók (p. 17 in 63VPS1; copied by Ditta in the fair copy, see p. 19 in 63VPFC2); this ending must have been composed during 1929; the UE 1st ed., which came out in December 1929, printed this version (and, also in 1929, Bartók used this ending for the orchestrated version). N.B. Sometime in the early 1930s Bartók speculated on a rather wild idea of a shortened version of the UE edition: in one of his copies[135] he marked *vi-de* from the last measure at the bottom of p. 23 to the 5th measure on p. 28, thus discarding two dance themes; we do not know whether he ever played it in this strange form.

134. This is a contemporary photocopy of the MS presented to Székely, with autograph additions serving as the printer's copy.
135. In Béla Bartók Jr.'s collection.

EXAMPLE 74   Rhapsody no. 2 for violin and piano: a section from the 3b ending.

EXAMPLE 75   Rhapsody no. 2 for violin and piano: the 3b ending.

3a ending = 49 mm., draft (p. 13 in 63VPS1ID1), from m. 19 on still very different from the final form (see Ex. 74). *3b ending* = 50 mm., partly a copy of *3a*, partly the draft of new ideas, but still with an old idea for the very end (see Ex. 75; on pp. 19–20 in 63VPS1ID1). *3c ending* = 63 mm., revision of *3b* with new continuation (on p. 22) that is by and large identical with the final form. Bartók copied this first in a 65-mm. form on standard music paper (ibid., pp. 26–27),[136] then in the final 67-mm. form on tissue master (ibid., pp. 24–25), together with further rewritten sections of the revised form of *Friss* (pp. 23–24) from which several sets of tissue copies were produced. Bartók sent a copy to UE in July 1935 (together with tissue copies of the similarly revised form of the orchestral version)[137] and prepared his own concert copies, using other tissue copies as pasted

136. Bartók used a copy of it written by Jenő Deutsch (BBA 2012) to prepare the orchestration of the new ending.
137. The *Lichtpause* tissues (with draft and tissue copies): PB 63TFSFC1. According to UE (April 16, 1936) in April 1936 the corrected pages had already been added to the performing material of the orchestral version.

insertions into revised copies of the UE edition at his concerts.[138] And there is a copy of the UE edition with manuscript corrections throughout, also a personal copy of Bartók's, which became the printer's copy of the posthumous B&H edition, erroneously marked as "revised 1945."[139]

138. A personal copy of Bartók's that, according to notes for the page turner, he certainly used in Italy (in March–April 1939 he toured with Ede Zathureczky in Italy and the second Rhapsody was on the program): PB 63VPFC3; another copy (with corrected violin part) that Bartók dedicated to Jenő Antal in Princeton Feb. 1941: BBA 3305.

139. PB 63VP/VFC4 (with violin part), Bartók's autograph changes in the printed music or on pieces of music paper pasted in suggest that it may have been Bartók's number one personal copy, already used in concerts in Europe (but the last two pages, the new ending, were written, or rather rewritten, on an American paper brand: Parchment 16-staff). The preparation of this copy as the printer's copy of the B&H edition had nothing to do with Bartók; the note under the name of the composer in the violin part and the vl.-piano form, "Revised Version 1945," was written by an editor in London.

8 · FINAL COPY, ORCHESTRATION, REDUCTION, ARRANGEMENT

AUTOGRAPH FAIR COPY AND COPYIST'S COPY

Although Bartók's notation was very clear and fast, like that of a good professional copyist, it was not at all his habit to copy new works in fair-copy handwriting unless he had to. His mother, Paula Voit, got young Bartók used to the convenience of a dedicated person in the family who took over the time-consuming work of producing a fair copy, and who at the same time was a careful first reader and critic. According to the existing sources, by the time he was seventeen Bartók's increasingly complicated music had outstripped his mother's ability to read and copy his drafts. Maybe his new teacher in Pozsony, Anton Hyrtl, advised him that a composer should write down his own music. Besides, Bartók's handwriting developed quickly and he had a sense for producing handsome scores. Sample facsimile pages in Dille/ *Verzeichnis* (pp. 287–289) give us insight into his quick maturation and ambition to produce a fair copy similar to the printed scores, with a neatly written German title at the top of the first page, and with the dignified (if not justified) form of his name as *B. von Bartók*. The autograph copy of the Violin Sonata in A major (BB 10, 1897) was still done in pencil,[1] that of the Piano Quartet (BB 13, 1898) and the orchestral song *Tiefblaue Veilchen* (BB 18, 1899) already in ink.

The fair-copy notational style written in ink was connected with Bartók's 1898 project to produce dedication copies of a number of his new works, for the third time starting a new opus-numbering with the Piano Sonata (BB 12, 1898) *Opus 1*, a large work Dille had believed to be lost.[2] This handsome autograph in which Bartók carefully scratched out and corrected the mistakes had well-proportioned size and layout but was not very practical for the performer, because Bartók left no empty

---

1. BB 11 *Scherzo oder Fantasie* (1897) is another copy in pencil.
2. László Somfai, "Újabb Bartók 'opusz 1'?" [A new "op. 1" by Bartók?], in *Muzsika*, no. 5, 1986: 3ff.

staves between the systems and therefore the lowest notes of the left hand and the top notes of the next system often collided.

Autograph copies in ink during Bartók's first Budapest years of study with Koessler were not so much fair copies as submission copies of his homework drafted in pencil. Compositions written not for the class — notably the works motivated by Bartók's love for his schoolmate Felicie Fábián (BB 20–21–22, 1900–1901) — come to us in two types of ink copies. The Scherzo based on the anagram motive F.F.B.B. (Fábián Felicie & Bartók Béla: *B* as B♭) is a genuine fair copy; from the *Liebeslieder,* drafted in ink, Bartók also made a fair copy, by no means restricted to mechanical copying: he always changed the music to some extent. The case of the third piece, Variations for piano, a long composition with Beethovenian and Schumannesque features, is less simple. From the draft in pencil Bartók made a copy in ink as a second notation, written in a quick and not very careful hand, on which he worked again and again by crossing, correcting, pasting cut-out pieces of music paper with the new version over the ground notation. (Bartók and Márta alike routinely used pasted corrections in the copies in ink; unfortunately without the help of a restorer to open these pasted pages we cannot know whether they were corrections of copying mistakes or corrections of the music itself.)[3] Finally Bartók began writing a typical fair copy of the Variations but after 8 measures abandoned the work.[4] Similar discarded pages and bifolios were often recycled: Bartók used them immediately or later for a sketch, or in a draft, or as a cover bifolio of the manuscript for another work.

In his first major chronological period (from the end of his studies in 1902–1903 until around 1909, when Márta took over the lion's share of the production of the copies) Bartók, as a grown-up composer, developed different styles and sizes of handwriting for different purposes. He generally used an ordinary running notation on standard music paper to make an engraver's copy or a copy for a musician friend. A smaller but neat notation appears in some of the dedication copies mailed on one or more postcards.[5] For chamber music or orchestral parts he adopted a large notation, well proportioned and easy to read;[6] a neatly written full-score notation for conductors to use;[7] and he was able to write in an absolutely impersonal style like a

---

3. Pages with pasted corrections in manuscripts held in the Budapest Bartók Archives were mostly opened in the 1960s and 1970s, but those in most of the manuscripts held by the American estate remain untouched.

4. Fol. 13ʳ of BBA 3330.

5. See, e.g., the facsimile edition of *Andante* A major for violin and piano (BB 26b, 1902) (EMB, 1980), the score on seven 6-staff pages, the violin part (with easy-to-read larger notation) on three 4-staff small pages.

6. E.g., Sonata for Violin and Piano 1903 and the Piano Quintet (BB 28, 33), Scherzo op. 2 and the Violin Concerto op. posth. (BB 35, 48a).

7. There exists, e.g., an extra full score of Rhapsody op. 1 for piano and orchestra (BB 36b) made for the Paris competition. In fact, some of the autograph full scores look like copies but may represent the original scoring (e.g., the full score of *Kossuth* BB 31, Scherzo op. 2 BB 35, perhaps even Suite no. 1 BB 39), while others look like a less meticulous notation that would be copied for the conductor (e.g., Suite no. 2 BB 40, Violin Concerto op. posth. BB 48a).

copyist.[8] (Incidentally he used ordinary running notation in making copies of music by other composers that he could not afford to buy.)[9]

Whether making a fair copy or a quick copy, Bartók automatically (1) revised the notes of the previous stage of his composition and (2) added the necessary markings such as tempo, dynamics, and performing signs to the basics (i.e., the bare notes and maybe a few dynamics in the draft that had been part of the original idea). Thus a characteristic feature of a copy of a Bartók work, independent of the graphic style, is that it has been furnished with performing instructions. In this respect, considering the function of the source, three crucially different materials may be very much alike, because all could have been sent to the publisher or the performer:

a draft, if Bartók in a next step furnished it with performing instructions;
an autograph copy;
a copy made by a copyist and revised by Bartók.

As mentioned in chapter 3, from 1910 until Bartók remarried in 1923, he had hardly needed to make copies at all. Márta made the ground notation (the actual copying of the previous stage) that he then completed. In the second chronological period when he himself made copies (from 1924 until ca. 1928–1929) his habits and styles in notation did not change considerably. It is indeed a fact that some-times — most typically in 1926 when he worked on a number of projects and wanted to produce the finished form quickly — Bartók made the copy at a premature stage; such manuscripts after the heavy correction became a second draft[10] that had to be copied again. A reader unfamiliar with Bartók's handwriting in different periods, genres, and situations might be surprised to find that the overall impression of an autograph copy is not very different from that of a draft. We presented such a case in chapter 7 (the first page of the Sonata 1926, Facsimiles 30–31, pp. 130–31).

A comparison of the first page of the original full score of Piano Concerto no. 1 (Facsimile 42), which strictly speaking is a draft, with the first page of the autograph copy of the score submitted to UE where it became the printer's copy (Facsimile 43), also proves that the difference is not striking at all. The one is not expressly a composing draft, and the other is not a mechanical copy. Bars drawn freehand here and with a ruler there, or the reduction of the 2-staff piano brace to the single active hand in the first system, do not change the general impression.

Of course for Bartók writing the first full score on the basis of a draft carefully prepared for the scoring meant, like the orchestration itself, a fairly mechanical task. And the composer's purpose in making a copy of this autograph full score was not to

8. Bartók actually wrote out a submission copy of a chorus by Mrs. Emma Gruber (later Mrs. Kodály) for a competition (BBA 497).

9. E.g., Gerald Tyrwhitt (Lord Berners), *Fragments psychologiques* (BBA BH 52; see *DocB/5*, facs. 7); Igor Stravinsky, *Pribaoutki* (Béla Bartók Jr.'s collection).

10. E.g., the Budapest manuscript of Sonata 1926 (deposit in the BBA), the second autograph MS of *Out Doors* (PB 56PFC1) and *Nine Little Piano Pieces* (PB 57PID1).

produce a score that would be easy for the conductor to read (UE was publishing it for the premiere conducted by Wilhelm Furtwängler), but to have a copy that he could send first to London[11] and later to the publisher, while he kept the original score in Budapest, among other things for making the 2-piano reduction.[12] The first score already had rehearsal numbers, metronome markings; thus Bartók accomplished the editing process (see chapter 9).

In another subchapter we discuss the similar production of traditional copies on music paper during the *Lichtpause* period.

THE BARTÓK COPYISTS

We cannot compare the present state of studies of Bartók's copyists with similar research concerning Bach, Haydn, and other composers of the past, for whom such research can be the key to the dating and authentication of their works. For Bartók we do not need such extensive and sophisticated research. The circle of individuals who produced copies of primary source value includes no more than thirty handwritings. These copyists worked under Bartók's supervision, or for him, or in direct connection with him, or their copies are the only existing source of a Bartók composition. A larger circle takes in professional copyists of the publishers (who provided the loan material of parts, occasionally the score too); copyists of opera houses, orchestras, choirs; occasionally Bartók let pupils or performers make a copy of an unpublished work. Such secondary copies will be of interest in the stemma of sources for the critical edition, whether or not they include correction or additional performing instruction directly or indirectly connected with Bartók.

The approximately thirty hands come from three groups: family members; musician friends and partners; professional copyists. Facsimiles 44–45 present short samples of ten handwritings among those documented and catalogued in the Budapest Bartók Archives.

Among the family members Paula Voit, the composer's mother, worked most intensively in 1890–1895 in Pozsony, and on the *Kossuth* in 1903, but occasionally later too.[13] She had a careful but not very fluent schoolteacher-type handwriting (Facsimile 44 no. 1).[14] In several of her copies young Béla's hand was also involved: for instance he began the copy, or he added the dynamics. Her sister, Irma Voit, as a casual help copied several duplicate parts for *Kossuth*. Bartók's sister, Elza, helped in 1903 not only with *Kossuth* but with the Violin Sonata too[15] (Facsimile 44 no. 2; Bartók added the words marked "BB").

11. Confirmed by Bartók's letter of Dec. 12, 1926, to UE.
12. See his letter of Feb. 3, 1927, to UE.
13. In the Appendix, e.g., BB 44, 48a.
14. Andante con variazioni op. 30 (DD 30 = BB 1/30, 1894).
15. See my description of the Vienna Österreichische Nationalbibliothek source of BB 28 in *Beiträge zur musikalischen Quellenkunde* (Tutzing: Schneider, 1989), 1–4.

FACSIMILE 42 Piano Concerto no. 1, p. 1 of the original full score (PB 58FSS1).

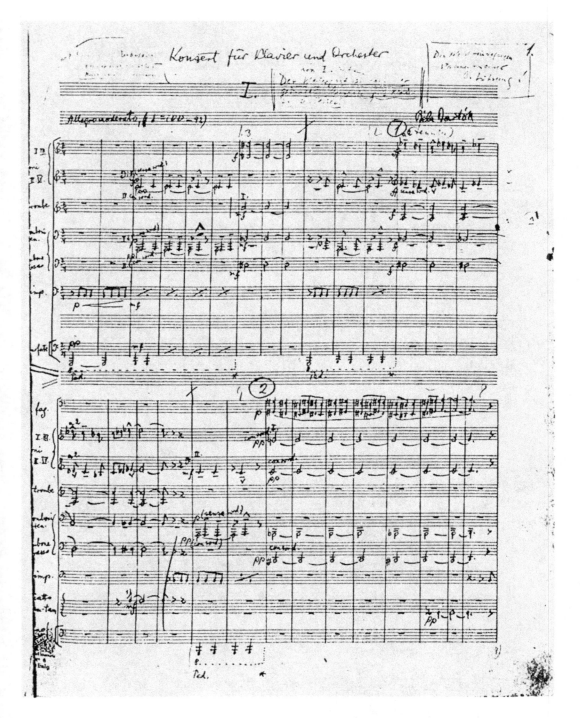

FACSIMILE 43　Piano Concerto no. 1, p. 1 of the autograph copy of the full score (PB 58FSFC1).

FACSIMILE 44 Samples of handwriting by Bartók's mother and by his sister, Elza (1–2); by Emma Kodály (3); by Márta (4); and by Ditta (5).

FACSIMILE 45 Samples of handwriting by copyists Anon. Y and Anon. X (6–7), Jenő Deutsch (8), Erwin Stein (9), and Tibor Serly (10).

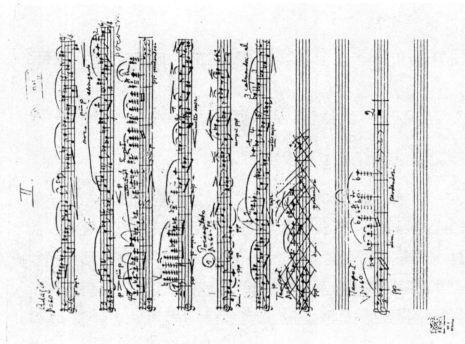

FACSIMILE 47 Sonata for Violin and Piano no. 1, Márta's copy of the violin part, 1921 (BBA 1987), with Bartók's additions and corrections (still with the original slurs in mm. 1–3).

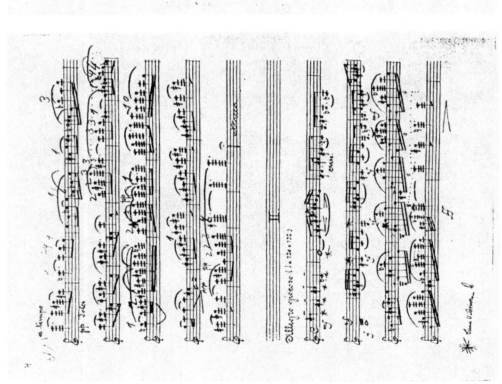

FACSIMILE 46 Violin Concerto op. posth., the solo violin part written by Anon. Y; fingering, etc., in Movement I added by Imre Waldbauer (1911); the footnote to the theme of Movement II by Bartók (BBA 4131c).

Márta Ziegler-Bartók, the composer's first wife, was a dedicated and trusted assistant in several kinds of copying (folk-music transcriptions; compositions; books and articles by Bartók; letters). Her handwriting in music was still inexperienced when she made the very first copies for Bartók, at the age of sixteen.[16] Then she quickly developed a good copying style (see Facsimile 44 no. 4, an excerpt from the 4-hand transcription of *The Miraculous Mandarin*), in many ways imitating her husband's writing habits, musical signs, and letters. She used two types of pens: one for ordinary writing, and another for a calligraphic writing that produced broader letters in text (see, e.g., *poco allarg.* in our example in contrast to the running type of the Hungarian text above the last measure). The parts she copied were easy for Bartók's chamber music partners to read (as in Facsimile 47, Mov. II from Sonata for Violin and Piano no. 1; Jelly d'Arányi played from this part with the composer in England and France in 1922).[17] For corrections and material inserted or pasted in, Bartók considered her handwriting equivalent to his own. Thus in correcting two manuscript full scores — the autograph and Márta's copy of *Four Orchestral Pieces*, for example — he would revise the copy as she corrected the autograph. A remarkable feature of her loyalty to her role as Bartók's chief copyist is that for some time after their divorce she still copied for Bartók and, as the shoulder-to-shoulder production of the full score and the 4-hand transcription of *The Miraculous Mandarin* witnesses, she helped Ditta learn the copyist's role.

Ditta Pásztory-Bartók, also a talented musician, who married the composer in late August 1923, was to take over the role of family copyist. She also imitated many features of Bartók's handwriting and did some work in 1924–1926 (e.g., versions of the *Village Scenes*), sporadically later too (see Facsimile 44 no. 5, the beginning of the *Petite Suite* copied ca. 1937). But for some reason — probably his wife's poor health and/or lack of persistence — from summer 1926 Bartók made the copies.

Of the second group, leaving out early acquaintances in Pozsony and elsewhere (Irmy Jurkovics and others thoroughly studied by Denijs Dille for the *Verzeichnis*), we need to begin with Mrs. Emma Gruber (later Mrs. Kodály). As a patron of the young composer and friend of the Bartók family, herself a composer,[18] she had access to and made copies of several of Bartók's works in an intermediary form, which gives to her copies[19] a distinctive feature (Facsimile 44 no. 3).

From the mid-1930s Jenő Deutsch, a former pianist pupil of Bartók, became his trusted copyist primarily for folk music. His handwriting is well known from the

16. BB 54 *Seven Sketches* no. 2.
17. The metronome and additional tempo markings are in Bartók's hand, as are the corrected measures.
18. It has long been recognized in Bartók literature that two folksong arrangements by Emma Kodály were printed under Bartók's name (see nos. 33–34 in the original Hungarian edition of the Slovak volumes of *For Children*).
19. In the Appendix, e.g., BB 24, 27, 30, 74, and 83 (a copy of five movements from the *Improvisations*: nos. 1, 5, 2, 7, 4, as I–V at that stage). N.B. Zoltán Kodály copied *Bagatelle* no. 6 in an intermediate form, and Emma's brother, Miklós Sándor, made a copy of *Bagatelle* no. 1, which is now in the Kodály collection of the National Library of Scotland, Edinburgh.

posthumous edition of Bartók's Rumanian and Turkish collections or from the records of Hungarian folk music[20] as well as from the facsimile edition of Bartók's choruses (BB 111–112) by Magyar Kórus. In fact his calligraphic handwriting with india ink was often mistaken for Bartók's autograph. Occasionally the composer asked Deutsch to make a quick copy (see Facsimile 45 no. 8, the new ending of Violin Rhapsody no. 2), or to correct the tissue masters under Bartók's supervision (String Quartet no. 5, 2-piano Sonata).

We discuss Erwin Stein's role as editor in the next chapter; here we reproduce his handwriting (Facsimile 45 no. 9, a reorganized and therefore rewritten passage in Mov. II of the Violin Concerto) as well as that of Tibor Serly (Facsimile 45 no. 10, from the 1948 piano reduction of the Viola Concerto).

The third group of Bartók's copyists, professionals hired by or for the composer, is the least known. Professional copyists seldom signed their work, so we either catalogue them as anonymous hands (with provisional codes, numbers, letters) or try to identify names known from a bill or a reference in Bartók's correspondence (e.g., Kajgliček, "that infamous man," mentioned in the letter of November 28/29, 1903) with the unsigned copies. The two most important such copyists in Budapest were Anon. X between 1907–1911 (see Facsimile 45 no. 7) and Anon. Y between 1903–1908 (Facsimile 45 no. 6 and Facsimile 46),[21] whose copies written as the engraver's copy or performing material Bartók revised and completed (on Facsimile 46, the *ohne Vibrieren* [without vibrato] instruction to the theme of Mov. II of the op. posth. Violin Concerto is a second thought, still missing from the autograph full score). More than a dozen hands directly working with or for Bartók are in evidence in one or two copies each from 1903–1911, 1926–1927, and later years, plus further copyists whose work he supervised to some extent, at Universal Edition in Vienna, Boosey & Hawkes in London and New York.

WORKING WITH *LICHTPAUSEN*

The introduction of *Lichtpausen* was the result of Bartók's dissatisfaction with the production of his orchestral scores by Universal Edition, Vienna. In a letter of September 10, 1927, after he was informed that the full score of Kodály's *Háry* was engraved, Bartók bitterly asked his publisher: "When will you finally have a full score of mine engraved?" He had reason to be unhappy. His chamber, vocal, piano works and choruses, the vocal score of his opera, and the piano reduction of the

---

20. See vols. I–II of *RFM*; the facsimile pages of the music in Benjamin Suchoff, ed., *Béla Bartók: Turkish Folk Music from Asia Minor* (Princeton: Princeton University Press, 1976); László Somfai, ed., *Hungarian Folk Music Gramophone Records with Bartók's Transcriptions* (Hungaroton LPX 18058-60, 1981). N.B. Deutsch — a good pianist and all-around musician — was able to make extremely detailed transcriptions of recorded folk music, which Bartók highly appreciated.

21. See, e.g., the sources of BB 27, 43, 48a (on which both worked plus Anon. Z), 50, 52, 54, 63.

ballet and the pantomime had been neatly engraved, but the full scores UE published up to 1927 were just lithographed,[22] and only the *Dance Suite,* as a commercial success for the publisher, was reedited in an engraved pocket score in the series *Philharmonia Partituren.* In 1929 Bartók made very special fair copies of the full score of the violin rhapsodies nos. 1–2 in larger size, clear notation[23] for reproduction in facsimile prints. The publisher, however, had them redone by a house copyist on *Lichtpausen* that Bartók had to proofread repeatedly. So in 1929 he made the first steps in writing the fair copy of his music on transparencies, making blue or brown prints (*Twenty Hungarian Folksongs*), which were not yet good enough for the publisher. But then in spring 1930 Bartók wrote the fair copy of *Four Hungarian Folksongs* for mixed choir directly on the sort of *Lichtpause* transparency that served to make a facsimile print. In June 1930 he visited the publishing house in Vienna to get detailed information about printing costs and procedures, specifically that of the *Lichtpause* process because, he argued, composers were entitled to some knowledge about the possibilities of reducing printing costs by using certain types of editions.[24] And with this a new chapter started both in Bartók's compositional process and in his ethnomusicological work.[25]

The *Lichtpause*—a transparent (or onionskin) tissue master sheet with preprinted staves on which one wrote with black india ink—was an ideal medium for Bartók. As to the preconditions, he had a beautiful handwriting in musical notation; he was quite skillful in correcting, cutting, setting the masters; and (this was crucial) he worked with rare concentration in the final stage of composition, and was able to produce the fair copy or the instrumentation with a minimum amount of correction. The *Lichtpause* was useful not only to produce a camera-ready copy but for the compositional process too. At different stages of writing on and adding to the tissue masters he could make working copies of two types:

1. *Negrokopie,* in the UE house jargon: single, direct print on one side of the paper only, with brownish or lilac lines on a lighter background of the same color;

2. black and white lithograph: mostly on both sides of the paper, usually produced in several copies, which Bartók sent to performers, to the publisher, or kept as his own concert copy. Practically all such copies contain corrections and thus we can call them corrected tissue proofs.

22. Suite no. 2, and *Rumanian Folk Dances* in 1922; *Four Orchestral Pieces* in 1923; *Dance Suite* (full score) in 1924 (the engraved pocket score appeared in 1925); *Bluebeard's Castle* (full score) in 1925; *Mandarin* suite, *Three Village Scenes,* and Piano Concerto no. 1 in 1927.

23. Rhapsody no. 1 in the Basel Paul Sacher Foundation; Rhapsody no. 2 in Peter Bartók's collection (63TFSFC2).

24. Unpublished letter of June 12, 1930.

25. His book *Melodien der Rumänischen Colinde* (Vienna: Universal Edition, 1935) was the first major work in which the music was printed from the *Lichtpausen* in Bartók's handwriting.

Just as in the case of the engraving technique the plate, if it survived, represents the last corrected version, there is a chance that after several steps of correction (documented on the tissue proofs, if there are any) the *Lichtpause* represents the final form rather than the original master.

The example of Piano Concerto no. 2 shows how many versions and chronological variant forms of the original *Lichtpause* came into existence. From the draft score (1930–1931) Bartók directly wrote:

1. the full score on *Lichtpause*[26] (without metronome numbers) and

2. separately the *Lichtpause* of the "2nd piano" part (the piano reduction of the orchestra, without MM).[27] From these two sets of tissues came the following versions:

3. a *Negrokopie* of (1), a full score, with additional MM numbers, etc., submitted to UE about fall 1932;[28]

4. a first handmade montage form of a 2-piano reduction of Movement I only, combining the *Negrokopie* of (2) and the solo piano part cut out from a *Negrokopie* of (1); this was Bartók's working copy during the preparations for the premiere and includes important corrections;[29]

5. another handmade 2-piano reduction, Movements I–III, combining (1) and (2), as in (4), with corrections;[30] this was used in 1938 as the printer's copy of the UE 10995 2-piano reduction (page 1: Facsimile 48);

6. after the revision of (1), a *first facsimile edition* of the full score (an *Aluminiumdruck*), printed in fifty copies in December 1932 for UE in Budapest (no plate number; on the title page marked copyright 1932 by UE). A copy of this edition was Bartók's concert copy between 1933–ca. 1937, with important corrections in several chronological layers;[31]

7. after another revision of (1), a *second facsimile edition* of the full score, marked copyright 1932 UE 10442, actually printed in April 1937 in Vienna. A copy of this edition, with autograph additions by Bartók, probably was a concert copy, and Ditta studied the solo part from this score.[32]

Not all cases are so rich in versions and so textually complex. And the use of *Lichtpausen* did not automatically result in a printed edition based on Bartók's hand-

26. In Peter Bartók's collection, 68FSFC1, but note that this is the corrected final form of the *Lichtpause*; see the variant (7).
27. 68TPSPFC1.
28. 68FSFC2.
29. BBA BH48a.
30. Béla Bartók Jr.'s collection (copy in the BBA).
31. BBA BH 48b.
32. Béla Bartók Jr.'s collection (copy in the BBA).

FACSIMILE 48 Piano Concerto no. 2, handmade 2-piano reduction based on the *Lichtpausen*, with corrections, ca. 1932 (Béla Bartók Jr.'s collection).

writing. The following survey of the fair copies of Bartók's compositions immediately preceding and during the *Lichtpause* period proves that he liked working with
Lichtpausen but was flexible and pragmatic. He still prepared traditional fair copies
on standard music paper, if he knew that the publisher would immediately engrave
or lithograph the edition (e.g., transcriptions for Rózsavölgyi; solo piano music for
UE) or that the presentation of the original manuscript was part of the commission
(Concerto for Orchestra). And he occasionally let Jenő Deutsch produce the *Lichtpausen* (for Magyar Kórus).

Fair copies in the *Lichtpause* period

1 fair copy on standard music paper
2 photoreproduction of MS fair copy
3 *Lichtpause* original tissue master
4 *Negrokopie* of *Lichtpause*
5 black & white copies of *Lichtpause*
6 facsimile edition from *Lichtpause* (**D** = *Lichtpause* written by Jenő Deutsch)
7 professional copyist's copy (loan material)
8 authorized printed edition (engraved or lithographed)

	1	2	3	4	5	6	7		8
String Quartet no. 3 1927	1	2							8
Rhapsody nos. 1–2 (vl.-piano) 1928	1	2							8
Rhapsody nos. 1–2 (vl.-orch.)	1								8
String Quartet no. 4 1928	1	2							8
Twenty Hungarian Folksongs 1929			3	4					8
Four Hungarian Folksongs 1930			3	4	5				8[33]
Cantata profana 1930, full score	1		3	4		6			
Cantata profana, vocal score			3[34]			6			
Piano Concerto no. 2 1930–31, full score			3	4		6			
Piano Concerto no. 2, 2-piano reduction			3	4					8
Dances from Transylvania 1931	1								8
Hungarian Sketches 1931	1								8
Forty-Four Duos 1931–32			3	4	5				8
Mikrokosmos (1926) 1932–39			3	4	5				8
Székely Folksongs 1932			3	4					8
Hungarian Peasant Songs 1933			3	4		6			
Five Hungarian Folksongs 1933	1						7		
Bartók–Országh, *Hungarian Folksongs* 1934	1								8
String Quartet no. 5 1934			3		5				8
Twenty-Seven Choruses a cappella 1935–36			D		D				
From Olden Times 1935			D		D				
Petite Suite 1936	1								8
Music for Strings, Percussion, and Celesta 1936								X[35]	8
Five choruses with orchestra 1937	1								8

33. **5** represents a provisional print of the choruses only with Hungarian text; **8** the printed edition
with German and English text.

34. Only the piano reduction of the orchestration, in the facsimile edition together with the vocal
parts cut from the *Lichtpause* of the full score.

35. Copy made by a Viennese copyist from Bartók's draft score.

2-piano Sonata 1937		3		5	8
Contrasts 1938		3	4	5	8
Violin Concerto, full score 1937–38		3		5	8
Violin concerto, piano reduction		3		5	8
Divertimento 1939		3		5?[36]	8
String Quartet no. 6 1939		3	4	5	8
Seven *Mikrokosmos* pieces[37] 1940		3		5	(8)[38]
Suite for two pianos 1941		3		5	(8)
Concerto for Orchestra 1943, full score	1	2			8
Concerto for Orchestra, piano reduction		3			
Sonata for Solo Violin 1944		3	4		(8)
Goat Song 1945		3			
Piano Concerto no. 3 1945, full score		3			

ORCHESTRATION

It is a general opinion that orchestration is not the strongest side of Bartók's music. He was very innovative in writing for strings and in using percussion instruments (or adopting the piano in the orchestra), but much less original in using the standard symphony orchestra. Specifically traditional is Bartók's treatment of the winds in many of his scores. Some of the safety doublings of wind parts (including a special kind of tutti woodwind unison known from the early to the latest scores)[39] could have been connected with Bartók's sad experience with Hungarian orchestras. Often the sound of his instrumentation was not sharp and loud, at other times not transparent enough. Because of the changing meter and the fragmented rhythm of the entries of the instruments, a few scores were and still are unnecessarily difficult (e.g., Piano Concerto no. 1). Bartók was not brilliant in handling the harp (or often two harps). He made strange choices of timbre — such as choosing saxophone for folk-song-like themes in *The Wooden Prince*; in this score he also miscalculated but later corrected the loudness of the xylophone tremolo. Some of his arrangements using additional orchestral accompaniment seem actually to weaken the general effect of the composition (e.g., the school orchestra accompaniment to five of the a cappella choruses; the quasi resonator role of the orchestral accompaniment in the concerto version of the 2-piano Sonata). And even if he created fascinating new sounds like that of the chamber orchestra of *Three Village Scenes* or the extremely fine scoring of the slow variation movement of the Violin Concerto,[40] not to mention the *Mandarin* score, which is one of the greatest scores of the century, Bartók was not sure

36. In the case of the Divertimento the engraver's copy, a (5)-type tissue proof, is missing.
37. Nos. 1–2, 4, 7 only.
38. Parentheses indicate a posthumous edition.
39. E.g., in Concerto for Orchestra, III, mm. 73–83.
40. See Somfai/*Strategies*, 189–200.

about the effect of his scoring for full orchestra until he heard a reliable performance, if he heard one at all.

All these problems related to Bartók's training. His having to score a Beethoven sonata movement or his own piano pieces as exercises (see items under BB 19) taught him that orchestration was a more or less mechanical work based on the already finished composition. No matter how much his concept developed in this respect, it is significant that in his mature years the orchestration was the only creative work in connection with a new composition that Bartók was willing to do for relaxation in the circle of his family. Márta remembered that occasionally he scored a new work at the big family table or even while sunbathing.[41] His elder son Béla recalls doing his homework during World War I at the same table, poorly illuminated by two or three candles, where Bartók did his orchestrations.[42]

Before the actual preparation for scoring Bartók made preliminary decisions about the size and makeup of the orchestra. For some time he differentiated between small and large orchestra. Following a certain German-Austrian-Hungarian tradition, for him *für kleines Orchester* meant woodwinds in pairs and a limited number of brasses;[43] *für grosses Orchester* — or simply for orchestra — mostly 3 woodwinds each,[44] 4 horns, 3 trumpets, 3 trombones, and 1 tuba,[45] with an adequately strong body of strings.[46]

As preparation Bartók used to take the short-score-form draft (see Facsimiles 49 and 52) or the already produced reduction (Facsimiles 50–51), revise it, and make his special notes for the orchestration. This usually included three types of notes, written in pencil:[47]

1. marks to show the beginning of each system in the full score (single / or double // strokes above the bar);[48]

41. Márta Ziegler, "Über Béla Bartók," in *DocB/4*, 175, 177.

42. My interview with Béla Bartók Jr., reprinted in Gillies/*Bartók Remembered*, 30.

43. For instance, in Suite no. 2 — according to the autograph score: *II. Suite (für kleines Orchester)* — he used 2–2–2–2 woodwinds, 3 horns, 2 trumpets, and no trombones; the *Rumänische Volkstänze für kleines Orchester* involved 2–0–2–2 (no oboes), and 2 horns, and Bartók suggested 8–8–6–4–3 (or 4) strings.

44. But Bartók employed 4–4 woodwinds and extras in *The Wooden Prince*: 4 horns, 4 trumpets, 2 cornets, 3 trombones, and 1 bass tuba, with percussion, 2 harps, and strings.

45. Bartók never used a combination of 3–3–2–1 of brass instruments, which was Tibor Serly's choice in the score of the Viola Concerto.

46. In a few cases Bartók suggested the number of the strings, e.g., 16–16–12–8–8 in *Bluebeard's Castle,* 10–10–6–6–6 in Piano Concerto no. 1. In the note in the score of the Divertimento for string orchestra he preferred a 6–6–4–4–2 composite but added, "it can also be played with a full body of strings." (Performances today often use an even smaller chamber orchestra, endangering Bartók's balance between solo instruments and tutti.)

47. Scattered references to the later scoring — the name of an instrument, such general notes as *Harm.* [wind instruments], *Cord.* [strings], or *Tutti* — written with the same ink as the notes of the draft, belong to the drafting process rather than to preparation for the scoring.

48. See the double stroke before m. 6 in system I in Facsimile 49, or the double strokes in Facsimile 52 with an additional number (e.g., 77 in system I, 79/1 and 79/2 in systems III and IV) indicating the page number in the full score.

2. sketchy notes about the assignment of voices or motives or single notes to a given instrument[49] or the type of instruments,[50] sometimes with partial sketches in pencil elaborating the actual voice leading or chords;[51]

3. a plan of the number of staves with or without the abbreviated list of instruments to be used in the individual systems of the full score.[52] Already at this stage Bartók carefully avoided the so-called *tote Zeilen* (empty staves without music) and considered the notation of pairs of instruments in one or two staves, and the direction of the stems when the two instruments played in parallel motion or unison.

After these preparations Bartók would write the autograph full score, clearly and regularly, so that the engraver could work from it without the help of an editor; often a conductor could use it without much ado. He allowed a somewhat careless form of the autograph score only if he had to work in haste (e.g., on the *Bluebeard* in 1911) and he knew that Márta would copy it immediately. From 1930 onward, with *Lichtpausen* available but not easy to correct, Bartók became very pragmatic, as mentioned above. If he knew that the score would go to the engraver without delay, he did the instrumentation quickly on standard music paper (e.g., *Dances from Transylvania, Hungarian Sketches*). If, however, several copies of the full score were needed soon, or a facsimile edition was made directly from Bartók's india-ink copy on the tissue, the *Lichtpause* process became essential. A most irregular case is the concerto adaptation of the Sonata for two Pianos and Percussion. No full score by Bartók's hand had been prepared. He wrote only the score sections (some still on European music paper, others on American),[53] which had to be added to the *Lichtpause* proofs of the piano and percussion parts.

PIANO REDUCTION

In Bartók's oeuvre there is no sharp dividing line between transcription and reduction. After all on what evidence should we assign a piano (or eventually a 2-piano, or a piano 4-hand) version of a symphonic score to this or that genre? whether it was the composer's intention to create a new piano version or the publisher needed a piano reduction for practical purposes? or whether the new version is easy to play on the piano or not?

49. E.g., in Facsimile 51 above m. 280 in the top left corner in Hungarian: *cel. hangjai* [notes of celesta], and *triang[ulum]* with an arrow pointing to the last note.
50. In Facsimile 51 in m. 286 the Italian word *arco* [strings].
51. In Facsimile 51 below mm. 280–284, 291–293.
52. E.g., in Facsimile 52, left margin, five such plans, some detailed, others only abbreviated, like *7 fa 5 vonós* [7 wood(winds), 5 strings, together:] *11* (N.B. originally 6 woodwinds).
53. See pp. 1–20 and 21–30 in 75TFSS1 in Peter Bartók's collection.

FACSIMILE 49   *The Miraculous Mandarin*, p. 9 of the draft (PB 49PS1), with additional notes for the orchestration.

FACSIMILE 50 *The Miraculous Mandarin,* p. 22 of the autograph copy of the piano 4-hand reduction, tempo and text added by Márta (PB 49TPPS1), with additional notes for the orchestration.

FACSIMILE 51   Violin Concerto (no. 2), Movement I, p. 11 of Bartók's violin-and-piano-form working copy (BBA 4091a), with additional notes and partial sketches for the orchestration.

FACSIMILE 52   Violin Concerto (no. 2), Movement III, p. 31 of the draft (PB 76VPS1), with additional notes for the orchestration.

In certain genres (concerto, stage work, major vocal work with orchestra) a piano reduction was needed for practical purposes, therefore automatically required by the publisher. In addition, the publisher could use a piano version of an orchestral score for promotion. It is not true that Bartók refused to make piano reductions.[54] (Of the concertos only the reduction of Piano Concerto no. 3 and the Viola Concerto is missing — for the obvious reason that the composer did not live to see the edition.)[55] Often he could use his original draft rather than make a brand-new reduction, even if he had to rewrite the more or less piano-score-like draft (the three stage works, *Cantata profana,* Piano Concerto no. 1). Rhapsody op. 1, being a transcription of the solo piano version, was a special case: here Bartók made the 2nd piano part of the reduction subsequently, just as he did in the case of Piano Concerto no. 2, which he drafted as a score. The Violin Concerto 1937–1938 was also a special case but in reverse: working with *Lichtpausen,* this time Bartók developed the by and large final form of the piano version of the orchestra before he scored it, one of the reasons why the piano part is a condensed score rather than a playable accompaniment. As a matter of fact, an easy to play répétiteur reduction was never Bartók's ideal:[56] with small notes in the two staves or in an extra staff (and even with percussion parts on a single line), or just with standard notes he often packed considerably more into the *Klavierauszug* than would have been desirable for an actual performance.

The really interesting cases are the reductions or transcriptions of orchestral works. And a crucial aspect seems to be whether the pianist/composer undertook the performance of these versions as piano works in his recitals or not. Except the 2-piano version of Suite no. 2 (BB 122), which Bartók hoped would become an attractive number in his duo recitals with Ditta in America, he considered none of the piano versions of his orchestral works to be an adequate form and therefore did not play them. Of the authorized printed versions, that of the *Two Pictures* is a quasi reduction (with references to the scoring and with names of instruments printed in the piano texture). The *Dance Suite* he carefully recomposed for piano but did not play: considering the rather limited number of larger and attractive solo piano works from Bartók's mature years, this in itself is a verdict.[57] (Incidentally Bartók did not play his piano transcription of "Marche funèbre" from *Kossuth* either.) Among the

54. In a 1969 interview Tibor Serly stated, incorrectly, that Bartók "did not like to make piano reductions; he always refused to do that" (see David Dalton, "The Genesis of Bartók's Viola Concerto," in *ML* 57, no. 2 [April 1976]: 121).

55. Of the posthumously printed works there is a 2-piano version of Scherzo op. 2 (a copy rather than the original draft; N.B. in 1962 EMB printed not this form but the reduction made from the full score by Olivér Nagy); of Violin Concerto op. posth. 1907–1908 only Mov. II survived in a violin and piano form.

56. One such reduction of the *Mandarin* for piano 2-hand (BBA 2155) was made for the Budapest Opera House and not for publication.

57. His pupil György Sándor played the premiere of the *Dance Suite* piano version in March 1945 in New York with certain changes suggested by Bartók to make the piano part more idiomatic; see Sándor's recollections in Bónis/*Így láttuk,* 192.

unpublished reductions the 2-piano autograph notation of *Four Orchestral Pieces*, preceding the scoring, seems to be an intermediary form from the years when there was no hope for publication; we do not know of a performance on two pianos.[58] The piano reduction of Concerto for Orchestra is another example of a répétiteur copy for a planned ballet performance, certainly not a genuine concert version.[59]

ARRANGEMENTS, AUTHORIZATION OF ARRANGEMENTS MADE BY OTHERS

Since Bartók's works based on folk-music themes are an integral part of his oeuvre, they are not included in the following discussion of arrangements, defined here "classically" as full or partial adaptations of works for another instrument or ensemble, whether motivated by a commission or by good chances of a performance,[60] by the popularization of his music,[61] by Bartók's own renewed interest in the composition,[62] or by some personal reason (such as the wish to create a public version of an intimately personal composition).[63] The source chain of the arrangements is usually quite simple: unless it was an orchestration, he hardly needed any preparation to produce the manuscript of the new version. He could even do it directly on the *Lichtpause* tissue: when working on the Suite for two Pianos, a revised and transcribed version of Suite no. 2 for orchestra, he drafted only Movements I and II and the rewritten sections and put Movements III–IV on tissue.

Incidentally Bartók made regular autograph manuscripts when he transcribed Italian keyboard music and a J. S. Bach organ sonata for piano in the late 1920s,[64] or he used *Lichtpausen* with no prior drafts.[65] But working on performing editions of piano music by Bach, Beethoven, Mozart, Haydn, Schumann, or Chopin, and on his Scarlatti and Couperin editions, Bartók employed a simpler process: he took a

58. A closer examination of this case is in Somfai, "Béla Bartók's Draft of *Four Pieces for Orchestra*"; see chapter 7 note 12.

59. The New York Ballet Theatre planned the performance in 1944–1945. In January 1944 Bartók made the piano score or piano reduction for this project (both terms occur in the correspondence with Boosey & Hawkes); Antal Doráti made a record of the reduction to be used for coaching the dancers. Although Bartók discussed the publication of the Concerto for Orchestra and even proofread the full score, he did not mention an edition of this version. The reduction, often written in 3–4 staves, can be played only with reasonable omissions (eventually with the help of a second player) but still does not contain all the crucial thematic material. György Sándor has recently played his arrangement of this unpublished Bartók reduction.

60. E.g., BB 36b, 76, 87b, 97, 111b, 115b, 120, 122, and the suite version of *The Wooden Prince* and the *Mandarin*.

61. See the versions of Violin Rhapsodies nos. 1–2, the orchestrations of *Dances from Transylvania*, *Hungarian Sketches*, and *Hungarian Peasant Songs*.

62. E.g., *Rumanian Dance* for orchestra (BB 61) or the *Petite Suite* for piano (from violin duos).

63. E.g., the piano version of *From Gyergyó* for recorder and piano (see BB 45a–b) or the *Two Portraits*, to save at least Mov. I of the Violin Concerto presented to Stefi Geyer (see BB 48a–b).

64. See BB A-4–5, and my introduction to the one-volume new edition of Bartók, *XVII and XVIII Century Italian Cembalo and Organ Music Transcribed for Piano* (New York: C. Fischer, 1990).

65. See BB A-6.

printed edition, or a copy of it, and furnished the performing instructions in red ink or pencil.[66]

Bartók works transcribed by others and published with his authorization are documented less reliably. The original manuscripts of the transcriptions he inspected are for the most part missing. Two valuable sources are André Gertler's transcription (from the mid-1920s), which Bartók not only thoroughly revised (ca. 1930) but used as his working copy for the orchestration of *Dances from Transylvania* (1931); and Tivadar Országh's transcription, which Bartók carefully rewrote and rearranged — for several pieces of *For Children* this 1934 version, not the 1943 revision, is his last word.

The authorized transcriptions follow (asterisks mark transcriptions that Bartók accepted but did not support):

For Children
1. Bartók–Szigeti, *Ungarische Volksweisen*, for violin and piano (1926), UE: Bartók approved the transcription (manuscript corrections exist) and recorded it with Szigeti.[67]
2. Bartók–Országh, *Hungarian Folksongs*, vols. I–II, for violin and piano (1931, rev. and transcribed by Bartók in 1934), Rózsavölgyi; a live broadcast performance of vol. I played by Ede Zathureczky and Bartók in 1939 has been recorded.[68]

Rumanian Folk Dances
1. Bartók–Székely, *Rumanian Folk Dances*, for violin and piano (1925), UE: Bartók recommended and approved the transcription (the printer's copy seems to be lost) and recorded it with Szigeti.[69]
*2. Wilke's transcription for salon orchestra (1922) and
*3. Willner's transcription for string orchestra (1928), UE: seen by Bartók (no manuscript is known).

Sonatina
Bartók–Gertler, Sonatina, for violin and piano (ca. 1930), Rózsavölgyi: considerably revised by Bartók.

Two Rumanian Dances
*Leo Weiner's orchestration (1939), Rózsavölgyi: printed with Bartók's permission.

Mikrokosmos
Tibor Serly, Five Pieces from *Mikrokosmos*, for string quartet (1941), B&H: approved by Bartók.

66. See Somfai/*19th-Century Ideas*, 78–87.
67. *Centenary Edition*, I:6/4.
68. *Centenary Edition*, II:9/1.
69. *Centenary Edition*, I:6/5.

9 · EDITING AND CORRECTING PROCESS

INTRODUCTION

"The extent to which composers have mastered editorial skill can often reveal interesting facets of their personalities, as well as some of their concern for their audiences of their own time. In the case of Béla Bartók, source material is plentiful," John Vinton pointed out in a pioneering study[1] and added, "Considering Bartók's prodigious accomplishment in the field of musical research, it is not surprising that he demanded a scholarly precision in editions of his music. Uniformity of language, spelling, punctuation and abbreviation was of as much concern to him as the accurate placement of note-heads on the staff."

As a general characterization this is true. Bartók, probably more intensively than many of his great contemporaries, strove for utmost precision and consistency in the notation of his music. We should count him among the professionals in editing music: the more than two thousand printed pages of Baroque and classical music in carefully revised performing editions alone made him an experienced music editor,[2] not to speak of the thousands of pages of meticulously transcribed and edited folk music. The precision and consistency in notation of his compositions, however, varies, depending on the period, genre, and other circumstances. Let us start by summarizing a few basic facts about Bartók's notation, edition, and revision.

(1) During his activity as a composer, Bartók repeatedly made considerable changes in his principles of notation. He started to write in a German-style notation of the late nineteenth century, as his teachers and the printed editions of the classic repertoire taught him. From around 1908 onward he introduced a variety of experi-

1. John Vinton, "Hints to the Printers from Bartók," in *ML* 1968: 224.
2. See a survey of Bartók's performing editions in Somfai / *19th-Century Ideas*, 84.

mental ideas in notation, unfortunately without being consistent with himself or persistent enough in fighting with the editors and house rules of his publishers.

(2) Bartók was a careful reader and by all means a terror for his publishers. Yet he was by no means a perfect proofreader. Mistakes in rhythm, the proper place of dynamics, the length of crescendo or diminuendo hairpins, for example, were points he usually noticed, but he often missed wrong notes, missing or misplaced accidentals. As a consequence, his manuscripts as well as the authorized editions contain many errors.

(3) There were prematurely printed Bartók scores (e.g., the composer's edition of Suite no. 2 in 1908; the 1927 first print of the full score of Piano Concerto no. 1).[3] Full scores lithographed after Bartók's handwriting (*Cantata profana*, Piano Concerto no. 2, *Hungarian Peasant Songs*) as well as the large-format lithographed old UE full scores of the stage works should be regarded as temporary forms rather than final public versions.[4]

(4) His relationship to house editors and thus the degree of outside interference (and help) in the revision of his scores varied. In Budapest Bárd, Rozsnyai, and Rózsavölgyi had no editor; Bartók dealt directly with the engraver. Universal Edition Vienna worked with good copy editors, but some (Herr Prof. J. V. Wöss, a stubborn old composer, for example) notoriously revised Bartók's notation. Bartók had first-class editorial assistance at Boosey & Hawkes (such as Erwin Stein, who moved from UE Vienna to London), but posthumous editions by B&H based on printer's copies authorized by Bartók may be controversial.

(5) Since Bartók's notation changed and the house rules of his publishers were different, the notation and its meaning in chronologically distant works (e.g., String Quartets nos. 1 and 6) are incompatible. Furthermore, in his piano music Bartók adopted definitely different genre notations that he used simultaneously: a detailed notation for works with a clear educational purpose, and a concert-style notation in pieces for his own performance, with intermediary forms in between.

(6) A revised reprint issued by the original publisher during Bartók's lifetime — never marked "revised," by the way — naturally overrules the text of the first edition, but in many cases there was no chance or time (or urgent need) to revise a reprint. A "revised edition" (a general revision, or perhaps partial recomposition, most often for another publisher) represents usually an improved version, but sometimes the revision involved such surgical operations — cuts and implants — that from the historical perspective we should rather characterize it an "alternative" version (e.g., the B&H edition of Suite no. 2, or Movement II of Violin Rhapsody no. 2).

---

3. On the circumstances see Iván Waldbauer, "Bartók's First Piano Concerto: A Publication History," *MQ* 1965: 336ff.

4. Occasionally an incomplete form was issued too, as a quasi temporary edition; of Rhapsody op. 1 for piano solo (1904) only the slow part was printed in 1908, followed in 1910 by the full edition of the transcription for piano and orchestra (1905), and finally in 1923 by the full edition of the solo version, the original form of the composition; see Somfai/*Exhibition*, 16–19.

(7) Printed copies from the collection of Bartók's one-time pupils with Bartók's autograph corrections and changes may eventually represent temporary versions (technically easier, or sometimes rather concert-style *ossia* forms) but contain no definitive changes. Bartók's own concert copies (manuscript and print alike, with autograph additions), however, contain important unpublished versions.

(8) Bartók's own recordings of his music definitely belong to the primary sources (see in detail in chapter 10).

MATURING THE FINAL VERSION

A long-felt gap in the study of Bartók's compositional process relates to the maturation of a composition: from the stage when Bartók had established its outlines (the notes, the basic performing instructions), to the point where he thought that the score was ready for publication. Even if we have ample examples of later revisions — corrections of mistakes and inconsistencies as well as considerable changes based on performing experience — this basic maturation of the rough musical text was of vital importance. At this stage Bartók checked not only the playability but the effect of the composition. Here indeed was the point when the sensitivity and experience of Bartók as a performer played a crucial role. Once he had let the piece on the paper come to life, it soon became public domain, and he more or less lost control over the realization and interpretation of the score (unless he decided to keep it unpublished for a while or forever).

In spite of the lack of major printed essays dedicated to this subject — quite understandably an underdeveloped branch of the Bartók literature, because it requires access to the full chain of the sources — the study of the maturation of the musical text is an important part of the source analysis within the framework of the complete critical edition in preparation in the Budapest Bartók Archives. An essential point for textual analysis is the ascertaining of a "test" performance (or rehearsal) in the presence of Bartók who could then make corrections before printing. In several cases there is no clear evidence of such a test. Each case is different, but there are common features within the different genres:

the solo piano works, and piano parts of concertos, chamber or vocal music
were naturally tested and finalized by Bartók himself;[5]
for difficult string parts he sometimes asked for expert opinion (wrote sample
pages at an intermediary stage;[6] asked the performer-commissioner of the

5. But in special questions of piano music for children he accepted expert advice (from Sándor Reschofsky, co-author of the Piano Method, or from Margit Varró).
6. The 1st violin part of String Quartet no. 4 Mov. I mm. 1–142 (BBA 1084, facsimile of 1st page in Somfai/*Exhibition,* 36) Bartók gave to Imre Waldbauer; the solo violin part of the 83 opening measures of the Violin Concerto with the so informative tempo indication *Tempo di verbunkos* (BBA BH46/14) he asked Zoltán Székely to check in 1937.

new work to advise him on technical questions),[7] and wanted to hear a performance before the publication;[8]

orchestral works could not normally be tested before the publication (but Bartók sometimes consulted with musicians about the technical capability of an instrument,[9] and he himself experimented with percussion instruments during the composition of Piano Concerto no. 1);[10]

vocal parts, whether in opera, in songs and folksong arrangements, in the *Cantata profana,* or in choruses, were elements he seldom discussed with experts.[11]

In general, with the years Bartók became not only more experienced and therefore more precise and demanding in his instructions for the editor and engraver, but at the same time more attentive too. He realized the potential help of musician partners in the appropriate notation of the intended style, for example, for a string solo part. And he realized the potential danger of expecting specific details of musical notation to have the identical meaning all over the world. The dramatic decrease of the instruction *rubato* in the scores of the last ten or fifteen years seems to reflect this recognition.

EDITING AND PROOFREADING

As discussed in several chapters, the edited version of a Bartók work, which became printer's copy (or engraver's copy; *Vorlage* in German), could be anything if Bartók properly prepared it for publication: the autograph draft, an autograph fair copy,

7. E.g., Zoltán Székely helped Bartók in the final articulation of the solo part of the Violin Concerto (as unpublished letters by Székely from 1938–1939, kept in the Budapest Bartók Archives, witness); in a letter of June 30, 1944, Bartók thanked Yehudi Menuhin "for the minute work you have spent in fingering and bowing of the [solo violin] sonata" (*Letters,* 332); and in the letter of Sept. 8, 1945, announcing the completion of the Viola Concerto to William Primrose, Bartók mentioned that "some passages will prove to be uncomfortable or unplayable. These we may discuss later, according to your observations." He welcomed his violinist partners' critical observations and suggestions, such as Szigeti's letter of April 20, 1927, about the Violin Sonata no. 2 (*DocB/3,* 134–136).

8. One such statement to UE, from Bartók's letter of Sept. 13, 1928 (in German), accompanied the printer's copy of String Quartet no. 3: "However, for the time being, as long as I have not heard it or it has not been performed, this cannot go to the printery."

9. On a bifolio (BBA 2016a) for instrumentation of *The Wooden Prince* Bartók drew up questions to ask a horn, a trombone, and a flute player about the capability of their instruments in holding notes (high and deep, in *ff* and in *pp*), doing repetition, legato, and glissando on trombone, *Flatterzunge* on flute, etc., with examples from *The Wooden Prince* score.

10. We have a vivid description thanks to Frank Whitaker, who visited Bartók in August 1926 ("The Most Original Mind in Modern Music," in *Radio Times,* Feb. 26, 1932, 504).

11. At the performance of a folksong arrangement Bartók was willing to make transpositions, and, probably following the advice of a chorus specialist, he changed the original key in the draft of several of the Twenty-Seven Choruses but wanted no compromises in solo vocal parts. There are two well-known exceptions: (a) in the mid-1930s Bartók agreed to make temporary changes in the Judith role for Mária Basilides, and for the 1936 Budapest revival of the opera some modifications in the Bluebeard role for

Márta's copy or anybody's copy, a photocopy of the Bartók manuscript, a *Lichtpause* proof, a revised printed copy. The easiest way to recognize that it functioned as an engraver's copy is to check the engraver's markings. For instance, in Facsimile 53 (Bartók's autograph of the transcription of J. S. Bach's 6th organ sonata, BB A-5, printed by Rózsavölgyi with plate number R & C° 5172), after m. 6, under the staves, the engraver marked the end of the printed system "1/"; after m. 11, "2/" etc.; after m. 22, "4/," with a circled "3" below it, marking that it is the last system on page 3 (according to the pagination of the printed edition). On this page, by the way, Bartók used red pencil (e.g., encircling staccati and slurs; see mm. 13–17) to mark his additions to the text of the old Bach edition that had to be engraved in smaller size and thin line respectively.

Unfortunately several printer's copies seem to be lost. Here follows a list of the major losses (aside from minor items before 1910, and preliminary prints in periodicals).

Missing printer's copies

* = the printer's copy was probably Márta's copy with Bartók's revision
\# = the printer's copy was a corrected tissue proof of Bartók's *Lichtpause*

composition	edition	title	publisher
1903	1904	*Four Piano Pieces*	Bárd
1908	1908	No. 3 of *Ten Easy Piano Pieces*	R
1909–1910	1911	**Four Dirges*	Rv
1913	1913	48 short pieces written for the Bartók-Reschofsky Piano Method	Rv
1915	1918	*Sonatina	Rv
1915	1918	**Rumanian Folk Dances* for piano	UE
1915	1918	**Rumanian Christmas Songs* for piano	UE
1916	1923	No. 5 of Five Ady Songs op. 16	UE
1914–1917	1920	**String Quartet no. 2	UE
1917	1918	**Slovak Folksongs* for male choir	UE
1917	1924	**Four Slovak Folksongs* for mixed choir and piano	UE
1935–1936	1937	Twenty-Seven Choruses and *From Olden Times*[12]	MK
1938	1942	#*Contrasts*	B&H
1937–1938	1946	#Violin Concerto (no. 2), full score	B&H
1939	1940	#Divertimento	B&H

The major part of Bartók's music, including his piano transcriptions and performing editions of other composers' keyboard music, was engraved; of the string quartets handsomely engraved pocket scores were printed. Hungarian music publishers

---

Mihály Székely, who had a deep basso tessitura, but Bartók did not consider these corrections (György Kroó, "Data on the Genesis of Duke Bluebeard's Castle," *SM* 1981: 120–123); and (b) in 1936, after a categorical first refusal ("It is impossible to alter anything there") he suggested a temporary change of a phrase with high C in the tenor solo of *Cantata profana* for Endre Rösler (*Letters*, 252).

12. These editions by Magyar Kórus were based on *Lichtpausen* written by Jenő Deutsch.

FACSIMILE 53   J. S. Bach's Sonata VI (BWV 530) transcribed for piano, Bartók's autograph (BBA BH221), the printer's copy of the Rózsavölgyi edition.

mostly worked with Leipzig engravers; UE had its own printing plant in Vienna; B&H produced excellent engraving in England, less satisfactory in the United States. Aside from scattered cases within the choral music, the problem area of the production — and Bartók's main complaint against the publication policy of Universal Edition — concerned full scores of orchestral music and stage works. UE preferred a lithographed full score based on the excellent handwriting of their copyists, which was printed in a limited copy number with a warning, *Aufführungsrecht vorbehalten*, performance rights reserved, preferably sold (or loaned) together with the parts. Bartók disliked this policy, because such a full score was still second-rate in quality; was expensive for a musician to buy for study purposes; and, last but not least, required a different correcting procedure that perhaps caused him to leave more mistakes in the score.

The percentage of lithographed scores in the group of compositions we discuss is surprisingly high.

Engraved full score (f.s.) and pocket score (p.s.)
    1912 Suite no. 1 (Rv: f.s.)
    1912 *Two Pictures* (Rv: f.s.)
    1912 *Two Portraits* (R: f.s.)
    1925 *Dance Suite,* 2nd ed. (UE/WPh: p.s.)
    1937 *Music for Strings, Percussion, and Celesta,* 2nd ed. (UE/WPh: p.s.)
    1940 Divertimento (B&H: f.s. and p.s.)
    1945–46 Violin Concerto (no. 2) (B&H: f.s. and p.s.)
    1945–46 Concerto for Orchestra (B&H: f.s. and p.s.)

Lithographed full score
    1907 Suite no. 2, 1st ed. (Bartók's own edition)
    1910 Rhapsody for piano and orchestra op. 1 (Rv)
    1922 Suite no. 2, 2nd ed. (UE)
    1922 *Rumanian Folk Dances* for orchestra (UE)
    1923 *Four Orchestral Pieces* (UE)
    1924 *The Wooden Prince* (UE)
    1924 *Dance Suite,* 1st ed. (UE)
    1925 *Duke Bluebeard's Castle* (UE)
    1927 *The Miraculous Mandarin,* Suite (UE)
    1927 *Three Village Scenes* (UE)
    1927 Piano Concerto no. 1, 1st ed. (UE)
    1929 Piano Concerto no. 1, 2nd ed. (UE)
    1931 Rhapsody no. 1, for violin and orchestra (UE)
    1931 Rhapsody no. 2, for violin and orchestra, 1st ed. (UE)
    1932 *Dances from Transylvania* (Rv)

1932 *Hungarian Sketches* (Rv)
1937 Five Choruses with orchestra (MK)
1937 *Music for Strings, Percussion, and Celesta,* 1st ed. (UE)

Facsimile edition based on Bartók's *Lichtpause*
1932 Piano Concerto no. 2, 1st ed. (UE)
1933 *Hungarian Peasant Songs* (UE)
1934 *Cantata profana,* full score and vocal score (UE)
1937 Piano Concerto no. 2, 2nd ed. (UE)

MS copy as loan material
1933 *Five Hungarian Folksongs* for voice and orchestra (UE)

Bartók's carefulness in editing his music before he sent it to the printer went to extremes. In a letter of August 4, 1945, written to Erwin Stein who as the editor at Boosey & Hawkes in London was responsible for the engraving of the full score of the Violin Concerto,[13] Bartók vehemently declared: "Perhaps you will believe that I am too fussy and pedantic about these editing questions. Yet, editing is a great art, and it is in the interest of both the composer *and the publisher* to obtain as perfect results as possible in this connection."[14]

Editing was indeed a great art for Bartók. In addition to making profound revisions in the notation and checking consistency in details, he often added special notes or warnings on the first page or the cover of the printer's copy addressed to the engraver. These *Anweisungen* (as they were usually called in German up to the B&H period) discuss practical questions raised either by a new phenomenon in Bartók's notation or by notorious mistakes in the engraving. In the *N.B. Stecher!* (N.B. Engraver!) instructions for the Leipzig engraver of *Fourteen Bagatelles*[15] in 1908 he asked for several irregular things: time signatures, such as 3/4, were to be printed above the staff; metronome markings, if included, were to be printed in a similar way, with a virgule between the note and the number; thick and thin cresc.–dim. hairpins were to be distinct (later the composer changed his mind about these three points). And among other matters Bartók explained the linear pedal sign.

Another characteristic list of instructions was written on the first page of the engraver's copy of the Piano Sonata 1926,[16] stressing that (1) the position of the dynamic marks should not be changed; (2) the angle of the cresc.–dim. hairpins should be similar to that in his manuscript, and the hairpins must be engraved with

13. This was the last major score Bartók discussed and proofread. His previous joint work with Stein was the full score of the Concerto for Orchestra (proofread in 1945); the violin and piano reduction of the Violin Concerto had already been printed.
14. Draft of a letter, BBA 186/20.
15. Facs. in Somfai/*MS vs. Urtext*, 61.
16. Peter Bartók's collection 55PFC2.

thicker lines than customarily; (3) possibly nothing should be changed or added;[17] (4) the size of the notes should not be large and the engraving should not be denser than that of the Suite op. 14; and (5) the Y-type stems[18] must be kept and not changed for the notation with a lying bracket favored by UE.

In the *N.B. Stecher!* note on the first page of the engraver's copy of String Quartet no. 5,[19] in addition to the general warning that everything must be done exactly as it was in the *Vorlage*, Bartók required that in triplet figures starting with one or two rests (e.g., mm. 1–4 in Mov. I) the beams be extended over the eighth-note rest(s) —a clever notation to avoid numbers and brackets marking the triplet or sextuplet units.

When Bartók switched to Boosey & Hawkes, he started again with renewed enthusiasm to teach the editors about general rules, his special signs and terms, and above all, about common sense and consistency. Probably the most extensive and informative of the existing memoranda are his instructions to the engraver of the 2-piano Sonata (and its Concerto version).[20] Written in January–February 1941 in two versions, Bartók's fifteen points covered every possible problem, including spelling, abbreviation, notation of percussions, the direction of stems in single-line notation, the proper typography of the time indications, that "staff-lines exclusively with rests are to be avoided," and (point 12) "Everything is to be engraved strictly in the same way as it is in the Ms; except what is in contradiction with the general printing rules." (In chapter 10 we return to his notes about the performance, also a part of the instructions.)

In a letter he wrote on June 14, 1945, three months before his death, Bartók spoke his mind.[21] This time he was angry because the note repetitions he had deliberately abbreviated in the Concerto for Orchestra had been engraved in full: "If you are still in doubt what to reinstate, what not, better ask me before going at work. And for the future, the best thing to do: to ask the composer — if he is still alive — about such intended changes before engraving a work."

And he discussed several questions in detail: (1) staccato should be placed either between the end of the slur and the note or rather outside the slur (we return to this question in chapter 10); (2) there is no reason to use capitals in Tutti, Tutte, Soli, Sole, "except that Germans did so which is no good reason"; (3) the end of the cresc. hairpin should never be clipped; (4) it is best to use larger-size time signatures printed through at least two staves, because "the conductors like it. And if they don't have it this way, then they introduce immense blue and red etc. signs into the score

17. The typical Bartókian formulation: "Womöglich nichts ändern oder hinzufügen."
18. See, e.g., in the middle part of the Sonata's Mov. II, correctly printed, as opposed to the UE print of the end of no. 2 in *Five Village Scenes* with a bracket, also written by Bartók with Y-type stem.
19. Peter Bartók's collection 71FSFC2.
20. Peter Bartók's collection 75TFSID1FC1, 13 pages.
21. Draft of a letter, BBA 186/18.

and spoil them" — but, according to Bartók, UE overdid this in the score of the *Music for Strings, Percussion, and Celesta*: "Look at it to see how it should *not* be done"; (5) how to distribute two instruments written in one staff into two staves if necessary; (6) if the "opposite" placement of a slur is unavoidable, that is, if the slur has to be placed on the stem side instead of the note side, it must go from the end of one stem to the end of the other rather than from head to head.[22]

Proofreading, the next step of the production, is a complicated matter with Bartók. There is an enormous amount of indirect data in the correspondence with his publishers, to show that proof sheets were sent and returned with or without the *Vorlage*; that further proofs were needed from the full material or just from single pages; that special notes were added to the proof sheets. Unfortunately, the majority of these documents themselves is missing. The reason is simple: the publisher kept only the last authorized step of the process. When the composer returned the corrected second proof sheets, the first became unnecessary; when Bartók authorized the edition, even the last proof sheets became expendable, because the corrected plates represented the final version. If any archival material remains, it is only the original *Vorlage*, the composer's manuscript or an equivalent corrected manuscript copy (remember the list of the missing printer's copies).

Therefore most of the existing corrected proof sheets survived in Bartók's possession rather than in the publisher's archives, and they do not represent the last stage of proofreading but a previous stage. Several times Bartók returned the corrected new proof sheets with a note that he had kept the previous ones; these are the proofs that come to us directly from Bartók's own material, or through someone who got proofs from him as a present and carefully kept them. In other words the very last document (the third, rarely the fourth, sometimes already the second proof), which could authorize the last changes appearing only in the printed first edition, is regularly missing. From the textual point of view this is a pity: we have to take it on faith that the last corrections were done by the composer himself and the engraver did not misunderstand him. Yet for the compositional process it is still fortunate that the ones that survived are just first or second proof sheets: these are more informative, because they contain the bulk of the corrections.

Here follows a checklist of the known corrected proof sheets (aside from material in collections still unknown to me), arranged according to the original publishers.

---

22. Probably the proofs of the Concerto for Orchestra, added to his illness, caused Bartók to work himself into a frenzy: "I got rather bewildered by the news that again those unsuitable, unskillful, incompetent, and stupid people should tamper with the proofs. After due consideration I must declare that I don't want to have anything to do with them: two trials were enough. Better to have never again published anything. I'll write a letter myself to London on this subject and explain the situation" (letter of Apr. 26, 1945, to Heinsheimer; see also Bartók's letter of May 5, Heinsheimer's letters of May 8, 15, June 13, Hawkes's letter of May 23).

Collections

BBA   Budapest Bartók Archives
BBJ   Béla Bartók Jr., Budapest
ENL   Edinburgh National Library[23]
Mil   Milroy collection, New York[24]
OSZK   Széchényi National Library, Budapest [Országos Széchényi Könyvtár]
PB   Peter Bartók, Homosassa, Florida
VSB   Vienna Stadt- und Landesbibliothek
WLC   Library of Congress, Washington, D.C.

Date	Title	Collection
Bárd (Budapest)		
1904.IV–V	Four Pósa Songs	BBA
1904.IV–V	*Four Piano Pieces*	BBA
Magyar Lant (Budapest)		
1905.V	*Kossuth,* "Marche funèbre"	BBA
B.K.[25]		
1906	BARTÓK–KODÁLY, *Hungarian Folk Songs*	BBA
Rozsnyai (Budapest)		
1908.VIII	*Ten Easy Piano Pieces*	BBA
1910.VII	*Two Elegies* (1st proof)	BBA
1910.VIII	*Two Elegies* (2nd proof)	Mil
1911.I	*For Children* III	Mil
1911.XI	MOZART (ed. Bartók), Piano Sonata no. 15, K284	BBA
1912.VII	*Seven Sketches*	BBA
Rózsavölgyi (Budapest)		
ca. 1908	Rhapsody op. 1, solo piano, short form	BBA
1910.VII	*Two Rumanian Dances*	Mil
1910.VIII	Rhapsody op. 1, 2-piano reduction	Mil
1910.X	String Quartet no. 1, pocket score	BBA
1911.VII	*Three Burlesques* (1st proof)	ENL
1911.VII?	*Four Dirges*	ENL
1911.XII	*Three Burlesques* (2nd proof)	BBA
1912.VII, X	*Two Pictures,* full score (1st & 2nd proof)	BBA
1912	*Two Pictures,* piano version (incompl.)	BBA
1918.X	Sonatina for piano	BBA
1931	BARTÓK–GERTLER, Sonatina (two proofs)	BBA
1937	*Young People at the Piano*	OSZK
Universal Edition (Vienna)		
1918.VIII	Suite op. 14	BBA
1921.X	*Bluebeard's Castle,* vocal score	PB

23. From Mrs. Emma Kodály's collection.
24. In June 1990 on sale (J. & J. Lubrano, Great Barrington, Mass.); present owner unknown. Nicholas R. Milroy is the son of Etelka Freund, who owned valuable Bartókiana.
25. Bartók and Kodály, private edition.

Universal Edition (Vienna), continued

1922.III, VIII	Ady Songs op. 16 (two proofs)	BBA
1927.IV	Piano Concerto no. 1, 2-piano reduction	BBA
1929	Rhapsody no. 1, vl.-piano	PB
1929	Rhapsody no. 1, cello part	BBA
1929	String Quartet no. 4, pocket score	PB
1936.V	String Quartet no. 5, pocket score (incompl.)	VSB
1938	*Petite Suite*	PB

Boosey & Hawkes (London)

1940	Violin concerto, vl.-piano reduction	BBJ
1940	String Quartet no. 6, score (2nd proof)	PB
1940	String Quartet no. 6, score (1st and 3rd proofs)	private coll.
1945.III	Violin Concerto, full score	WLC

How much did Bartók modify the composition during the proofreading? As a rule he changed more in the years of the Rozsnyai and Rózsavölgyi editions than later, but not much at all. On our first sample page (see Facsimile 54: the first page of *Seven Sketches* for piano, a Rozsnyai print from 1912) he added the metronome marking; restored the original notation (see the marginal note about the time signature; the omission of dots after the tempo marking; the place of the dim. hairpin in m. 3;[26] the missing natural — these were engraver's errors); added a missing tie and corrected a wrong note in the left hand (errors in the engraver's copy Bartók had not noticed); revised some changes in the title suggested by the publisher (no capital letter in the title); suggested that after the deletion of the word *zongora* [piano] the first measure be moved to the left. The notes are in German, because the engraving was done at Röder in Leipzig. In other proof sheets he occasionally changed the music slightly, or asked for an enharmonic notation,[27] or added a variant rhythm or melody with small notes in the vocal part to fit the translation, etc.[28]

Was Bartók a good proofreader? Indeed he was, and although not perfect in every respect, over the years he grew more and more experienced. But his early scores lack his later neatness and accuracy; furthermore, he was not watchful or insistent enough in demanding perfection from copyists at intermediary stages or in discovering and correcting deviations from his manuscript. For instance, Bartók overlooked the following misprints or details in four measures of Movement I of String Quartet no. 1 in the first edition (Facsimile 55, upper brace: a Rózsavölgyi pocket-score edition from 1909 based on a copy made by a professional copyist that Bartók revised).[29]

26. In the top right corner is a special remark that the cresc.–dim. hairpins must be in line.

27. See the facsimile reproduction of p. 18 of the 1912 full-score proofs of *Two Pictures* (Somfai/*Exhibition*, 26): Bartók accepted Kodály's suggestion on writing the violins in the measure before no. 11 with flats and so instructed the engraver; in those years Kodály often read Bartók's new works in manuscript or proofs.

28. See p. 15 of the *Ady Songs* op. 16 reproduced in facsimile in the Hungaroton Complete Edition, Vocal Music 1 (SLPX 11603), 5.

29. BBA BH37.

FACSIMILE 54   *Seven Sketches*, first page of the Rozsnyai edition, corrected proof sheets (BBA 1997).

FACSIMILE 55   String Quartet no. 1, excerpt from Movement I in the Rózsavölgyi pocket score edition (upper brace) and in the draft (lower brace) (PB 20FSS1).

The dynamics of each voice should be printed in line (see the two *p* signs above the notes in vl. 1, the misplaced *mf* in vl. 2), which the narrow and overcrowded disposition here did not allow — no improvement on Bartók's own manuscript[30] (Facsimile 55, lower brace).

In the measure before no. 6: (vl. 1) the cresc. hairpin should end with the high D, the end of the motive, followed immediately by *cresc.*; twice there should be marcatissimo ʌ instead of marcato >);[31] (vlc.) Bartók wanted to have a much wider cresc. hairpin with *molto* inside it.

In the measure after no. 6: the angle of all the dim. hairpins should be much wider, suggesting a strong decrescendo; (vl. 1–2) *espr.* should clearly belong to vl. 2 (as in the next measure).

30. PB 20FSS1.

31. Copyist X automatically turned the autograph's marcatissimo signs into marcato signs that Bartók did not correct consistently, either because he revised the copy without the autograph or was careless.

In the second measure after no. 6: the angle of the dim. hairpins is too
narrow.

In the third measure after no. 6: (vl. 1–2) all three cresc. hairpins are
misplaced; they belong to the three-note motive and should eventually be
placed slantwise.

Of course we must recognize that Bartók's autograph score opened the door to
such confusion, because his notation in these years was not careful enough; furthermore he was not accurate enough in correcting and editing the printer's copy.

In his late years, on the contrary, Bartók was a model editor of his music and his
Lichtpause fair copies provided an extremely clear concept of what should be done. It
is easy to understand that he became irate when the editor of the publishing house or
the engraver interfered with his basic principles (by, e.g., turning consciously abbreviated forms into full ones), or with the carefully designed special rules and signs of
his notation (e.g., placement of the trill not above but under the slur; the so-called
Bartók-pizzicato sign; or the already mentioned differentiation of the slur-and-dot
combination with the staccato dot inside or outside the end of the slur), or with his
correction of notorious misspellings in everyday musician's Italian (e.g., Bartók
insisted on *leggero* and *sonoro* instead of the outdated *leggiero* and *sonore*). Sometimes
the best musician-editor became the chief target of Bartók's sharp criticism, as did
Schoenberg's pupil Erwin Stein in 1945, because he thought that he knew enough
about everything to come up with useful changes and suggestions.

A crucial finding of recent years is the proofs of the full score of the Violin Concerto, the penultimate proof sheets read by Bartók, full of his extensive notes, with
additions by Stein for the engraver.[32] Our sample (p. 51, see Facsimile 56) is a typical
page: there is a precise explanation of how the special pizzicato sign should be
printed and what compromise Bartók would tolerate; furthermore there are detailed
typographical instructions for the footnotes,[33] accepted by Stein (bottom left corner). On other pages there are several Bartók notes addressed to the editor starting as
"Question of principle"; discussions on punctuation in English and about the proper
use of Italian; criticism of the tiniest mistakes in the engraving (such as different size
of numbers in triplets, quintuplets on the same page; a glissando line not leading
directly from note to note). But there are extensive explanations of his notational
principles too. In view of Bartók's reserved attitude, it is quite surprising that he
accounted for the mysterious "(*sic*)" at note B for harp in Movement II, m. 35:[34] "I

32. This source, which should originally have belonged to the Boosey & Hawkes archive material,
came in a partly obscure way via Erwin Stein to Hans Moldenhauer's possession and finally to the Library
of Congress, Washington, D.C. (Moldenhauer Archives, Hungarian Box).

33. Bartók wrote "parenth." but actually referred to quotation marks.

34. See Somfai/*Strategies*, 198–199: in Variation II Bartók apparently set for himself a strict rule that
bound a certain material to a certain octave, so that the harp's part should not go below B even if the rule

FACSIMILE 56   Violin Concerto (no. 2), p. 51 of the corrected proof sheets of the Boosey &
Hawkes full score (Library of Congress, Washington, D.C., Moldenhauer Archives,
Hungarian Box).

have the experience that (good) musicians believed this to be a misprint for 'a.' It would be advisable (though unusual) to add a (*sic*)."

CORRECTED AND REVISED EDITIONS

The twentieth-century philosophy of music publishing holds that the maintenance and the necessary correction of the text of a copyright-protected work are the mutual interest of the composer and the publisher. Therefore the announcement of a corrected reprint on the title page is considered unnecessary. From the market-oriented business point of view, such an announcement might even cut into the sales of remaining copies of the previous print. Its absence, however, ignores the interest of those who might buy older copies although entitled to the correct (latest) edition.

As a result of this practice, the existence of unchanged editions along with corrected reprints from Bartók's lifetime has led to a state of absolute chaos. Without a page-by-page collation of copies that seem to come from different reprints — a project now under way for the complete critical edition and thematic index — not even the catalogues of the largest collections of Bartók's music can offer reliable assistance. Such studies start from two directions: collecting data on the reprints, and collating the first edition with the available contemporary printed copies.

First, in Bartók's correspondence with UE and B&H we find many references to reprints:[35] the publisher asked whether Bartók had corrections; he got a copy to record the changes; the corrected copy was sent; proofs of the correction were returned; Bartók sent an additional list of errors, etc. But the documents in question, the corrected copies and proofs and lists, seldom survived (see details in the list of works and primary sources).

Second, we collect old prints from Bartók's lifetime and try to date and identify them. Advertisement on the back cover, for instance with the recent list of Bartók's works edited by UE, was usually dated at the bottom (e.g., "VIII.1927," or "VIII/27"), the approximate date of the print within a month or two. Since the edition kept the original plate (or publisher's) number in the corrected reprint even if it introduced re-engraved pages, first we check the printing style of the plate number at the bottom of the page.[36] And of course we compare the metronome numbers in the different editions and check whether there is timing at the end of the movements or not.

---

meant a distortion of the octave parallel motion (N.B. When I wrote this study I was not aware of the existence of the corrected proof sheets).

35. Bartók discussed such questions with the Hungarian publishers in person or by telephone, so hardly any document survived.

36. I recognized the re-engraved pages in the 4-hand *Mandarin* edition by this method: rather than the original form with period at the end, "U. E. 7706.," the redone plates had "U.E.7706" without period.

The most typical areas of Bartók's corrections in ordinary reprint are the following:

First, revision of metronome markings: changing the number or correcting the note value, if it was misprinted in the previous edition. Bartók's changes of tempi had different motivations: carelessly given MM numbers in the early years; malfunction of his metronome, as he discovered it in the mid and late 1920s; correction of the intended speed after performing experience; and occasionally slight changes of tempi in his own performance during the years (see detailed discussion of tempo in chapter 10).

Second, introduction of timing (*Aufführungsdauer — durée d'exécution*) from spring 1930 onward (see also in chapter 10).

Third, revision of dynamics, accents, other performing signs.

A "revised edition," marked as such, is of course another matter. Before we visit complex examples of revised editions, we need to consider a few facts about Bartók's publishers and their interest or willingness to make corrected reprints and/or revised editions. Bárd did not reissue the two 1904 Bartók editions. Rozsnyai was very active in 1908–1913[37] but later practically disappeared from the market; in 1936 Rózsavölgyi officially took over Rozsnyai's Bartók editions. Rózsavölgyi, in 1908–1912 the rival of Rozsnyai,[38] managed to publish a few new Bartók works and transcriptions during the UE period too, and kept him active in making revisions, among others for two collections (both with revised MM numbers and additional timing): *Young People at the Piano*, vols. 1–2, 1937,[39] *Bartók Album* for piano,[40] revised in March 1940.[41] Magyar Kórus played a limited role in the distribution of choral music (1937–); Schott's Söhne sold only eighteen of the Duos in Erich Doflein's violin albums.

Universal Edition had the longest intensive connection with Bartók as his chief publisher (1918–1938) and therefore, and because of the expansion of Bartók's

37. In addition to Bartók compositions Rozsnyai published the larger part of Bartók's performing editions (see Somfai/*19th-Century Ideas*, tb. 3 on 84) and was willing to bring out two volumes of Bartók's four-volume edition of the *Well-tempered Clavier*, in revised form too, probably the most instructive example of Bartók's revised editions (cf. pls. 5–6 in the same essay).

38. As a result of by and large parallel editions issued by Rózsavölgyi (Rv) and Rozsnyai (R), and the carelessness of Bartók, there is a confusion of opus numbers in the first edition of piano works from 1908–1911 that was corrected in later editions:

	orig.	*corr.*	*title*	*contracted*
Rv	op. 8	op. 8a	*Two Rumanian Dances*	June 11, 1910
	op. 8b	op. 9a	*Four Dirges*	May 30, 1911
	op. 8c		*Three Burlesques*	May 30, 1911
R	op. 8	op. 8b	*Two Elegies*	July 6, 1910
	op. 9	op. 9b	*Seven Sketches*	June 26, 1911

39. Selected pieces from *For Children* (11 plus 7 pieces) and the *Ten Easy Piano Pieces* (no. 1 plus nos. 2–3 and 8).

40. The selection included *Bagatelles* nos. 2–3, 5, 10, 14, *Burlesques* nos. 1–2, *Two Rumanian Dances* no. 1, *Seven Sketches* nos. 1–2 and 5–6, and *Ten Easy Piano Pieces* nos. 5 and 10.

41. Printed only posthumously.

music between the two wars, they issued the largest number of reprints and corrected reprints in genres that sold well, such as solo piano music. Bartók's abrupt break with UE in 1938 after the Nazis took over the firm in Vienna and his switch to Boosey & Hawkes in London (with the help of former UE staff member Alfred Kalmus) caused several problems in the continuous reprint and correction of Bartók's published works: first, UE continued issuing reprints, but now without the composer's cooperation; second, B&H issued photographic reprints of the UE editions, with the text "Copyright assigned 1939 to Hawkes & Son (London) Ltd. for the British Empire, U.S.A. and all countries of South and Central America," or with a similar text on the first page — unfortunately often printing old versions (with wrong MM numbers, etc.), based on a copy available in London or New York, instead of the latest ones; finally, in the United States Bartók received such B&H reprints and made extensive revisions without having his last corrections done for UE at hand, thus making variant corrections, often forgetting the revision of basic matters like MM numbers.

Boosey & Hawkes (publishing original editions of Bartók's music from 1940) supported revised editions with a new copyright, which Bartók partly welcomed, because it gave a chance to publish previously revised versions (e.g., Violin Rhapsody no. 2), or to make a systematic revision, which was on his agenda (e.g., *For Children*). Furthermore, the insufficient copyright protection of works published in Hungary a long time ago urged him around 1943 to make revised editions at least from piano solo works that, as he hoped, could so be copyrighted. B&H was interested in *Three Burlesques*. The New York publisher E. B. Marks planned a volume titled "Béla Bartók Masterpieces for Piano"[42] — these came out posthumously in Benjamin Suchoff's archive edition — and Delkas printed in 1945 the revised version of *Four Dirges*.

Here is a quick survey of the accessibility of Bartók's revisions from the American years: what is available in print, what is authenticated, and where the problem zones lie.

American revisions proofread and mostly printed in Bartók's lifetime:
> *Three Hungarian Folktunes* (Paderewski Album)
> Four choruses a cappella (from the Twenty-Seven Choruses)
> Five choruses (from the Twenty-Seven Choruses) with orchestra[43]
> *For Children* (rev. 1943, proofread 1944, printed 1947)[44]
> *Petite Suite* (enlarged six-movement form)

42. Including the *Bagatelles*, the *Easy Pieces*, the *Sketches*, the *Two Elegies*, and the *Two Rumanian Dances*, with Bartók's introduction (see in *Essays*, 432).

43. Four of the five, together with the two choruses orchestrated in 1941, were published in 1942.

44. On the title page: "revised and arranged by the composer, January 1945," which does not fit the known facts (MS of the rewritten pieces dated *1943*, PB 22PFC2).

Revised versions attributed to the American years, published posthumously:
   Suite no. 2 for orchestra (printed 1948, see below)
   Rhapsody no. 2 for vl.-piano and vl.-orch. (both rev. 1935,[45] arbitrarily
      marked as "rev. 1944" and "rev. 1945," resp., printed 1946)

Revised copies intended for publication but not printed in Bartók's lifetime
(see above):
   Fourteen Bagatelles
   Ten Easy Piano Pieces
   Seven Sketches
   Three Burlesques
   Two Rumanian Dances[46]

Revised copies of B&H reprints of UE editions:
   Improvisations op. 20 (detailed corrections)
   Forty-Four Duos (with fingering by Rudolf Kolisch)
   (see also minor corrections, added timing, etc., in *Allegro barbaro*;
      Rumanian Folk Dances for piano; Suite op. 14; Sonata 1926; Three
      Rondos)

Revised copies of original UE prints corrected in America:
   String Quartet no. 2 (pocket score 1st ed.; basic revision but unfinished)

Studies dedicated to the analysis of chronological variant forms of individual works, including the composer's recording(s),[47] have already pointed out that the correction and revision of the printed music in several cases did not arrive at a form that could be taken as definitive. I would like to add another example, very much limited in scope but complicated, about the authentic tempi in the corrected reprints of the *Rumanian Folk Dances* for piano.

In Fig. 24 I compare the MM numbers and timings, if there are any, from various printed editions and corrected Bartók copies (A–H), supplemented with the measured data of tempo and length on Bartók's recordings (X–Z), and the MM numbers of the original folk dances recorded on phonograph by Bartók (R-1–2):

A = (1) the original piano version 1915; MM added 1917; printed by UE
      1918; (2) the 1917 scoring for small orchestra; MM added 1921;

B = Székely's arrangement for violin and piano 1925, authorized by
      Bartók; printed by UE 1926;

45. The 1935 revision was made for UE (but not printed); the preparation of the printer's copies for B&H, based on the 1935 version, happened in America.
46. The revised copy of *Two Elegies* and *Four Dirges* seems to be missing.
47. László Somfai/*Rubato-Stil* (on "Evening in Transylvania"), in extended form: Somfai/*Tizennyolc*, 117–132; Somfai/*Allegro barbaro*, in extended form: Somfai/*Tizennyolc*, 133–149. See also my commentaries to the facsimile edition of *Two Rumanian Dances* (Budapest: EMB, 1974).

		A	B	C	D		E		F		G		H	
		1917, 1921	1925	1928	1934		193?		1939		194?		1948-	
I	Allegro moderato ♩	80	80	90	**104**	*57"*	104	*57"*	**80**	*57"*	100	{58" or *1'03"*[a]	104	*57"*
II	Allegro ♩	144	144		144	*26"*	144	*26"*	144	*25"*	144	*25-26"*	**134**	*25"*
III	Andante ♩	112	**90**		**116**	*45"*	116	*45"*	**90**	*45"*	108	*45-46"*	116	*45"*
IV	Moderato ♩	100	100	**74**	100	*35"*	100	*70"*[b]	100	*35"*	100	*1'05"*[c]	**74**	*35"*
V	Allegro ♩	152	152		152	*31"*	152	*31"*	152	*31"*	146	*31"*	**132**	*31"*
VI	Allegro ♩	152	152		152	*13"*	152	*13"*	152	*13"*	146	*13-14"*	**132**	*13"*
	Più allegro ♩	160	160		160	*36"*	160	*36"*	**144**	*36"*	152	*36"*	144	*36"*
						4'15"		*4'50"*						

[a] The piano version and the vl.-piano version, respectively
[b] Twice as long as in the piano version
[c] The vl.-piano version

		X		Y		Z		R-1[d]	R-2[e]
		1915 Bartók's phonogr. cylinder		1928 Bartók's Welte-Lic. piano roll		1930 Columbia record played with J. Szigeti			
I	Allegro moderato ♩	c92	*c58"*	c92-112	*55"*	c100-96	*1'07"*	♩ 96	92
II	Allegro ♩	—[f]		c152	*27"*	c160-144	*24"*	♩ 92	92
III	Andante ♩	c104	*40"*	c112-110	*48"*	c100-96	*52"*	♩ 132	130-8
IV	Moderato ♩	c100	*38"*	c92-76	*1'17"*[g]	c80-72	*1'30"*	♩ 138	♪ 570
V	Allegro ♩	c144	*33"*	c160	*29"*	c138-144	*32"*	♩ 120-6	145
VI	Allegro ♩	c136		c160		c126-132	*15"*	♩ 138	138
	Più allegro ♩	c136[h]	—	c168	*48"*	c160-168	*36"*	♩ 160	160
					4'47"		*5'19"*		

[d] Orig. Rumanian folk dance according to Bartók's first transcription
[e] Orig. Rumanian folk dance as printed in the *RFM*, vol. 1
[f] Missing
[g] Played with repetition
[h] Incomplete

FIGURE 24   *Rumanian Folk Dances* for piano: metronome and timing in different editions and sources.

C   = only two pieces printed in *Musik der Zeit* vol. 5 (UE), 1928;

D   = the piano version revised October 1934, with timing;[48]

E   = Bartók's corrected copy of D, probably from the late 1930s;[49]

F   = B&H 1939 reprint of the UE piano version with partly new MM numbers (source unknown);[50]

G   = Bartók's corrected copy of F and, with an extra page titled *Helyes tempo* [correct tempo], Bartók's data of MM numbers, timings, plus the considerably different MM numbers of the peasant performances; no date (from the 1940s); N.B. this list refers to the piano version as well as to the violin and piano transcription, see Movements I[51] and IV;

H   = UE prints of the piano version after the composer's death (source[s] of the contamination unknown);

X   = private recording on wax cylinders, ca. 1915, see *Centenary Edition of Bartók's Records* (Hungaroton 1981), LPX 12334-A/4–5 (incomplete recording);

Y   = Welte-Licensee Roll 7767, 1928 (the actual speed of the performance cannot be reconstructed with certainty), see *Centenary Edition,* LPX 12329-B/4;

Z   = 1930 studio recording issued 1934 Col.LB6, see *Centenary Edition,* LPX 12328-B/5;

R-1 = the MM of the orig. dance on phonograph cylinder, as measured by Bartók in his first transcription;

R-2 = as printed after a revision in *RFM*, vol. I.

Which form is the *Fassung letzter Hand* (final version) of the metronome? On the one hand, D is the last documented revision of Bartók for UE,[52] and a reliable source: with all the printed versions available, and still active as a concert pianist, he measured his established performance and considered the necessity of changing MM numbers. On the other hand, G seems to be Bartók's last choice, expressly the

48. The corrected copy used by UE (and dated by UE "3/XI 34"), now in Béla Bartók Jr.'s collection, is one of the rare corrected copies sent to the publisher and returned to the composer — thus it survived.

49. Béla Bartók Jr.'s collection.

50. The MM numbers corrected in London go back to B, except the last one, which must be a misprint (a slower tempo for the Più mosso!). A B&H 1939 reprint of the violin and piano version has identical MM numbers except the last two (Mov. VI): 152, 160; a corrected copy is in Peter Bartók's collection 37TVPFC1.

51. In the B&H edition, added to the printed 57″, Bartók's note: *vagy 58, bevezetéssel +5* [or 58, with introduction plus 5 (seconds)]. The violin transcription — following Bartók's transcription for small orchestra — has a 4-measure chordal introduction.

52. Version E diverges from it only in the performance of Movement IV with repetition, which was Bartók's personal choice in recitals; see already Y.

correct tempi, again with measured timing,[53] but we should perhaps keep in mind that the latest UE edition was not available for Bartók in the United States; also, these tempi seem to apply to the solo piano form as well as the violin transcription, although some movements (e.g., Mov. III) are considerably different in the two versions; and finally, at the time of the correction Bartók was occupied with the edition of his great Rumanian collection and obviously checked the correspondence of the tempi of the composition and of the original peasant dances. All in all, G is not an unambiguous revision of D; they are rather variant revisions.[54]

As another example, a serious case of revised versions, I summarize the recent views on the issue of Suite no. 2 for orchestra,[55] without going into details. We used to think in terms of three successive printed versions, plus the 2-piano transcription that was also an intermediary step toward the *Fassung letzter Hand* third full score:

1st edition: *Selbstverlag* 1907 (in 50 lithographed copies);
2nd edition: UE 1921;
(Suite for 2 pianos: 1941, B&H posth. ed. 1960);
3rd edition ("revised 1943 edition"): B&H posth. ed. 1948.

Thanks to the analysis of the Budapest manuscript orchestral parts[56] and a close look at the two scores of the American years,[57] we have a more nuanced picture. It came to light that the 1907 printed form was matured in several steps in connection with Bartók's performance experiences (as a conductor on one single occasion,[58] otherwise as a listener); that his printer's copy for the UE 2nd edition was the last thorough revision of the complete work; that the revision from about 1942 did not go beyond the short cut in Movement III and the inclusion of rewritten pages in Movement IV, which was actually not a general revision; and that any further revision in the posth. B&H 3rd edition, including changes in the notation and transpositions of instruments, were arbitrarily done by the B&H editor. Thus the critical edition of Suite no. 2 has to face the unusual situation of working with the fully authentic 1921 score combined only with the cuts and insertions of the American version.

53. It is suspicious that in F and H the corrected MM numbers did not involve changes in the timing.
54. In the "New Edition 1993 / Revision: Peter Bartók," UE 5802, MM numbers taken from source G are joined to timings taken from D; although the differences in MM numbers are modest, it should be noted that this is an arbitrary combination.
55. I discussed this case in Somfai/*MS vs. Urtext*, 25–26, as yet without access to the American sources.
56. See BB 40 in the Appendix. For the BBCCE László Vikárius made a preliminary analysis of the parts copied for the premiere and still used in the 1920s–1930s with the UE score, after repeated revision that included Bartók's autograph additions.
57. Bartók's personal copy, a UE score plus rewritten pages (PB 12FSFC1); the printer's copy of the B&H edition, with no traces of Bartók's hand at all (PB 12FSFC3).
58. This performance on Jan. 2, 1909, in Berlin was of Movement II only; see *DocB/2*, 62–66.

10 · ON BARTÓK'S NOTATION AND PERFORMING STYLE

TEMPO, METRONOME, DURATION

Among performers the question of the proper tempo is the key issue for interpreting Bartók and overshadows other — no less crucial — aspects and problems of his notation. With good reason, we must add, because the interpreters of his works know from personal experience that a major constituent of a successful Bartók performance is indeed the just tempo, the proper contrast between tempi, the choice of a basic speed allowing adequate gestures to articulate the tempo (with ritardandos and accelerandos), and a natural declamatory rubato. Reading the available printed music and listening to the supposedly authentic oral transmission of the Bartók interpretation, performers find contradictions between one and another printed edition, between the metronome marking and the duration at the end of a piece, between the edition and Bartók's recorded performance.

A quick survey of facts and circumstances, based on the primary sources, will clarify several misunderstandings and may help to define the genuine problem areas.

First of all, until he started to transcribe recorded folk music, Bartók, the composer, was not specific about giving exact tempo indications. From the (mostly German) editions of the repertoire of his piano studies he naturally knew the phenomenon of the composer's metronome markings from Beethoven onward as well as the editor's MM suggestions in nineteenth-century performing editions. Occasionally he gave MM in very early manuscripts of his compositions,[1] but up to 1906–1907 usually there was no MM in the manuscripts of Bartók's works, not even in those that were used at performances (including *Kossuth,* Sonata for Violin

---

1. Three cases are known: BB 11 *Scherzo oder Fantasie* for piano (1897), added by Bartók to the copy his mother made; BB 21 Scherzo for piano (1900); BB 22 Variations for piano (1900–1901), to one variation only.

and Piano 1903, Piano Quintet),[2] and no MM in the first printed editions either ("Marche funèbre" from *Kossuth; Four Piano Pieces; Four Pósa Songs;* Bartók–Kodály, *Hungarian Folksongs*).

A new habit appeared in 1907–1908: from now on the public form of his music bore MM numbers.[3] This change could have had various external motivations. For one thing, in 1907 Bartók started intensive production of performing editions of the piano literature, among other editorial additions with the suggestion of the proper tempo by MM markings.[4] For another, after the years of scattered publications, from 1908 on two Budapest publishers brought out his new works as soon as he wrote them (Rozsnyai and Rózsavölgyi, who also printed the performing editions).[5] Bartók used to add the MM numbers after he finished the last revision of the printer's copy before giving it to the publishers,[6] or as he read the proofs.[7] Interestingly enough he gave no MM to the 1908–1909 version of *For Children* (because they were folksong arrangements? or because they were works for beginners?). And orchestral parts, lithographed or copied, usually did not have the MM markings of the score; the just tempo was the decision of the conductor and not of the orchestral musician.[8] As to the graphic style of the MM marking in this period, Bartók was not yet consistent: / or = between the note value and the number — for example, $\quarternote/60$ or $\quarternote = 60$ — occurred with equal frequency,[9] with or without parentheses.

The years between the end of the regular Rozsnyai and Rózsavölgyi editions and the beginning of the Universal Edition era — roughly between 1912 and 1918, including the war years — were interesting from the point of view of the MM markings too. For a longer time Bartók did not introduce metronome numbers into his manuscripts, because there was no pending edition and thus no need for final editing of his music. For instance *Duke Bluebeard's Castle* (1911) was premiered in Budapest under Egisto Tango (1918) from a score (and parts for the singers, vocal score for the répétiteur, all manuscript) without MM markings[10] — and Bartók liked the

2. One exception is the autograph full score of BB 35 Scherzo op. 2 for orchestra and piano, from which the conductor was already rehearsing the work with the Budapest Philharmonic Orchestra in March 1905 when Bartók, deeply worried by the orchestra's lack of preparation, rejected the performance. (N.B. The metronome markings of Suite no. 1, written in 1905 but printed only 1912, seem to be later additions in the autograph score that served as the engraver's copy.)

3. Even the Violin Concerto op. posth., although not prepared for publication, has MM markings throughout its MS sources.

4. See Somfai/*19th-Century Ideas*, 83–89.

5. Remember that in December 1907, before the two publishers started to print Bartók's music, 50 copies of his own edition of Suite no. 2 were lithographed; this full score also has MM markings (later additions in the autograph full score that served as the engraver's copy).

6. Quite often first he wrote it in pencil and in a next step finalized it in ink.

7. See the existing corrected proof sheets of the *Seven Sketches* and the *Two Rumanian Dances.*

8. In some orchestral parts the copyists of the MS parts of the Violin Concerto op. posth. dutifully copied the MM numbers from the score, yet no orchestral parts of the same material Bartók copied have MM (BBA BH34).

9. In the autograph copy of *Fourteen Bagatelles* and the copyist's copy, which was sent to the engraver, both the / and = forms appear but in print only the / form.

10. Bartók added the MM numbers to the printer's copy of the vocal score only (Peter Bartók's collection 28VoSFC1).

performance. On the contrary the Budapest manuscript score of *The Wooden Prince* (premiered in Budapest already in 1917, "in a perfect manner under the direction of Maestro Egisto Tango," according to the autobiography)[11] already had MM markings. We see that for Bartók, at least in some periods of his life, if he trusted the performer and had a chance to attend rehearsals, the metronome was of secondary importance.

From 1918 Universal Edition issued the new works, and their 1st editions in the first years included several gross errors in MM numbers. Bartók made errors in both note values and numbers. Famous cases of the former occur in *Allegro barbaro* and Movement III of Suite op. 14 for piano: in both instances the 1918 1st edition gave the MM number for a quarter instead of a half note,[12] obviously a slip on Bartók's part that he did not notice in the proofs. No matter how critical he was in several aspects of notation, he often made such mistakes and left them in the proofs.

But there were also problems with the MM numbers themselves. Around 1930 Bartók became aware of gross errors in the early editions. Writing in German a little later to the violinist Max Rostal[13] (who worked with his string quartet on Bartók's String Quartets nos. 1 and 4) and referring primarily to errors in the Rózsavölgyi pocket score edition of the first quartet as well as to the earlier editions in general, Bartók gave what is probably the most sensible explanation of the wrong MM numbers:

> I should add . . . that in my earlier works MM signs are very often inexact, or rather they do not correspond to the correct tempo. The only explanation I can think of is that I metronomized too hastily at that time, and perhaps my metronome was working imperfectly. I have phonogrammes made 20 years ago of some of my piano pieces played by myself,[14] and they show that I play them today in exactly the same tempo as I did then. Now I use a pendulum metronome,[15] which, of course, cannot show any considerable differences from the correct oscillation number. [November 6, 1931][16]

11. *Essays*, 411.

12. Bartók made similar mistakes in earlier editions too: in the Rozsnyai 1st ed. of *Fourteen Bagatelles* he gave MM for no. 4 in eighths (instead of quarters).

13. German original in János Demény, ed., *Béla Bartók: Ausgewählte Briefe* (Budapest: Corvina, 1960), 146–148; the crucial section quoted in Somfai/*Allegro barbaro*, 272.

14. Bartók very probably referred to phonograph recordings he made in his home from 1912–ca. 1915 of piano pieces from the *Bagatelles, Ten Easy Pieces, Seven Sketches, For Children*, and the *Rumanian Folk Dances* (see *Centenary Edition*, II:1/1–5).

15. Bartók's famous pendulum metronome, a pocket metronome his contemporaries often mentioned (trademark, Dr. Jhlenburg's Metronom, which is now kept in the Budapest Bartók Archives) has on one side of the band a *Secunden-Zähler* grading from MM 200 to 60, on the other side cm 1–100; see photo in *Centenary Edition*, I:57. For a trustworthy account of Bartók's use of the pocket metronome in fixing tempi with the conductor for the revival of *The Wooden Prince*; of the composer's comments on the ideal performance of the *Dance Suite* (no longer than 15 minutes); and of Bartók's usually asking for faster tempi, see János Ferencsik's memoirs in Bónis/*Így láttuk*, 242. Iván Engel, a former pupil of Bartók and his friend in the late 1930s, states (in Bónis/*Így láttuk*, 136) that he showed his Swiss watch-metronome to Bartók, who was fascinated by the clever little gadget, and that Engel presented it to the composer. I have no reason to question Engel's account but know of no evidence that Bartók ever worked with a watch-metronome.

16. *Letters*, 218.

Before studying the 1931 revision of MM numbers in String Quartet no. 1, let us recall Bartók's shocking experience with the *Allegro barbaro*, a case that set off his basic reconsideration of tempo markings.[17] The leader of an outstanding Belgian band, Arthur Prévost, made an instrumentation of *Allegro barbaro* that Bartók saw and authorized.[18] Then a gramophone record was sent to Bartók and he must have realized that the arrangement had been based on a "fatal misprint" of the MM in the 1st edition (which he obviously did not notice for twelve years, simply because he played *Allegro barbaro* dozens of times by heart, and as a proofreader he missed such details easily). So he decided:

> I have the intention from now on in every published work to supply the duration of the performance too, at the end of each piece or individual movement, respectively; roughly thus:
>
> *Aufführungsdauer:* ⎱
> *Durée d'exécution:* ⎰ *cca 2' 35".*

> I believe that this will prevent misunderstandings (as happened, for example, with the military-orch. recording of "Allegro barbaro," which became — probably as a result of a fatal misprint of the MM marking in the 1st edition — an "Adagio barbaro"!). [May 30, 1930, letter to UE]

The "fatal misprint" was ♩ = 96–84, which Bartók corrected in a revised reprint to ♩ = 78–84 (but, as we will see when examining his recordings, he habitually played it even faster: ♩ = ca. 94–98 in the opening measures, with a significant oscillation of tempo).

From 1930 on whenever UE reprinted an earlier edition, Bartók not only revised (and often changed) the MM numbers but added the duration. The first original editions supplemented with duration were the Three Rondos for piano (printed in 1930), *Twenty Hungarian Folksongs* for voice and piano, *Four Hungarian Folksongs* for mixed choir (both printed in 1932); the first editions with additional partial durations for the sections of the individual movements were String Quartet no. 5 (ed. 1936), and the *Music for Strings, Percussion, and Celesta* (ed. 1937). Incidentally the division into sections involved the composer's analysis of the basic contours of the form, a phenomenon that is certainly worth studying.[19]

The accuracy of these durations giving minutes and seconds with authoritative precision is a major source of frustration for musicians today. But Bartók's intention was not at all "unmusical," as he explained it in a text that unfortunately few musicians know, because it was printed, hidden to some extent, in a piano reduction:

> Timings, noted from an actual performance, are given for sections of movements, and, at the end of each movement, for the whole thereof. It is not suggested that the

17. See Somfai / *Allegro barbaro*, 272.
18. Letters May 7, 18, 25, 31, June 18, 1929, and May 30, 1930, of the correspondence with UE.
19. László Somfai, "Self-Analysis by Twentieth-Century Composers," in Edward Olleson, *Modern Musical Scholarship* (Stockfield: Oriel Press, 1978), 167–179, esp. 175.

duration should be exactly the same at each performance; both these and the metronomic indications are suggested only as a guide for the executants. It appears to me better to present them as exact timings, rather than attempt them into round figures. [Bartók's "Note" in the violin and piano reduction of the Violin Concerto (no. 2), Boosey & Hawkes; written 1939, printed 1941]

This statement is entirely characteristic of Bartók, who was at once a genuine scholar and a pragmatic musician. It makes clear that he measured timings against actual performances (and for piano music, as we guess, very probably his own),[20] presumably by a stopwatch just as he did for transcriptions of folk-music recordings; that timings as well as MM numbers were only suggestions;[21] that as one of the possibilities Bartók preferred to give precise rather than approximate data.

A further important Bartók text, the validity of which also goes beyond the given case, was printed in German among the general remarks to the UE/W.Ph. pocket score edition of *Music for Strings, Percussion, and Celesta*:

Movement IV can under certain circumstances (acoustic conditions, etc.) be played somewhat slower too.[22]

The message of this suggestion by Bartók can hardly be misunderstood. Neither the technical difficulty nor the capability of the given orchestra, but the assurance of a clear presentation of the dense (contrapuntal, etc.) texture could influence the tempo.[23] For quick movements, however, he usually preferred an even faster tempo than given in the MM numbers. In the letter quoted above written to the violinist Rostal, speaking of String Quartet no. 4, Bartók declared:

All the MM figures are *correct* here.
In the 2nd movement the main tempo should, if possible, be ♩. = 98 or even quicker,[24] not slower (of course with legato bowing, and *in no case spiccato!*); from bar 78 to 101 (of the middle part) ♩. = 88 is better; from 102 on, the main tempo again. The 5th movement can eventually be played somewhat quicker than indicated by the MM figures.

Let us return to Bartók's statement about his wrong metronome in the letter to Rostal and the revision of the MM numbers in String Quartet no. 1, also consider-

20. The timing measurement for the Violin Concerto happened in March 1939 in Paris, where Bartók and Zoltán Székely checked and rehearsed the concerto from the working copy BBA 4091.
21. In the preface to *Mikrokosmos* (1939, printed 1940) Bartók suggested less prominently that "the metronome markings and indicated duration should be regarded only as a guide, particularly in volumes 1–3"; "in volumes 5 and 6 tempo indications must be adhered to."
22. Bartók put it at the end of a list, *Änderungen in "Mus. f. Saiteninstrumente,"* enclosed with the corrected copy of the UE full-score edition (PB 74FSFC1).
23. In his letter of Dec. 2, 1936 to Paul Sacher, Bartók also allowed a somewhat slower tempo for the last movement: "By all means, it is better to play somewhat slower but clearly [*klar*] than in full tempo but unclearly."
24. In the printed score ♩. = 88–98.

ing similar revisions in the complete Bartók source material. Since in the revisions the acceleration of the tempi clearly dominates, the mentioned old metronome may well have been slow (although the immense material of Bartók's folk-music transcriptions and their later revisions do not give conclusive proof thereof).[25] The corrections in String Quartet no. 1 and in other scores revised around 1930 were, however, not linear in all tempo regions and in all movements. Therefore Bartók's other explanation, that he "metronomized too hastily," seems more likely to be the chief source of wrong MM numbers.

A comparison of the old (Rózsavölgyi 1909) and revised (1931; in later editions, incl. EMB) MM numbers in String Quartet no. 1 gives us insight into the very nature of the reconsideration of tempi. Here are the tempo instructions and MM numbers (in eighths throughout) in Movement I.[26]

measure	old	new
1	50	60 (63–56)
28–29	—	poco rit. – – – a tempo
32	—	poco rit. (calando)
33	—	a tempo 76 (76–70)
41[27]	—	poco a poco più tranquillo
44	a tempo	a tempo 66
50	rit.	rit.: a half note earlier
52	—	poco rit.
53	—	a tempo 63
59–61–63	—	poco stringendo – – 72 – – 80
65	—	60

This example shows that as a second thought Bartók made a considerably more detailed elaboration of the tempi (he wrote to Rostal: "in Quartet [no.] 1 the tempo should be very elastic all through"), but such refinements expose a number of problems to be faced by the Bartók interpreter here and in other scores:

1. there are "from-to" MM instructions, sometimes as an addition to the basic (one-number) MM number, and in the pair of numbers often the larger number (the faster tempo) is the first; does it mean that the performer should rather follow the first number?

25. Yet another document from an earlier time refers to a much too fast metronome. In his letter of Sept. 2, 1925, discussing misprints in the lithographed full score of the *Dance Suite*, Bartók wrote to UE that just by chance he discovered that between rehearsal nos. 9–59 all MM numbers were wrong, ca. 10–20 faster than intended. He found no other explanation for these wrong numbers than his having at that time [1923] "ein schlechtes Metronome."

26. Bartók's letter referred to the rehearsal number and the number of the measure after or before it; here I refer to the measure number in recent editions. As a source of data in addition to the letter, I used Bartók's personal copy, a Rózsavölgyi pocket score with MS corrections of the tempi (Béla Bartók Jr.'s collection).

27. Clearly in m. 41 in Bartók's personal copy but printed in m. 42 in the revised editions.

2. the return to the original tempo (a tempo) often has a MM slightly different from the first (see, e.g., m. 53, and specifically m. 44);[28]

3. in a longer movement a new section, a contrasting part of the form after a rit., often starts with "a tempo" that Bartók has, however, specified as another tempo (see m. 33);

4. in similarly complex cases the affiliation of a few "a tempo" markings without MM number is not clear and the intended speed is a question of interpretation (see m. 51: probably MM 66 of m. 44?).

Another problem crops up in Movement II of String Quartet no. 1. Bartók's letter tells that here "the MM figures are generally right (the data below are corrected from ♩. to ♪)," and thus he corrected the ♩. 46 to ♩ 138. The opposite happened in String Quartet no. 2 in the 1937 revision of the MM numbers:[29] together with a genuine revision of the tempi, the specification of the first MM number in Movement I changed from ♪ 138–150 to ♩. 60–56 and so forth. While the motivation of this second type of correction — giving the beat in a 9/8 Moderato opening movement in three-eighths — is easy to understand, the cutting of the whole-bar beat in a 3/4 Allegretto sonata-form movement (Mov. II of no. 1) into quarters is a Bartókian phenomenon that the performer must understand properly.

As an interpreter Bartók knew the traditional relationship of tempo and pulsation in German-Austrian classical music as one knows one's mother tongue (think of his performance of Beethoven's "Kreutzer" Sonata or the Brahms F minor).[30] But if as a composer he faced two possibilities, he usually chose the smaller rhythmic unit for giving the MM number in the edition of his own music and to some extent in his performing editions of Haydn, Mozart, Beethoven, and other composers too. In fast 2/4 or 4/4 he often gave MM for a quarter instead of a half (in the quartets see, e.g., Mov. II of no. 2, Mov. V of no. 4) and in his mature oeuvre he did not make much use of the alla breve time signature even if the music, to an outsider, seems unmistakably to have an alla breve drive. Does this mean that he preferred to have a faster beat in his music with lots of accented quarters? Perhaps he did, although his recordings partly speak against this interpretation. Another sensible explanation

28. Here I do not consider superficially corrected editions like the rev. 2nd ed. of Piano Concerto no. 1, Mov. I, in which the basic Allegro tempo ♩ = 130 of the 1st ed. dropped to ♩ = 116 but in m. 249 the Allegro and in m. 333 the Tempo I (Allegro) remained ♩ = 130 and 138, respectively; and the Meno vivo in m. 181 after the revision remained the original ♩ = 120, which is not "less vivid." See Somfai/*Piano Year*, 51–52.

29. Bartók sent the list *Richtigstellung der M. M. Zahlen* to UE Aug. 7, 1937; André Gertler also got a copy of the list (see the facsimile in "Bela Bartok: L'homme et l'oeuvre," *La Revue Musicale*, numéro spécial 224 [1955]: 104–105). Recent editions follow these MM numbers. The recording by the Amar–Hindemith Quartet, with some extremely slow tempi, followed the 1st edition; see J. Breuer, "Die erste Bartók-Schallplatte — Das II. Streichquartett op. 17 von Béla Bartók in der Einspielung des Amar–Hindemith Quartetts," in *Hindemith-Jahrbuch* 1976/V (Mainz: B. Schott's Söhne, 1977), 123–145.

30. *Centenary Edition*, I:11–12/1; II:7–8/1–2.

(and I myself consider it the obvious one) is that in his folk-music transcriptions, in agreement with Kodály, Bartók developed certain principles in creating the rhythmic notation of orally transmitted music. For instance, dance steps = quarters; syllables in vocal music = eighths and quarters in 4/4 rather than sixteenths and eighths in 2/4.[31] And in his own music he tended to use similar notation.[32]

One final word about the supposed malfunction of Bartók's old metronome. There is evidence that even during the pendulum metronome era, Bartók made considerable changes in the carefully elaborated network of MM numbers, because his original concept changed and matured after a number of performances. Such was the case with Piano Concerto no. 2 that he played some eighteen times between the 1932 first facsimile edition and the April 1937 revised second facsimile edition:

measure	tempo	1st ed.[33]	2nd ed.	recording[34]
Movement I				
1	Allegro	♩ = 96	104	[94–102]
74	Mosso	104	108	[100–104]
82	Tranquillo	88	88	[80–88]
254	Più mosso	120	126	—[35]
Movement II				
1	Adagio	♩ = 60	66–69	[42–50][36]
23	Più adagio	♪ = 80	80–72	[70–80][37]
1	Presto	♩ = 150	184	—
Movement III	⋮			
1, 45	Allegro molto	♩ = 108	150	[140–156]
6	Più allegro	138	188	[140–180]
196	Meno vivo	84	94	—[38]
211	Più allegro	138	168–178	[160–180]
255	Presto	♩ = 168	♩. = 88	—
292	—	♩ = 132	132	

31. See my notes on "Bartók's transcriptions" in László Somfai, ed., *Hungarian Folk Music: Gramophone Records with Béla Bartók's Transcriptions* (Budapest: Hungaroton, 1981; LPX 18058–60), Commentaries, 20–24.

32. Bartók seldom changed the metric/rhythmic notation from sketch to final form whether by diminution or augmentation. One exceptional case is Mov. III of String Quartet no. 2: the sketches are in 4/4 but in diminished values (see *DocB/5*, 182–186), the draft already in 4/4 with augmented rhythm, so the short quasi-syllables of the declamatory melody (at no. 2, etc.) are eighths.

33. I compare only the characteristic main tempi.

34. *Centenary Edition*, II:3—fragments only, of a broadcast concert, Budapest, March 22, 1938, cond. Ernest Ansermet; the Hungarian orchestra was mediocre, which may explain the tempi being slower than Bartók preferred them. The speed of Bartók's performance on this record was measured with a DB-66 "Dr. Beat" pocket instrument; the numbers are approximate, owing to the procedure of the measurement and even more to the great oscillation of the tempo in Bartók's performance.

35. This section as well as the Presto section in Mov. II are missing from the record.

36. The slow tempo of the Adagio of the strings was probably Ansermet's choice, not Bartók's.

37. In mm. 39–53 with greater freedom: between 76–ca. 100.

38. The poor recorded quality precluded measurement of mm. 196ff. and 255ff.

We can ask whether most of these data are relevant to musicians today. After all, do we not use the latest editions, the recent printings, which are supposed to contain the corrected MM numbers, if there are any? But how do we know they do so? In the previous chapter it was pointed out first, that the original publisher of Bartók's music did not announce that the text was revised; second, that several printings could not have been revised by Bartók during his lifetime; third, that different revisions made by Bartók at different times led to authentic "variant forms" and in this respect the metronome or the duration marks were no exception (see Fig. 24 again).

In the following table I compare the MM numbers and durations given to pieces from the series *For Children* incorporated into the 1937 2-volume Rózsavölgyi set *Zongorázó ifjúság* (*Jugend am Klavier*; *Young People at the Piano*) with those given in the 1943 revised version published by Boosey & Hawkes, and with the actual durations of Bartók's 1945 recordings of some of these pieces. (There are four additional pieces taken from the *Ten Easy Piano Pieces*; here the 1943 revision for the planned volume "Béla Bartók Masterpieces for Piano," published in the Archive Edition, is used as a revised version.)

Young People at the Piano (1938), Vols. 1–2

1.1 (etc.) = *For Children* vol. I no. 1 (etc.)
2.6 (etc.) = *For Children* vol. II no. 6 (etc.)
no. 1 (etc.) = *Ten Easy Piano Pieces* no. 1 (etc.)
1937   = 1937 rev. for *Young People at the Piano*
1943   = 1943 rev. for the B&H edition of *For Children*
      and the rev. ed. of *Ten Easy Piano Pieces* (in the Archive Edition)

Source	1937	1943	1937	1943	Bartók's Recording (1945)[39]
Vol. 1					
1 = 1.1	♩ = 112	♩ = 92	30″	32″	
2 = 1.2	♩ = 76	♩ = 74	50″	48″	
3 = 1.3	♩ = 66	♩ = 65	45″	45″	ca. 51″
4 = 1.4	♩ = 144	♩ = 120	50″	58″	ca. 48″
5 = 1.6	♩ = 160	♩ = 144	45″	50″	ca. 45″
6 = 1.10	♩ = 160	♩ = 160	38″	40″	ca. 42″
7 = 1.26	♪ = 184	♪ = 150	45″	40″	ca. 41″
8 = 2.14	♩ = 96	♩ = 85	35″	34″	
9 = 2.23	♩ = 69	♩ = 72	40″	40″	
10 = 2.6	♪ = 150*	♩ = 138	36″	40″	
11 = 2.7	♩ = 80	♩ = 84	50″	50″	
12 = no. 1	♩ = 60–66	♩ = 60–66	50″	1′	

*recte = ♪?

39. *Centenary Edition*, I:15.

Source	1937	1943	1937	1943	Bartók's Recording (1945)
Vol. 2					
1 = 1.15	♩ = 116	♩ = 112	30″	28″	ca. 31″
2 = 1.22	♩ = 112	♩ = 114	51″	52″	
3 = 2.18	♩ = 116	♩ = 100	38″	36″	
4 = 2.24	♩ = 78	♩ = 80	48″	50″	
5 = 2.8	♩ = 144	♩ = 120	33″	37″	
6 = 2.26	♩ = ca. 60	♩ = ca. 63	55″	1′	
7 = 2.30	♩ = 160	♩ = 138	50″	57″	
8 = no. 2	♩ = 69	♩ = 69	1′22″	1′45″	
9 = no. 3	♩ = 144	♩ = 144	47″	50″	
10 = no. 8	♩ = 80	♩ = 69	1′05″	1′04″	

Bartók did not have the *Young People* volumes at hand in America. Therefore the 1943 tempi are not reconsidered as revised versions of the 1938 ones, but independent data. In both cases, as we presume, he made up his mind, for the duration used his stopwatch, and arrived at more or less different tempi. All together four of the twenty-two have the same MM only, but at least the duration is different in these cases too. If we do a little experimentation with playing Bartók's variant MM instructions and measuring the duration of each performance, plus listening to Bartók's own performance of the six pieces, we see that depending on the suspension of the last chord, on the amount of ritenuto and rubato, and so forth, the duration might vary considerably. And we see that the Bartókian phenomenon of metronome vs. duration in most cases is neither contradictory nor confusing, but natural and musical.

However, for the time being there are problematic editions, variant editions, misprints,[40] mistakes even in Bartók's own corrections,[41] leading to contradictory cases that cannot easily be handled in a commercial edition but in the future complete critical edition only. As an example let us take the *Fourteen Bagatelles* for piano. The 1908 Rozsnyai 1st edition, after unaltered later prints, as a whole was re-engraved for the two successors of the nationalized publishing house Rózsavölgyi (ed. in 1952 by Suvini Zerboni, Milan; in 1953 by Zeneműkiadó [later, Editio Musica], Budapest). None of the new editions contained Bartók's revisions made

40. A famous misprint of a metronome number came in Concerto for Orchestra, Mov. II: Bartók clearly wrote ♩ = 94 (PB 80FSID1), but the photostat of the MS serving as the engraver's copy of the B&H edition (PB 80FSFC2) cut off the top of the page (with the old title, "II Presentando le coppie"), making it 74! Koussevitzky had the correct MM in his copy and, as his 1944 recorded performance proves, conducted it in the right tempo.

41. An interesting example is the wrong MM of *Four Dirges* no. 3, ♩ = 50 in the Rózsavölgyi 1st ed. and in the Archive Edition, although based on Bartók's American revision. In the late 1930s Iván Engel pointed it out to Bartók, who corrected the MM to ♩ = 60–70 (facs. of corrected copy in Bónis/*Így láttuk*, 136).

around 1943 in the United States[42] for the planned "Masterpieces" album mentioned above (with new MM in six pieces and duration given to all, with fingering, orthographic changes, etc.). Nor did the Boosey & Hawkes "New Version Cop. 1950" (B&H 16980) follow these corrections. Then the 1981 Archive Edition finally made use of the composer's revision, unfortunately not without mistakes (see, e.g., the duration of no. 2, and the MM value in no. 14):

Fourteen Bagatelles (1908, rev. ca. 1943)

No.	Old MM[43]	New MM if different	Duration	Bartók's Recording
1	♩ = 66		1′20″	
2	𝅗𝅥 = 76	𝅗𝅥 = 84	1′48″*	45″; 44″[44]
3	𝅗𝅥. = 46	♩ = 126	45″	
4	♪ = 69	♩ = 69[45]	1′10″	
5	𝅗𝅥 = 84		1′10″	
6	𝅗𝅥 = 69		1′35″	
7	♩ = 70		1′57″	1′56″[46]
8	♩ = 54–60		1′45″	
9	♩ = 50	𝅗𝅥. = 62	1′37″	
10	𝅗𝅥 = 92		2′35″	2′16″[47]
11	𝅗𝅥 = 56		—	
12	♩ = 72	♪ = 72	3′6″	
13	♩ = 60–72		1′46″	
14	♩ = 108	𝅗𝅥. = 120[48]	1′55″	

We discuss further aspects of Bartók's authentic tempi in the context of his own recorded performances.

SELECTED PROBLEMS OF BARTÓK'S NOTATION

The aim of the following discussion of selected problems is not to give a systematic guide to Bartók's general performance practice — that purpose requires further extensive studies and a whole book[49] — but to shed light on the need for a chronology-

42. Bartók corrected his own copy of the 1st edition (PB 18PFC2). N.B. For the *Bartók Album* in 1940 in Budapest he selected nos. 2, 3, 5, 10, 14 of the *Bagatelles*. The printer's copy of the belated (posthumous) edition has not survived, but Bartók made orthographic changes and corrected the MM value in *Bagatelle* no. 14 from quarter to dotted quarter.

43. Only the first MM of a piece is marked here.

44. HMV recording 1929; Continental recording 1942 (see *Centenary Edition*, I:1/3a and I:16/1). The asterisked duration 1′48″ in the revised copy is an error; it should read 48″.

45. Quarter value in the Archive Edition; but the eighth not corrected in Bartók's copy.

46. Private recording for wax cylinder ca. 1912 (*Centenary Edition*, II:1).

47. Private recording for wax cylinder ca. 1912 (*Centenary Edition*, II:1).

48. Quarter in the Archive Edition, dotted quarter in the *Bartók Album*.

49. In addition to articles and recollections, see Benjamin Suchoff, *Guide to Bartók's Mikrokosmos* (London: Boosey and Hawkes, 1957, rev. ed. 1971).

oriented study in this subject; to show examples of how some aspects of the notation reflect basic problems of the true acoustic form of a Bartók composition; and finally, to clear up a few fundamental questions of Bartók's music for the performer.

The first group of selected topics deals with general problems, followed by special questions for strings, for orchestra, and for piano.

Tempo inscriptions, tempo articulation. For Bartók, Italian was the language of verbal instructions in musical notation.[50] From his study years on he was quite good at expressing himself with great subtlety (and, in contrast to the MM numbers, without much hesitation, as the manuscripts prove). But his vocabulary changed and the inscriptions grew more and more suggestive. Typical changes are that rit., ritard. gradually decreased and ritornando al, tornando al, allarg., rallent. increased, along with attributes that refined them (poco, etc.). Or that for the presentation of a slower statement in his music, instead of quieto or più quieto, later sostenuto[51] or poco sost. predominated. The words Più mosso or Meno mosso (instead of a conventional tempo indication or a slightly faster or slower MM) seem to refer to the same tempo/character class but with more, or less, agitation in the performance. The combination of speed and character is often very suggestive: a tempo, ma tranquillo; Più mosso, pesante; Più lento, espressivo; Più presto, scorrevole; Allegretto capriccioso[52] (poco rubato); Allegretto con indifferenza; agitato e rubato (examples from String Quartets nos. 5–6). In earlier printings, following the manuscript, the shades of the basic tempo (rall., accel., etc.) were often printed under the stave (between the two staves for piano) together with the dynamics, which Bartók later changed by transferring all tempo instructions above the stave.

The sign ⌢ is often supplemented by *breve* or *lunga*, with or without parentheses; in earlier works the first, the fermata breve, above the bar (e.g., in String Quartet no. 1) perhaps means something like a ⁹ in the later notation. He explained a crucial distinction to the editor of Boosey & Hawkes (letter of December 7, 1939):[53]

---

50. But in 1908–1911 Bartók used a number of Hungarian words, most typically in piano music between two staves, to express the suggested character more strongly than the established Italian words did: *harsány hangon* [in a loud voice] (*Seven Sketches* no. 5), *dülöngélő ritmusban* [in stumbling rhythm; rev. ed., molto rubato], *kicsit durván* [a bit rudely], *száraz tónussal* [with a dry tone; rev. ed., secco] (*Three Burlesques* no. 2, mm. 1, 16, 30); or in German: *gedehnt* [drawling] (*Fourteen Bagatelles* no. 12, m. 2). Some such very expressive instructions were left out of Bartók's American revision (see the Archive Edition).

51. In the explanation of signs he used in his Beethoven sonata editions, Bartók made this distinction: "*Sostenuto* = abrupt hold back; *ritard.* and *riten.* = gradual hold back." In the note to the 1908 edition of *Fourteen Bagatelles* he wrote: "*Sostenuto* indicates a sudden slowing down of the tempo, *ritard.* or *riten.*, a gradual slowing down."

52. A misprint in String Quartet no. 2, Mov. II: not "Allegro molto capriccioso" (i.e., molto capriccioso fast piece), as in the UE ed., but "Allegro molto, capriccioso" (MS).

53. In an earlier text, the 1916 preface to Bach's *Notenbüchlein für Anna Magdalena*, Bartók was more specific about the length of the comma: "Hardly perceptible stop."

, (comma) means not only an interruption, but also an additional rest (*Luftpause*);
I means only an interruption (division of sound) without extra rest.[54]

A note about the Bartókian use of the term rubato. The performer must know that earlier compositions have a great amount of rubato instructions, but works from the 1930s have much less. The shift is misleading, because what changed was not Bartók's music but his confidence that musicians coming from other schools, nations, generations would understand the proper meaning of his rubato, poco rubato, molto rubato. When Bartók prescribed rubato he did not refer to eighteenth-century "stolen time" (free performance within the bar), but for a time to Lisztian free rhythm, and after 1908 mostly to the parlando-rubato of folk music. The latter is not a rhapsodic rendition per se with romantic slowing down, but a characteristic declamation, often quite agitated, as if there were a text behind the themes. Fortunately Bartók's recordings give ample examples of the different rubato styles of his concept.

Dynamics and characters. Bartók was indefatigable in giving precise dynamic instructions and supplying more or marking changes if needed. He knew that the grade of dynamic volume between *pp* and *ff* (or *ppp* and *fff*) alone is fictitious, but additional Italian words would help a lot to find the proper volume and character, to specify the function of a given voice in the texture. Here are some samples in combination with *piano*:[55]

p, senza calore	*p, ma con calore*
p, semplice	*p, ma espressivo*
p, grazioso	*p, dolce*
p, leggero, grazioso	*p, più dolce, lontano*
p, leggerissimo	*p, distinto*
p, leggero, in rilievo	*p, marcato*
p, oscuro	*p, subito*
p, meccanico	*sempre p*

In Bartók's notation *in rilievo* (or in a given context, *espr.*) had a meaning similar to Schoenberg's *Hauptstimme* sign. For accent he used the grades between *sff* and –; in the explanation of signs in the performing edition of pieces from J. S. Bach's *Notenbüchlein für Anna Magdalena* Bartók gave the following instructions:[56]

sf = strongest accent
∧ = still "rather strong" accent[57]

54. There are, however, misprints in the commercial editions: in String Quartet no. 2, Mov. II, between no. 22–23 the signs , must be understood as I .
55. Selected from String Quartets nos. 5–6.
56. See the facsimile of the German original in Somfai/*19th-Century Ideas*, 82.
57. Unfortunately around 1908–1910 Bartók was not consistent enough to require the distinct use of — as I call it — marcatissimo (∧) and marcato (>) signs of his autograph score in copies and engraving. As a result the printed text of String Quartet no. 1 (see Facsimile 55) in this respect is unreliable in all editions.

> = weak accent

– = the tenuto sign above single note(s) in slurred passages means a gentle emphasis by means of a different tone quality.[58]

Cresc.–decresc. hairpins involved trouble for Bartók. His habit was to write a variety of hairpins with a wider angle than is traditional in modern engraved music (sometimes with an additional *molto* in the hairpin), occasionally with a slanting direction of small hairpins following the rising motive. But for a long time he did not put his hairpins into their exact position in the engraver's copy, and the engravers were careless: a hairpin might end before the bar (although it should have led to the next dynamic mark) or might not align with the other dynamic signs, and so on. So Bartók corrected, made angry notes in the margin of the proofs, but finally gave up. After all corrections on an engraved plate were expensive and often impossible without the re-engraving of whole systems.[59]

For a short time in his music (*Bagatelles*) as well as in performing editions (e.g., *Well-tempered Clavier*) Bartók differentiated between thin and bold-line hairpins in print.[60] As he explained in the revised edition of the latter: "The thin type . . . denotes a slight *cresc.* and *decresc.* restricted rather to one voice whereas the heavy type . . . a larger and more general *crescendo* affecting all voices alike." For instance in *Bagatelle* no. 1 only the diminuendo hairpin in mm. 13–14 was printed in bold,[61] a differentiation that unfortunately vanished in the later photoreproductions and new engravings.

Performing signs in articulation. The composer's text on the Anna Magdalena Bach pieces gives the essentials of Bartók's understanding of the signs of articulation. From staccatissimo to legato he listed:

1. the wedge, staccatissimo, "which goes together with a certain kind of accentuation and sharper tone quality";

2. the dot, the normal staccato, the length of which "oscillates between the very short and ca. half of the note value";

3. the portato (the slurred staccato),[62] where the length is "almost half of the note [value]" and is connected "with a certain specific coloring";

---

58. At my inquiry, Bartók's one-time chamber music partners confirmed the double function of the tenuto sign.

59. With recent printing techniques such corrections present no major problem. Corrected reprints of B&H and UE editions, prepared since 1989 by Peter Bartók, handle dozens of such inaccuracies. But the wide angle and the slanting direction of certain hairpins are elements of Bartók's notation that can be properly reconsidered only in the context of a complete edition.

60. See the facsimile of Bartók's instructions to the engraver of the *Bagatelles*, item 4, in Somfai/*Ms vs. Urtext*, 61.

61. See plate 2 in Somfai/*19th-Century Ideas*, 76.

62. Bartók mistakenly wrote "portamento"; see Somfai/*19th-Century Ideas*, n. 36, for possible reasons.

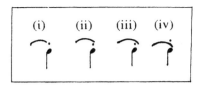

FIGURE 25   Slur-and-staccato ending
in Bartók's notation.

4. ⊤ the half-staccato (*das Zeichen der Halbkürze*), which should be longer than half of the value;[63]

5. the tenuto sign, which "above individual notes means that the note is to be held out in full length, above a series of notes means that the notes, without being slurred together, [are to be rendered] possibly in full note value";

6. the slur, the sign for legato,[64] but one that "in legato passages, lacking another sign, we also use for marking the phrase" (Bartók refers to the traditional two-level slur-above-slurs notation).

Bartók made a special warning, revealing that in his youth the eighteenth-century (C. P. E. Bach, etc.) keyboard traditions were still alive:

> The end of a slur marking the phrase by no means indicates that the note under the end of the slur is played staccato, or that the duration of it should be shortened at all. This is the case only if there is a staccato sign (dot) above the last note of the phrase or a sign of division (|) after it.[65]

For the major part of his oeuvre the notation of the slur-and-staccato ending was conventional in Bartók's handwriting (Fig. 25): the dot either continued the curve of the slur (see Fig. 25i) or was between the end of the slur and the note (Fig. 25ii); sometimes (if the articulation was above and not under the notes), whether intentionally or not,[66] it was outside the curve (Fig. 25iv). Then, beginning with the works written around 1938 and printed by Boosey & Hawkes (Violin Concerto, Divertimento, String Quartet no. 6, *Contrasts*, but *Mikrokosmos* too) Bartók sud-

63. It was not until 1908 that Bartók discovered the importance of a shade of touch in the half-staccato (*Bagatelles*, his 2nd volume of the *Well-tempered Clavier*), see Somfai / *19th-Century Ideas*, 76–79 and pl. 4.

64. In his performing editions Bartók described — and in his own music as a pianist used — the legatissimo that (in the phrase explaining signs for the Beethoven sonatas) "means an exaggerated *legato* (when every note is sustained somewhat longer than the beginning of the next [note])."

65. He added that between staccato notes the sign of division (|) means the end of the phrase.

66. Such a contradictory case is the two-note figure in m. 20, etc., in the autograph draft score of Mov. III of String Quartet no. 1.

EXAMPLE 76   Examples of the two types of the slur-and-staccato ending in the Violin Concerto,
Contrasts, and String Quartet no. 6.

denly became fussy about whether the dot was inside (Fig. 25iii, which I call "portato separation") or outside (Fig. 25iv, which I call "end-staccato").[67] He carefully
differentiated it in his manuscripts and corrected in the proofs. In his letter to
Boosey & Hawkes (December 7, 1939) Bartók made a clear distinction:

> in string (bow-) instruments[68] (a) ⁀ and (b) ⁀ or (a) ‿ and (b) ‿ have different
> meaning. (a) means an interruption before the last quaver, (b) means a shorter sound
> of the last note, without any interruption.

A few examples (Ex. 76) from late scores can convince us that such a differentiation between the portato-like separation (a special bow stroke) and the conventional staccato ending is highly meaningful and a considerable help for the string
player. There are scattered signs that also in earlier scores, as a special effect, Bartók
wanted to have the dot expressly under the slur.[69] In some UE scores, the end
staccato, although conspicuously outside the slur in the engraver's copy, appeared in
the negligent neutral form.[70] There is evidence that in America Bartók worked on
the revision of the neutral-position slur-and-staccato endings in earlier prints.[71]
Despite such aids, a full retrospective revision of hundreds of ambiguous places in
scores published before the authorized B&H editions must follow the intuition of
the interpreter rather than the arbitrary decision of the editor of a new printing.

Pitch notation: accidentals, glissandi, micro intervals. In 1908 in the preliminary note to
Fourteen Bagatelles Bartók announced, "Accidentals affect only those notes which are

67. I have not yet succeeded in discovering the source of this distinction, which may have come as
advice from a string player or violin tutor.
68. But Bartók used it in the notation of other instruments too, including the piano.
69. E.g., in the proofs of the 1st ed. of String Quartet no. 1 he made a clear correction at no. 38 of
Mov. III.
70. E.g., in mm. 24–26 of vl. 1 in Mov. III of String Quartet no. 5.
71. String Quartet no. 2, Mov. II, from m. 5 before no. 2 to no. 37 (where the revision broke off): the
staccato throughout outside the slur (PB 42FSFC1); likewise in Forty-four Duos nos. 16, 29, 35 (PB
69VVFC2).

EXAMPLE 77   Examples of glissando notation in String
Quartet no. 2, in *The Wooden Prince*, in
Sonata for Violin and Piano no. 1,
and in the *Four Orchestral Pieces*.

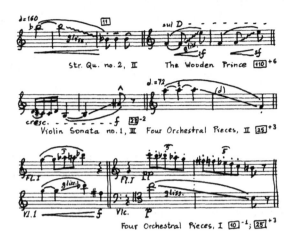

on the same line or in the same space, and only within one measure. . . . An exception is made only when notes are tied over into the next measure." He added music examples.[72] For a few years Bartók edited his music according to this strict formula. However, with the years — perhaps under the influence of experience in teaching and performing, but perhaps with the intention to show that he wrote tonal compositions — Bartók stepped back to some extent. For instance in the revised edition of *For Children* he introduced key signatures; in the American revision of the *Bagatelles* and other sets he applied cautionary accidentals;[73] as early as the 1910s–1920s he used key signatures in folksong arrangements, and occasionally in so-called original compositions as well (e.g., in *Nine Little Piano Pieces* nos. 1, 4, 6, 9).

A little detail about Bartók's pitch notation: If a chord or cluster (typically on piano) included two notes on the same line — for example, B♭–B♮ — he wrote Y-shaped stems. Herr Wöss, senior editor at UE, changed these to simple stems with a ⊔-form bracket.[74] In the early 1920s Bartók had to accept the change but did not agree with it.

The glissando notation in Bartók's scores is not uniform. Wavy line from note to note (in early scores), straight line but with a little gap between the note and the line (early 1920s), straight line "directly from the note head into the other note head"[75]

72. With the key signature in no. 1 (4 sharps vs. 4 flats) he had a special purpose of course.
73. E.g., in *Bagatelle* no. 12: naturals in the first chord of m. 11, naturals to d¹ in the left hand in mm. 11–12.
74. E.g., m. 19 in Mov. II of *Five Village Scenes* (see the editor's note in PB 54VoPFC2).
75. From the 1929 "Hints to the engraver" of String Quartet no. 3.

(from ca. 1928) are chronological variants of the same sign, often with the verbal instruction *gliss.*, *gliss.* or *quasi gliss.* to accompany progressions of normal-size notes or small notes too. The combination of tied notes with following glissando under the slur (see Ex. 77) is the more significant, because this is the only way Bartók indicated the delayed beginning of a slide.

Otherwise, glissandi were to be played as Bartók specifically demanded in the note to *Music for Strings, Percussion, and Celesta* (and elsewhere, and as his chamber music partners clearly remember):[76]

> All of the glissandi marked for strings as well as for timpani should be played so that the starting tone is immediately left and a slow but constant slide during the full value of the first note is executed.

In pizzicato–glissando combinations only the first note is plucked.

Bartók was very interested in micro-intervals — quarter tones, and otherwise narrowed intervals of the 12-tone system (there can be little doubt that for Bartók it was an equal-tempered system). In the transcription of recorded folk music he invented a system to differentiate intervals of approximately a quarter tone (marked ♯/2, ♭/2) and less than a quarter tone (by using ↑ and ↓ above the note).[77] In composition the full score of *The Miraculous Mandarin* (1924) made the first use of quarter tone as color: to fill F♯–E♭ with four descending tones (at no. 84 in the cello) and to play a narrow *bariolage* on A and a quarter tone lower (after no. 85 in vl. 1), in both cases using the reversed flat sign with a footnote: *senkt um einen Viertelton*. In the late 1930s Bartók returned to the idea, this time using ↑ and ↓ for a quarter tone higher and lower, in combination with open string (Violin Concerto I, m. 303) or as a *Dorfmusikanten*-type "mistuned" effect in the "Burletta" (String Quartet no. 6, III, m. 26). The only piece in which the quarter tone affects the concept of the form itself is of course the original version of the Presto in the Sonata for Solo Violin (1944), which was not available to the public for decades, as only the alternative (easier) version appeared in print. Note that in addition to quarter tones marked with arrows, in mm. 57–62 "equal division of the distance c♯–d♯ (2/3 tones)"[78] was also required.

Special instructions in string parts. Bartók used a number of refined instructions for the player of his quartets and other string parts, mostly Italian terms but some French ones too, probably acknowledging the vernacular of his partners from the

76. Here too the recordings of the Hungarian String Quartet have documentary value, and younger groups who studied with the members of the quartet, the Takács Quartet for example, keep the tradition.

77. See my comments on "Bartók's transcriptions" in László Somfai, ed., *Hungarian Folk Music Gramophone Records with Béla Bartók's Transcriptions* (Budapest: Hungaroton, 1981), LPX 18058–60.

78. Bartók's note in the autograph *Lichtpause* fair copy; cf. m. 58 in the 1994 Urtext Edition (Boosey & Hawkes).

Hubay school. Special notes such as *con tutta la lunghezza dell'arco* appeared in String Quartet no. 3, and at the same time he became rigorous in demanding round ○ for harmonics and oval ○ for open string. Double circle indicated a special fingernail pizz. (Quartet no. 5, II, m. 32), + normal left-hand fingernail pizz. (Quartet no. 4, IV, m. 36). The so-called Bartók pizzicato first appeared in Quartet no. 4. The composer had a clear idea about the graphic representation of this pizzicato, as his comment on Facsimile 56 (in the previous chapter) shows.

The subject of down-bow and up-bow signs in Bartók's strings parts — in solo parts, string quartets, even orchestral string parts — has not yet been studied extensively and can perhaps be handled only in the context of the critical edition satisfactorily. It is a fact that from the mid-1910s (String Quartet no. 2, *The Wooden Prince*) onward, but most typically from the 1920s (Violin Sonatas nos. 1–2, *Dance Suite*, the orchestration of the *Four Orchestral Pieces* and the *Miraculous Mandarin*), down-bow and up-bow signs occur already in the draft score to express the intended proper effect. Their presence gives us indirect information about Bartók's experience with the Hungarian school: the down-bow was still the natural accent, whereas the up-bow meant an upbeat-like gentler beginning of a phrase. Therefore the majority of Bartók's authentic bowing signs must be understood not as technical aids but as primarily musical suggestions for the accentuation of unusual or ambiguous places: for example, vl. 1 in the Seconda parte of String Quartet no. 3, after no. 3. At the same time, however, in concert copies of difficult string parts (such as manuscript sources of the Violin Sonatas nos. 1–2, manuscript parts of String Quartet no. 3), the technically motivated bowing of Bartók's musicians has survived. Bartók adopted some of the bowings for the printed version and rejected others. There is enough evidence in his correspondence that Bartók asked his string players (such as Székely and Menuhin) to check their difficult solo parts and send copies furnished with the necessary performing signs so that he could consider them for the printed edition. This request had a special purpose: Bartók wanted to know how to put on paper unambiguously the form they developed orally during rehearsals.

Vibrato and non vibrato instructions rarely appear in Bartók's string parts, but the occasional presence of them is telling evidence that he regarded a constant vibrato as neither obligatory nor beautiful. Molto vibrato plus wavy line, clearly suggesting an unusually heavy shake in *fff*, appears before the end of the Seconda parte in String Quartet no. 3. Wavy line with *(vibrato)* in parentheses (actually *vibrando* in the 1905 layer of the autograph score), together with molto espr., in a place marked ritardando molto for solo violin in Suite no. 2 (Movement II, before no. 35) is an early example of exaggerated vibrato as a special effect. The strings play non vibrato in the 1st Adagio of Piano Concerto no. 2. And there is a famous case, the series of non vibrato alternating with vibrato in the Non troppo lento Movement III of String Quartet no. 4 (mm. 1–35, 47 and 52).

The notation of the beginning of this slow movement developed in three stages (see Facsimile 57): in the sketchy first draft, in the continuity draft, and in the fair

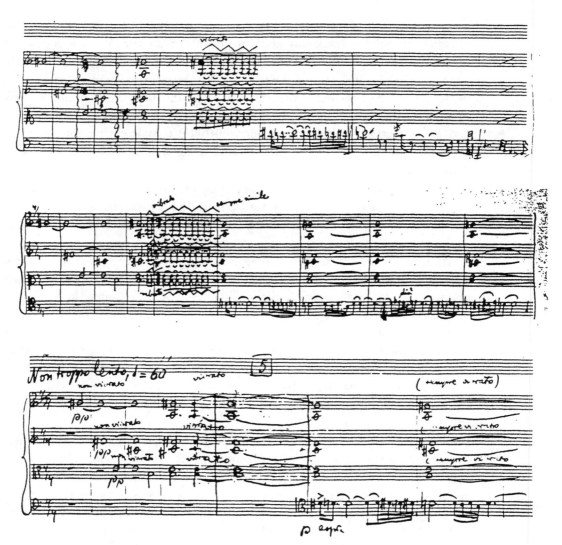

FACSIMILE 57   String Quartet no. 4, the beginning of Movement III in the sketchy draft (top), in
the full draft (middle), and in the autograph copy (bottom) (PB 62FSS1, p. 32 and
p. 9; 62FSFC1, p. 11).

copy from which Bartók had erased the previous form.[79] The exact meaning of the
tied eighth-note repetition with the zigzag and the vibrato above it in this tempo
(quarter = 60) is an enigma. Since we have no knowledge that Bartók was aware of
the eighteenth-century technique of *Bogenvibrato*,[80] our best guess is that he intended a special kind of increasing / decreasing vibrato, with peaks on the 2nd eighth

79. See p. 32, p. 9 in PB 62FSS1, and p. 11 in 62FSFC1.
80. Although from the score of the late Beethoven string quartets Bartók was familiar with the
phenomenon of the pulsation of tied chords at the end of slow movements, which is a subtle rhythmic
bow vibrato, as at the end of Mov. I of Op. 131 or Mov. III of Op. 132.

note, the 4th, and so on — that is, as syncopation. It would be a stylized and sublime version of the *dűvő* accompaniment in instrumental folk music. We cannot rule out the possibility that Bartók tried out this special effect with the Waldbauer Quartet, was not satisfied, and corrected the fair copy. The retreat to a simple vibrato above the long notes, as opposed to the non vibrato chords, in spite of the tremendous effect of cold and warm in this formulation, certainly seems to be a compromise. Today's conventionally exaggerated contrast between completely straight-toned and heavily throbbing voices in an over-vibrated string style could hardly have been Bartók's ideal.

A survey of the general styles of string playing in Bartók's time, supplemented by the recordings of his favored violinist partners and the expression marks in his notation, demonstrates that Bartók's espressivo, molto espress. ma con calore, cantabile, and similar indications are primarily instructions for vibrato in performance. By contrast, hardly any modern vibrato seems needed when the score indicates leggero, semplice, or marcato. Even grazioso and dolce could be a genuine contrast to espressivo, to be played with not much vibrato. As an example: in the Lento Movement III of String Quartet no. 2 the dolce entries after no. 2 require a minimum amount of vibrato, the espr. entries after 8 measures considerably more; the quasi non vibrato chords at no. 4 with a warm vibrato from the espr. molto cresc. seem to be an authentic tradition; the *pp* sotto voce Debussy reference (before no. 7) is another place for quasi non vibrato performance; and the Più andante before no. 9 needs vibrato in the molto espr. vl. 1 and vlc. parts but even tones in the middle voices.

We cannot and would not wish to change performances that have transformed the taste of audiences today. We have come to expect a sound quite different from that of older chamber music ensembles, a sound that sometimes makes older ensembles seem antiquated. Yet musicians who play Bartók's works must be aware of the composer's expectations of great variety of timbres, must study and adopt, transform and translate them into the instrumental language of our times — possibly without heavy losses.

Orchestral seating, percussion. There are two known seating plans printed in a score: the semicircular position of the special orchestra in *Music for Strings, Percussion, and Celesta*; and the grouping of the various instruments, an actual seating plan with proportionate drawings, in the Sonata for two Pianos and Percussion. As to the second, the only significant difference between the printed plan and Bartók's own drawing[81] is that he added a small drawing to a note of the seating plan according to which the *gran cassa* (bass drum) was a modest-size one that in upright position could be placed under the stand of the xylophone (Fig. 26).[82] Here indeed is

81. See p. 16 in PB 75TFSID1FC1.
82. This note with the drawing was left out of the printed score. In a letter of July 22, 1942, Erwin Stein wrote from London to Hans Heinsheimer in New York: "Our expert just told me that a Xylophon

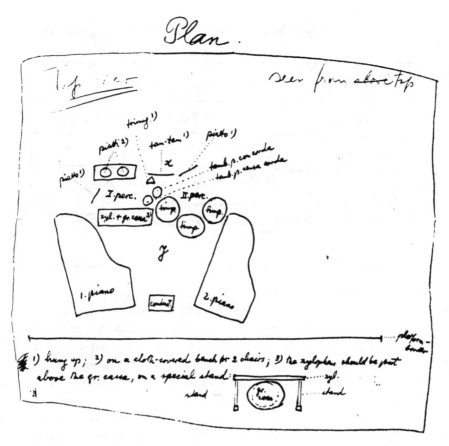

FIGURE 26   Sonata for two Pianos and Percussion: Bartók's diagram of the seating plan
with a sketch of the place of the bass drum.

evidence from a historic performance — think of the huge drums often used today
that might have a grand sound but disrupt the balance in Bartók's score.[83]

As to the seating plan in the pocket score of *Music,* it is not exactly the same as that
drawn by Bartók (Fig. 27);[84] he put the timpani in the axis, but in the last row (not
before the double basses, as printed) and specified the place of the harp, etc., behind
the piano.

---

cannot be placed on a special stand above the Bass Drum. The modern Xylophones are fixed on a stand,
from which resonance tubes are hanging down (similar to the vibraphone) so there is no place for the
Bass Drum. Will you please tell this to Bartok so that he may decide whether it should be altered or not"
(BBA 202/19). Bartók perhaps agreed to the deletion. The original note, however, tells us that in
Bartók's experience the xylophone had no resonance tubes; he was writing for this older form of the
instrument.

83. Modern timpani with plastic heads instead of leather have a similarly demolishing effect on Bartók
performances.

84. On an extra page in PB 74FSFC1.

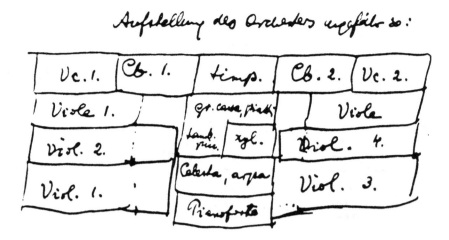

FIGURE 27 *Music for Strings, Percussion, and Celesta*: Bartók's diagram of the seating plan.

This placement is an important part of the acoustic concept of the work and it is a crucial matter whether the string basses in the back of the stage embrace the ensemble or keep it apart, or whether the musical punctuation at so many points of the movements comes exactly from the center or not. (It is too bad that most modern performances let the drums take their normal place outside the semicircle.)

One more indisputable document shows that Bartók liked to have the percussion instruments in the middle, with the piano. In a list of misprints in the full score of Piano Concerto no. 1,[85] written in German, he added to the notes:[86] "The percussion (including timpani) must be placed directly next to the piano (behind the piano)."

On the analogy of this note we might place the percussion group also in Piano Concerto no. 2 (and eventually in other scores with orchestral piano?) in the kernel of the orchestra. Furthermore, we know that even in the Violin Concerto (no. 2) Bartók suggested placement of the percussion, as far as possible, inside the orchestra.[87]

Bartók's notation for the special use of sticks, drums, cymbals (suspended or in a pair, their clashing indicated with "a 2"), for the proper place of the hit, the technique for sordino, etc., changed during the years, but he gave good instructions from the score of the *Rumanian Dance* (1911) through the Piano Concerto no. 1 to

85. BBA, a page from Béla Bartók Jr.'s collection.
86. Several generations of the UE edition of the pocket score and full score omitted this note, restored in recent printings.
87. Zoltán Székely wrote to Bartók shortly after the March 23, 1939, Amsterdam world premiere: "Az ütőhangszereket kivánságodra lehetőleg a zenekarban helyeztük el" [As you requested, as far as possible we placed the percussion instruments inside the orchestra] (unpublished letter of Apr. 3, 1939, BBA).

the 2-piano Sonata. Incidentally, the list of instruments on the page before a printed score is often incomplete.

Notation of piano works in different styles. The performer has to recognize that from about 1908 two basic styles occur in the notation of Bartók's piano music (with transitory forms and irregular cases):

1. piano works in a quasi performing-edition-like elaboration: with detailed pedaling and fingering instructions, appropriate for educational use (e.g., *For Children, Ten Easy Piano Pieces, Rumanian Folk Dances, Rumanian Christmas Songs*), and

2. piano works in a concert-style notation, intended primarily for Bartók's own performance: here pedaling and fingering instructions appear mostly when they are a part of the intended effect in harmony or touch[88] (e.g., Suite op. 14, the piano part of Violin Sonatas nos. 1–2, Sonata 1926, *Out Doors,* Piano Concertos nos. 1–2).

There is no sharp dividing line between the two styles. For instance *Improvisations* (1920), one of Bartók's most original arrangements of peasant music and a favorite item on his recitals, was edited so carefully that there is hardly a note for which the touch is not precisely indicated. Why? We can only guess that in the early Universal Edition years Bartók was especially careful in fixing the style of works based on folk material because he supposed that the intended style was alien to listeners or musicians. Yet in *Mikrokosmos,* after all an exemplary instructive collection of progressive piano pieces, a fairly precise but considerably simpler notation is manifest. Probably Bartók recognized that the precise meaning of performing signs was understood and taught differently in different conservatories, countries, cultures. Nor is *Mikrokosmos* by any means typical of the whole piano oeuvre of Bartók, in music or notation. The dominating role of it in teaching (and analyzing) Bartók, beyond the obvious profit, may have a disadvantageous influence too.

Taking only pedal signs in Bartók's piano parts (Fig. 28), we see that their frequency has been polarized between professional and didactic notation but with irregular cases on both sides: relatively few in *Mikrokosmos,* none in the *First Term at the Piano,* a lot in the *Improvisations* and Violin Sonata no. 1. In Fig. 29 I catalogue

88. See for instance the use of the pedal signs and (at the end) the 1 + 2 fingering in Mov. II of the Suite op. 14. It is confusing, however, that difficult concert-style works (e.g., the Three Studies, Piano Concerto no. 2) often have Bartók's fingering, typical of his own technique and his own hands, which he supplied when learning the piece from the MS that then became the engraver's copy. Why did he not delete these fingerings? We can rule out sheer carelessness, and Bartók did not explain. Perhaps he remembered Liszt's fingering in concert-style works, which, even if inconvenient for another pianist, give useful ideas about the intended performing style.

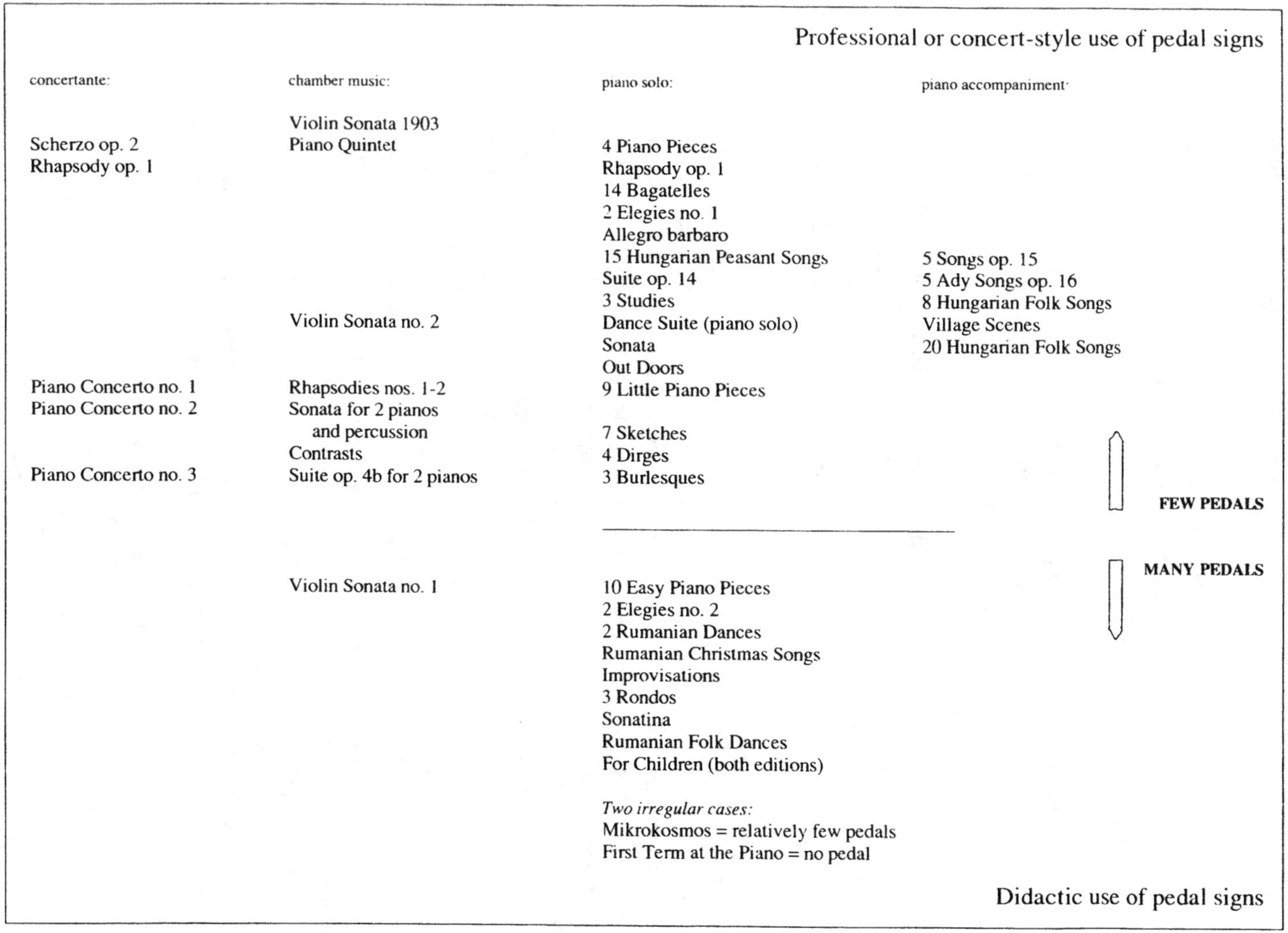

Professional or concert-style use of pedal signs

concertante:	chamber music:	piano solo:	piano accompaniment:
Scherzo op. 2	Violin Sonata 1903	4 Piano Pieces	5 Songs op. 15
Rhapsody op. 1	Piano Quintet	Rhapsody op. 1	5 Ady Songs op. 16
		14 Bagatelles	8 Hungarian Folk Songs
		2 Elegies no. 1	Village Scenes
		Allegro barbaro	20 Hungarian Folk Songs
		15 Hungarian Peasant Songs	
		Suite op. 14	
	Violin Sonata no. 2	3 Studies	
		Dance Suite (piano solo)	
		Sonata	
		Out Doors	
		9 Little Piano Pieces	
Piano Concerto no. 1	Rhapsodies nos. 1-2	7 Sketches	
Piano Concerto no. 2	Sonata for 2 pianos and percussion	4 Dirges	
	Contrasts	3 Burlesques	
Piano Concerto no. 3	Suite op. 4b for 2 pianos		

FEW PEDALS ⇦

MANY PEDALS ⇨

	Violin Sonata no. 1	10 Easy Piano Pieces	
		2 Elegies no. 2	
		2 Rumanian Dances	
		Rumanian Christmas Songs	
		Improvisations	
		3 Rondos	
		Sonatina	
		Rumanian Folk Dances	
		For Children (both editions)	

Two irregular cases:
Mikrokosmos = relatively few pedals
First Term at the Piano = no pedal

Didactic use of pedal signs

FIGURE 28   Frequency of pedal signs in Bartók's piano parts.

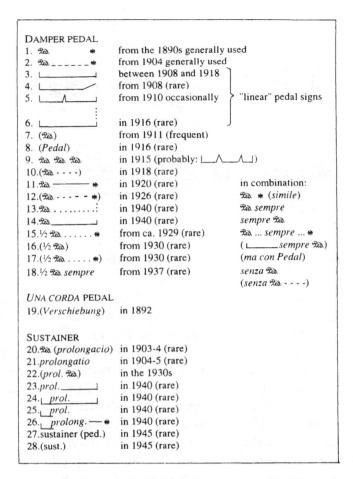

DAMPER PEDAL
1. 🎵 ∗	from the 1890s generally used	
2. 🎵 _ _ _ _ _ ∗	from 1904 generally used	
3. ⌐_____⌐	between 1908 and 1918	
4. ⌐_____╱	from 1908 (rare)	
5. ⌐__∧__⌐	from 1910 occasionally	"linear" pedal signs
6. ⌐_____⌐	in 1916 (rare)	
7. (🎵)	from 1911 (frequent)	
8. (*Pedal*)	in 1916 (rare)	
9. 🎵 🎵 🎵	in 1915 (probably: ⌐__∧__∧__⌐)	
10.(🎵 - - - -)	in 1918 (rare)	
11.🎵 ――――― ∗	in 1920 (rare)	in combination:
12.(🎵 - - - - - ∗)	in 1926 (rare)	🎵 ∗ (*simile*)
13.🎵 . . . .⋮	in 1940 (rare)	🎵 *sempre*
14.🎵_____⌐	in 1940 (rare)	*sempre* 🎵
15.½ 🎵 . . . . . . ∗	from ca. 1929 (rare)	🎵 ... *sempre* ... ∗
16.(½ 🎵)	from 1930 (rare)	(⌐_____*sempre* 🎵)
17.(½ 🎵 . . . . . ∗)	from 1930 (rare)	(*ma con Pedal*)
18.½ 🎵 *sempre*	from 1937 (rare)	*senza* 🎵
		(*senza* 🎵 - - - -)

UNA CORDA PEDAL
19.(*Verschiebung*)	in 1892

SUSTAINER
20.🎵 (*prolongacio*)	in 1903-4 (rare)
21.*prolongatio*	in 1904-5 (rare)
22.(*prol.* 🎵)	in the 1930s
23.*prol.*_____⌐	in 1940 (rare)
24.⌐ *prol.* ⌐	in 1940 (rare)
25.⌐ *prol.*	in 1940 (rare)
26.⌐ *prolong.* ― ∗	in 1940 (rare)
27.sustainer (ped.)	in 1945 (rare)
28.(sust.)	in 1945 (rare)

FIGURE 29   Survey of pedal signs and instructions in Bartók's
manuscripts and in the authorized editions.

pedal signs as they appear in manuscripts and authorized editions: damper, una corda, and sustainer pedal signs, with the date of their first use. In addition to the basic forms are variants in parentheses, most of which indicate a warning or free choice. Some represent typographical variants only; others are experiments or rare exceptions.

Between 1908–1918 Bartók clearly preferred the bracket-form linear pedal signs that could fix the exact point of pressure and release, gradual release, or quick half-changes much better than the conventional sign.[89] He was not consistent, although

89. The idea of the linear pedal sign may have come from a professor (such as Szendy or Chován) in the piano department of the Liszt Academy of Music, since Bartók adopted it in the performing edition of the *Well-tempered Clavier*; see Somfai/*19th-Century Ideas*, 78ff.

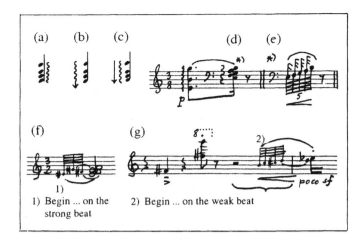

FIGURE 30   Experimentation in Bartók's notation.

mixing the signs usually meant a practical solution,[90] and Universal Edition was not in favor of the linear sign.[91] From 1921 onward the "Ped. ❋" type and its variants dominate, with an interesting bunch of combination forms ("Ped." plus bracket, etc.) in the fair copy of Suite op. 4b (1941) for 2 pianos. As a piece of general advice, before we make up our mind about pedaling in Bartók's works we should listen to the composer's own recordings, printed music in hand, in order to appreciate the amount and refined variety of pedaling in his performance.

Another general suggestion for pianists today is to experiment with old pianos that Bartók knew as the best in his youth in Budapest (Bechstein,[92] or Bösendorfer,[93] for example). To bring off certain pianistic effects in the given tempo on the latest Steinway or similar instrument requires special tricks.[94]

Special signs. An interesting quirk of Bartók's was his sudden burst of passion in inventing new solutions in his notation, an ardent fight for the exact printed realization of his ideas, then an equally sudden change of mind or loss of interest. His experimentation with the downward arpeggio is well known (Fig. 30): he aban-

90. In the *Rumanian Folk Dances* for piano Mov. IV, mm. 4–10, 11–12, 16–18 had the pedal sign no. 9 (= quick changes), the other movements the linear sign. In the *Ady Songs* op. 16 the pedal signs include, in addition to nos. 3 and 6 for special pedal effects, also no. 8, as a warning not to play without pedal.

91. E.g., the sign no. 11 at the beginning of *Improvisations* no. 8 in the UE edition was the publisher's solution for a simple no. 3 linear sign. It is less precise, but Bartók accepted it.

92. See his note on the half-pedal on a Bechstein, in connection with Beethoven op. 2 no. 2, II, m. 28.

93. During a relatively well-to-do period in Budapest he had Bösendorfer instruments. He also used the extra low keys of the Bösendorfer grand during the piano year 1926 (e.g., Sonata Mov. II).

94. Malcolm Bilson has pointed out that the opening F♯ in the left hand of the Sonata for Violin and Piano no. 2 would last longer on a modern Steinway concert grand than on pianos of the 1920s; thus a pianist using Bartók's metronome markings and dynamics needs tricks with the pedal to recreate the intended effect.

doned the earlier works' strange form of the wavy line on the wrong side of the chord (Fig. 30a)[95] for the very clear wavy arrow (Fig. 30b), as in Piano Concerto no. 2, whereas in later works he preferred a combination of arrow plus wavy line (Fig. 30c). Another idea, actually two seemingly different ideas, occurred to him in writing "The Night's Music" (*Out Doors* no. 4, 1926). Their common root was that in Bartók's experience small notes or groups of notes were usually played before the beat. So in the peasant-flute style episode he made a differentiation between upbeat and on-beat left-hand arpeggio chords (represented by standard and larger wavy lines in the UE printing; see Fig. 30d–e),[96] and with two footnotes (plus a bracket in the g-type notation) on the first page he indicated which small-note groups should begin on the beat and which before the beat.

Bartók was not persistent in using such little inventions. Of course we must realize that in his scores there are hundreds of solutions for irregular cases written in standard-size notation. Besides he knew well enough the limits of musical notation and recognized that beyond a certain point musicians do not like irregular or complicated scores. To some extent he used recordings as supplementary documents for his compositions and kept painstakingly exact notation for his transcription of folk music.

THE SIGNIFICANCE OF BARTÓK'S OWN RECORDINGS

Bartók firmly believed that his own recordings formed an essential part of the authentic transmission of his works. Writing about sound recording procedures in 1937, he stated that "our notation records on music paper the idea of the composer more or less inadequately; therefore the existence of instruments with which one can record precisely every intention and idea of the composer is indeed of great importance."[97] On the occasion of the reprinting of Suite op. 14 for piano, when he added the timing too to the score, he ventured to ask UE (letter May 13, 1937) to put a phrase on page 2, above the copyright or under the note "All rights reserved": *Authentische Grammophon-Aufnahme (Vortrag des Komponisten): His Master's Voice AN 468, 72–671/2*,[98] a surprising formulation.[99] But in his essay "Mechanical Music" mentioned above he also stressed that "the composer himself, when he is the

95. The first print's last page of the *Two Elegies* mixed up Bartók's original intention, because in the autograph his explanatory footnote said that the sign after the chord meant upwards (!) arpeggiation. He did not notice this error in the proofs (BBA 489 and 1995); later revised editions corrected it but made new errors. The notation is quite clear, however, in Mov. III of Violin Sonata no. 1.

96. Since in the autograph printer's copy both wavy lines were standard size and only the footnote specified the on-beat type, someone at UE may have suggested the graphic representation.

97. "Mechanical Music," *Essays*, 298.

98. This text was still included in some prints after 1945 but later vanished.

99. The formula *authentische Aufnahme* occurs for the *Allegro barbaro* too. In his German letter of July 13, 1936, to UE Bartók mentioned that the text was correct, he needed to add only the timing and the "gram. record-number of the authentic recording."

performer of his own composition, does not always perform his work exactly the same way. Why? Because he lives; because perpetual variability is a trait of a living creature's character."

This is of course a serious warning for us who scrutinize the documentary value of a composer's recordings: one recording alone may have lots of nonce features; two or more Bartók recordings of the same piece with identical or similar deviations from the printed text may mark intentional changes. A basic rule in handling Bartók's recordings is of course to consider the date and how the recording fits into the revisions of the printed music chronologically, and the genre of the recording, because the player had a chance to hear, judge, and eventually reject studio takes of a gramophone record but had no control over the live recordings of recitals or amateurs' recordings of broadcast concerts.

In the extensive commentaries to Vols. I–II ("Bartók at the Piano"; "Bartók Record Archives") of the 1981 *Centenary Edition of Bartók's Records (Complete)* I gave detailed documentation on the types of recordings:[100]

1. studio recordings, 1928–1942 (all together 262');[101]
2. piano rolls, 1928 (18');[102]
3. private phonograph recordings, 1910–ca. 1915 (12½');
4. recorded public recital, 1940 (70');
5. studio recordings of broadcasts, 1932–1945 (47');
6. phonoamateur recordings of broadcasts, 1936–1939 (177')

Some recordings were made very close to the time of the work's composition, and thus the interpretation was still fresh (e.g., nos. 3 and 6 of *Seven Sketches* on the 1910 and 1912 cylinders; the "Bagpipe" movement of *Petite Suite* on the Patria disc; the May 1940 studio recording of *Contrasts*). Others were refined in the course of twenty or thirty years (e.g., Violin Sonata no. 2 in the 1940 Library of Congress concert; the American recordings of pieces from the *Improvisations, For Children*). We should by all means know what Bartók played at the peak of his powers as a pianist (in studio recordings between 1928–1937), and what he played in the last years with an already painful shoulder.

100. In the rearranged CD version of vol. I, *Bartók at the Piano 1920–1945* (Budapest: Hungaroton, 1991; HCD 12326–31), and vol. II, *Bartók Recordings from Private Collections* (Budapest: Hungaroton Classic, 1995; HCD 12334–37), the commentaries, although they include some new data, were considerably reduced.

101. In each category are non-Bartók works too, in addition to piano solos, also chamber music, and accompaniment of singers.

102. Based on a recent study by János Mácsai ("Törölhető kérdőjelek?" [Superfluous question marks?], *Muzsika* 37, no. 1 [January 1994]: 14–16), the supposed date "1920–1922" given in the *Centenary Edition* (I:8) should be corrected to 1928. These Welte-Licensee-type paper rolls were made in New York. Following Mácsai's studies I now suggest that the supposed piano rolls made for Pleyela in 1922 in Paris (cf. *Centenary Edition*, II:1/6–9) are fragments of a recorded studio concert for the Hilversum Radio on Jan. 31, 1935.

Here are the recordings of his own music that exist in two or more versions (in the chronological order of composition):

Bagatelle no. 2 (1908): (1) 1929 His Master's Voice (HMV); (2) 1942
   Continental.
"Evening in Transylvania" (*Ten Easy Piano Pieces* no. 5, 1908): (1) 1928
   Welte-Licensee; (2) 1929 HMV; (3) 1935 Hilversum Radio; (4) 1945
   Vox.
"Bear Dance" (*Ten Easy Piano Pieces* no. 10, 1908): (1) 1912 wax cylinder;
   (2) 1929 HMV; (3) 1935 Hilversum Radio; (4) 1945 Vox.
For Children I no. 10 (ca. 1908): (1) 1912 wax cylinder; (2) 1945 Vox.
Two Rumanian Dances no. 1 (ca. 1909): (1–2) 1929 HMV (two takes);
   (3) 1935 Hilversum Radio.
Allegro barbaro (1911): (1) 1929 HMV; (2) 1935 Hilversum Radio.
Rumanian Folk Dances (1915): 1915 wax cylinder; 1928 Welte-Licensee.[103]
Suite op. 14 (1916): (1–2) 1929 HMV (two takes).
Three Rondos no. 1 (ca. 1916–1927): (1) 1936 Patria; (2) 1942
   Continental.
Rhapsody no. 1 for violin and piano (1928): (1) 1939 phonoamateur
   recording (with Ede Zathureczky); (2) April 13, 1940, Library of
   Congress, Washington, D.C., concert, recording of the library; (3) May 2,
   1940, Columbia[104] (both with Joseph Szigeti).
"Bagpipe" (from *Petite Suite*, 1936): (1) 1936 Patria; (2) 1942 Continental.

Each of these cases is different. The tempo sometimes changed drastically (e.g., in the piece from *For Children*), sometimes not at all (*Bagatelle* no. 2). The three performances of Rhapsody no. 1 make a fascinating comparison that not only shows differences between a live concert and studio work, even with the same partner, but proves that Bartók was willing to adjust his performance to various concepts and temperaments. The two studio takes of Suite op. 14 and the first *Rumanian Dance*, made presumably on the same day, represent crucial evidence in the study of the possible variability of a well-established production and of Bartók's judgment. (He preferred a faultless rendition to another that was more poetic but had wrong notes.)[105] And of course the four recordings, which span nearly two decades, in spite of the very different sound quality, make "Evening in Transylvania" and "Bear Dance" special cases.

103. A related third recording: Bartók–Székely, *Rumanian Folk Dances,* for violin and piano (1925): 1930 Col. (with Joseph Szigeti).
104. New York studio.
105. On the reserve take at the end of Mov. IV in the midst of the extremely inspired performance Bartók had a memory lapse. Contemporary recollections witness similar lapses, presumably because new ideas came to him when he was in an excited mood and could not put them aside; therefore he usually played from the score except for famous numbers of his solo repertoire.

Compared to recordings by his greatest contemporaries (except maybe Stravinsky), the heritage of Bartók's recordings of his own music is an extremely large, many-sided, and important one. However, crucial areas are fully missing or the existing documents are much too distorted and fragmentary to give us a fair picture of his interpretation. It is a pity that there is no recording of the Piano Concerto no. 1 (and the series of fragments of Concerto no. 2 is a distorted document),[106] or the Sonata 1926, or concert-style sets like the Three Studies and *Out Doors* (cycles, e.g., the *Improvisations,* are represented only by selections). Violin Sonata no. 2 is probably the best evidence of Bartók playing one of his large-format works, but we miss the Sonata no. 1. And there is a great performance of the *Contrasts,*[107] but only a very uneven one of the 2-piano Sonata (because the 1940 broadcast is problematic despite great moments created at the first piano by Bartók, owing to the partners including dropouts in Ditta's piano part).

Therefore it is especially important that we have Bartók's performances of grand-scale works by Beethoven, Brahms, Liszt, Debussy that show him as a chamber musician in action; it is fortunate also to have a large amount of outstanding vocal production of Kodály's folksong arrangements with Bartók's accompaniment at the piano that help to reconstruct the style in similar genres of his oeuvre. And there are fascinating samples from his repertoire of works by Bach (e.g., the Passepied from BWV 829), Scarlatti (four sonatas), Mozart (2-piano Sonata K 448), Chopin (Nocturne op. 27 no. 1), and Brahms (Capriccio op. 76 no. 2) — all these performances give a horizon to the study of Bartók's relation to the musical notation in general, outside his innermost world. In this respect recordings of works that also exist in Bartók's performing edition belong to the most valuable documents, as for instance the four Scarlatti sonatas (L 286, 135, 293, 50) and the fragment of Beethoven's Six variations op. 34.

In the commentaries to the *Centenary Edition* I discussed the source value and the problems of Bartók's records from the angle of the professional performer. Here I focus on a somewhat different angle, their source value in connection with the revised editions and the intended *Fassung letzter Hand.* There are indeed burning questions of methodology for us in handling the composer's recordings. Is Bartók's own performance an interpretation of the version already fixed in musical notation, or rather the recreation of a latent original? Is it crucial whether he played ex tempore or from the score? Should we acknowledge a recorded form in certain cases as the last authenticated version or must we always handle it as a variant form? And can we always differentiate between established correction and improvised variation,

106. In addition to the generally poor quality, the single microphone directed toward the piano made the orchestra's sound faint.

107. Benny Goodman's understanding of Bartók's style and intentions on this 1940 recording is a miracle. His noble *verbunkos* tone in Mov. I, the gentle quasi rubato in the Trio of Mov. III, the jazzy coloring of the last pages of the score, surpass Szigeti's contribution.

between intentional change and pianistic error? Other questions concern practical methods. Has the performer to listen only to Bartók's recording or does he need a transcription of it in normal musical notation (shorthand or detailed; samples only or full pieces)? How far is Bartók's performance an object for imitation? How are we to differentiate indisputable corrections and *ossia* readings, which may belong to the main text of Bartók's score, from case-studies of general phenomena in his performance (like the rubato), which constitute the background information?

This may not be the place to answer all methodological questions that have to be solved in the complete critical edition. We can, however, take and discuss selected examples, starting with the obvious ones and moving on to the more difficult.

Additional notes (ad libitum addition; unpublished Konzertfassung *version).* Pieces written for young people with pedagogical considerations, without octaves, Bartók played in a progressive form, most typically with octaves in the melody here and there. In the case of the *Rumanian Christmas Songs* (UE 1918) he added *Änderungen für den Konzertvortrag* in the 1936 UE reprint as an appendix. He played similar variants by heart in the three 5-piece groups from *For Children* (1945); see for instance mm. 18–35 r.h., and m. 24 l.h. in no. 26 of the Hungarian volume, or compare the printed version and the Welte-Licensee recording of nos. 2 and 4 of the *Rumanian Folk Dances,*[108] which can easily be transcribed and added to the printed text as an *ossia.*

Revised version: different notes, additional or deleted measures in Bartók's recording. Most typically in the "soft" part of his forms — such as repeated figures, between two themes, or in the coda — Bartók sometimes played more or less music. For example, listen to the end of no. 5 in the "Six Dances in Bulgarian rhythm" (extension; changes in the texture); or the end of "All'Ungherese" (*Nine Little Piano Pieces* no. 9), where he left out half a measure of the repeated figure.[109]

Allegro barbaro is an extreme example of printed vs. performed authentic versions. The case must be studied with special care, because different aspects of correction are involved: the "fatal misprint" of the basic metronome that was discussed above;[110] the characteristic oscillation of tempo and the supplemented accents, both of which we examine below; and last but not least, the correction of the phrase length of repeated ostinato measures, our focus now. The piece has an unusual source chain (Fig. 31):[111] it matured in two more or less independent channels that can probably

108. There are interesting little variants and additional ornaments in no. 1 of the *Rumanian Folk Dances.*
109. Half the first measure in the last system.
110. See p. 255.
111. For a detailed list of the sources (excluding the Hilversum recording) see Somfai/*Allegro barbaro*, 260, and (a rev. version, including the Hilversum) Somfai/*Tizennyolc*, 134.

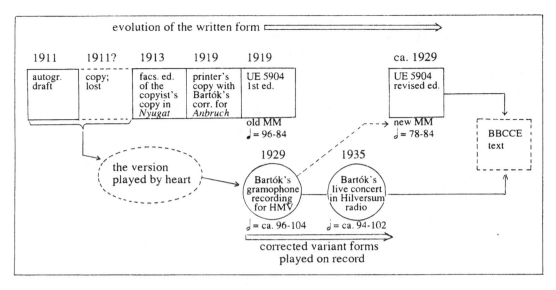

FIGURE 31   *Allegro barbaro*'s source chain.

only be synthesized in the critical edition. The astonishing fact is that on his 1929 HMV recording Bartók changed the number of repeated measures at three places (Ex. 78); on the 1935 Hilversum recording there were two identical corrections and two different ones. A close look at the form, the metric characteristics of the themes,[112] and the phrase structure of *Allegro barbaro* (Fig. 32), suggests sound reasons why Bartók played the length of certain ostinato phrases differently — if it was a conscious change. After all he played *Allegro barbaro* by heart, even before it was printed, and he played and matured it for a long time before the HMV recording.

The presentation of themes (except the agitated, asymmetrical phrases of Theme III) goes in 8 measures; modulation (m. 13, m. 109) and diminuendo-ostinati in 6 or 12 measures, with the compressed recapitulation in 4 measures. According to this presumed rhythm of the phrase structure, the 13-measure calming down at m. 88 seems to be rather a chance occurrence whereas a phrase of 12 is appropriate;[113] a 6-measure diminuendo at m. 50 is better than 8. The 8-measure diminuendo, instead of 7, leading to the sostenuto, dolce sigh gesture (m. 150) seems to be a more

112. In a predominately 2-bar pulsation, Themes I and II have 8-measure contours, both with upbeat phrase structure: the first with a 2-bar (or one double-measure) upbeat, the second with a 1-bar upbeat (this explains the 7-measure transition between the two themes that maintains the steady 2-bar pulsation). Theme III, as a contrast, brings asymmetrical phrase length in the theme (4, 4, 5½, 3) and in the ostinati in between (5, 5, 3 in the print and on the HMV recording, 6, 5, 3 on the Hilversum recording).

113. Corrections of phrase length occurred already in the autograph MS (BBA 176) and the preliminary print (*Nyugat*): mm. 45–48 was a second thought, an insertion; m. 114 was added in the engraver's copy of the *Anbruch* version; and the 13-measure ostinato was at first 10 measures long in the MS, with typical ∕. repeat signs, then Bartók added 2 more ∕. in the MS margin that the copyist who made the fair copy for the *Nyugat* print misread as 13 (a slip that seems to have escaped Bartók's attention).

EXAMPLE 78   *Allegro barbaro*: repetitions left out or added on Bartók's His
Master's Voice recording.

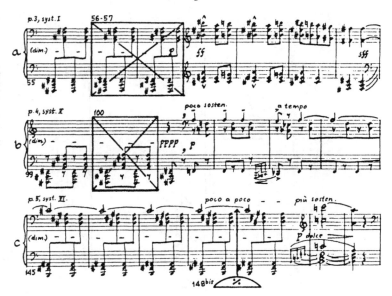

complicated issue. But even here the maintenance of the 2-bar pulsation is the
natural cause of the spontaneous correction (Ex. 79). The phrase length and the
accentuation of the end of *Allegro barbaro* vary on the two Bartók recordings (see
Fig. 32 again), as if he hesitated between playing the *sff* sostenuto climax as the
beginning of the closing 8 + 4 diminuendo (Hilversum) or as an independent
gesture before the ostinato (1 + 8 + 4 on the HMV and in the printed version).
Either these were alternative versions for Bartók, or the 1935 performance was
merely an improvised variant. Without more recordings one cannot decide. But
Bartók himself recognized the HMV recording as "the authentic recording."[114]

Additional or different articulation, touch, dynamics. Occasional improvements of
slurs, accents, or similar details missing from the printed notation, as well as slightly
different articulation are recurring phenomena on Bartók's records. For instance in
Allegro barbaro (Ex. 80) he played additional strong accents that significantly
change the character (Ex. 80a–b, e–g), added important slurs (Ex. 80c–d), used
interruptions that underline the phrasing (Ex. 80b, h).

In piano works with concert-style notation, as described above, Bartók often
realized the quasi non legato bare notation with a variety of touches from staccato to
slurred notes. In Ex. 81 we see the beginning of the right-hand melody of "All'Ungherese" (no. 9 of *Nine Little Piano Pieces*), a theme in the manner of a Hungarian

114. See note 99 above.

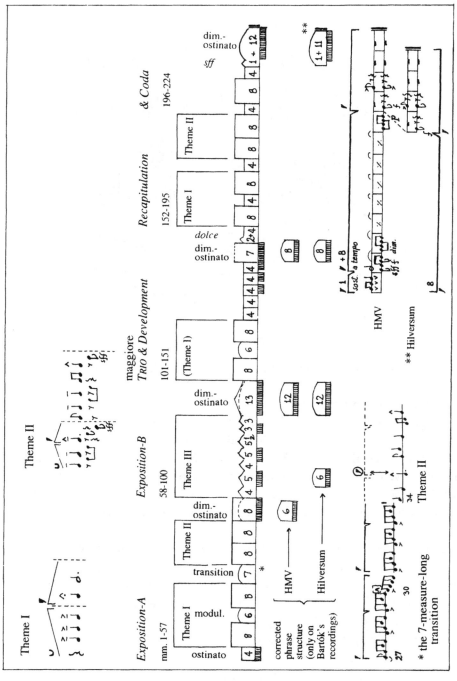

FIGURE 32   Form and phrase structure of *Allegro barbaro*, with an interpretation of the corrections on Bartók's two recordings.

EXAMPLE 79   *Allegro barbaro*: an added measure after
              m. 148 on both recordings of Bartók.

EXAMPLE 80   *Allegro barbaro*: significant changes in
              the accents on Bartók's recordings.

EXAMPLE 81   No. 9 of *Nine Little Piano Pieces*:
              the beginning of the right-hand melody
              of "All'Ungherese" as printed and as
              Bartók articulated it.

folksong in the so-called new style, as it was printed and as Bartók played it. Isolated cases of such authentic deviations from the printed score may not authorize the pianist to create his own articulation in other Bartók compositions. But on the one hand these deviations correct the printed score of the given piece, and on the other hand they give a lesson in how Bartók decorated the bare notes with touch and articulation. An extensive study of all the composer's records would give useful ideas to the performer.

Tempo and tempo oscillation. Adding to what we observed in the first part of this chapter about metronome markings, duration, misprints, and corrected editions, we must touch upon the tempo oscillation in Bartók's performance. The study of the complete recorded material shows that Bartók tended to play his music considerably faster than the tempi given by the authentic MM numbers in the printed notes, although there are examples that go in the opposite direction too; this was particularly true in studio recordings during his best years. The speeded-up performances may, however, be the mark of Bartók the *pianist* and must be considered, along with the printed MM instructions, only as suggestions concerning the tempo — extremes on both ends — and not as obligatory amendments.

Bartók's tendency to play in a lively, natural motion with lots of unmarked rit. and a tempo, with a rich variety of unmarked slight changes of tempo in the presentation of sections with different functions in the composition is an integral part of his general musicianship, not only of his piano music. He did not practice or favor mechanically even tempi at all.[115] His education encouraged a natural way of articulation and differentiation of the tempo of individual phrases, sentences, themes, modulations, transitions; even without written instructions, these elements belonged to musical conventions, to good taste.

The diagram of the tempo oscillation in Bartók's performance of *Allegro barbaro* on the HMV recording is a typical case history (Fig. 33). Rather than invite us to imitate the details of this single performance, it helps us to understand the Bartókian message. In his music there are themes and connecting phrases and the two are not equally important. Depending on the specific nature of a piece, even the maintenance of the basic tempo at the beginning and the end can be irrelevant. In case of *Allegro barbaro* the gradual disintegration of the steady Tempo giusto,[116] with the widening range of tempo oscillation, directly leads to the explosion of the form.

Another fine example of the differentiation of tempo is the Quasi pizzicato movement of *Petite Suite*, 21 measures without the slightest change of the $\jmath$ = 116 tempo in the printed music. On the 1942 Continental record Bartók starts in a slower

115. It is typical that even in the most "even-motion" rhythmic style of his music, in pieces in the so-called Bulgarian rhythm, Bartók never played in a Stravinsky-like giusto of mechanical rhythmic execution but had a variety of tempo giusto with more or less freedom. Compare Bartók's recording of nos. 1 and 2 from "Six Dances in Bulgarian Rhythm."

116. In Bartók's folk-music terminology Tempo giusto is rigid rhythm, but not a mechanically even motion: it has the flexibility of a dance with steady bars but natural movement within the beats.

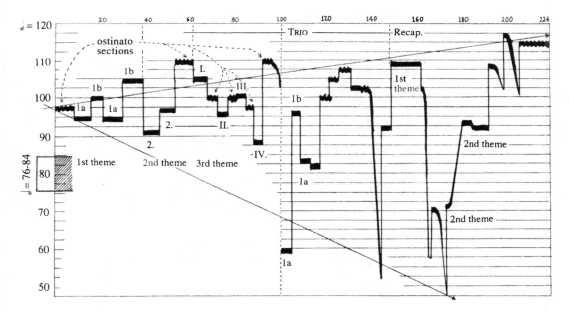

FIGURE 33 *Allegro barbaro*: diagram of the tempo in Bartók's 1929 recording (His Master's Voice).

tempo ca. MM 80–92;[117] in the second stanza, from m. 5, he introduces a more fluent motion of 96–100; in m. 9 the tempo goes back to 92–88; from the end of m. 11 a rall. leads to m. 13, which suddenly starts in 100–116; then, after slowing down, an accel. follows in m. 14, and 112 in m. 15; from m. 16 the tempo is 100–104. The oscillation of the tempo seems to suggest that the piece as a whole has a story, a humorous narrative in Bartók's performance that has nothing to do with the text of the original folk song.[118]

Rubato rhythmic styles in Bartók's performance. Owing mostly to the special folk-music sources of his creative world, Bartók's music is rich in rhythmic styles that he thought either impossible and impractical to note exactly, or so complicated as not to fit into the concept of the piece. We are not speaking of subtle nuances of rhythm in the composer's performance. It is a fundamental question — even a weakness — of Bartók's notation that rubato or parlando-rubato themes, sections, and movements in his music, be it a folksong arrangement or an original composition, have a skeleton notation of the rhythm only. Anyone who has listened to dozens of live and recorded performances of, let us say, "Evening in Transylvania," or the elegy movement of the *Improvisations* (no. 7), or the first solo of the piano in Movement II of the Piano Concerto no. 2 played in the customary lifeless rhythm by non-Hungarians as well as Hungarians (some claiming to represent the authentic tradition), will admire Bartók's own performance.

117. Measured, approximate tempo.
118. Lampert/*Quellenkatalog*, 146.

EXAMPLE 82 The melody of no. 31 in Volume I of *For Children,* as Bartók recorded it in 1945.

With three extracts we take samples from three types of Bartók's rubato. The first case (Ex. 82), no. 31 in vol. I of *For Children,* is the arrangement of a Hungarian folksong. In the 1st edition it was Andante sostenuto (written in 2/4 with diminished rhythm), in the 1943 revision Andante tranquillo, *p,* dolce. However, in 1945 Bartók played it as a typical non-tranquillo but parlando-rubato[119] piece. As my approximate transcription shows (see the note values under the stave), even the halves of the measures are very different in length (instead of 8, they fluctuate between 4- and 15-sixteenths values), and the declamation of the melody is extraordinarily free. Note for instance that the opening 4-note group of each line of the stanza has a slightly different quick and nervous rhythm.[120]

The second case (Ex. 83), a short sample from Bartók's rhythmic performances of "Evening in Transylvania" — the most-demanded encore at his recitals — is a reminder for everybody who studies or plays his music: it is imperative to listen carefully to these four (!) recordings (1928, 1929, 1935, 1945).[121] In many respects this case is unique. Astonishingly enough, Bartók's interpretation did not fundamentally change at all.[122] With the years the amplitude of the micro-oscillation

119. The original folksong was not parlando but Tempo giusto; see Lampert/*Quellenkatalog,* 58.

120. These rhythms correspond neither with "Amerre én járok" (see Lampert) nor with "Csillagok, csillagok," a better known text of the same melody; Bartók probably played a free rhythm without any particular text in mind, a Hungarian rubato in a wider sense.

121. See my complete transcription of the three rubato sections (and samples from the tempo-giusto Vivo) based on the two studio recordings in Somfai/*Rubato-Stil,* and in an extended form, based on all four Bartók recordings in Somfai/*Tizennyolc,* 117–132.

122. My essays quoted above discuss a few changes in the left hand and the relation of the performed version to the 1st printed edition and the revised edition.

EXAMPLE 83 "Evening in Transylvania," no. 5 of *Ten Easy Piano Pieces*: a comparison of the rhythm of four Bartók recordings.

EXAMPLE 84　"A bit drunk," no. 2 of *Three Burlesques*: the approximate speed of Bartók's recording.

R. és Tsa 3437

of the motion between the long notes (beginning and end of a melody line) and the short notes (i.e., the declamation in between) perhaps grew wider. The composer's physical condition also emerges from the general impression of the rubato: the 1945 Vox version is a bit manneristic or nervous; the 1929 HMV recording is probably the best, and certainly the one that he authorized, an exemplary performance of his rubato. Yet the special quality of speech-like rhythm — without actual words, since after all this theme is not a folksong but Bartók's own melody[123] — did not change in nearly two decades.

What is important is the artistic message of the case. With minimum rubato this is a lovely piece for a child, no more and no less. With Bartók's rubato it is a great piece of music: confession about his musico-national identity, about his immense respect for the creative world of his beloved peasants, a transfiguration in which he becomes one with the people, with accumulated experiences of generations and centuries.

The third case points toward another type of rubato in Bartók's performance that has no link to folk music: the grotesque rubato, mostly with "a bit drunk" mood — which actually is the title of no. 2 of the *Three Burlesques*; we see its beginning in Ex. 84. In box lines I have added the approximate MM speed and the abrupt changes of the tempo, furthermore the very pointed "hiccup" stops (ꝑ), and the rhythm of mm. 6 and 8 in Bartók's 1929 recording. Many things I did not mark: for example, the different micro-rhythm of the breaks between the left and the right hand, the slightly stumbling internal rhythm of the pairs of eighth notes with a sharply differentiated staccato and tenuto touch. Our conclusion for the third case is like that for the second. With a cautious rubato or a different-style rubato this is just a slightly odd character piece. With Bartók's exaggerated rhythmic freedom that, however, has cohesion and directionality, we have an extraordinary piece, a key to similar characters and episodes in several major works by Bartók (scenes in the *Wooden Prince*, in the Violin Sonata no. 2, and elsewhere).

Throughout his music special forms of the rubato are connected to espressivo instructions. Furthermore anything that Bartók takes to have a valse's swing, even that of a tragic slow valse (e.g., the Più sostenuto section in Mov. IV of Suite op. 14), has in Bartók's performance a very special sort of rubato.

Bartók's arpeggiando performance of chords. It is a general feeling among listeners to Bartók's recordings today that the typical broken chords or left-hand anticipations belong to a turn-of-the-century pianistic mannerism and thus we do not have to take any notice of it. I think that this opinion is anachronistic. For Bartók this was a forceful tool for underlining and accentuating dissonances between the voices of the

123. "Evening in Transylvania is an original composition . . . with themes of my own invention but . . . the themes are in the style of the Hungarian-Transylvanian folk tunes. . . . The first one is [in] a parlando-rubato rhythm," etc.; listen to Bartók's statement in the English-language interview (July 2, 1944) in *Centenary Edition*, II:10/4, and commentaries, 26–27.

two hands, in polyphonic texture, in the presentation of a dissonant chord. This bears little resemblance to the usual rolling of chords in arpeggio to make them lovelier, or louder, or softer — which Bartók often used in his notation. Dozens of places show that he expressed the growing level of the tension with a broader chord-breaking to give enough time for the appreciation of the dissonance or linear motion.[124] Therefore instead of neglect, a close study of the phenomenon can be recommended.

I conclude with an attempt to summarize the artistic testimony of Bartók's own performance.

The general trend of interpretation of the decades since Bartók's death (1945) has not favored really good Bartók performances. The greater virtuosity of musicians today has made his scores more accessible, and many of his works — string quartets, symphonic and piano music — have, in perfectly executed performances, acquired the features of classic (and sometimes even classicist) masterworks.

The importance of Bartók's own performance partly lies in the fact that it shows up the exaggeratedly clear-cut and harmonious interpretation of his works. His music is, fundamentally, *not classical*, even if some of his major instrumental works between 1928 and 1937 expressed thoughts and feelings in forms of truly classical perfection. His life's work as a whole and his personality as an artist obviously rest on *romantic* foundation.

The search for the experience of *catharsis* is extraordinarily strong in Bartók's piano playing. He reaches the catharsis repeatedly and with different intensity in large-scale works: in the Violin Sonata no. 2, in the first movement of the 2-piano Sonata, sometimes in triumph, sometimes in an incantatory manner, or with dream-like music of silence. Even in the shorter pieces he produces penultimate moments or conclusions that the score does not reveal to other performers.

Bartók's playing does justice to each of his stylistic periods. A later compositional manner is not a criticism of an earlier style but simply a search for new directions. In his repertoire the decades-old work coexists, survives, and ripens together with the novelties. He liked his old pieces because they knew things that were missing from the new ones. No one should be allowed to conduct Bartók's *Music for Strings, Percussion, and Celesta* who is not prepared to undertake also the *Four Orchestral Pieces, The Wooden Prince,* the *Two Pictures.*

Bartók shows in his own interpretation that an objective and correct reading of a score and virtuosity are no substitutes for *personality*, for the courage and imagination of the genuine performing artist. He would certainly not have agreed with

124. Listen, e.g., to Bartók playing the first page of "Minor Seconds, Major Sevenths" (*Mikrokosmos* no. 144) or the Violin Sonata no. 2 from no. 12 in Mov. I, from no. 29 in Mov. II.

Stravinsky who suggested that one just "realize" his works. *Expression* and rich musical characters are more important than correct technique — the proof is in Bartók's own recordings. Characters and allusions within his oeuvre — perhaps similar to Mozart's instrumental characters with reference to his operas — interconnect Bartók's stage works (the lake of tears, his wooden prince, etc.) and instrumental pieces with or without character titles (dirges, elegies, burlesques, "A bit drunk").

Even greater numbers of styles and characters refer, however, to *folk music* — and that is where we all are very poor readers of Bartók's scores. There is no way and perhaps no need to be familiar with all the folk music Bartók ever knew, but we must pay attention to the likely sources of his characters. Otherwise our understanding of Bartók will be sterile — rather like that of a Bach interpreter unfamiliar with the basics of Bach's symbolism, Lutheran chorales, liturgy, and eighteenth-century dance music.

Finally I touch on a very delicate subject: is Bartók's music *Hungarian,* or a *universal idiom?* Are there secrets in the understanding and interpretation of Bartók that are open only to those whose native language is Hungarian, and whose musical training took place in Hungary? It would be a commonplace to register all the reasons why a musician who inherited the rhythm of the Hungarian language, who remembers hundreds of folksongs, who has been playing Bartók right from the start will understand more easily and more naturally his most advanced music too. But this conditional advantage evens out and is, moreover, insufficient for an ideal preparation for Bartók's style. A musician should also absorb Rumanian, Slovak, and other folk music; should understand the musical atmosphere, repertoire, and training of musicians that at the beginning of this century at the Budapest Liszt Academy of Music formed the taste and made artists of Bartók and his generation, the violinist Joseph Szigeti, the conductor Fritz Reiner, and others. Perhaps anyone will understand Bartók better after studying his interpretation of Bach, Couperin, Scarlatti, Haydn, Mozart, Beethoven, documented in Bartók's 1907–1921 performing editions. The style of Bartók's age is as much part of the past, of a submerged culture, for young Hungarian artists as it is for non-Hungarian ones. Fortunately we possess a reliable guide, if we learn how to use it: the recordings of Bartók the pianist.

APPENDIX: LIST OF WORKS AND
PRIMARY SOURCES

The new BB numbers given in the following list are those used in the forthcoming Bartók thematic catalogue, which presents the whole oeuvre, including the juvenilia, in chronological order. Thus the previous routine (e.g., in *The New Grove Dictionary of Music and Musicians*) of identifying the Bartók works prior to 1904 by the Dille number and the rest of the oeuvre by the Szőllősy number (with the two sets of numbers overlapping for several compositions) — or further by a third, non-public numbering by Waldbauer that is integral to the call-numbering in the American estate, the largest collection of primary sources — can now be put aside. Note (a) that in a few cases one BB number stands for a group of works (BB 1, 19, 26) or for several lost works written at approximately the same time (BB 7, 9); (b) that the arrangement or variant forms of a composition, depending on the case, may occur as *a* and *b* under the same number, or as independent numbers (see Somfai, "Problems of the Chronological Organization of the Béla Bartók Thematic Index in Preparation," *SM* 34 [1992]: 345–366); (c) that although in most cases the official English title is given, in some cases, following tradition, a German or French title may be used, if it is an authorized one; and (d) that the size — number of pages — of the individual sources is only an approximation, since many sources include cover sheets, empty pages, pages with notes not belonging to the given work that may or may not have been included in the count.

Letters used in the call numbers of the American estate refer, after the Waldbauer number, to the instrument(s) and score-type of the sources first, e.g.:

P	= piano	SATB	= soprano, alto, tenor, bass
PP	= two pianos	O	= orchestra
V	= violin	FS	= full score (of chamber music, concerto,
C	= cello		symphonic work, major vocal work,
D	= percussion		etc.).
Vo	= voice (solo)		

This is followed by a classification of the source, with serial number (but number 1 usually stands not for the chronologically first, but for the final, the "primary" version):

S = sketch
ID = intermediary draft
FC = final copy, finished form of the composition.

The letter T before the whole complex means "transcription" from the original form; Y refers to collections of youthful works. Here is an example:

TVPFC2 = transcription (T) for violin and piano (VP), final copy (FC), source no. two (2).

NB: Throughout this list as well as in the book as a whole, page numbers in manuscripts of the American Estate (PB) are given according to the librarian's arbitrary pagination printed on the original manuscript, which often differs from the original pagination and order of the MS as well as from the pagination on photocopies previously known by scholars.

Abbreviations of Collections and Publishers

B&H	Boosey & Hawkes
BB	the *Béla Bartók Thematic Catalogue* number
BBA	Budapest Bartók Archives (Bartók Archívum, Budapest)
BH	Bartók Hagyaték (Bartók estate) in the BBA
DD	Dille number
EMB	Editio Musica Budapest (Zeneműkiadó)
MK	Magyar Kórus
OSZK	Országos Széchényi Könyvtár (Széchényi National Library, Budapest)
PB	Peter Bartók's archive (Homosassa, Florida)
R	Rozsnyai
Rv	Rózsavölgyi
Sz	Szőllősy number
UE	Universal Edition
W	Waldbauer number

BB 1 (DD 1–31): **Early piano pieces, opp. 1–31** (first opus numbering) **(1890–1894)**[1]
Autogr. drafts of the child Bartók exist only from **op. 27 Loli Mazurka** and **op. 29 Elza Polka** (1894), 2 pp. (in Béla Bartók Jr.'s collection). The rest of the pieces, written down by Bartók's mother, with additions by Bartók, are in six small oblong-format school music copy-books, 106 + 6 + 27 pp. (Béla Bartók Jr.; BBA 180; PB Y1TVFC1 and Y4.7–911.13PFC1), and on one sheet (BBA BH1). ■*Autogr. fragments* from ca. 1894–1895, DD B1–7, all together 16 + 2 pp. (BBA BH46/1, 7–8, 12a, and PB "Miscellaneous" C-27/25), and *autogr. sketches* from ca. 1894–1895, DD E6–22, 10 pp. (BBA BH46/9–10).

BB 2 (DD 32–33): **Sonata G minor, op. 1** (second opus numbering) and **Scherzo, for piano (1894)**
Mother's fair copies, 11 + 3 pp. (Béla Bartók Jr.).

---

1. For a piece-by-piece description of the sources of the individual compositions from Bartók's childhood see Dille/*Verzeichnis,* 53–76.

BB 3 (DD 34): **Fantasia A minor, op. 2, for piano (1895)**
Mother's fair copy, 6 pp. (Béla Bartók Jr.).

BB 4 (DD 35): **Sonata F major, op. 3, for piano (1895)**
Sketch, 1 p. (BBA BH46/12a). Mother's fair copy with *autogr. additions*, 22 pp. (BBA BH2).

BB 5 (DD 36): **Capriccio B minor, op. 4, for piano (1895)**
Mother's copy with *autogr. additions*, 10 pp. (BBA BH3).

BB 6 (DD 37): **Sonata for Violin and Piano, op. 5 (1895)**
Sketches for Mov. I in a small hand-ruled booklet, 10 pp., DD E23–54 (Béla Bartók Jr.). Mother's copy, but the beginning Bartók's *autogr. copy*, 27 pp. (BBA BH4). See also the *autogr. fragment* for vl. and piano, C major, 1 p., DD B8 (BBA BH46/12b).

BB 7 (DD 38–44 = opp. 6–12, lost works from 1895–1897)
An *autogr. fragment* titled "III. Sonata op. 6" for piano (see DD 38), 2 pp. (BBA BH46/10a).

BB 8 (DD 45): **Drei Klavierstücke, op. 13 (1897)**
Copy by unidentified hand, but mm. 11–35 of no. 3 is Bartók's *autogr. addition,* 6 pp. (BBA 178).

BB 9 (DD 46–48 = opp. 14–16, lost works from 1897)

BB 10 (DD 49): **Sonata for Violin and Piano A major, op. 17 (1897)**
Sketch in Bartók's Greek textbook (BBA). *Autogr. copy* written in pencil [the earliest existing major autograph score], 36 pp.; in Mov. II only the vl. part is elaborated (BBA BH5; at the end of the MS a musical joke, fugue on the theme "DACH," DD D1).

BB 11 (DD 50): **Scherzo oder Fantasie, op. 18, for piano (1897)**
Sketch in Bartók's Greek textbook of the *Odyssey* (BBA). *Autogr. copy* (in pencil), 11 pp. (BBA BH6), and mother's fair copy with Bartók's additions, 11 pp. (BBA 179).

BB 12 (DD 51: "missing"): **Piano Sonata, op. 19 (1898)**
Sketches in Bartók's Greek textbooks (*Herodoti Epitome* and *Odyssey*), including DD E57–58, 64, 69–71 (BBA). *Autogr. fair copy*, 30 pp., a dedication copy marked **op. 1** (third opus numbering) (New York Pierpont Morgan Library, Robert Owen Lehman Collection on deposit). Revised form of Mov. III, *autogr. fragment* (=DD A12), 2 pp. (BBA BH48).

BB 13 (DD 52): **Piano Quartet, op. 20 (1898)**
Sketches in Bartók's *Herodoti Epitome*, DD E59, and in school copy-books (BBA). *Autogr. fair copy* of the score and the 3 string parts, 59 + 8 + 10 + 10 pp. (BBA BH8).

BB 14 (DD 53): **Drei Klavierstücke, op. 21 (1898)**
Sketch for no. 2, DD E60, in Bartók's *Herodoti Epitome* (BBA). *Autogr. fair copy* marked **op. 5,** 11 pp. (BBA BH7).

BB 15 (DD 54): **Drei Lieder, for voice and piano (1898)**
Autogr. fair copy, 9 pp. (until 1978 in private collection; BBA 4996). An *autogr. copy* of no. 3 only, 1 p., submitted to Prof. Koessler, in the MS complex "Dolgozatok II" [Exercises II] (BBA BH48).

BB 16 (DD 55): **Scherzo B minor, for piano (1898)**
Autogr. fair copy, 12 pp. (BBA BH9).

BB 17 (DD 56): **String Quartet F major (1898)**
Autogr. fair copy, 50 pp. (BBA BH10).

BB 18 (DD 57): **Tiefblaue Veilchen, for voice and orchestra (1899)**
Draft score in pencil, 20 pp., and *autogr. copy* of the score in ink, 20 pp. (BBA BH11a–b).

BB 19 (DD 58–61, 65, A1, 3–11, 13–15, B10–13): **Studies in composition (1899–1901)**, submitted to and corrected by H. Koessler

- (a) *"Dolgozatok I"* [Exercises I], MS complex from ca. 1900, 76 pp. (BBA BH47), including choral harmonization, counterpoint exercises, fugues, and *drafts* (=DD E87–88, A15).
- (b) *"Dolgozatok II,"* MS complex from ca. 1900, 77 pp. (BBA BH48), including choral harmonization, counterpoint and fugue exercises, furthermore *sketches* and *fragments* (=DD A3–14), and chorus pieces (=DD 61a-c).
- (c) *"Dolgozatok III,"* MS complex from ca. 1900, 40 pp. (BBA 1310), including counterpoint exercises, chorus pieces, and exercises in writing "phrase," "sentence," "period," etc. (=DD E97–99).
- (d) **Scherzo in Sonatenform, for string quartet** (1899–1900), *autogr. copy*, 5 pp. (BBA BH14).
- (e) **Scherzo B-flat minor, for piano** (ca. 1900), *autogr. copy*, 5 pp. (BBA BH12).
- (f) **Six dances, for piano; nos. 1–2 for orchestra too** (ca. 1900), *autogr. draft*, 6 + 16 pp. (BBA BH18); no. 1 was written down again by Bartók in 1913 (?) and, with the title **Danse orientale**, reproduced in facsimile in *Preßburger Zeitung* 1913 (and reprinted in *Új Zenei Szemle* 1959).
- (g) **Scherzo B-flat major, for orchestra** (ca. 1901), fragment, *draft* (with Trio) and *autogr. score* (Scherzo only), 2 + 6 pp. (BBA BH19; see also another "Scherzo-trio" in E-flat, *draft score*, 10 pp.: BBA BH13).
- (h) Bartók's orchestration of BEETHOVEN, C minor ("Pathétique") Sonata op. 13, Mov. I,1–194 only, *draft score* (DD A1, 1900?), 25 pp. (BBA BH51).
- (i) Further fragments and sketches, including: three **Piano quintet** fragments (DD B10, 12, ca. 1899–1900), *autogr. draft*, 22 pp. (BBA BH45).

BB 20 (DD 62): **Liebeslieder, for voice and piano (1900)**
Draft and *autogr. fair copy*, 13 + 22 pp. (BBA BH15a–b).

BB 21 (DD 63): **Scherzo ("F.F.B.B."), for piano (1900)**
Autogr. copy, 12 pp. (BBA BH16).

BB 22 (DD 64): **Variations, for piano (1900–1901)**
Draft, 17 pp. (BBA 3330). *Autogr. copy* with considerable revision, 19 pp. (BBA BH17).

BB 23 (DD 66): **Tempo di minuet, for piano (1901)**
Autogr. copy, on 2 postcards (Budapest Institute for Musicology Major/C-483).

BB 24 (DD 67 / W 1): **Four Songs (L. Pósa), for voice and piano (1902)**
Autogr. copy of no. 4 (but in A-flat), 1 p. (BBA BH21a). Copy of nos. 3, 4 (in A-flat), and 2, in a version different from the printed form, by Mrs. Gruber (later Emma Kodály), 4 pp. (Budapest Kodály Archives Ms.mus.779, pp. 58–61), and a copy of no. 1 by "Sándor K.," preliminary version too, 2 pp. (Budapest Kodály Archives Ms.mus.ext.7). Corrected proof sheets of the 1904 Bárd 1st edition, 8 pp. (BBA BH21b). A corrected copy of the 1st edition (PB 1VoPFC1).

BB 25 (DD 68 / W 2): **Symphony, for orchestra (1902)** (fragment, except Mov. III: Scherzo)
Draft in piano short score form, Movements I–IV (but Mov. I only up to the recapitulation, and from Mov. III only the Scherzo part without Trio), 25 pp. (photocopy BBA). *Score-draft fragment*, mm. 1–62 of Mov. I, and *sketches* for Mov. IV, 8 pp. (BBA). Mov. III, **Scherzo**, *fragment of the score*, 4 pp. only (BBA); the rest of the movement survived only in parts. Orchestral parts of Mov. III for the Feb. 29, 1904, premiere, copied by Kejglíček, 68 fascicles (BBA BH54).

BB 26 (DD 69–70): **Pieces for violin (1902): (a) Duo for two violins; (b) Andante A major, for violin and piano**
(a) *Autogr. draft* and *copy*, 1 p. (BBA 3342). *Autogr. dedication copy* presented to Adila Arányi, on a postcard (Sotheby & Co., London, May 16, 1967, auction no. 388). — (b) *Draft*, 2 pp. (BBA BH46/3). *Autogr. dedication copy* presented to Adila Arányi, 7 + 3 pp., mailed as postcards (BBA 3341; facsimile edition EMB, 1980).

BB 27 (DD 71 / W 6): **Four Piano Pieces (1903)**
Draft, no. 1 only, titled *Szonáta*, 9 pp. (PB 6PS1). *Autogr. copy*, no. 2 only, a version different from the printed form, dedicated to Mrs. Gruber (later Emma Kodály), 4 pp. (BBA 480; a copy of it, written by Copyist Y, in private collection). Copy by Mrs. Gruber (Emma Kodály) of no. 3 only, 7 pp. (BBA 500). Corrected proof sheets of the 1904 Bárd 797, 800, 801 1st editions of nos. 1, 3–4 only (BBA BH22).

BB 28 (DD 72 / W 4): **Sonata for Violin and Piano (1903)** (and a fragment, DD B14)
Draft, Mov. III only, 12 pp. (BBA BH23b). *Autogr. copy*, complete, 34 pp., with several layers of corrections (Bartók's concert copy; BBA BH23a, e). *Autogr. vl. part*: (a) Mov. I, 2 pp.; (b) Mov. III, 4 pp., concert copy of the June 8, 1903, performance (BBA BH23c–d; Elza Bartók's copy of Mov. I of the vl. part: in private collection in Belgium). Complete vl. part, Mov. I copied by Elza, Mov. II in Bartók's *autogr.*, Mov. III copied by a Berlin copyist, the whole revised by Bartók, performing copy used in 1904 and 1905, 4 + 3 + 7 pp. (Vienna Österreichische Nationalbibliothek Mus.Hs.39549). ▪ *Autogr. fragment*, an **Andante** for vl. & piano, 2 pp. (BBA BH46/4).

BB 29 (DD 73 / W 5): **Evening, for voice and piano (1903)**
No autogr. MS is known. Irmy Jurkovics's copy, 3 pp. (BBA BH25a).

BB 30 (DD 74 / W 5): **Evening, for male choir (1903)**
Autogr. fragment, mm. 17–47 only, 1 p. (BBA BH25c). *Autogr. copy*, 3 pp. (BBA 481). Copy by Mrs. Gruber (later Emma Kodály), submitted to a competition, 4 pp. (BBA BH25b).

BB 31 (DD 75 / W 3): **Kossuth, for orchestra (1903)** (and **Marche funèbre, for piano, 1903**)
Sketches, 2 pp. (BBA 3344a–b; the draft missing). *Autogr. full score*, 89 pp. (PB 3FSFC1); a copy of the full score written by mother and Elza, 89 pp. (in Béla Bartók Jr.'s collection). Orchestral parts, 75 fascicles, copied by Elza, Irma Voit, two professional copyists, and (additional parts) by two English copyists (BBA BH55). ▪ **Marche funèbre**, for piano: no autogr. MS is known; a fragment (2 pp. only) of the corrected proof sheets of the 1905 Magyar Lant 1st edition (BBA BH24a, and BBA 1029).

BB 32 (DD 76): **Four Songs, for voice and piano (1903)** (lost)

BB 33 (DD 77 / W 7): **Piano Quintet (1903–1904)**
Sketches and the draft are missing. *Autogr. score*, 77 pp., with layers of later corrections (BBA 2002a), with *autogr. string parts*, 23 + 22 + 22 + 21 pp., with corrections (BBA 2002b1–4). Copyist's copy of the score, 91 pp. (PB 7FSFC1), with copied string parts, 40 + 34 + 34 + 33 pp. (PB 7PartsFC1).

BB 34 (DD C8 / Sz 30): **Székely Folksong ("Piros alma"), for voice and piano (1904)**
No autogr. MS is known.

MATURE WORKS: FINAL OPUS NUMBERS

BB 35 (Sz 28 / W 9): **Scherzo for Orchestra and Piano, op. 2 (1904)**
No sketch exists. *Draft* (? fair copy character) in 2-piano form, 32 pp., with preparatory notes for the orchestration (BBA BH29b). *Autogr. full score*, 95 pp. (BBA BH29a). Orchestral parts, 41 fascicles (one vlc., one cb., woodwind, brass, percussion, harp partly copied by Bartók, all together 183 leaves; BBA BH30).

BB 36a (Sz 26 / W 8): **Rhapsody, op. 1, for piano solo (1904)**
No sketch or draft exists. *Autogr. fair copy* (dated Oct.–Dec. 1904), 23 pp., dedicated to Mrs. Gruber (later Emma Kodály); pp. 10–23 used as the printer's copy of the 1923 Rv 3199 edition of the full form (BBA 484); pp. 1–10 copied by an unknown hand (BBA BH26a), revised by Bartók and used as the printer's copy of the 1908 Rv 3199 edition of the shortened form (corrected proof sheets: BBA BH26b, with a revised printed copy), another revised copy of the Rv 3199 edition of the short form (Béla Bartók Jr.).

BB 36b (Sz 27 / W 8): **Rhapsody, op. 1, for piano and orchestra (1905)**
Two *autogr. full scores*, both originally titled *Morceau de Concert*: (1) the original instrumentation, 43 pp., after revision, the printer's copy of the 1910 Rv edition (no plate no.; PB 8TFSS1); (2) an *autogr. copy* written for the 1905 Paris competition, 40 pp. (BBA 35). (Revised printed copies of the 1st edition and the Rv 4154 new edition, with parts: BBA 2006.) ■ 2-piano reduction: (1) *draft*, Piano 2 only, 18 pp., printer's copy of the 1910 Rv 3337 edition (PB 8TPPS1; corrected proof sheets: former Freund collection); (2) discarded p. 1 of the *autogr. copy* (BBA BH28b); (3) fully revised copy of the 1st edition, marked *(II. Edition)*, printer's copy of the 1919 rev. edition (BBA BH28a; a printed copy with autogr. notes: BBA 3346).

BB 37 (Sz 29 / W —): **Hungarian Folksongs (1st series), nos. 1–4, for voice and piano (ca. 1904–1905)**
Draft (no title beyond "I. sorozat" [first series]; no. 4 is incomplete), 4 pp. (BBA BH46/13).

BB 38 (Sz 29 / W —) **Petits Morceaux, for piano (1905)** (from **BB 37/2** and **BB 24/1**)
Autogr. fair copy, 3 pp. (BBA BH31b; a copy written by an unknown hand: BBA BH31a).

BB 39 (Sz 31 / W 10): **Suite no. 1, op. 3, for orchestra (1905)**
No continuity sketch or short score exists (but 12 mm. partial sketches for Mov. V: BBA BH46/15). *Autogr. full score*, 162 pp., with instructions for the engraver of the Rv 3531 edition, with unpublished Hungarian titles of the five movements (PB 10FSS1). Corrected proof sheets of the 1912 Rv score (BBA 2000); a corrected printed copy, with cuts and revision, and the printer's copy of the page *Zur Beachtung* to the conductors (Béla Bartók Jr.).

BB 40 (Sz 34 / W 12): **Suite no. 2, op. 4, for orchestra (1905–1907)**
Sketches (incomplete): (1) fragmentary continuity sketches for Movs. I–II, and IV, 10 pp. (PB, in 12FSS1ID1); (2) partial sketches, 3 pp. (BBA, in 2002a). *Autogr. full score*, originally titled *Szerenád* [Serenade], 64 pp., printer's copy of the composer's 1st edition (*Selbstverlag* with "B.B." plate no.), with a later revision of pp. 29–32 (PB 12FSS1ID1). Revised copies of the 1st edition: (1) Bartók's personal copy (BBA BH32); (2) copy of the Budapest Philharmonic Society (BBA 2131); (3) the printer's copy of the 1921 2nd edition, UE 6981 (Wiener Stadt- und Landesbibliothek; a slightly revised copy of the 2nd edition: Béla Bartók Jr.). MS orchestral parts, copyist's work (heavily corrected, representing the text of the 1st and 2nd editions), with Bartók autogr. corrections (Budapest F. Liszt Academy of Music, deposited in BBA). American revision: (1) a copy of the UE edition with rewritten pages in Mov. IV, ca. 1942 (photostat of the [missing?] MS pages: PB 12FSFC1); (2) printer's copy of the 1948 3rd edition, B&H 16160 "revised 1943 edition" (without Bartók's hand, PB 12FSFC3). ■ 2-piano version: **BB 122.**

BB 41 (Sz 32 / W 11): **Children's Songs ("For the little 'tót'"), for voice and piano (1905)**
Autogr. dedication copy, 9 pp. (private collection; photocopy in BBA).

BB 42 (Sz 33 / W 13): **Hungarian Folksongs, for voice and piano (1906)** (nos. 1–10: Bartók; nos. 11–20: Z. KODÁLY)
Drafts, including 3 unpublished songs, 6 + 4 pp. (BBA 485 and PB 13VoPS1). *Autogr. fair copy*, 4 pp., printer's copy of the R 1906 1st edition (plate no. "B.K.") (together with Kodály's autogr.: BBA 485; facsimile edition EMB, 1970). Corrected proof sheets of the R 1st edition (BBA 1998). (No sources of the 1938 Rv rev. edition known.) ■ Rewritten form of five songs, see **BB 97.**

BB 43 (Sz 33a / W—): **Hungarian Folksongs (2nd series), for voice and piano (1906–1907)**
Draft, 11 pp. (BBA 2013; six of the ten songs copied by Copyist X: BBA 2014).

BB 44 (Sz 33b / W—): **Two Hungarian Folksongs, for voice and piano (1907)**
Draft, 2 pp. (BBA 486; mother's copy: PB 70VoPFC1).

BB 45a (Sz 35 / W 14): **From Gyergyó, for recorder and piano (1907)**
Draft, 2 pp. (in private collection; facsimile in Dille/1979).

BB 45b (Sz 35a / W 14): **Three Hungarian Folksongs from Csík, for piano (1907)** (from **BB 45a**)
No autogr. MS is known. Corrected proof sheets of the R 418 1st edition (Béla Bartók Jr.).

BB 46 (Sz 35b / W—): **Four Slovak Folksongs, for voice and piano (ca. 1907)**
Draft, 8 pp., no. 2 missing (BBA 491).

BB 47 (Sz 64 / W 17): **Eight Hungarian Folksongs, for voice and piano (nos. 1–5: 1907; nos. 6–8: 1917)**
Draft, 7 pp. (nos. 2–3 missing; PB 17VoPS1; a copy of nos. 1, 4, 5, and 2, revised by Bartók: Bibliothèque Laloy in France). Four MS copies, mostly written by Márta and revised by Bartók, represent new versions (PB 17VoPFC1, 17VoPID1). Printer's copy of the 1922 UE 7191 1st edition, written by Márta (PB 17VoPFC2). Two ad hoc performing copies (incomplete), written by Ditta and Bartók (BBA 2003, and Bucharest Composer's Society).

BB 48a (Sz 36 / W 15): **Violin Concerto, op. posth. ("no. 1," 1907–1908)**
Sketches: (1) short memos, 1 p. (BBA BH39); (2) 1 p. (fol. 1ʳ of Black Pocket-book, BBA BH206); (3) continuity sketches, 13 + 1 pp. (Black Pocket-book, fol. 2ʳff, and PB 12FSS1ID1). *Draft* in vl.-piano short score form, Mov. II only, 17 pp. (BBA 4130); copied by Copyist Y: BBA 4131b). *Autogr. full score*, 31 pp. (Basel: Paul Sacher Stiftung; a corrected copy, written by Copyist Z and Copyist X: BBA 4129; see **BB 48b** too). Solo violin part in different versions, written by Bartók, his mother, and a copyist (BBA 4131a, c–f; PB 15VFC1; and Basel: Paul Sacher Stiftung). Orchestral parts (1911), 40 fascicles, partly written (13 pp.) and fully revised by Bartók (BBA BH34).

BB 48b (Sz 37 / W 16): **Two Portraits, op. 5 (1907–1911)**
I (= Mov. I of **BB 48a**) revised copy of the score written by Copyist Z (PB 16TFSID1; the rest of the MS, i.e., Mov. II of **BB 48a**: BBA 4131b); II (= instrumentation of **BB 50** no. 14) *autogr. full score*, 9 pp. (PB 16TFSID1); this autogr. MS was the printer's copy of the R 767 1st edition (a printed copy with Bartók's corrections: Béla Bartók Jr.).

BB 49 (Sz 41 / W 21): **Two Elegies, op. 8b, for piano (1908–1909)**
Sketch on fol. 8ʳ of Black Pocket-book (BBA BH206) and on one page (PB 21PS1). *Draft*, 12 pp., the printer's copy of the R 478 1st edition (BBA 489). Corrected proof sheets of the R edition (1910; BBA 1995; another set: former Freund collection; a corrected copy: Béla Bartók Jr.).

BB 50 (Sz 38 / W 18): **Fourteen Bagatelles, op. 6, for piano (1908)** (and fragments)
Sketches: (1) in the Black Pocket-book (BBA BH206), fol. 8ᵛ–9ʳ: nos. 8, 9, 13 (and a fragment, 17 mm.), fol. 33ʳ–34ʳ: no. 14 (further unrealized plans, fragments: fol. 32ʳ, 34ᵛ, 10 + 6 mm.; a Fugue fragment, 17 mm.: fol. 9ᵛ–10ʳ); (2) on one page (BBA 495b) no. 14 and the Fugue theme. *First draft*, 7 pp., nos. 1–4 and 6 only (BBA 488a–f; no. 6 in Z. Kodály's copy too). *Complete draft*, 28 pp. (PB 18PFC1). A corrected copy, written by Copyist Y, was the printer's copy of the 1908 R 338 1st edition (BBA BH35 and 2010). A copy of the R edition, revised in the 1940s (PB 18PFC2). ■ See **BB 48b** too.

BB 51 (Sz 39 / W 19): **Ten Easy Piano Pieces (1908)**
First draft, nos. 8 and "0" [= Dedication] only, 1 + 1 pp. (BBA 488 and PB 19PS1). *Draft*, incomplete (no MS of no. 3), 15 pp.: "Dedication" and nos. 1–2, 4, 6–10 (PB 19PS2), and 2 pp.: no. 5 (Budapest Institute for Musicology Fond 2/27); this draft was the printer's copy of the 1908 R 293 1st edition. Corrected proof sheets of the 1st edition (BBA BH36). A corrected copy of the rev. 2nd (Rv) edition (PB 19PFC1). — Printer's copy of nos. 1, 2, 3, 8, a revised version, prepared for the 1937 selection **Young People at the Piano, 1–2** (as no. 12 in vol. 1 and nos. 8–10 in vol. 2) (Budapest OSZK Ms.Mus.3190). ■ See **BB 103** too.

BB 52 (Sz 40 / W 20): **String Quartet no. 1, op. 7 (1908–1909)**
Sketches: (1) four memos on one page (BBA BH39); (2) short memos in the Black Pocket-book (BBA BH206), fol. 9ʳ, 11ʳ, 12ʳ, 31ᵛ, 32ᵛ; on fol. 9ʳ a short continuity sketch too. *Draft score*, 25 pp. (PB 20FSS1). Revised copy, written by Copyist X (BBA BH37), the printer's copy of the 1909 Rv 3287 1st edition. Corrected proof sheets (BBA BH38). A corrected copy of the 1st edition (Béla Bartók Jr.).

BB 53 (Sz 42 / W 22): **For Children, for piano (1908–1909)**
Hungarian I–II = Vol. I of the rev. edition: *Drafts*: (1) no. 23, 1 p. (BBA 487); (2) nos. 13–18 as "I–VI," 2 pp. (PB 22PS1); (3) a collection of the melodies for II, 2 pp. (BBA

BH46/23); (4) complete draft of **I–II**, 39 pp., the printer's copy of the R 376–377 1st edition (PB 22PI.ID1). ■ Slovak **III–IV** = Vol. II of the rev. edition: *Drafts*: (1) 16 pp., nos. 1–12, 14, 17–22, and 30–32, 42 (PB 22PII.ID2); (2) 25 pp., nos. 13, 15–16, and 23–29, 35–41, 43 (together with Márta's copy of nos. 30–32, and Emma Kodály's autogr. MS of her arrangements, nos. 33–34), the printer's copy of **IV**, R 728 (BBA 487, 499). Márta's copy of **III**, nos. 1–22, with Bartók's corrections, the printer's copy of R 634 (BBA 2015). Corrected proof sheets (former Freund collection). ■ Revisions: Bartók's copies of R 376–377 with notes (and on one page: preparations for the orchestration of **BB 103/V**; Béla Bartók Jr.). Revised copies of the R edition, prepared for the 1937 Rv 6171–6172 selection **Young People at the Piano**, 1–2 (11 plus 7 pieces), the printer's copy (Budapest OSZK Ms.Mus.3190). ■ 1943 revised version: (1) *autogr. copy*, 10 pp., the 13 rewritten pieces, dated 1943 (PB 22PFC2, with 14 revised printed pages from the R 1st edition); (2) camera-ready printer's copy for the B&H 15936–15937 rev. edition, 148 pp., Bartók's autogr. revision partly covered by the printer's corrections (PB 22PFC1). ■ J. SZIGETI, arr. for vl. and piano: **Ungarische Volksweisen (1926)**, Szigeti's MS corrected by Bartók, 16 + 7 + 2 pp. (Wiener Stadt- und Landesbibliothek MHc 14300). ■ See **BB 109** too.

BB 54 (Sz 44 / W 23): **Seven Sketches, op. 9b, for piano (1908–1910)**
Draft, nos. 4–7 on 5 pp. (PB 23PID1); no. 3 with the draft of **BB 58/III** (PB 26PID1); nos. 1–2 missing; nos. 4–7 were engraved for R 769 from the draft. *Dedication copy* of no. 2, noted down in spiral form (PB 23PFC2). Printer's copy of nos. 1–3, written by Copyist X (no. 1) and Márta, revised by Bartók (BBA 2011). Corrected proof sheets (BBA 1997). A revised copy from the 1940s (PB 23PFC1).

BB 55 (Sz 47 / W 24): **Three Burlesques, op. 8c, for piano (1908–1911)**
Sketch, for no. 1 only, in the Black Pocket-book (BBA BH206), fol. 10ʳ⁻ᵛ. *Draft*, no. 1 only, 4 pp. (PB 24PS1); no autogr. MS of nos. 2–3 is known. A mixed copy of no. 1, 4 pp., written by Márta (pp. 1–2) and Bartók (pp. 2–4; PB 24PID1) was the printer's copy of the Rv 3237 1st edition. Two sets of corrected proof sheets (July and Dec. 1911; Edinburgh National Library, and BBA 1999). A copy of the Rv 1st edition contains (a) preparatory notes for the orchestration of no. 2 (**BB 103/IV**) and (b) a full revision from 1944 (PB 24PFC1).

BB 56 (Sz 43 / W 25): **Two Rumanian Dances, op. 8a, for piano (1909–1910)**
Draft, 14 pp. (BBA 490; facsimile edition: EMB, 1974), the printer's copy of the 1910 Rv 3333 1st edition. A copy of no. 1 written by Márta (PB 25PID1). Corrected proof sheets of the 1st edition, July 1910 (former Freund collection). Revised copies of the 1st edition: (1) (Béla Bartók Jr.); (2) the printer's copy of the 2nd Rv edition (BBA BH70); (3) revision (with rewritten sections in no. 2) in America for the E. B. Marks edition (PB 25PFC1). ■ See **BB 61** too.

BB 57 (Sz 58 / W 39): **Two Rumanian Folksongs, for female choir (ca. 1909)**
Draft, one page (PB 39SAS1).

BB 58 (Sz 45 / W 26): **Four Dirges, op. 9a, for piano (ca. 1909–1910)**
Sketches, nos. 1 and 3 in the Black Pocket-book (BBA BH206), fol. 11ʳ, 12ʳ. *Draft*, nos. 1–4 (with the draft of **BB 54/III**, and Márta's copy of no. 1, together 7 pp.; PB 26PID1). (The printer's copy is missing.) Corrected proof sheets of the Rv 3438 1st edition (Edinburgh National Library). (The printer's copy of the 1945 Elkan rev. edition is missing.) ■ See **BB 103** too.

BB 59 (Sz 46 / W 27): **Two Pictures, op. 10, for orchestra (1910)**
Sketches, fol. 12ʳ–13ᵛ in the Black Pocket-book (BBA BH206). (The draft short score is missing.) *Autogr. full score*, 46 pp. (PB 27FSS1), the printer's copy of the Rv 3557 edition; corrected proof sheets, 2 sets (BBA 1993). Sample pages of a fair copy of the full score, 4 pp., written by Márta (BBA 2018). ■ *Draft of the piano reduction*, a mixed-form autogr. MS, pp. 1–4 and 4–13 (PB 27TPS1), partly the printer's copy of the Rv 3558 piano reduction; corrected proof sheets of this edition (BBA 2019).

BB 60 (Sz 50 / W 30): **Four Old Hungarian Folksongs, for male choir (1910–1912, rev. ca. 1926)**
Draft (1910), 4 pp. (BBA 117; a copy, dated Dec. 1910, revised by Bartók: BBA 2016). *Draft* (new version, ca. 1926?), 3 pp. (PB 30TBS1). *Autogr. copy*, 3 pp., printer's copy of the 1927 UE 8891 edition (PB 30TBFC1).

BB 61 (Sz 47a / W 25): **Rumanian Dance, for orchestra (1911),** (from **BB 56/I**)
Autogr. full score, 13 pp. (PB 25TFSS1). (The EMB Z.4692 posth. 1st edition was based on MS orchestral parts: Budapest F. Liszt Academy of Music.)

BB 62 (Sz 48 / W 28): **Duke Bluebeard's Castle, op. 11, opera in one act (1911)**
Sketch, one theme on fol. 12ᵛ of the Black Pocket-book (BBA BH206); no further sketches survived. *Draft* (or copy of the first draft?) in vocal score form, 68 pp., with variants of the ending (BBA 492; with Emma Kodály's unpublished German translation). *Autogr. full score*, 118 pp., with inserted new ending (PB 28FSS1). Copy of the full score, 149 pp., written by Márta, Bartók (pp. 31–36, 143–149), and a professional copyist (pp. 105–128) (probably the 1911 competition copy; PB 28FSFC2; Márta's copy of an earlier ending, pp. 195–200: PB 28FSID1). A copy written for the Budapest Opera House by a professional copyist (BBA 2156; vocal parts for the first performers, dated 1917 and 1936: BBA 2157). A copy for UE (ca. 1922), written by a Viennese copyist (PB 28FSFC1). ■ Vocal score: Copy written by Márta, revised by Bartók, the printer's copy of the UE 7026 ed., 68 pp. (PB 28VoSFC1); corrected proof sheets, Oct. 1921 (PB 28VoSFC2); a corrected copy of the 1st ed. (Béla Bartók Jr.).

BB 63 (Sz 49 / W 29): **Allegro barbaro, for piano (1911)**
Draft, 4 pp. (BBA 176; the next MS form probably missing). A copy written by Copyist X and reprinted in facsimile in *Nyugat* (1913); a revised copy of the facsimile edition, used as the printer's copy of the 1919 *Musikblätter des Anbruch* and the UE 5904 editions (Wiener Stadt- und Landesbibliothek MH14293c). (The revisions for the 1927 and 1936 new UE prints are missing.) A revised copy of the 1939 Hawkes 15190 print (PB 29PFC1).

BB 64 (Sz 51 / W 31): **Four Orchestral Pieces, op. 12 (1912, orchestration 1921)**
Sketches, two ideas possibly connected with Mov. II, on fol. 34ʳ of a folksong collecting pocket-book (BBA BH110). *Draft* (?) in 2-piano form, 25 pp. (partly first draft, partly rewritten from a lost form [?] for 2 pianos; with preparatory notes for the orchestration; PB 31TPPS1; with the beginning of Mov. III in Márta's copy). *Autogr. full score*, 84 pp. (with authorization of performances of Movs. I–II or IV–III–II too; London British Library). Márta's copy with Bartók's additions, the printer's copy of the UE 7270 edition (PB 31FSFC1).

BB 65 (Sz 59 / W 40): **Nine Rumanian Folksongs, for voice and piano (ca. 1912)**
Draft, 10 pp. (PB 40VoPS1; no. 8 in a fragmentary new version, written in America, too).

BB 66 (Sz 52–53 / W 32): **Piano Method** (with S. Reschofsky) **(1913); First Term at the Piano (1929)**
(No autogr. MS of the 48 [?] pieces written by Bartók for the Piano Method and the 18 pieces re-edited separately as the **First Term at the Piano** exist.) Revised copy of the Piano Method for a planned new edition (Béla Bartók Jr.).

BB 67 (Sz 57 / W 38): **Rumanian Christmas Songs, Series I–II, for piano (1915)**
Draft, on pp. 1–5 and 13–19 of a MS complex (PB 36–37–38PS1). (The printer's copy of the 1918 UE 5890 1st edition missing.) *Autogr.* of the *Änderungen für den Konzertvortrag*, Jan. 1936, 5 pp. (PB 38PFC1, together with a revised copy of the 1st edition: PB 38PFC2).

BB 68 (Sz 56 / W 37): **Rumanian Folk Dances, for piano (1915)**
Draft, on pp. 5–9 of a MS complex, with a discarded first dance (PB 36–37–38PS1). (The printer's copy of the 1918 UE 5802 1st edition missing.) A revised copy of the 1st edition, used by UE in Nov. 1934 for the correction of a new print (Béla Bartók Jr.). Revised copy of a B&H print (PB 37PFC1). ■ No printer's copies of the authorized transcriptions are known: for vl. and piano by Székely (1925); for string orch. by Willner (1928); for "Salon-orchester" by Wilke (1922, new version 1928). A revised copy of the 1926 UE 8474 1st edition of Székely's transcription, with Bartók's corrections (Béla Bartók Jr.). ■ See **BB 76** too.

BB 69 (Sz 55 / W 36): **Sonatina, for piano (1915)**
Draft, on pp. 9–12 and 19 of a MS complex (PB 36–37–38PS1). (The printer's copy of the 1918 Rv 3919 1st edition missing.) Corrected proof sheets of the Rv 1st edition (BBA 1994). A revised copy of the 1st edition, used by Rv for the corrected new print (Béla Bartók Jr.). ■ See also **BB 102a–b**.

BB 70 (Sz 62 / W 43): **Suite, op. 14, for piano (1916)**
Draft, 15 pp. (including a fifth, an Andante movement, see Facs.40; PB 43PS1). *Printer's copy* of the 1918 UE 5891 1st edition, I–III and the Andante (as no. 2) written by Márta, IV by Bartók (PB 43PFC2; a copy of the 5-movement form written by a pupil, Irén Egri, with Bartók's additions: BBA 5412; a copy of IV by Márta, with Bartók's additions: BBA 2009). Corrected proof sheets of the 1st edition, Aug. 1918 (BBA 1995). (The copy with the 1927 revision is missing; timing and Bartók's reference to his HMV record: letter May 13, 1937). Revised copy of a B&H print with the new timing (PB 43PFC1).

BB 71 (Sz 61 / W 41): **Five Songs, op. 15, for voice and piano (1916)**
Drafts: (1) 14 pp., no. 3 (in F-sharp), 4, 2, 5, 1 (among the "Reserved songs," PB 41VoPS1); (2) 4 pp., no. 3 (in G-sharp) (PB 41VoPID1). *Printer's copy* of the planned *Drei Lieder* UE edition (1918–1923), 16 pp., nos. 1–3, pp. 3 and 11–16 written by Bartók, pp. 4–10 by Márta (PB 41VoPFC1), Márta's copy of nos. 4–5, 10 pp. (BBA 2027a–b). End of no. 1 written down by Bartók and reproduced in facsimile in *Ma* 1917. *Autogr. copy* of no. 1 (together with **BB 73**), 4 pp., in 1922 dedicated to M. Calvocoressi (PB 41Calvo).

BB 72 (Sz 63 / W 44): **Five Songs (E. Ady), op. 16, for voice and piano (1916)**
Draft, 18 pp. (with the beginning of a fair copy of no. 1; PB 44VoPS1). *Printer's copy* of the 1923 UE 6934 1st edition, 20 + 4 pp., pp. 1–3 and 5–20 written by Márta, no. 5 on pp. 21–24 by Emma Kodály (nos. 1–4 revised by Bartók; no. 5 with notes by Z. Kodály; PB 44VoPID1FC2). Autogr. vocal part of nos. 1–2 with Emma Kodály's German text, 1 p. (BBA 493). (Missing are: the actual printer's copy of no. 5, which was reproduced in facsimile in

Ma 1917, and printed in *Musikblätter des Anbruch* 1921; the *autogr. fair copy* of no. 1 printed in facsimile in *Nyugat* 1919.) Corrected proof sheets of the UE 1st edition, two sets (BBA 1988). Corrected UE copy with new German text (PB 44VoPFC1).

BB 73 (Sz 63a / W —): **Slovak Folksong ("Krutí Tono vretena"), for voice and piano (1916)**
Draft, 2 pp. (BBA 2004; Márta's copy, with Hungarian and German text added by Bartók, BBA 2028). *Autogr. copy* (together with **BB 71/I**), 2 pp. (dated *1916.I.*), in 1922 dedicated to M. Calvocoressi (PB 41Calvo).

BB 74 (Sz 60 / W 33): **The Wooden Prince, op. 13, ballet in one act (1914–1917)**
Sketches: (1) on fol. 13ᵛ–14ᵛ of the Black Pocket-book (BBA BH206); (2) 4 pp., memo notes, plan of a scene (and on extra pages: notes about instruments; BBA BH222, 2016). *Draft* in piano short score form: (1) from p. 7 onward, 42 pp. (a mixed-form MS with later additions, by Márta's hand too; PB 33PS1.PFC1); (2) pp. 1–2, 7–8 (= 5 pp.), the beginning of the draft, incomplete (dedicated on Dec. 21, 1915, "Sándor Mikinek"; Edinburgh National Library). *Autogr. full score*, 195 pp. (with additions by Márta's hand; PB 33FSFC3). Copy for the Budapest Opera House, 193 pp., mostly Márta's copy with Bartók's additions (BBA 2158, with discarded pages: BBA 2017). Bartók's personal copy of the 1924 UE 6638 lithographed full score, with corrections, cuts, versions (Béla Bartók Jr.). ■ Piano reduction: *Printer's copy* of the 1921 UE 6635 1st edition, 55 pp., written by Bartók, Márta (pp. 2–10, 29–31, 33–45), and Emma Kodály (pp. 1–2, 5) (PB 33PFC2). Corrected copy of the 1st edition, with preparatory notes for a 7-part "Suite" (Béla Bartók Jr.). ■ Suite versions: (1) "small suite": 3 dances (see letters Jan. 16, 1921, June 22, 1925, and 3 pp. *autogr. draft*: PB 33TFSID1; and 4 pp. autogr., photostat in Béla Bartók Jr.'s collection); (2) 1932 suite: 2 pp. *autogr. draft* (PB 33TFSID2, and a revised copy of the UE lithogr. full score, with one page tissue-proof, p. 178: PB 33TFSFC2). Autogr. MSS marking the cuts and changes, 7 + 4 + 2 + 1 + 2 pp. (PB 33FSFC1, TFSID1–2, FSFC2, TFSFC1).

BB 75 (Sz 67 / W 42): **String Quartet no. 2, op. 17 (1914–1917)**
Sketches: (1) fol. 13ᵛ in the Black Pocket-book (BBA BH206); (2) continuity sketches for Mov. III (BBA 494a). *Score draft and copy*, a MS complex (PB 42FSS1): (1) 11 + 14 pp., draft of I and II; (2) 18 pp., Márta's copy of II, corrected; (3) 4 pp., autogr. fair copy of III. (The printer's copy of the 1920 UE 6371 1st edition missing. Revised MM numbers in letter Jan. 31, 1936.) *Revision*, from the 1940s, unfinished, in a copy of the UE 1st edition (PB 42FSFC1).

BB 76 (Sz 68 / W 37): **Rumanian Folk Dances, for small orchestra (1917)** (from **BB 68**)
Autogr. full score, 10 pp. (BB 37TFSFC1), printer's copy of the UE 6545 1st edition.

BB 77 (Sz 69 / W 46): **Slovak Folksongs, for male choir (1917)**
Draft, 5 pp. (PB 46TBS1). (The printer's copy of the 1918 UE 6101 1st edition missing.)

BB 78 (Sz 70 / W 47): **Four Slovak Folksongs, for mixed choir and piano (1917)**
Draft, 8 pp. (PB 47SATBPS1). (The printer's copy of the 1924 UE 7595 1st edition missing.)

BB 79 (Sz 71 / W 34): **Fifteen Hungarian Peasant Songs, for piano (1914–1918)**
Draft: (1) (1914 layer) 10 pp., nos. 2, 4, 7–15, with **BB 80a**, and three unpublished pieces; (2) (1918 layer) 7 pp., nos. 1, 3, 5–6, with **BB 80b/II–III**, and three unpublished pieces

(the whole MS complex: A. Fassett's collection). *Printer's copy* of the 1920 UE 6370 1st edition, 26 pp., corrected copy written by Márta: nos. 1–4 (with **BB 80a**, crossed, as the planned "no. 1"), "nos. 5–6" (discarded pieces), nos. 7–15, nos. 5–6 (PB 34PFC1; Márta's other copy of **BB 80a**, nos. 3, 2, and "no. 6": PB 34PFC2). ■ See **BB 107** too.

BB 80a, 80b (Sz 65–66 / W 35): **(a) "Leszállott a páva" (1914); (b) Three Hungarian Folktunes, for piano (1914–1918)**
(80a) *Draft*: see **BB 79**. *Autogr. fair copy* (*"Leszállott a páva,"* old form of **80b/I**): the orig. missing; facsimile reproduction in *Periszkóp* 1925. — (80b) *Printer's copy* of the 1942 B&H edition in the "Homage to Paderewski" album, written down in 1941, Ditta's copy with Bartók's additions (PB 35PFC1). Corrected copy of the 1942 B&H print (PB 35PFC2).

BB 81 (Sz 72 / W 48): **Three Studies, op. 18, for piano (1918)** (and fragments)
Draft: (1) 17 pp., nos. 1–3 (PB 48PS1); (2) 1 p., fragment of a planned piece (PB miscell.C-26/6, see Facs.17; a sketch probably meant an *Etude*, on p. 53 of **BB 75** in PB 42FFS1, see Ex. 30). *Printer's copy* of the 1920 UE 6498 1st edition, 23 pp., Márta's copy with corrections (PB 48PFC1). A copy of the 1st edition with timings (Béla Bartók Jr.).

BB 82 (Sz 73 / W 49): **The Miraculous Mandarin, op. 19, pantomime in one act (1918–1919, orchestration 1924)**
Continuity sketches: fol. 15ʳ–24ᵛ (from the pursuit scene till the end) in the Black Pocket-book (BBA BH206). *Draft* in 2-piano/piano-4-hand mixed form, 48 + 4 pp., with additional preparatory notes for the orchestration (with variant endings in piano 4-hand form, including the 1931 ending too, and partial sketches for the orchestration; PB 49PS1). *Autogr. full score*, 127 pp., with the concert-suite ending (2 pp.) and the new ending (draft and fair copy, 20 pp.) (PB 49FSFC1–2). Copy for the Budapest Opera House, 127 pp., written by Ditta and Márta, with Bartók's additions (BBA 2165; another copy by copyist O. Chamouk 1925, with the 1931 ending too: BBA 2154). A corrected copy of the 1927 UE 8909 lithographed full score of the **Suite** (Béla Bartók Jr.). ■ Piano 2-hand répétiteur copy for the Budapest Opera House: 40 pp., written by Bartók, pp. 1–2, and Márta, with additions by Ditta, corrected (BBA 2155B). ■ Piano 4-hand reduction: *Autogr. copy*, 66 pp., text additions by Márta (partly used for the preparations of the orchestration too; PB 49TPPS1). *Printer's copy* of the 1925 UE 7706 1st edition, 54 pp., written by Ditta and Márta (pp. 29–48), with Bartók's additions (ca. 1923; PB 49TPPFC1; 2 sample pages, fair copy, printed in facsimile in *Nyugat* 1923). Bartók's personal copy of the 1st edition, with one page autogr. ending of the Suite (for 4-hand performance), with corrections, and preparation for the new end (Béla Bartók Jr.).

BB 83 (Sz 74 / W 50): **Improvisations on Hungarian Peasant Songs, op. 20, for piano (1920)**
Sketch for no. 1: with **BB 75** (p. 53 of PB 42FSS1). *Draft*, 16 pp., in three layers, with revisions, no. 2 in two versions (PB 50PS1; nos. 1, 5, 2, 7, 4 copied by Emma Kodály as "I–V": BBA 501). *Printer's copy* of the 1922 UE 7079 1st edition: (1) *Zwei Klavierstücke* (= nos. 2, 8), 5 pp., Márta's copy with Bartók's revision (PB 50PID1); (2) *8 impromptu zongorára* (but nos. 1, 3–7 only), 10 pp., Márta's copy revised by Bartók (PB 50PFC1). Corrected UE copy (BBA BH69); revised B&H print from the 1940s (PB 50PFC1).

BB 84 (Sz 75 / W 51): **Sonata for Violin and Piano no. 1 ("op. 21") (1921)**
Sketches: fol. 24ᵛ–27ʳ in the Black Pocket-book (BBA BH206). *Draft*, 31 + 5 pp. (PB

51VPS1). *Concert copy* (with vl. part), 48 + 18 pp., Márta's copy revised by Bartók (BBA 1987). *Printer's copy* of the 1923 UE 7247 1st edition (with vl. part), 47 + 22 pp., Márta's copy revised by Bartók (PB 51VPFC2 and VFC2). Corrected copy of the UE edition (with vl. part; PB 51VPFC1 and VFC1).

BB 85 (Sz 76 / W 52): **Sonata for Violin and Piano no. 2 (1922)**
Sketches: fol. 27ᵛ–30ᵛ in the Black Pocket-book (BBA BH206). *Draft*, 21 pp. (PB 52VPS1). *Autogr. copy* of the first page (orig. missing; in facsimile reproduced in *Az Est Hármaskönyve* 1923). *Autogr. copy, vl. part*, 17 pp., with Márta's additions (PB 52VS1), concert copy and the printer's copy of UE 7295a. *Printer's copy* of the 1923 UE 7295 1st edition, 45 pp., Márta's copy revised by Bartók (PB 52VPFC2). Corrected copy of the 1st edition (vl. part too; PB 52VPFC1 and VPC1).

BB 86 (Sz 77 / W 53): **Dance Suite, for orchestra (1923), and for piano (1925)**
Sketch: to the ritornello theme (together with partial sketches for **BB 82**: p. 48 in PB 49PS1). *Draft* in piano short score form, 14 pp., with one discarded movement between Movs. II and III (on 3 additional pages: partial sketches for the orchestration; PB 53PS1; further partial sketches, 3 pp.: BBA BH92, BH213, BH495b). *Autogr. full score* (and dedication copy), 62 pp. (and 2 pp. corrections; Budapest History Museum). *Printer's copy* of the 1924 UE 7545 full score, 68 pp., Márta's copy revised by Bartók (with E. Dohnányi's retouches; PB 53FSFC1). Revised copies of the full score: (1) Bartók's personal copy (Béla Bartók Jr.); (2) printer's copy of the W.Ph.V. 200 pocket score 1st edition (Wiener Stadt- und Landesbibliothek MHc14299). Corrected copies of the W.Ph.V. pocket score (BBA BH91; Béla Bartók Jr.). ▪ Piano solo version: *Autogr. copy* (with considerable changes), printer's copy of the 1925 UE 8397 1st edition, 17 pp. (PB 53TPFC1). Corrected copy of the UE 1st edition, with timings and new MM numbers (Béla Bartók Jr.).

BB 87a (Sz 78 / W 54): **Five Village Scenes, for voice and piano (1924)**
Draft: 17 pp. (no. 1 in 1st and 2nd drafts; nos. 4, 3, 5 as "I–II–III"; PB 54VoPS1). *Autogr. copy* (but no. 3, pp. 3–5, in Ditta's copy with Bartók's additions), printer's copy of the 1927 UE 8712 1st edition, 14 pp. (PB 54VoPFC2). Corrected UE copy with timings (PB 54VoPFC1).

BB 87b (Sz 79 / W 54): **Three Village Scenes, for 4 or 8 women's voices and orchestra (1926) (from BB 87a/III–V)**
Autogr. full score, 54 pp. (PB 54TFSS1). *Revised copy*, 54 + 3 pp., written by Ditta (pp. 1–22) and a copyist, with Bartók's additions (used by UE as the printer's copy of the lithographed 8714 full score, then sent to The League of Composers in New York; Washington, Library of Congress ML 30.3c3.83). ▪ Vocal score: *Autogr. copy*, printer's copy of the 1927 UE 8713 1st edition, 15 + 2 pp. (PB 54VoSFC2); revised copy, 16 + 1 pp., written by Ditta (pp. 11–16) and a copyist (PB 54TVoSFC1).

BB 88 (Sz 80 / W 55): **Sonata for piano (1926)**
Sketches: (1) thematic memos for Mov. III (p. 33b of PB 58PPS1); (2) continuity sketch to Mov. I, one page (BBA BH214). *First draft* in a MS complex of **BB 88–89**: Mov. I on pp. 21–24, Movs. III and II on pp. 12–19 (PB 55PS1). *Second draft* (the urform of **BB 89/III** still an episode in Mov. III of the Sonata), 15 pp. (with side sketches for the revision of III; Budapest OSZK Ms.Mus.998 deposited in BBA; facsimile edition: EMB, 1980). *Autogr. copy*, printer's copy of the 1927 UE 8772 1st edition, 11 pp. (PB 55PFC2). Corrected copy of a 1939 B&H print with timings (PB 55PFC1).

BB 89 (Sz 81 / W 56): **Out Doors, five piano pieces (1926)**
Sketches: (1) continuity sketch of no. 1 and thematic memo for no. 2, 2 pp. (–1981: Ditta Bartók's collection; photocopy in BBA); (2) theme for no. 4 (p. 37 of PB 58PPS1). *First draft* in a MS complex of **BB 88–89**: nos. 1–2 on pp. 9–12, nos. 4–5 on pp. 3–7 (no. 3 see **BB 88/III**; PB 56PS1). *Second draft*, 11 pp., nos. 1–2 and 4 (as "I–II–III") and no. 5 (without number; PB 56PFC1). *Autogr. copy*, printer's copy of the 1927 UE 8892 one-volume 1st edition, 16 pp. (written in sequence II–V, I; PB 56PFC2). Changes and corrections in copies of the UE edition (BBA BH62c; Béla Bartók Jr.); timing for II and IV (Béla Bartók Jr.). ▪ **No. 1 for orchestra**, fragment: 2 pp., mm. 1–31 only (BBA BH46/17).

BB 90 (Sz 82 / W 57): **Nine Little Piano Pieces (1926)** (and fragments)
Sketch of no. 5 (on p. 10 of PB 56PS1, see **BB 89**). *Continuity sketches and drafts*, 10 pp., nos. 1, 9/I, 6, 3, 5, 4, 7, 2 (and **BB 105 no. 146** and **no. 137**; PB 57PS1). *Second autogr. MS*, 13 pp., nos. 1, 9, 7, 3, 2, 4, 6, 5 (and **BB 105 no. 81**; PB 57PID1). *Autogr. copy*, the printer's copy of the 1927 UE 8920–8921–8922 1st edition, 14 + 1 pp. (written in sequence nos. 1–4, 8, 5–7, 9; PB 57PFC2). *Autogr. dedication copy* (for Ditta), 2 pp., no. 1 (and the beginning of no. 9; BBA BH215). Corrected copies of Vols. I and III of the UE edition (PB 57PFC1). ▪ (Piano pieces, fragments, ca. 1926 [?]): (1) 1 p. (ca. 34 mm., p. 36 of PB 58PPS1); (2) 1 p., two Hungarian folksongs (33 + 21 mm.; BBA BH46/5); see also **BB 93**.

BB 91 (Sz 83 / W 58): **Piano Concerto no. 1 (1926)**
Sketches: (1) memo for Mov. I (on p. 10 of the MS complex PB 55–56PS1); (2) 5 pp., memos and unrealized plans for I–II–III (on pp. 5, 25a–b, 33a–b, 34 in PB 58PPS1); (3) memo perhaps connected with the concerto (back of the page BBA BH214, see **BB 88**). *Draft* in 2-piano form, 38 + 8 pp. (with sketches; PB 58PPS1). *Autogr. full score draft* (Bartók's personal copy), 73 pp. (PB 58FSS1). *Autogr. copy*, printer's copy of the 1927 UE 8777 full score 1st edition, 104 pp. (PB 58FSFC1). *Revised copy* of the 1st edition, printer's copy of the 1929 UE (unmarked) 2nd edition (BBA BH41; two slightly corrected copies: BBA BH67, PB 58FSFC2; a corrected copy of the 2nd edition: Béla Bartók Jr.) ▪ 2-piano reduction: *Autogr. copy*, 42 pp. (with revision and Bartók's outline of the form of Mov. I; PB 58TPPFC1). *Printer's copy* of the 1927 UE 8779 1st edition, 42 pp., written by Bartók (pp. 1–23) and an unknown hand (PB 58TPPFC2); corrected proof sheets, Apr. 1927 (BBA). Corrected copy of the 1st edition (Béla Bartók Jr.).

BB 92 (Sz 84 / W 45): **Three Rondos on Folktunes, for piano (1916–1927)**
No. 1 (ca. 1916 version = 3 separate Slovak folksong arrangements; the autogr. draft of the ca. 1916 form missing; ca. 1927 version = recomposition in one movement). *Dedication copies* of the 1st episode only: (1) autogr. fair copy, dedicated to E. Hertzka, Sept. 1925, titled *Tót népdal*, 1 p. (New York Pierpont Morgan Library R. O. Lehman deposit); (2) another autogr. fair copy, titled *Tót népdal*, dated 1916 (but presumably written down later), 1 p. (in facsimile reproduced in *Zenei Szemle* 1928; Budapest Institute for Musicology Fond 2/32). *Printer's copy*, 6 pp., Márta's copy of the three original folksong arrangements, the rondo *couplets* and the recomposition in Bartók's handwriting (PB 45PFC2; a copy of the not yet definitive version, written by Ditta: Béla Bartók Jr.) — Nos. 2–3 (1927): *Draft*, titled *2 (3) kis rapszódia*, 14 pp., no. 3 ("I") in one, no. 2 (with a discarded folksong theme) in two versions with variant forms (New York Pierpont Morgan Library R. O. Lehman deposit). *Printer's copy* of the 1930 UE 9530 1st edition: (nos. 2–3) pp. 7–16, Ditta's copy with Bartók's revision and addition on p. 12 (PB 45PFC2). Corrected B&H copy (PB 45PFC1).

BB 93 (Sz 85 / W 60): **String Quartet no. 3 (1927)**
Draft score (and sketches; on p. 17 an unidentified sketch, possibly for piano; PB 60FSS1).
Autogr. final copy, 20 + 3 pp. (later dedicated to the Musical Fund Society in Philadelphia;
University of Pennsylvania, Philadelphia). *Competition copy* (sent 1928 to Philadelphia), 30
pp., written by Bartók and by two unknown hands (pp. 3–8 and 9–14 respectively) (University of Pennsylvania, Philadelphia). *Printer's copy*, photostat of the autogr. final copy (see
above) with Bartók's MS additions, 20 pp. (PB 60FSFC1), used 1928–1929 for the UE
9597 1st edition. — (Parts:) 16 + 14 + 15 + 14 pp., written by a copyist, with Bartók's
additions (and notes by performers), printer's copy of the 1929 UE 9598 1st edition
(Wiener Stadt- und Landesbibliothek MHc14297).

BB 94 (Sz 86–88 / W 61): **Rhapsody no. 1, (a) for violin and piano (1928), (b) for
violin and orchestra (–1929), (c) for violoncello and piano (–1929)**
(a) *Draft*, 12 + 10 pp. (with several endings, some belong to the vlc. version; with a drawing
of the location of the notes on *cimbalom*; PB 61VPS1). *Autogr. copy* (the orig. MS missing?;
photocopy from the property of J. Szigeti: PB 61VPFC1), 18 pp. (with the 2nd ending;
Cadenza breve on p. 15; with the later discarded Allegretto scherzando section at no. 12).
Printer's copy of the 1929 UE 9864 1st edition, a contemporary photocopy of the missing
Szigeti copy, 13 + 2 pp., with Bartók's additions, and autogr. supplement to p. 13 (Rubato,
quasi cadenza; without the Allegretto scherzando section; with scattered preparatory notes
for the instrumentation; Basel: Paul Sacher Stiftung). Autogr. vl. part, 7 pp. (PB 61VFC1).
Corrected proof sheets of the UE 1st edition (also served as Bartók's concert copy;
PB61VPFC4); a corrected copy of the UE print (in connection with the vlc. version too;
Basel: Paul Sacher Stiftung); another copy with timings (Bartók's concert copy; Béla Bartók
Jr.) — **(b)** *Draft score*, 33 + 7 pp. (with variant endings, with the Allegretto scherzando
section; PB 61TFSS1). *Autogr. fair copy*, 43 + 2 pp., printer's copy of the 1931 UE 9858 1st
edition (Basel: Paul Sacher Stiftung); the second ending, 7 pp. (PB 61TFSFC1). A copy
of the UE print, the printer's copy of the B&H edition (without Bartók's hand;
PB 61TFSFC2). — **(c)** *Draft of the Vlc. part* and changes in the piano part, 10 pp. (PB
61TCPFC1). Corrected proof sheets of the vlc. part only, UE 9866, marked by Bartók and a
performer (BBA BH63; a copy of the UE print, Bartók's concert copy: Béla Bartók Jr.).

BB 95 (Sz 91 / W 62): **String Quartet no. 4 (1928)**
Draft score (with sketches), 35 pp. (PB 62FSS1); autogr. sample pages of vl.1 of Mov. I,1–
142, 4 pp. (BBA 1084). *Autogr. final copy*, 39 pp. (Mov. IV as a later insertion; PB
62FSFC1); a photocopy of the same, with MS additions by Bartók, the printer's copy of the
1929 UE 9788/W.Ph.V.169 1st edition, 39 pp. (PB 62FSFC2); Bartók's German draft of
the text *Formübersicht*, Dec. 1929, 2 pp.: BBA 3923; Bartók's instructions for the engraver of
the parts: Wiener Stadt- und Landesbibliothek. Corrected proof sheets of the UE/W.Ph.V.
pocket score, 16 pp. only (PB 62FSFC3).

BB 96 (Sz 89–90 / W 63): **Rhapsody no. 2, (a) for violin and piano (1928, rev. 1935),
(b) for violin and orchestra (–1929, rev. 1935)**
(a) *Draft*, 13 pp. (and on pp. 14–22 plus 3 pp. different variants of the ending, and versions;
PB 63VPS1ID1). *Autogr. final copy* (the orig. sent to Z. Székely), 19 pp.; a photocopy of it
with Bartók's additions, the printer's copy of the 1929 UE 9891 1st edition, 19 pp. (PB
63VPFC2); autogr. vl. part, 8 pp. (with Székely's writing on p. 8; PB 63VFC1). Corrected
copies of the UE 1st edition: (1) with marking a major cut (Béla Bartók Jr.); (2) with
crossings etc. (PB 63VPFC1); (3) a copy with pasted-in lithographed corrections, dedicated

Feb. 1941 to J. Antal (BBA 3305); (4) another copy with pasted-in corrections, used by Bartók as concert copy in Italy (PB 63VPFC 3); (5) a revised copy with Bartók's autogr. insertions, with vl. part, the printer's copy of the 1946 B&H 15890 rev. edition (PB 63VP/VFC4). — (b) *First autogr. full score*, 39 pp. (PB 63TFSS1). *Autogr. fair copy*, 73 + 2 pp., printer's copy of the 1931 UE 9867 1st edition (PB 63TFSFC2); a corrected copy of the 1st edition, with autogr. preparations for the revision (Béla Bartók Jr.). The *revision* of Mov. II: 9 + 7 pp. draft, pp. 18–26 of the autogr. fair copy on tissues (PB 63TFSFC1; preparatory notes for the scoring of the new ending, in a copy of the vl.-piano form written by J. Deutsch, 2 pp., BBA 2012); tissue-proofs of the corrections, 9 pp. in 5 copies (BBA BH42). A revised copy of the UE 1st edition, printer's copy of the 1949 B&H 16230 rev. edition (PB 63TFSFC3).

BB 97 (Sz — /W —): **Five Hungarian Folksongs, for voice and piano (1928)** (recomposed from **BB 42**)
Drafts: (1) nos. 2, 1, 5, 3, and no. 4 in two versions; (2) shorthand notation of nos. 1–5 (2 + 1 + 2 pp.; BBA BH212).

BB 98 (Sz 92 / W 64): **Twenty Hungarian Folksongs, Vols. I–IV, for voice and piano (1929)**
Draft, 31 pp. (and 1 p. sketch for no. 8; PB 64VoPS1). *Autogr. copy*, 68 pp. (unusual format with hand-rastral, with considerable changes and revision), printer's copy of the 1932 UE 1521–1522–1523–1524 1st edition (PB 64VoPFC1); blue and brown contact copies, 29 + 23 pp. (with Bartók's revision, and partly with German text too, BBA 2008); a full set of brown contact copies, 66 pp. (with R. St. Hoffmann's German translation; PB 64VoPFC2).
■ See **BB 108** too.

BB 99 (Sz 93 / W 65): **Four Hungarian Folksongs, for mixed choir (1930)**
Sketches to II, III (in PB 65SATBS1). *Draft*, 10 + 1 pp. (written in sequence I–II, IV, III; PB 65SATBS1). *Fair copy on tissue*, 20 pp., incl. discarded pages (PB 65SATBFC1). *Tissue-proofs*, Bartók's working copies: (1) 28 pp. (German translation; PB 65SATBFC2); (2) 17 pp., with English text, the printer's copy of the 1932 UE 10371 1st edition (PB 65SATBFC3).

BB 100 (Sz 94 / W 67): **Cantata profana, for tenor, baritone, double chorus, and orchestra (1930)**
Sketch of two themes on p. 10 of the draft of **BB 99**. *Draft* in vocal score form, 24 + 3 pp. (sketches on pp. 26–27; up to p. 20 written for Rumanian text; on 30 extra pages: the formation, translation, and preparation for edition of the text in Rumanian, Hungarian, German, and — from a later time — English; PB 67VoSS1). *Draft score*, 67 + 2 pp. (German translation written by B. Szabolcsi; PB 67FSS1; the first page copied by Ditta: BBA BH46/6a). *Fair copy on tissue*, originally the full score plus the piano part for the vocal score written together (in this form, 70 + 1 pp., corrected tissue proofs as admission copy for UE: PB 67FSFC2), then the tissues were cut and rearranged for the 1934 UE *facsimile edition* (UE 10613 full score, UE 10614 vocal score), 70 and 36 pp. (PB 67FSFC1 and 67PFC1; a preliminary version of the vocal score made from tissue proofs, with Bartók's corrections, 29 pp., and corrected copies of the facsimile edition of the full score and the vocal score: Béla Bartók Jr.).

BB 101 (Sz 95 / W 68): **Piano Concerto no. 2 (1930–1931)**
Draft score, 75 pp. (including sketches on pp. 31, 46, 48, 53; PB 68FSS1). *Fair copy on tissue* of the score (=A) and of "Piano 2" for the 2-piano reduction (=B), written at the same time

(PB 68FSFC1). *Tissue-proof working copies* ("negrocopy" style), presumably in the sequence: (B.1) 19 pp., hand-montage 2-piano form of Mov. I only, with considerable autogr. changes (BBA BH48a); (A.1) 98 pp., full score, admission copy for UE (PB 68FSFC2); (B.2) 43 pp., handmade new 2-piano form, Movs. I–III (Béla Bartók Jr.). The 1932 UE *1st facsimile edition* of the full score ("aluminum print" without plate no., from the corrected autogr. tissues printed in Budapest); a copy of this edition (A.2) was Bartók's concert copy (with corrections and changes; BBA BH48b). The 1937 UE 10442 *2nd facsimile edition* (from the newly corrected tissues printed in Austria); a copy of this edition (A.3) has Bartók MS insertions, was used by Ditta (Béla Bartók Jr.). ■ 2-piano reduction: The printer's copy of the 1941 UE 10995 1st edition was B.2, see above. A handmade copy for a planned B&H edition (PB 68TPSPFC1).

BB 102a (Sz 55 / W 36): (BARTÓK–GERTLER) **Sonatina, for violin and piano (ca. 1930)** (from **BB 69**)
Draft, 12 + 2 pp., a copy of Gertler's transcription fully revised by Bartók (with notes for the orchestration of **BB 102b** too; PB 36TVPS1). Corrected proof sheets of the 1931 Rv 5374 1st edition, 2 sets (BBA 1989; a copy of the Rv edition with Bartók's notes: Béla Bartók Jr.).

BB 102b (Sz 96 / W 36): **Dances from Transylvania, for orchestra (1931)** (from **BB 69** and **102a**)
Autogr. score, 11 + 3 pp., printer's copy of the 1931 Rv 5440 full score (PB 36TFSS1).

BB 103 (Sz 97 / W A1): **Hungarian Sketches, for orchestra (1931)** (from **BB 51/V, X, 58/II, 55/I, 53-I/xlii**)
Autogr. score, 27 pp. (the preparation for the orchestration of Movs. IV–V: see **BB 55** and **53**), printer's copy of the 1931 R/Rv 5442 1st edition (PB A1TFSS1); a copy of the 1st edition with Bartók's revision of Mov. II (Béla Bartók Jr.).

BB 104 (Sz 98 / W 69): **Forty-Four Duos, for two violins (1931–1932)**
Draft, 26 pp. (one discarded duo on p. 19; nos. 2, 26, 30 = nos. 8, 16, 36 of the orig. numbering; missing; PB 69VVS1). *Autogr. copy on tissue*, 27 pp., 44 + 1 pieces (two sets of numbering; with corrections; PB 69VVFC1). *Corrected tissue-proofs*: (1–2) 18 pieces written for E. Doflein and Schott's Söhne (1: the original, once in Doflein's collection, missing, copy in BBA; 2: PB 69VVID2); (3) 47 pp., printer's copy of the 1933 UE 10391–10394 edition (PB 69VVFC3). Corrected copy of the 18 duos printed by Schott in *Spielmusik für Violine: Neue Musik* III and IV, and a corrected copy of the UE 10452 one-volume edition (Béla Bartók Jr.). *Autogr. performing copy* of 7 duos, 3 pp., written in America (PB 69VVID1). Corrected copy of the B&H (2nd) edition (with R. Kolisch's fingering; PB 69VVFC2).

BB 105 (Sz 107 / W 59): **Mikrokosmos, Vols. I–VI, 153 pieces for piano (1926, 1932–1939)**
Sketches from 1926 (nos. 81, 137, 146) in the draft of **BB 90**; sketch of no. 98 in the draft of **BB 111**; a sketch probably for the *Mikrokosmos*, see p. 25 of the draft of **BB 115**. *Draft*, 90 + 2 pp., including 9 unpublished pieces but 14 pieces and several variant forms missing (PB 59PS1). *Autogr. final copy on tissue*, 82 pp., including discarded pieces, versions, and drafts too (PB 59PID1-ID2). *Working copies* made from *tissue proofs*: (1) 35 pp., used for Peter Bartók's lessons (Béla Bartók Jr.); (2) personal copy, 56 pp.: pp. 1–7 orig. MS (21 pieces), pp. 8–50 and 56 black & white proof, corrected, pp. 51–55 lilac proof (PB 59PFC1); (3) submission copy for B&H, 51 pp., without the orig. pp. 9–12, 33–36, black & white proof, corrected

(PB 59PFC3); (4) *printer's copy* of the 1940 B&H 15196, 15197, 15192, 15191, 15189, 15187 1st edition, 99 + 17 pp., black & white and lilac proofs and MS copies pasted and rearranged (with several additional hands, including M. Seiber, E.S.E.; PB 59PFC4). Corrected printed copies: (1) Vols. III and VI (with notes for the 2-piano transcription **BB 120/2** and 7; PB 59PFC2-TPPS1); (2) Vol. VI, dedicated by Bartók to J. Deutsch (BBA 182). ▪ The 2-piano transcriptions, see **BB 120**.

BB 106 (Sz 99 / W 70): **Székely Folksongs, for male choir (1932)**
The draft is missing. *Autogr. copy on tissue*, 9 pp. (PB 70TBFC1). *Corrected tissue proofs*, 2 sets of lilac proofs, 9 + 9 + 4 pp. (BBA 2001). On his copy of the 1939 MK 418 1st edition Bartók corrected the title *Székely dalok* to *Székely népdalok* (Béla Bartók Jr.).

BB 107 (Sz 100 / W 34): **Hungarian Peasant Songs, for orchestra (1933)** (from **BB 79/6–15**)
No draft or preparatory notes for the orchestration are known. *Autogr. full score on tissue*, 30 pp., used for the 1933 UE 10573 facsimile 1st edition (PB 34TFSFC1). Tissue-proofs, 28 pp., submission copy for UE, with editor's and Bartók's notes (PB 34TFSFC3). Corrected copies of the *facsimile edition*: (1) (BBA BH71); (2) printer's copy of the 1949 B&H 16167 edition (revised not by Bartók; PB 34TFSFC2); (3) a copy with Bartók's notes about the distribution of the copies (Béla Bartók Jr.).

BB 108 (Sz 101 / W 64): **Five Hungarian Folksongs, for voice and orchestra (1933)** (from **BB 98/1, 2, 11, 14, 12**)
Autogr. full score, 26 pp. (Mov. IV added later), used for producing the copy made at UE for hire (PB 64TFSS1).

BB 109 (Sz 42 / W 22): (ORSZÁGH–BARTÓK) **Hungarian Folksongs, Vols. I–II, for violin and piano (1934)** (from **BB 53**)
Based on T. Országh's 1931 transcription of 11 pieces from *For Children* (PB 22TVPFC2, with Bartók's preliminary notes for a revision, with additional "Changes"), Bartók's own *draft*, 10 pp., 9 pieces only (PB 22TVPS1, and vl. part, 3 + 1 pp., 22TVFC1). Corrected copy of the Rv 1699 1st edition (PB 22TVPFC1).

BB 110 (Sz 102 / W 71): **String Quartet no. 5 (1934)**
Draft score with sketches, 44 pp., and discarded pages, sketches, partial sketches on 18 pp. (PB 71FSS1). *Autogr. fair copy on tissue*, 50 pp. (Washington, Library of Congress ML 29c B29, with a copy of the tissue proofs ML 29e B29). *Corrected tissue proofs*: (1) with MS additions by Bartók and J. Deutsch, 50 + 9 pp., printer's copy of the 1936 UE 10736 1st edition (PB 71FSFC2); (2) the corrected tissue proofs cut and pasted together as the 4 parts, 21 + 20 + 21 + 22 pp., printer's copy of the 1936 UE 10737a–d 1st edition of the parts (PB 71PartsFC1). Corrected copies of the pocket score 1st edition (Wiener Stadt- und Landesbibliothek MHv14297; Béla Bartók Jr.).

BB 111 (Sz 103 / W 72): **Twenty-seven Two- and Three-part Choruses, (a) a cappella (1935/36), (b) Seven Choruses with orchestra (1937–1941)**
(a) *Draft*, 26 pp. (PB 72SAS1), probably the direct source of the (missing) fair copy on tissue, written by J. Deutsch and reproduced in facsimile in the 1937 MK 1st edition. *Autogr. copies* of "Huszárnóta" and "Lánycsúfoló," 2 + 3 pp. (BBA 181, BH216). Corrected copies of the MK 1st edition: (1) 103 pp., with German and English titles and a still unpublished new

numbering (PB 72SAFC1); (2) 24 pp., printer's copy of 4 choruses edited by B&H 15339–15342 (PB 72SAFC2); (3) a copy of 18 choruses with Z. Kodály's comments (Béla Bartók Jr.). — **(b)** Nos. 1–5 (1937): *draft score*, 16 pp. (with instructions for the MK copyist; PB 72SAOS1). *Draft score* of no. 6 "Only tell me" (ca. 1941), pp. 17–22 (PB 72SAOS1), and no. 7 "Teasing Song," 7 pp. (G. Selden-Goth collection; present owner unknown). *Revised version* of nos. 1–5 with English text, a copy of the MK 1st edition with Bartók's additions, 13 + 4 + 6 + 6 + 14 pp., printer's copy of the 1941 B&H edition (including a new numbering of the 7 choruses; PB 72SAOFC2; photostat of nos. 1–3 and 5–7, 64 pp., copyist's copy with Bartók's corrections, English and German text: PB 72SAOFC1). Sketch and short score of a 103 mm.-long fragment: orchestral episode for the planned revised version of "Hussar" (from the 1940s; see PB 80FSS3).

BB 112 (Sz 104 / W 73): From Olden Times, for male choir (1935)
Draft, 12 + 5 pp. (together with "Teasing song" from **BB 111**; PB 73TBBS1-ID1), probably the direct source of the (missing) copy on tissue, written by J. Deutsch and reproduced in facsimile in the 1937 MK 321 1st edition. Corrected copies of the 1st edition (PB 73TB-BFC1; Béla Bartók Jr.).

BB 113 (Sz 105 / W 69): Petite Suite, for piano (1936) (from BB 104)
Draft of the orig. 5-movement form, 5 pp. (PB 69TPS1). *Printer's copy* of the 1939 UE 10987 1st edition, 10 + 1 pp., copied by Ditta, with Bartók's revision (Wiener Stadt- und Landesbibliothek MH14296c). Corrected proof sheets (PB 69TPFC3) and a corrected copy of the UE 1st edition, and of a B&H reprint of the UE edition (PB 69TPFC1-2). *Draft* of the additional Mov. I^bis (ca. 1942), based on **BB 104/32** (played on Bartók's 1942 Continental 4005/Set 102 gramophone record), 1 p. (PB 69TPS2).

BB 114 (Sz 106 / W 74): Music for Strings, Percussion, and Celesta (1936)
Draft score, 71 pp., with sketches and discarded pages on pp. 72–83 (PB 74FSS1), with instructions to the copyist of the printer's copy for the 1937 UE 10815 full score. Corrected copies of the UE full score: (1) first correction of misprints, with changes and additional 5 pp. MS including the seating plan of the orchestra (PB 74FSFC1); (2) a copy with the extra page *Änderungen* and corrections (Béla Bartók Jr.); (3) printer's copy of the 1937 UE 10888/W.Ph.V.201 pocket score, with additional 3 pp. MS including Bartók's text *Aufbau* (PB 74FSFC2). A corrected copy of the pocket score (Béla Bartók Jr.).

BB 115 (Sz 110 / W 75) and BB 121 (Sz 115 / W 75)
(a) Sonata for two Pianos and Percussion (1937), (b) Concerto for two Pianos and Orchestra (1940)
(a) Sketches on p. 71 of the draft of **BB 105** (PB 59PS1), together with sketches of **BB 117** (T. Spivakovsky's collection). *Draft*, 36 pp. and 3 extra pp. with the ca. 1939 recomposed retransition of Mov. I,229–273 (PB 75FSS1). *Autogr. copy on tissue* of the score of **(a)**, 42 pp., with corrections, still with the orig. retransition but marked "vi-de" (PB 75FSID1-ID3), with separate percussion parts III–IV, 11 pp. (PB 75DID1). *Corrected tissue proofs* of score **(a)**: (1) Bartók's concert copy, 42 pp. (old retransition; PB 75PSID2A); (2) copy with dedication of June 1939, 42 pp. (old retransition; J. Sólyom's collection, Stockholm); (3) **(a + b)** Bartók's new concert copy, the Sonata and Concerto versions together, 46 pp., with preparatory notes for the orchestration (new retransition; PB 75TPPPFC1); (4) **(a + b)** Ditta's concert copy of the Sonata and Concerto versions, 46 pp. (new retransition; PB 75TPSPFC1). Corrected tissue proofs of the *percussion parts*: (I–II) 11 + 11 pp. (BBA

BH44; and extra copies written by the percussionists of the Budapest performance: BBA); (III–IV) 11 + 11 and 11 + 11 pp., old, and revised new forms (PB 75DID2). Other sets of percussion parts: (I–II) 21 + 21 pp., copies for the 1940 New York performance (partly revised by Bartók; PB 75DID3). *Printer's copy* of the 1942 B&H 8675 1st edition of the score (a), 42 pp., a tissue proof prepared by E. Stein (PB 75(T)PSPFC2), and of the B&H 8816 1st edition of the percussion parts, 11 pp. (PB 75(T)DFC4; a copy of the printed part with one correction: PB 75TDFC2). — (b) Score-sections for the Concerto version: *autogr. copy*, 30 pp. (pp. 1–20 still on European paper; PB 75TFSS1).

BB 116 (Sz 111 / W 77): **Contrasts, for violin, clarinet, and piano (1938)**
Draft with sketches, 15 pp. (another sketch with **BB 117**), written in sequence I, III, II, with preparatory notes for copying (PB 77FSS1). *Autogr. copy on tissue*, 18 pp., the beginning of Mov. III still follows Mov. I (PB 77FSFC1). Tissue-proofs of pp. 7–8 only (= Mov. II), corrected (PB 77FSFC2; a complete tissue proof copy, dedicated to D. Dille, in private collection; the tissue proof printer's copy of the 1942 Hawkes B.Ens.49–73 1st edition missing).

BB 117 (Sz 112 / W 76): **Violin Concerto (no. 2, 1937–1938)**
Sketches, 2 pp. (T. Spivakovsky's collection). *Draft* in vl.-piano short-score form, with sketches, 36 pp. (in Mov. III only: notes for the orchestration; PB 76VPS1); autogr. sample page of the vl. part, Mov. I, 83 mm., titled *Tempo di verbunkos* (BBA BH46/14). *Autogr. copy of the vl.-piano form on tissue*, 35 + 2 pp., with changes (PB 76TVPFC1). Corrected tissue proofs of the vl.-piano form: (1) Bartók's *working copy*, 21 + 16 + 16 pp., in Movs. I–II considerable revision, preliminary notes for the orchestration, preparation for the edited form; Mov. III in two different, slightly revised forms (on p. 21 sketch for **BB 116**; BBA 4091a–c); (2) copy sent to Z. Székely (private collection); (3) printer's copy of the 1941 B&H 8296 1st edition of the vl.-piano reduction, prepared by E. Stein (PB 76TVPFC2; corrected proof sheets of the 1st edition, dated Sept. 1939: Béla Bartók Jr.; a corrected copy of the B&H print: PB 76TVPFC2). *Autogr. full score on tissue*, 98 pp. (PB 76FSID1). Corrected tissue proof of the full score, 98 pp., with list of errors (PB 76FSFC1–2; the printer's copy of the 1946 B&H 9003 1st edition missing). Corrected proof sheets of the B&H full score, pp. 1–132, with important marginal notes on problems of the notation (Washington, Library of Congress, Moldenhauer Archives, Hungarian box).

BB 118 (Sz 113 / W 78): **Divertimento, for string orchestra (1939)**
Draft score, 22 pp. (sketches on pp. 2 and 19; sketches for **BB 119** on p. 14), the movements written in sequence I, III, II (PB 78FSS1). *Autogr. full score on tissue*, 26 pp. (PB 78FSID1; the printer's copy tissue proof missing). A corrected copy of the 1940 B&H 8326 full score, with corrections for the pocket score edition (PB 78FSFC1).

BB 119 (Sz 114 / W 79): **String Quartet no. 6 (1939)**
Sketches in the draft of **BB 118**. *Draft score*, 20 pp., with sketches on pp. 1 and 9; the fragment of a planned fast finale on pp. 17–19 (PB 79FSS1). *Autogr. copy on tissue*, 26 + 1 pp., with later additions (PB FSFC1). Corrected tissue proof, 15 pp., the printer's copy of the 1941 B&H 8437 1st edition (PB 79FSFC2; another copy: BBA 5660; a copy with R. Kolisch's notes: in private collection, photo in BBA). Corrected proof sheets of the B&H edition, three sets (the 2nd with Bartók's corrections, incomplete, pp. 20, 32, 34, 36–38, 41 missing: PB 79 FSFC3; the missing pages, together with the 1st and 3rd corr.: private collection; photocopy in BBA).

BB 120 (Sz 108 / W 59): **Seven Pieces from Mikrokosmos, for two pianos** (–1940) (from **BB 105**)

Sketches: notes for the transcription of nos. 2 and 7 in printed copies of Vols. III and VI of *Mikrokosmos* (PB 59PFC2-TPPS1). *Draft*, 4 pp., no. 2 ("2nd version") and no. 3 (photo: PB 59TPPS2). *Autogr. copy on tissue*, nos. 1, 4, 2, 7 only, 7 pp. (PB 59TPPID1); corrected tissue proofs of nos. 4, 2, 7 only, 6 pp. (PB 59TPPFC2). Printer's copy for B&H, 19 pp., a mixed-form MS: nos. 1–2, 4, 7: corrected tissue proofs; no. 3 ("1st version"): 4 pp. autogr. MS; nos. 5–6: rearranged-revised from the printed *Mikrokosmos* edition (PB 59TPPFC1).

BB 121, see **BB 115**

BB 122 (Sz 115a / W 12): **Suite for two Pianos, op. 4b** (1941) (from **BB 40**)

Fragmentary draft (but probably the complete form of the source), 12 pp.: Mov. I full, Mov. II,1–38, 223–227 (twice, sketch and draft), Mov. IV,43–64 and 124–145 (i.e., the rewritten sections). *Autogr. copy on tissue*, 31 pp., with corrections (PB 12TPPID1). Corrected tissue proofs, two concert copies, 31 + 31 pp. (Piano I = Ditta, Piano II = Bartók; PB TPPFC1-TPSPFC1).

BB 123 (Sz 116 / W 80): **Concerto for Orchestra** (1943)

Sketches and continuity draft (complete), on pp. 10–98 of the Turkish field-book of Bartók (including unrealized sketches too; PB 80FSS1; see also **BB 129** [a]), continued on standard music paper, 12 + 1 pp. (with notes for the orchestration, including partial sketches too; PB 80FSS2; further sketch with **BB 128**). *Autogr. full score*, 92 pp. (one ending only), the dedication copy (Washington, Library of Congress ML 30.3c2.B3, Koussevitzky Music-Foundation). 2 photostat copies of the autogr. MS: (1) Bartók's *personal copy*, 1 + 92 pp., with notes and corrections (PB 80FSFC1); (2) printer's copy of the 1946 B&H 9009 full score 1st edition, 92 pp., with the *autogr. MS* of the alternative (2nd) ending from 1945, and changes on pp. 93–100 (PB 80FSFC2; the proof sheets which Bartók corrected in 1945 are missing). A tissue proof of the full score written for S. Koussevitzky by copyists Turner and Weisleder (with a few additions by Bartók; Washington, Library of Congress ML 30.3e2.B3). ▪ Reduction for **piano solo** (1944); *autogr. MS on tissue*, 43 pp. (PB 80TPFC1).

BB 124 (Sz 117 / W 81): **Sonata for Solo Violin** (1944)

Sketches and continuity draft (complete), on pp. 37–64 of the Arab field-book of Bartók (PB 81FSS1; sketches for the preliminary form of the fugue theme (?) on p. 95 of the Turkish field-book, see **BB 123**). *Autogr. copy on tissue*, 10 pp. (PB 81VFC1). Tissue-proofs: (1) 10 pp. (the first copy seen by Menuhin?; PB 81VFC2); (2) 10 pp., Bartók's *personal copy* with notes (PB 81VFC4); (3) 10 pp., rearranged, R. Kolisch's copy (BBA 2410; another version in private collection); (4) 10 pp., Y. Menuhin's personal copy (private collection; photo in BBA); (5) 10 pp., printer's copy of the 1947 B&H 15896 1st edition (Menuhin's edition, prepared for publication by E. Stein; PB 81VFC3).

BB 125 (Sz 118 / W 83): **Goat Song (The Husband's Lament), for voice and piano** (1945)

Draft, 2 pp., Ukrainian folksong with Hungarian text and title ("A férj keserve"), dedicated to P. Kecskeméti (private collection; facsimile: BBA and PB). *Autogr. copy on tissue*, 2 pp., without title, with Hungarian and English texts (PB 83VoPFC1).

BB 126 (Sz — / W. 82): **Three Ukrainian Folksongs, for voice and piano (ca. 1945)**

Draft, 3 pp., Ukrainian text only (partly fragmentary form; PB 82VoPS1 = pp. 3–5 in "Reserved Songs").

BB 127 (Sz 119 / W 84): **Piano Concerto no. 3 (1945)**
Sketch of I, first theme: on p. 69 and 67 of the Arab field-book (see **BB 124**; see also the sketch on p. 95 of the Turkish field-book, **BB 123**); Bartók's notation of birdsong themes, including the theme of II,64–67: on a small tissue (PB "Miscellaneous" Box C-27 55b). *Draft* in 2-piano form (complete; with sketches and partial sketches too, and notes for the orchestration), 19 pp. (PB 84FSS1). *Autogr. full score on tissue*, 62 pp. (the last measures on pp. 61–62 filled by T. Serly's hand; performing marks in Mov. III missing; Bartók's corrections in pencil in Movs. II–III, disregarded in the posth. 1st ed; PB 84FSFC1). (N.B. The printer's copy of the 1947 B&H 9122 posth. 1st edition seems to be missing.)

BB 128 (Sz 102 / W 85): **Viola Concerto (1945)** (draft, realized and scored by T. Serly)
Draft in viola-piano short score form, 14 pp. on 4 bifolios, including sketches and material not used by Serly, and some notes for the orchestration not realized in the score (PB 85FSS1; on p. 16 sketch for **BB 123**; facsimile edition: Bartók Records, 1995). — *T. Serly's MSS*: full score (missing?); copies on tissue: (1) viola-piano reduction, dated Dec. 15, 1947 (with tissue proof); (2) viola part (with tissue proof, edited by W. Primrose); (3) violoncello part of the Violoncello Concerto version by T. Serly (PB 85TVaP1-VaID1-TVaFC1-CID1).

BB 129: Fragments of unrealized compositions, 1943–1945 (or earlier without date)[2]
(a) 12 mm., piano 2-hand-form sketch (slow piece?; planned slow movement for the Concerto for Orchestra?), not later than 1943: on p. 85 of the Turkish field-book, see **BB 123** (further sketches on pp. 17–18, 79–80 in the same sketch-book may or may not belong to the Concerto for Orchestra, those on p. 95 may belong to the Piano Concerto no. 3 **BB 127**).
(b) ca. 22 mm., string-quartet-like beginning with short-score-form continuation (slow movement?; sketch for the planned **String Quartet no. 7?**), ca. 1944 or 1945: on pp. 65–66 of the Arab field-book, see **BB 124**; notation of the rhythm of m. 6 on p. 98 of the Turkish field-book, see **BB 123**.
(c) ca. 50 mm., **fragment for violoncello and strings** (slow piece; planned concerto?), ca. 1907–1908? (BBA BH46/11).

AUTOGRAPH SOURCES OF BARTÓK'S TRANSCRIPTIONS AND CADENZAS[3]

BB A-1: Rákóczi March, for piano 4 hands (1896) (= DD C-2)
Autogr. draft in pencil, 4 pp. (BBA BH50).

BB A-2: Cadenza to Movement I of BEETHOVEN's **Piano Concerto no. 3 C minor (1900)**
Autogr. copy, 2 pp. (BBA BH12b).

BB A-3: Orchestration of BEETHOVEN's **Erlkönig (WoO 131) (ca. 1905)**
Autogr. full score, 10 pp. (University of Illinois, Urbana).

2. *Fragments* that presumably belong to finished mature works are listed with **BB 50, 81, 89, 90, 91, 110, 111, 115, 123** (see also **BB 28**); fragments that may not belong to the set are listed with **BB 50, 90, 93**. *Discarded* pieces, movements, or significant longer sections are listed with **BB 42, 53, 79, 86, 94, 104, 105**.
3. Bartók's autograph copies of other composer's music (Zoltán Kodály, Emma Kodály, Stravinsky, Lord Berners, etc.) and the extant primary sources of his performing editions (see Somfai/*19th-Century Ideas*, 84) are not included here.

BB A-4a–k: 17th- and 18th-century Italian harpsichord and organ music (MARCELLO, ROSSI, DELLA CIAIA, FRESCOBALDI, ZIPOLI), transcribed for piano (1926–1927)
Autograph MS exists only to five of the eleven pieces: (b–c–d) Michelangelo Rossi, "9. Toccata," "1. Toccata" (Corrento), *autogr. copy*, 9 pp., Bartók's concert copy; (i) Girolamo Frescobaldi, "Toccata" in G, *autogr. copy*, 3 pp., Bartók's concert copy; (k) Domenico Zipoli, "Pastorale," *autogr. copy*, 2 pp., Bartók's concert copy (BBA BH208, BH209, BH207). (The printer's copies of the 1930 C. Fischer edition of the 11 vols. missing.)

BB A-5: J. S. BACH–BARTÓK, Sonata VI (BWV 530), transcription for piano (ca. 1929)
Autogr. copy, 13 pp., printer's copy of the Rv 5172 1st edition (BBA BH221).

BB A-6: PURCELL–BARTÓK, Two Preludes, transcription for piano (ca. 1929)
Autogr. draft, 3 pp., and *autogr. copy. on tissue*, 4 pp. (BBA BH211a–b).

BB A-7: Cadenzas to Movements I and III of MOZART's Concerto for two pianos K365 E-flat major (ca. 1939)
Autogr. draft, 4 pp. (PB M1).

INDEX OF BASIC TERMS

Only those pages containing the definition of the term or an extensive discussion of it are included.

abbreviations in Bartók's MSS, 121
acoustic (performed) form, 13
Albumblatt, 34
alternative endings, 171
Aluminiumdruck of *Lichtpause,* 216
American revisions, 247
arbitrary pagination in Bartók's MSS, 99
arrangements, 227
articulation signs, 265

bifolio (one folded sheet), 96
bi-functional MS, 113, 142
birdsong, 54
black and white lithography based on *Lichtpause,* 215
Black Pocket-book (sketch-book), 69
Bogenvibrato, notation of, 271
bowing marks, 270
bridge form (arch form, palindrome form), 19

calligraphic vs. running notation, 205, 215
comma and *Luftpause,* 263
composer's recordings, 279
composing vs. copying notation, 206
concert copy, 29
concert-style notation for piano, 275
continuity draft, 34
continuity sketch, 68
copyists (family members, friends, professionals), 207
corrected edition, 245

corrected proof sheets, 238
correcting process, 121, 179, 229

dating, 118
dedication, 120
dedication copy, 204
destroyed drafts, 26, 114
destroyed sketches, 26, 35
discarded movements, 84, 189
draft, 113
draft complex, 175
düvő rhythm, 193
dynamics, 264

editing procedure, 232, 236
editors' work on Bartók's MS, 236
engraver's (or printer's) copy, 232
expression marks, 264

facsimile print, 216
fair copy, 205
Fassung letzter Hand, 282
field-book (pocket-sized). *See* sketch-book
final copy, 204. *See also* fair copy
formation of a work, 144
fragment, 83
fragmentary exercises in composition, 86
full-score draft, 117

gathering (*Heft*) from bifolios, 98
glissando, notation and performance, 267

Handexemplar (personal copy), 29
handmade (montage) copy, 217
hora lungă, 71
house rules of Bartók's publishers, 230

ink and pencil in Bartók's MSS, 30, 80, 204
instructions to publisher (engraver), 236

language and spelling in Bartók's scores, 243, 263
layout (plan for scoring), 220
Lichtpause, 32, 96, 215
lithographed full score, 235
Luftpause and comma, 263

memo (sketch), 37
metronome, pocket (Bartók's), 254
metronome numbers, 252
micro-chronology of the composition, 99
missing corrected proof sheets, 26, 238
missing drafts, 114
missing printer's copies, 233
mixed-form MS, 113, 206
music paper, 96

Negrokopie of *Lichtpause,* 215
notation. *See* articulation signs; bowing marks;
    comma and *Luftpause*; concert-style notation
    for piano; dynamics; expression marks; glis-
    sando; pedal notations; performance instruc-
    tions; performing edition; pitch notation and
    micro-intervals; rules of notation; tempo;
    vibrato

omitted movements or sections, 84, 189
onionskin. See *Lichtpause*
orchestral seating plans, 272
orchestration. *See* preparatory notes for orches-
    tration; scoring

pagination in Bartók's MSS, 99
partial sketch, 34, 78
particella. See short score
paste-ups (paste-overs) in Bartók's MSS, 105,
    205
pedal notations, 275
pencil. *See* ink and pencil in Bartók's MSS
performance instructions, 206
performing edition, 227; notation style, 275
personal copy, 29
photocopies of Bartók's MSS, 99

photoprints, corrected, 31
piano reduction, 221
pitch notation and micro-intervals, 269
plan of layout in MS, 81
preliminary memo sketch, 33, 37, 56
preparatory notes for orchestration, 142, 220
printer's (or engraver's) copy, 232
proofs, corrected, 238

rastrum, 96
reconstruction of bifolios, 98
reorganization of form, 100, 185
répétiteur piano reduction, 226
reprint, corrected, 245
restoration of Bartók's MSS, 99
revised edition, 230, 246
revised version on Bartók's recordings, 283
revision(s) of MSS, 206
rubato styles and notations, 289
rules of notation, 236

scoring, 219. *See also* preparatory notes for or-
    chestration
Selbstverlag, 251
short score, 116
side sketch, 34, 61
sketch, 33. *See also* continuity sketch; memo; par-
    tial sketch; preliminary memo sketch; side
    sketch
sketch-book, 34, 69
source chain, 28
stemma, 30
submission copy, 206

tempo (indication, correction), 252
test performances, 231
timing (*durée d'exécution*), 255
tissue master. See *Lichtpause*
tote Zeilen (empty staves), 221
trademark of music paper, 96
transcription, 48; of Bartók's recordings, 291; of
    folk music, 81

unrealized plans, 84

variant endings, 171
vibrato, notation of, 270
vocal-score-form short score, 116

working copy, 215

INDEX OF BARTÓK'S COMPOSITIONS

Page numbers in italic refer to the description in the Appendix: List of Works and Primary Sources.

PIANO MUSIC

Allegro barbaro (BB 63), xxi, 6, 26, 214, 248, 254–55, 276, 281, 283–89, *306*

Bartók Album, 246, 262
"Bear Dance." See *Ten Easy Piano Pieces*
"A Bit Drunk." See *Three Burlesques*

Cadenza to Beethoven's Piano Concerto no. 3 (BB A-2), *319*
Cadenzas to Mozart's Concerto for two pianos, K365 (BB A-7), *320*
Capriccio B minor (BB 5), *299*
Colindas. See *Rumanian Christmas Songs*
Csík. See *Three Hungarian Folksongs from Csík*

Danse orientale (BB 19/e), *300*
Dance Suite, for piano (BB 86), 6, 226, 276, *310*
Drei Klavierstücke, 1897 (BB 8), *299*
Drei Klavierstücke, 1898 (BB 14), *299*

early fragments and sketches, 1894/5 (BB 1), 113, 298–300
early piano pieces, opp. 1–31 (BB 1), 207, *298*
"Elle est morte." See *Fourteen Bagatelles*
Elza Polka (BB 1/29), *298*
Esquisses. See *Seven Sketches*
Etudes pour le piano. See Three Studies
"Evening in Transylvania." See *Ten Easy Piano Pieces*

Exercises [*Dolgozatok*] (BB 19), 26, 30, 33, 86, 115–16, 299, *300*

Fantasia A minor (BB 3), *299*
Fifteen Hungarian Peasant Songs (BB 79), 6, 26, 84, 175, 186, 191–92, 276, *308–9*
First Term at the Piano (BB 66), 275–76, *307*
For Children (BB 53), 84, 175, 186, 191, 213, 228, 239, 246–47, 253–54, 260–61, 268, 275–76, 280–81, 283, 290, *304–5,* 315
Four Dirges (BB 58), 37, 43–45, 233, 239, 246–47, 261, 276, *305*
Four Piano Pieces (BB 27), 114, 213–14, 233, 239, 253, 276, *301*
Fourteen Bagatelles (BB 50), 11–12, 37, 41–43, 87, 213–14, 236, 246–48, 253–54, 261–63, 266–68, 276, 281, *304*
fragments, unrealized compositions, 41, 44–45, 87–91, 304, *309, 311, 319*

Homage to Paderewski. See *Three Hungarian Folktunes*

Im Freien. See *Out Doors*
Improvisations (BB 83), 85, 89, 213, 248, 275–76, 278, 280, 282, 289, *309*
Italian keyboard music (Marcello, Rossi, Della Ciaia, Frescobaldi, Zipoli), transcribed for piano (BB A-4a-k), 227, *320*

juvenilia. *See* early piano pieces

Kezdők zongoramuzsikája. See *First Term at the Piano*

"Leszállott a páva" (BB 80a), 192, *309*
Little Suite. See *Petite Suite*
Loli Mazurka (BB 1/27), *298*

"Ma mie qui danse." See *Fourteen Bagatelles*
Marche funèbre, for piano, from *Kossuth* (BB 31), 226, 239, 253
Mikrokosmos (BB 105), 6, 47, 50–51, 53, 69, 84–85, 91, 132, 134, 143, 175, 179, 218, 228, 256, 262, 266, 275–76, 283, 288, 294, *314–15,* 318
"Musettes." See *Out Doors*; Sonata, 1926

"The Night's Music." See *Out Doors*
Nine Little Piano Pieces (BB 90), 50, 57, 85, 91, 120, 179, 206, 268, 276, 283, 285, *311*

Out Doors (BB 89), 6, 37, 47, 50, 56–57, 85, 89, 91, 171, 175–78, 206, 275–76, 278–79, 282, *311*

Petite Suite (BB 113), 210, 213, 218, 227, 240, 247, 280–81, 288, *316*
Petits Morceaux (BB 38), *302*
Piano Method (Bartók–Reschofsky; BB 66), 114, 231, 233, *307*

Quatre nénies. See *Four Dirges*

Rákóczi March, for piano 4 hands (BB A-1), *319*
Rhapsody for piano solo (BB 36a), 37, 81, 114, 230, 239, 276, *301*
Rumanian Christmas Songs (BB 67), 175, 191, 233, 275–76, 283, *307*
Rumanian Folk Dances (BB 68), 6, 84, 175, 186, 191, 233, 248–51, 254, 275–76, 278, 281, 283, *307*

Scherzo, 1894 (BB 2), *298*
Scherzo ("F.F.B.B."; BB 21), 205, 252, *300*
Scherzo B-flat minor (BB 19e), *300*
Scherzo B minor (BB 16), *299*

Scherzo oder Fantasie (BB 11), 38, 204, 252, *299*
Seven Pieces from Mikrokosmos, for two pianos (BB 120), 219, 227, *318*
Seven Sketches (BB 54), 87, 114, 213–14, 239–41, 246–48, 253–54, 263, 276, 280, *305*
Six Dances, 1900 (BB 19f), *300*
Sonata, 1898 (BB 12), 38, 204, *299*
Sonata, 1926 (BB 88), 6–7, 37, 47–50, 120–21, 130–31, 144, 151–54, 168, 170–75, 186, 189–90, 206, 236–37, 248, 275–76, 282, *310*
Sonata F major (BB 4), *299*
Sonata G minor (BB 2), *298*
Sonata VI (J. S. Bach, transcribed by Bartók; BB A-5), 227, 233–34, *320*
Sonatina (BB 69), 175, 191, 233, 239, 276, *307*
Suite for two Pianos (BB 122), 219, 227, 250, 276, 278, *318*
Suite op. 14 (BB 70), 84, 140, 144, 186, 194, 237, 239, 248, 254, 275–76, 279, 281, 293, *307*

Tempo di minuet (BB 23), *300*
Ten Easy Piano Pieces (BB 51), xiv, xxii, 114, 233, 239, 246–48, 254, 260, 275–76, 281, 289–91, *304*
Three Burlesques (BB 55), 43, 114, 168, 239, 246–48, 263, 276, 292–93, *305*
Three Hungarian Folksongs from Csík (BB 45b), 114, *303*
Three Hungarian Folktunes (BB 80b), 191–92, 247, *309*
Three Rondos (BB 92), 26, 114, 186, 191–93, 248, 255, 276, 281, *311*
Three Studies (BB 81), 15, 84, 87–89, 275, 282, *309*
Two Elegies (BB 49), 43, 239, 246–47, 276, 279, *304*
Two Pictures. See under Orchestral and Stage Works
Two Preludes (Purcell, transcribed by Bartók; BB A-6), *320*
Two Rumanian Dances (BB 56), 7, 35, 113, 120, 144, 228, 239, 246–48, 253, 276, 281, *305*

Variations (BB 22), 205, 252, *300*

Young People at the Piano, 239, 246, 260–61, *304–5*

CHAMBER MUSIC

Andante, for violin and piano, fragment (*see* BB 28), *301*
Andante A major, for violin and piano (BB 26b), 205, *301*

Contrasts for violin, clarinet, and piano (BB 116), 60–61, 64, 66, 116, 119, 139, 143, 219, 233, 266–67, 276, 280, 282, *317*

Duo for two violins, 1902 (BB 26a), *301*

Forty-Four Duos, for two violins (BB 104), 6, 69, 84, 218, 248, 267, *314*
From Gyergyó, for recorder and piano (BB 45a), 227, *303*

Hungarian Folksongs (Országh–Bartók), for violin and piano (BB 109), 218, 228, *315*

Piano Quartet (BB 13), 38, 204, *299*
Piano Quintet (BB 33), 37–38, 79, 114, 253, *302*
piano quintet fragments (BB 19i), *300*

Rhapsody no. 1, for violin and piano (BB 94a), 171, 186, 193–95, 218, 227, 240, 276, 281, *312*
Rhapsody no. 1, for violoncello and piano (BB 94c), 171, 194, 218, 240, *312*
Rhapsody no. 2, for violin and piano (BB 96a), 186, 199–203, 211, 214, 227, 230, 247–48, 276, *312–13*
Rumanian Folk Dances, arr. for violin and piano (Székely), 228, 248–51, 281, *307*

Scherzo in Sonatenform, for string quartet (BB 19d), *300*
Sonata for Solo Violin (BB 124), 6, 53, 70, 75–78, 95, 113, 119, 219, 232, 269, *318*
Sonata for two Pianos and Percussion (BB 115), xiv, 9, 14, 69, 80, 82, 116, 119, 137–38, 158, 168, 186, 196–98, 214, 219, 221, 237, 272–73, 275–76, 282, 294, *316–17*
Sonata for Violin and Piano, 1895 (BB 6), *299*

Sonata for Violin and Piano, 1897 (BB 10), 38, 204, *299*
Sonata for Violin and Piano, 1903 (BB 28), 37–38, 114, 205, 207, 210, 252, 276, *301*
Sonata for Violin and Piano no. 1 (BB 84), 6, 71, 104, 115, 201, 212–13, 268, 270, 275–76, 279, 282, *309–10*
Sonata for Violin and Piano no. 2 (BB 85), 71–74, 104, 115, 168, 232, 270, 275–76, 278, 280, 282, 293–94, *310*
Sonatina (Bartók–Gertler), for violin and piano (BB 102a), 228, 239, *314*
String Quartet in F, 1898 (BB 17), *300*
String Quartet no. 1 (BB 52), 11, 37, 39–41, 45, 115, 136, 143, 211, 214, 230, 239–40, 242–43, 254–58, 263–64, 266–67, *304*
String Quartet no. 2 (BB 75), 37, 43, 69, 89, 248, 258–59, 263–64, 268, 270, 272, *308*
String Quartet no. 3 (BB 93), 6, 69, 91, 102–4, 144–51, 218, 232, 268, 270, *312*
String Quartet no. 4 (BB 95), 14, 19, 61, 63, 85, 100–102, 155–58, 164, 192, 218, 231, 240, 254, 256, 258, 270–71, *312*
String Quartet no. 5 (BB 110), 6, 19–20, 34, 80, 135, 141, 164, 179, 181–89, 214, 218, 237, 240, 255, 263–64, 267, 270, *315*
String Quartet no. 6 (BB 119), 60, 105, 107–9, 133, 179–80, 219, 230, 240, 263–64, 266–67, 269, *317*
String Quartet (no. 7?), fragment (BB 129b), 86, 94–95, *319*
string quartets, 9, 119

Ungarische Volksweisen (Szigeti), for violin and piano (BB 53), 228, *305*

ORCHESTRAL AND STAGE WORKS; VOCAL WORKS WITH ORCHESTRA

"Ballet Symphonique" (planned composition), 84–85
Beethoven: C minor (*Pathétique*) Sonata op. 13, scored by Bartók (BB 19h), 220, *300; Erlkönig,* scored by Bartók (BB A-3), *319*
Bluebeard. See *Duke Bluebeard's Castle*

Cantata profana (BB 100), 36, 57–58, 80–81, 85, 117, 120, 218, 226, 230, 232–33, 236, *313*
Concerto for Orchestra (BB 123), 6, 14, 36, 53–55, 70, 72–73, 75, 80, 85, 91–92, 113, 120, 171, 186, 196, 198–99, 218–19, 227, 235–38, 261, *318, 319*
Concerto for two Pianos and Orchestra (BB 121), 116, 196, 219, 221, 227, *316–17*

Dance Suite, for orchestra (BB 86), 14, 17–18, 56–57, 80, 84, 116, 186, 215, 226, 235, 257, 270, *310*
Dances from Transylvania, for orchestra (BB 102b), 116, 218, 221, 227–28, 236, *314*
Divertimento, for string orchestra (BB 118), 36, 57–60, 64, 66, 102–3, 109, 116, 119, 219–21, 233, 236, 266, *317*
Duke Bluebeard's Castle, opera (BB 62), 36, 43, 56, 114, 116, 119, 171–72, 215, 220, 226, 232–33, 236, 239, 253, *306*

Five Choruses, with orchestra. See *Seven Choruses*
Five Hungarian Folksongs, for voice and orchestra (BB 108), 218, 227, 236, *315*

Four Orchestral Pieces (BB 64), 36, 66, 68, 70, 116, 119, 124, 142, 213, 215, 227, 236, 268, 294, *306*
fragments, unrealized compositions, 85–86, 91–95, *300, 311, 319*

Hungarian Peasant Songs, for orchestra (BB 107), 116, 218, 227, 230, 236, *315*
Hungarian Sketches, for orchestra (BB 103), 116, 218, 221, 227, 236, *315*

Kossuth, for orchestra (BB 31), 14, 34, 36, 38, 78, 114, 205, 207, 252, *301*

The Miraculous Mandarin, pantomime and suite (BB 82), 36, 56, 64, 70, 87, 116, 171–72, 186, 210, 213, 215, 219, 222–23, 226–27, 236, 245, 269, *309*
Morceau de Concert. See Rhapsody for piano and orchestra
Music for Strings, Percussion, and Celesta (BB 114), 9, 14, 20–21, 36, 63, 80, 105–6, 115, 117–19, 122, 129, 143, 164–65, 169, 218, 235–36, 238, 255–56, 269, 272–74, 294, *316*

Piano Concerto no. 1 (BB 91), 6, 36, 47, 49, 51–53, 56–57, 63–64, 89–90, 117, 119, 169, 176, 206–9, 215, 219–20, 226, 230, 232, 236, 240, 274–76, 282, *311*
Piano Concerto no. 2 (BB 101), 6, 14, 19, 36, 66–68, 102–3, 115, 117, 119, 128, 143, 163–67, 169, 216–18, 226, 230, 236, 258–59, 270, 274–76, 279, 282, 289, *313–14*
Piano Concerto no. 3 (BB 127), 6, 36, 54–55, 63–65, 95, 107, 109–12, 117, 127, 142, 219, 226, 276, *319*

Rhapsody for piano and orchestra (BB 36b), 14, 38, 116, 118, 205, 226–27, 230, 236, 239, 276, *302*
Rhapsody no. 1, for violin and orchestra (BB 94b), 116, 171, 194, 215, 236, *312*
Rhapsody no. 2, for violin and orchestra (BB 96b), 116, 171, 199–203, 215, 236, 247–48, *312–13*
Rumanian Dance, for orchestra (BB 61), 116, 227, 274, *306*

Rumanian Folk Dances, arr. for salon orchestra, for string orchestra (Wilke, Willner; BB 68), 228, *307*
Rumanian Folk Dances, for small orchestra (BB 76), 6, 86, 116, 215, 220, 227, 236, 248–49, *308*

Scherzo B-flat major, for orchestra (BB 19g), *300*
Scherzo for Orchestra and Piano (BB 35), 205, 226, 247, 253, 276, *302*
Seven Choruses (and *Five Choruses,* resp.), with orchestra (BB 111b), 92–93, 116, 218, 227, 236, *315–16*
Six Dances, 1900 (BB 19f), 116, *300*
Suite no. 1, for orchestra (BB 39), 14, 36, 38, 81, 114, 205, 235, 253, *302*
Suite no. 2, for orchestra (BB 40), 14, 35–36, 38–39, 79, 114, 116, 119, 186, 205, 215, 220, 226–27, 230, 236, 248, 250, 253, 270, *303*
Symphony (BB 25), 116, *301*

Three Village Scenes, for women's voices and orchestra (BB 87b), 116, 213, 215, 219, 227, 236, *310*
Tiefblaue Veilchen, for voice and orchestra (BB 18), 117, 204, *300*
Two Pictures, for orchestra (BB 59), 43, 56, 114, 116, 226, 235, 239–40, 294, *306*
Two Portraits, for orchestra (BB 48b), 116, 227, 235, *304*

Village Scenes. See Three Village Scenes
Viola Concerto (BB 128), xxii, 36, 83, 95, 110–12, 116, 126, 142, 144, 211, 214, 220, 226, 232, *319*
Violin Concerto ("no. 1") op. posth. (BB 48a), 11, 35–36, 38–39, 70, 86–87, 114, 116, 118, 205, 207, 211–12, 214, 226–27, 253, *304*
Violin Concerto ("no. 2"; BB 117), xxii, 26, 36, 60–62, 116, 119, 125, 158–66, 171, 186, 196, 211, 214, 219, 224–26, 231–33, 235–36, 240, 243–44, 256, 266–67, 269, 274, *317*

The Wooden Prince, ballet and suites (BB 74), 36, 43, 46–47, 114, 116, 119, 123, 142, 171, 219–20, 226–27, 232, 236, 254, 268, 270, 293–94, *308*

VOCAL MUSIC

A férj keserve. See Goat Song
A kicsi "tót"-nak. See Children's Songs
Ady-Songs. See Five Songs op. 16

Children's Songs, for voice and piano (BB 41), *303*

Drei Lieder, for voice and piano, 1898 (BB 15), *299*

Eight Hungarian Folksongs, for voice and piano (BB 47), 35, 114, 276, *303*

Elmúlt időkből. See *From Olden Times*

Evening, for male choir (BB 30), 213, *301*

Evening, for voice and piano (BB 29), 114, *301*

Five Hungarian Folksongs, for voice and piano (BB 97), *313*

Five Songs op. 15, for voice and piano (BB 71), 6, 276, *307*

Five Songs (Ady) op. 16, for voice and piano (BB 72), 233, 240, 276, 278, *307–8*

Five Village Scenes, for voice and piano (BB 87a), 6, 237, 268, 276, *310*

Four Hungarian Folksongs, for mixed choir (BB 99), 57, 215, 255, *313*

Four Old Hungarian Folksongs, for male choir (BB 60), 116, *306*

Four Slovak Folksongs, for mixed choir and piano (BB 78), 233, *308*

Four Slovak Folksongs, for voice and piano (BB 46), *303*

Four Songs (lost; BB 32), *301*

Four Songs (Pósa; BB 24), 114, 210, 213, 239, 253, *300*

From Olden Times, for male choir (BB 112), 212, 218, 233, *316*

Goat Song, for voice and piano (BB 125), 83, 219, *318*

Hungarian Folksongs (1st series), for voice and piano (BB 37), *302*

Hungarian Folksongs (2nd series), for voice and piano (BB 43), 214, *303*

Hungarian Folksongs (Bartók–Kodály), for voice and piano (BB 42), 84, 144, 239, 253, *303*

"Krutí Tono vretena." See *Slovak Folksong*

Liebeslieder, for voice and piano (BB 20), 205, *300*

Magyar Népdalok (Bartók–Kodály). See *Hungarian Folksongs*

Nine Rumanian Folksongs, for voice and piano (BB 66), 83, *306*

Piros alma. See *Székely Folksong*

Pósa-Songs. See *Four Songs*

"reserved songs" (MS collection), 307, 318

Slovak Folksong, for voice and piano (BB 73), 83, *308*

Slovak Folksongs, for male choir (BB 77), 233, *308*

Székely Folksong, for voice and piano (BB 34), 114, *302*

Székely Folksongs, for male choir (BB 106), xiv, 114, 218, *315*

Three Ukrainian Folksongs, for voice and piano (BB 126), 83, *318*

Twenty Hungarian Folksongs, for voice and piano (BB 98), 215, 255, 276, *313*

Twenty-Seven Choruses, a cappella (BB 111a), 92, 120, 134, 143, 214, 218, 232–33, 247, *315–16*

Two Hungarian Folksongs, for voice and piano (BB 44), 207, 218, *303*

Two Rumanian Folksongs, for female choir (BB 57), 83, *305*

Ukrainian folksong: A férj keserve. See *Goat Song*

unrealized compositions, 85

Village Scenes. See *Five Village Scenes*

GENERAL INDEX

"Anon. X," "Anon. Y," "Anon. Z" (copyists), 211, 214, 242, 303–6
Adorno, Theodor W., 16
Ady, Endre, 233, 240, 276, 278, 307
Albrecht, Sándor, 85
Amar-Hindemith Quartet, 258
America. *See* United States
Amsterdam, 200, 274
Anatolia, 72
Anbruch (Vienna), 284, 306, 308
Anschluss of Austria, 26
Ansermet, Ernest, 259
Antal, Jenő, 203, 313
Antokoletz, Elliott, xix, 3, 5, 61, 155
Arab collection, field-book, 18, 54, 70, 75, 95, 318–19
Arányi (d'Aranyi), Adila, 26, 301
Arányi (d'Aranyi), Jelly, 213
Arauco, Ingrid, xv
Asheville, North Carolina, 32, 70
Austria, 26, 258, 314

Babbitt, Milton, 3
Bach, Anna Magdalena, 263–65
Bach, Carl Philipp Emanuel, 266
Bach, Johann Sebastian, 85, 169, 207, 227, 233–34, 246, 263–66, 277, 282, 295, 320
Bárd (music publisher), Budapest, 27, 230, 233, 239, 246, 300–301
Bárdos, Lajos, 3, 152
Bartha, Dénes, 3, 23
Bartók Archives (Bartók Archívum), Budapest, xiv, xix, 2, 4–6, 27–28, 81, 99, 192, 205, 207, 231–32, 239–40, 254, 298–320
Bartók Archives, New York. *See* Béla Bartók Archives
Bartók, Béla Jr., xv–xvi, xix, 2, 5–6, 27–28, 119, 121, 206, 216, 220, 239–40, 250, 257, 274, 298–99, 301–17
Bartók, Elza, 207, 210, 301
Bartók estate: in Hungary, 2, 81, 298; in the United States, xiv, 2, 6, 27, 81, 205, 297–98. *See also* Béla Bartók Estate, New York
Bartók, Mrs. *See* Pásztory, Ditta (second wife); Voit, Paula (mother); Ziegler, Márta (first wife)
Bartók, Peter, xv–xvi, xxi, 6, 10, 27–28, 54, 86, 99, 144, 155, 216, 236–37, 239–40, 250–51, 253, 265, 298–99, 302–20
Bartók's mother. *See* Voit, Paula
Basel, 196, 215; Chamber Orchestra, 117. *See also* Paul Sacher Stiftung
Basilides, Mária, 232
Bator, Victor (Bátor, Viktor), 2, 4, 27
Bechstein piano, 278
Bécs. *See* Vienna
Beethoven, Ludwig van, 33, 35, 69, 104, 165, 205, 220, 227, 252, 258, 266, 271, 278, 282, 295, 300, 319
Béla Bartók Archives, New York, 2, 99–100, 177
Béla Bartók Complete Critical Edition (BBCCE), 7, 284
Béla Bartók Estate, New York, 2, 99
Béla Bartók Thematic Catalogue, 7, 297–98
Belgium, 301

Belwin, Inc., New York, 110
Berg, Alban, 13
Berkeley, University of California, xiii–xiv
Berlin, 14, 251, 301
Berners, Lord. *See* Tyrwhitt, Gerald Hugh
Beu, Octavian, 18
Bilson, Malcolm, 278
Bloch, Ernest, xiii–xiv
Bónis, Ferenc, xx, 5, 226, 254, 261
Boosey & Hawkes, London, and Boosey & Hawkes, Inc., New York, NY, xix, 27–28, 32, 84–86, 120, 171, 198–200, 203, 214, 230, 233, 235–37, 243–45, 247–51, 256, 260, 262, 266–67, 298, 303, 305, 307, 309–19
Bösendorfer piano, 278
Boston, 198
Brahms, Johannes, 258, 282
Bratislava. *See* Pozsony
Brett, Philip, xiv
Breuer, János, 16, 258
Brinkmann, Reinhold, xv
British Library, London, xv, 27, 306
Bucharest, Composer's Society, 303
Budapest, 2, 14, 26, 28, 31, 33, 35, 60, 102, 117–21, 154, 173, 178, 192, 196, 207, 214, 216, 239, 251, 253–54, 278, 314, 317; History Museum, 27, 310; Hungarian National Museum, 178; Institute for Musicology, xiv, 300, 304, 311; Liszt F. Academy of Music, xiv, 25, 250, 277, 295, 303, 306; Opera House, 226, 232–33, 306, 308–9; Philharmonic Orchestra, 253; Philharmonic Society, 303; Széchényi National Library (OSZK), xxi, 27, 121, 178, 239, 304–5, 310
Bulgarian rhythm, 61, 183, 186, 288

Calvocoressi, Michel Dimitri, 26, 307–8
Carnegie Hall, 198
Centenary Edition of Bartók's Records (Complete). See Hungaroton records
Chamouk, Otto, 309
Chopin, Fryderyk, 227, 282
Chován, Kálmán, 277
Ciaia. *See* Della Ciaia
Columbia records (England; United States), 249–50, 281
Continental records, 262, 281, 288, 316
Corvina Press, Budapest, xviii
Couperin, François, 227, 295
Cowell, Henry Dixon, 15
Craft, Robert, 16
Creel, Wilhelmine (Mrs. Driver), 26, 192–93
Croll, Gerhard, 76

Dalmatian rural music, 22
Dalton, David, 226
Debussy, Claude Achille, 272, 282
Delius, Frederick, 12
Delkas (music publisher), Los Angeles, 247
Della Ciaia, Azzolino Bernardino, 320
Dellamaggiore, Nelson, xxii, 111, 144
Demény, János, xx–xxi, 3, 15, 23
Deutsch, Jenő, 143, 202, 211, 213–14, 218, 233, 313, 315–16
Deutsch, Otto Erich, 35
Dille, Denijs (Denis), xiv, xx, 4, 10, 12, 25, 35, 84, 86, 118, 120, 144, 204, 213, 297–98, 303, 317
Doflein, Erich, 314
Dohnányi, Ernő (Ernst von), 310
Doráti, Antal, 227
Duckles, Madeline, xiv

Eberle, J. E. & Cº (music paper), 96–98, 101–3, 105–7, 176, 178
Edinburgh, National Library of Scotland, 213, 239, 305, 308
Editio Musica Budapest, xx, 226, 257, 261, 298, 303, 305–6, 310
Egri, Irén, 194, 307
Elkan (publisher), 305
Engel, Iván, 254, 261
Engelmann, Hans Ulrich, 3
England, 213, 235, 301
Eötvös, Péter, xv
Est Hármaskönyve, Az (Budapest), 310
Europe, 15–16, 109, 200, 203, 221, 317

Fábián, Felicie, 205
Falvy, Zoltán, xiv
Fassett, Agatha (Illés, Ágota), 26, 309
Ferencsik, János, 196, 254
Fibonacci numbers, 81, 152, 197
Fischer, C., Inc., New York (music paper; publisher), 110–11, 227, 320
Forte, Allan, 3
France, 213, 303
Fränzl, Ágost (August), 38
French music, 16
Frescobaldi, Girolamo, 320
Freund, Etelka, 239, 302, 304–5
Frid, Géza, 200
Furtwängler, Wilhelm, 207

German folksongs, 85
German music, 16, 252, 258
Germany, 2, 6

Gertler, André (Endre), 228, 258, 314
Geyer, Stefi, 11, 26, 37, 39, 227
Gillies, Malcolm, xiv, xx, 6, 158
Gombocz, Adrienne, xiv, xix
Gombosi, Otto, 2
Goodman, Benny, 282
Gratzer, Wolfgang, 76
Gruber, Mrs. *See* Kodály, Emma
Gyergyó (Transylvania), 303

Harvard Lectures, 10, 12, 15–16, 18, 21–23, 60, 201
Hawkes, Ralph, 85–86, 95, 238
Hawkes & Son, Ltd., London, 247, 306, 317
Haydn, Joseph, 207, 227, 258, 295
Heartz, Daniel, xiv
Heinsheimer, Hans W., 85, 198, 238, 272
Herodoti Epitome, 38, 299
Hertzka, Emil, 311
Hilmar, Ernst, xv
Hilversum Radio, 280–81, 283–86
His Master's Voice (HMV) records, 262, 279, 281, 284–86, 288, 293
Hoffmann, Rudolf Stephan, 313
Homer, 38
Homosassa, Florida, 6, 27, 99
Horatio Appleton Lamb Fund, 15
Howat, Roy, 81
Hubay, Jenő, 270
Hungarian Academy of Sciences. *See* Budapest: Institute for Musicology
Hungarian folk (peasant) music, 14, 16, 61, 85, 91, 189, 193, 214
Hungarian music, 16, 18, 270, 289, 295
Hungarian National Museum, Budapest, 178
Hungaroton records, 240, 250, 259, 262, 280, 282, 293
Hungary, xiii, 2, 6, 8, 27, 33, 109, 219, 245, 247, 259
Hunkemöller, Jürgen, 6
Hyrtl, Anton, 204

Italy, 203, 313

Jászberény, 39, 118
Jhlenburg metronome, 254
Jurkovics, Irmy, 213, 301

Kajglíček (Kejglíček; copyist), 214, 301
Kárpáti, János, 5
Kecskeméti, Pál, 318
Kenneson, Claude, 158
Kerman, Joseph W., xiv

Kiss, Gábor, 192
Kocsis, Zoltán, xv, xx, 195
Kodály, Emma (Gruber, Emma), 26–27, 69, 78, 86, 206, 210, 213, 239, 300–302, 305–9, 319
Kodály, Zoltán, 4, 11, 13, 17, 23, 26, 35, 66, 68, 142, 213–14, 239–40, 259, 282, 303–4, 307, 316, 319
Kodály Archívum, Budapest, 300–301
Koessler, Hans (János), 26, 30, 33, 86, 114–16, 205, 299–300
Kolisch, Rudolf, 314, 317–18
Koussevitzky, Serge, 171, 198, 261, 318
Kovács, Sándor, 5, 111
Kroó, György, xiv, 5, 84, 170, 233
Kurtág, György, xv

Laloy, Bibliothèque, 303
Lampert(-Deák),Vera, xiv, xx, 4, 69, 199, 289–90
LaRue, Jan, xxi
László, Ferenc, 35
League of Composers, New York, 310
League of Nations, 35
Lehman, Robert Owen, 192, 299, 311
Leipzig, 235–36, 240
Lendvai, Ernő, 3, 19, 21, 81, 197
Lenoir, Yves, xx, 5
Library of Congress. *See* Washington, D.C.
Ligeti, György, 3
Lindmayr, Andrea, 76
Liszt, Franz (Ferenc), xxi, 13, 16, 104, 264, 282
Liszt F. Academy of Music. *See under* Budapest
London, 27, 86, 203, 207, 236, 238, 247, 250, 272; Wigmore Hall, 86. *See also* British Library
Lubrano, J. & J., Great Barrington, Mass., 239
Lucas sequence numbers, 81

Ma (Budapest), 307
Mácsai, János, 280
Magyar Kórus (music publisher), Budapest, xxi, 27, 214, 218, 233, 236, 246, 298, 315–16
Magyar Lant (Budapest), 239, 301
Major, Ervin (collection), 300
Maramureş, 168
Marcello, Benedetto, 320
Marks, E. B. (music publisher), New York, 247, 305
Mason, Colin, 3
Melos (Berlin), 14
Menuhin, Yehudi, 158, 232, 270, 318
Metzger, Heinz-Klaus, 5
Michael, Frank, 5
Mihály, András, 3
Milhaud, Darius, 23

Milroy, Nicholas R., 239
Moldenhauer, Hans, 243, 317
Moreux, Serge, 3
Móricz, Klára, 5, 120
Mozart, Wolfgang Amadeus, 33, 227, 239, 258, 282, 295, 320
Müller-Widmann, Annie, 33
Mureş, 191
Musik der Zeit (Vienna), 250
Musikblätter des Anbruch. See *Anbruch*

Nagy, Olivér, 226
National Library of Scotland. See Edinburgh
New York, 2, 27, 70, 110–11, 158, 196, 198, 214, 226, 247, 272, 280–81, 310, 317; Carnegie Hall, 198; New York Ballet Theatre, 227; Pierpont Morgan Library, xv, 27, 192, 299, 311
Newcomb, Anthony, xiv
Nüll, Edwin von der, 15
Nyugat (Budapest), 284, 306, 308–9

Odyssey, 38, 299
Olleson, Edward, 255
Oramo, Ilkka, 5
Ormandy, Eugene (Ormándy, Jenő), 86
Országh, Tivadar, 228, 315
Österreichische Nationalbibliothek. *See under* Vienna
OSZK, Országos Széchényi Könyvtár. *See* Budapest: Széchényi National Library

Paderewski, Ignacy Jan, 191, 319
Parchment (music paper), 110–11, 203
Paris, 120, 205, 256, 280, 302
Pásztory, Ditta, 2, 6, 10, 27, 31, 37, 47, 79–80, 102, 120, 177–78, 196, 201, 210, 213, 216, 226, 282, 303, 309–11, 313–14, 316, 318
Patria records, 281
Paul Sacher Stiftung, Basel, xv, 27, 215, 304, 312
Pennsylvania, University of. *See* Philadelphia
Periszkóp (Budapest), 309
Perle, George, 3
Péteri, Ignác, 26
Petersen, Peter, 5
Philadelphia: Free Library, 27, 312; Musical Fund Society, 312; University of Pennsylvania, 27, 312
Philharmonia Partituren (Vienna), xxii, 169, 215, 235, 256, 310, 312, 316
Pierpont Morgan Library. *See under* New York
Pleyela recordings, 280
Portugal, 86

Pósa, Lajos, 114, 210, 213, 239, 253, 300
Poulenc, Francis, 23
Pozsony (Pressburg, now Bratislava), 27, 38, 204, 207, 213
Preßburger Zeitung (Pozsony), 300
Prévost, Arthur, 255
Primrose, William, 111, 232, 319
Princeton, New Jersey, 203
Pro Arte Quartet, 20
Pro Musica (New York), 14
Pruett, James W., xv
Purcell, Henry, 320

Radvány, 79, 119
Rákóczi (march), 319
Rákoskeresztúr, 35, 119
Rákospalota, 119
Ravel, Maurice, 23
Reiner, Fritz (Frigyes), 295
Reschofsky, Sándor, 231, 233, 307
Révész, Dorrit, v, xv, 12
La Revue Musicale (Paris), 258
Riehn, Rainer, 5
Rimaszombat, 79
Röder (engraver), Leipzig, 240
Roesner, Edward H., xxi
Rösler, Endre, 233
Rossi, Michelangelo, 320
Rostal, Max, 254, 256–57
Rózsavölgyi (music publisher), Budapest, xxi, 27, 120, 191, 218, 228, 230, 233, 235–36, 239–40, 246, 253, 257, 260–61, 298, 302–7, 314, 320
Rozsnyai (music publisher), Budapest, xxi, 27, 191, 230, 233, 235, 239–40, 246, 253–54, 261, 298, 303–5
Rumanian folk music, 18, 70–71, 81, 85, 190–91, 193, 199, 214–15, 249–50, 295

Saanen, 60
Sacher, Paul, xv, 11, 105, 117–18, 256. *See also* Paul Sacher Stiftung
The Sackbut (London), 14
St. Martin's Press, New York, NY, xviii
Sándor, György, 226–27
Sándor, Miklós, 213, 308
Saranac Lake, New York, 32, 70, 110–11
Scarlatti, Domenico, 227, 282, 295
Scherchen, Hermann, 56
Schoenberg, Arnold, 10, 13, 23, 33, 85, 158–59, 243, 264
Schott's Söhne, Mainz, 246, 314
Schumann, Robert, 205, 227

Searle, Arthur, xv, 116
Sebestyén, János, xx
Sebő, Ferenc, 5
Seiber, Mátyás, 2, 315
Selden-Goth, Gisella, 316
Serly, Tibor, 85, 111–12, 211, 214, 220, 226, 228, 319
Shilkret, Nathaniel, 85
Siemens Foundation, Munich, xv
Slovak folk music, 18, 70, 85, 114, 190, 192–93, 295
Sólyom, János, 196, 316
Sotheby & Co., London, 301
Spain, 86
Spivakovsky, Tossy, 26, 158, 316–17
Stein, Erwin, 211, 214, 230, 236, 243, 272, 317–18
Steinway piano, 278
Stern, Isaac, 195
Stevens, Halsey, 3, 192
Stockholm, 196, 316
Stravinsky, Igor, 10, 14, 16–17, 23, 56, 85, 166, 169–70, 206, 288, 295, 319
Suchoff, Benjamin, xix–xxi, 2, 4, 12, 105, 214, 247, 262
Switzerland, 26–27, 33
Szabó, Miklós, 5–6
Szabolcsi, Bence, xiv, 3–4, 23, 313
Széchényi National Library. *See under* Budapest
Székely, Mihály, 233
Székely, Zoltán, xv, 26, 158, 195–96, 200–201, 228, 231–32, 248, 256, 270, 274, 307, 312, 317
Szelényi, István, 3
Szendy, Árpád, 277
Szervánszky, Péter, 196
Szigeti, Joseph (József), 26, 64, 171, 195, 228, 232, 281–82, 295, 305, 312
Szőllősy, András, xx, xxii, 3, 12, 297–98
Szombathely, International Bartók Seminar, xiv

Takács Quartet, 269
Tallián, Tibor, xiv, xix, 4, 11–12, 18, 190
Tango, Egisto, 253–54
Taruskin, Richard F., xiv, xv
Tóth, Aladár, 23
Traimer, Roswitha, 3
Transylvania, 71, 119, 199
Treitler, Leo, 3
Trianon Treaty, 18, 27
Turkish collection, field-book, 53, 55, 70, 81, 120, 214, 318–19
Turner (copyist), 318

Turner, J. Rigbie, xv
Turner, Malcolm, 116
Tyrwhitt, Gerald Hugh (Lord Berners), 206, 319

Uhde, Jürgen, 3
Új Zenei Szemle (Budapest), 300
Ujfalussy, József, xiv, 3
Ukrainian folksong, 318
United States, 2, 6, 8, 12, 14–15, 23, 27–28, 31, 53, 56, 70, 75, 80, 95, 120, 158, 195, 197, 200, 203, 221, 226, 235, 247, 251, 261, 262, 263, 267–68, 280, 303, 305–6, 314
Universal Edition, Vienna (Universal Edition, Ltd., London), xxii, 26–27, 31–32, 84–85, 91, 105, 117–21, 171, 178, 191, 194, 199–203, 206–7, 214–16, 218, 228, 230, 232–33, 235–37, 245–51, 253–57, 263, 267–68, 274–75, 278–79, 283–84, 298, 303, 306–16
Urbana, University of Illinois, 319

Varró, Margit, 231
Vecsey, Ferenc, 86
Versailles, Treaty of, 18, 27
Vienna, 14, 118–19, 214–15, 218, 235, 239, 247, 306; Österreichische Nationalbibliothek, 27, 207, 301; Wiener Stadt- und Landesbibliothek, xv, 27, 239–40, 303, 305–6, 310, 312, 315–16
Vikárius, László, 5, 120, 251
Vinton, John, 4, 229
Voit, Irma, 207, 301
Voit, Paula, 25, 109, 204, 207–8, 213, 299–301, 303–4
Vox records, 281, 293

Wade, Bonnie C., xiv
Wagner, Richard, 13
Waldbauer, Imre (Waldbauer Quartet), 231, 272
Waldbauer, Iván, xxii, 4, 178, 230, 297–98
Washington, D.C., Library of Congress, xv, 27, 195, 239–40, 243, 280–81, 310, 315, 317–18
Weiner, Leó, 228
Weisleder (copyist), 318
Weiss(-Aigner), Günter, 5
Welte-Licencee piano rolls, 249–50, 280–81, 283
Welte-Mignon piano rolls, 249–50
Whitaker, Frank, 232
Wiener Stadt- und Landesbibliothek. *See under* Vienna
Wiener, Barry, 192
Wiesengrund-Adorno, Theodor, 16
Wigmore Hall, 86
Wilheim, András, xiv, 5

Wilke, Arnold, 228, 307
Willner, Arthur, 228, 307
Wolf, Eugene K., xxi
Wöss, Josef Venantius von, 230, 268

Zathureczky, Ede, 203, 228, 281
Zenei Szemle (Temesvár), 311

Zeneműkiadó. *See* Editio Musica Budapest
Zerboni, Suvini (Milan), 261
Ziegler, Márta, 11, 23, 31, 41, 115, 119, 142, 144, 194, 205–6, 210, 212–13, 220–21, 233, 303, 305–10
Zipoli, Domenico, 320